BECOMING

BECOMING

ADAPTED FOR YOUNG READERS

MICHELLE OBAMA

DELACORTE PRESS

Library of Congress Cataloging-in-Publication Data is available upon request.
ISBN 978-0-593-30374-0 (trade) — ISBN 978-0-593-30375-7 (lib. bdg.) —
ISBN 978-0-593-30376-4 (ebook)

The text of this book is set in 11.5-point Minion Pro.
Interior design by Andrea Lau
Jacket design by Christopher Brand
Jacket photograph by Miller Mobley

PRINTED IN THE UNITED STATES OF AMERICA
10 9 8 7 6 5 4 3 2 1
First Edition

To all the people who have helped me become:

the folks who raised me—Fraser, Marian, Craig,
and my vast extended family,

my circle of strong women, who always lift me up,

my loyal and dedicated staff, who continue to make me proud.

———————

To the loves of my life:

Malia and Sasha, my two most precious peas,
who are my reasons for being,

and finally, Barack, who always promised me an interesting journey.

CONTENTS

A NOTE TO READERS

WHEN I BEGAN THE PROCESS OF WRITING THIS BOOK, I wasn't sure what shape it would ultimately take, let alone what the title might be. One thing I did know was that I wanted to be honest—and this edition for young readers is no different. Growing up on the South Side of Chicago in the 1960s and '70s, my parents, Fraser and Marian Robinson, always kept it straight with me and my brother, Craig. They never sugarcoated hard truths or presented their reality as anything other than what it was—because they knew we could handle it. I want to give you all that same respect.

So my promise to you is to give you my story in all its messy glory—from the time I struggled on a question in front of my kindergarten class, to my first kiss and the insecurities I felt growing up, to the chaos of a campaign trail and the strange experience of shaking hands with the Queen of England.

But I hope you don't get too swept up in the glitz of the White House, because the most meaningful parts of my story aren't the ball gowns or state dinners. Instead, they are the little things: the way my grandfather smiled when he put his favorite album on the record player, the smell of our house when my mom cleaned it each spring, the sound of an ice scraper on a car window in the middle of a Chicago winter.

During the writing process, I realized that there is no memory too small. Every last bit of our story has meaning. Some memories can bring a twinge of pain, particularly those that happen when we are young. I can still feel the embarrassment when I failed in front of my classmates at a young age. I can still feel the knot in my stomach after someone doubted me. And I still feel the pain and the emptiness that came with losing those closest to me. At some point, we all experience the kind of hurt that we can't fix on our own.

But those tender spots—the ones that we try the hardest to keep hidden—are often the parts of ourselves that are most worth sharing. Feelings like discomfort and struggle are signs that we're doing the hard work of discovering the greatest truths about ourselves. And when I look back at my own life, I see that it's only through those moments of great difficulty that I was able to find the strength to make a change or search more purposefully for who I wanted to be.

These kinds of things aren't usually what we feel comfortable sharing with one another. We're usually most concerned with what I like to call our statistics—our test scores, our exploits on the sports field, the kind of jeans our family can afford to buy. But truly, what's most important is our story—our whole story, including those moments when we feel a little vulnerable. So often, it's in sharing those parts of our stories that we see the beauty not only in our own journey, but in someone else's.

So I hope that as you're reading my story, you'll also think about your own—because it's the most beautiful gift you'll ever have. The bumps and bruises, the joys and triumphs and bursts of laughter—they all combine to make you who you are. And who you are is not some static, unchanging thing. It will change every day and every year, and none of us know what shape our lives will ultimately take. That's what becoming is all about. And just like you, I still have a whole lot of becoming left to do, too.

PREFACE

WHEN I WAS A KID, MY DREAMS WERE SIMPLE. I WANTED a dog. I wanted a house that had stairs in it—two floors for one family. For some reason, I wanted a four-door station wagon instead of the two-door Buick that was my dad's pride and joy. I used to tell people that when I grew up, I was going to be a pediatrician. Why? Because I loved being around little kids and I quickly learned that it was a pleasing answer for adults to hear. *Oh, a doctor! What a good choice!* In those days, I wore pigtails and bossed my older brother around and managed, always and no matter what, to get As at school. I was ambitious, though I didn't know exactly what I was shooting for. Now I think it's one of the most useless questions an adult can ask a child— *What do you want to be when you grow up?* As if at some point you become something and that's the end.

So far in my life, I've been a lawyer. I've been a vice president at a hospital and the director of a nonprofit that helps young people build meaningful careers. I've been a working-class Black student at a fancy mostly white college. I've been the only woman, the only African

American, in all sorts of rooms. I've been a bride, a stressed-out new mom, a daughter torn up by grief. And until recently, I was the First Lady of the United States of America. Being First Lady challenged me and humbled me, lifted me up and shrank me down, sometimes all at once. I'm just beginning to process what took place over these last years—from the moment in 2006 when my husband first started talking about running for president to where we are now. It's been quite a ride.

When you're First Lady, America shows itself to you in its extremes. I've been to fund-raisers in private homes that look more like art museums, houses where people own bathtubs made from gemstones. I've visited families who lost everything in Hurricane Katrina and were tearful and grateful just to have a working refrigerator and stove. I've encountered people I find to be shallow and false and others—teachers and military spouses and so many more—whose spirits are so deep and strong it's astonishing. And I've met kids—lots of them, all over the world—who crack me up and fill me with hope and who blessedly manage to forget about my title once we start rooting around in the dirt of a garden.

I've been held up as the most powerful woman in the world and taken down as an "angry Black woman." I've wanted to ask those people what they didn't like about me—was it that I was "angry," or that I was Black, or that I was a woman? I've smiled for photos with people who call my husband horrible names on national television, but still want a framed keepsake. Some people on the internet have questioned everything about me, right down to whether I'm a woman or a man. A U.S. congressman has made fun of my butt. I've been hurt. I've been furious. But mostly, I've tried to laugh this stuff off.

There's a lot I still don't know about America, about life, about what the future might bring. But I do know myself. My dad, Fraser, taught me to work hard, laugh often, and keep my word. My mom, Marian, showed me how to think for myself and to use my voice. Together, in our cramped apartment on the South Side of Chicago, they helped me see the value in our story, in my story, in the larger story of our country. Even when it's not pretty or perfect. Even when it's more real than you want it to be. Your story is what you have, what you will always have. It is something to own.

For eight years, I lived in the White House, a place with more stairs than I can count—plus elevators, a bowling alley, and an in-house florist. I slept in a bed that was made up with fancy linens. Our meals were cooked by a team of world-class chefs and delivered by professionals more highly trained than those at any five-star restaurant or hotel. Secret Service agents, with their earpieces and guns and serious expressions, stood outside our doors, doing their best to stay out of our family's private life. We got used to it, eventually, sort of—the strange grandeur of our new home and also the constant, quiet presence of others.

The White House is where our two girls played ball in the hallways and climbed trees on the South Lawn. It's where my husband, Barack Obama, sat up late at night, reading briefings and drafts of speeches in the Treaty Room, and where Sunny, one of our dogs, sometimes pooped on the rug. I could stand on the Truman Balcony and watch the tourists posing with their selfie sticks and peering through the iron fence, trying to guess at what went on inside. There were days when I felt suffocated by the fact that our windows had to be kept shut for security, that I couldn't get some fresh air without causing a fuss. There were other times when I'd be awestruck by the white magnolias blooming outside, the everyday bustle of government business, the majesty of a military welcome. There were days, weeks, and months when I hated politics. And there were moments when the beauty of this country and its people so overwhelmed me that I couldn't speak.

Then it was over. Even if you see it coming, even as your final weeks are filled with emotional good-byes, the day itself is still a blur. A hand goes on a Bible; an oath gets repeated. One president's furniture gets carried out while another's comes in. Closets are emptied and refilled in the span of a few hours. Just like that, there are new heads on new pillows—new personalities, new dreams. And when it ends, when you walk out the door that last time from the world's most famous address, you're left in many ways to find yourself again.

So let me start here, with a small thing that happened not long ago. I was at home in the redbrick house that my family recently moved into. Our new house sits about two miles from our old house, on a quiet neighborhood street. We're still settling in. In the family room, our furniture is arranged the same way it was in the White House. We've got mementos around the house that remind us it was all real— photos of our family time at Camp David, handmade pots given to me by Native American students, a book signed by Nelson Mandela. What was strange about this night was that everyone was gone. Barack was traveling. My younger daughter, Sasha, was out with friends. My older daughter, Malia, was living and working in New York before going to college. It was just me, our two dogs, and a silent, empty house like I haven't known in eight years.

And I was hungry. I walked down the stairs from our bedroom with the dogs following on my heels. In the kitchen, I opened the fridge. I found a loaf of bread, took out two pieces, and laid them in the toaster oven. I opened a cabinet and got out a plate. I know it's a weird thing to say, but to take a plate from a shelf in the kitchen without anyone first insisting that they get it for me, to stand by myself watching bread turn brown in the toaster, feels as close to a return to my old life as I've come. Or maybe it's my new life just beginning to announce itself.

In the end, I didn't just make toast; I made cheese toast, moving my slices of bread to the microwave and melting a fat mess of gooey ched- dar between them. I then carried my plate outside to the backyard. I didn't have to tell anyone I was going. I just went. I was in bare feet, wearing a pair of shorts. The chill of winter had finally lifted. The air smelled like spring. I sat on the steps of our veranda, feeling the warmth of the day's sun still caught in the slate beneath my feet. A dog started barking somewhere in the distance, and my own dogs paused to listen, seeming momentarily confused. It occurred to me that it was a jarring sound for them, given that we didn't have neighbors, let alone neighbor dogs, at the White House. For them, all this was new. As the dogs loped off to explore the perimeter of the yard, I ate my toast in the dark, feeling alone in the best possible way. I wasn't thinking about the guards with guns sitting less than a hundred yards away at the custom-built command post inside our garage, or the fact that I still can't walk down a street without security. I wasn't thinking about the new president or for that matter the old president, either.

I was thinking instead about how in a few minutes I would go back inside my house, wash my plate in the sink, and head up to bed, maybe opening a window so I could feel the spring air—how glorious that would be. I was thinking, too, that the stillness was affording me a first real opportunity to think about so many things. As First Lady, I'd get to the end of a busy week and need to be reminded how it had started. But time is beginning to feel different. My girls, who arrived at the White House with their Polly Pocket dolls, a blanket named Blankie, and a stuffed tiger named Tiger, are now teenagers, young women with plans and voices of their own. My husband is making his own adjustments to life after the White House, catching his own breath. And here I am, in this new place, with a lot I want to say.

BECOMING

Becoming Me

1

I SPENT MUCH OF MY CHILDHOOD LISTENING TO THE sound of striving. It came in the form of bad music, or at least amateur music, coming up through the floorboards of my bedroom—the *plink plink plink* of students sitting downstairs at my great-aunt Robbie's piano, slowly and imperfectly learning their scales. My family lived in the South Shore neighborhood of Chicago, in a tidy brick bungalow that belonged to Robbie and her husband, Terry. My parents rented an apartment on the second floor, while Robbie and Terry lived on the first. Robbie was my mom's aunt and had been generous to her over many years, but to me she was kind of a terror. Prim and serious, she directed the choir at a local church and was also our community's resident piano teacher. She wore sensible shoes and kept a pair of reading glasses on a chain around her neck. She had a sly smile but didn't appreciate sarcasm the way my mom did. I'd sometimes hear her chewing out her students for not having practiced enough or chewing out their parents for delivering them late to lessons.

"Good night!" she'd exclaim in the middle of the day, with the same blast of exasperation someone else might say, "Oh, for God's sake!" Few, it seemed, could live up to Robbie's standards.

The sound of people trying, however, became the soundtrack to our life. There was plinking in the afternoons, plinking in the evenings. Ladies from church sometimes came over to practice hymns. Under Robbie's rules, kids who took piano lessons were allowed to work on only one song at a time. From my room, I'd listen to them attempting, note by uncertain note, to win her approval, graduating from "Hot Cross Buns" to "Brahms's Lullaby," but only after many tries. The music was never annoying; it was just persistent. It crept up the stairwell that separated our space from Robbie's. It drifted through open windows in summertime, accompanying my thoughts as I played with my Barbies or built little kingdoms made out of blocks. The only break came when my dad got home from an early shift at the city's water treatment plant and put the Cubs game on TV, boosting the volume just enough to blot it all out.

This was the tail end of the 1960s on the South Side of Chicago. The Cubs weren't bad, but they weren't great, either. I'd sit on my dad's lap in his recliner and listen to him narrate how the Cubs were playing or why Billy Williams, who lived just around the corner from us on Constance Avenue, had such a sweet swing from the left side of the plate. Outside the ballparks, America was in the midst of a massive and uncertain change. The Kennedys were dead. Martin Luther King Jr. had been killed standing on a balcony in Memphis, setting off riots across the country, including in Chicago. The 1968 Democratic National Convention turned bloody as police went after Vietnam War protesters with batons and tear gas in Grant Park, about nine miles north of where we lived. White families, meanwhile, were moving out of the city to the suburbs, drawn by the promise of better schools, more space, and probably more whiteness, too.

None of this really registered with me. I was just a kid, a girl with Barbies and blocks, with two parents and an older brother who slept each night with his head about three feet from mine. My family was my world, the center of everything. My mom taught me how to read early, walking me to the public library, sitting with me as I sounded out words on a page. My dad went to work every day dressed in the blue uniform of a city laborer, but at night he showed us what it meant to love jazz and art. As a boy, he'd taken classes at the Art Institute of Chicago, and in high school he'd painted and sculpted. He'd been a competitive swimmer and boxer in school, too, and as an adult was a fan of every televised sport, from professional golf to the NHL. He appreciated seeing strong people excel. When my brother, Craig, got interested in basketball, my dad propped coins above the doorframe in our kitchen, encouraging him to leap for them.

Everything that mattered was within a five-block radius—my grandparents and cousins, the church on the corner where we were not quite regulars at Sunday school, the gas station where my mom sometimes sent me to pick up a pack of cigarettes, and the liquor store, which also sold Wonder bread, penny candy, and gallons of milk. On hot summer nights, Craig and I dozed off to the sound of cheers from the adult-league softball games going on at the nearby public park, where by day we climbed on the playground jungle gym and played tag with other kids.

Craig and I are not quite two years apart in age. He's got my dad's soft eyes and optimistic spirit, my mom's sense of calm. The two of us have always been tight, in part thanks to a constant and natural loyalty he seemed to feel for his baby sister right from the start. There's an early family photograph of the four of us sitting on a couch, my mom smiling as she holds me on her lap, my dad appearing serious and proud with Craig perched on his. We're dressed for church or maybe a wedding. I'm about eight months old, a pudge-faced, no-nonsense baby in diapers and an ironed white dress, looking ready to slide out of my mom's clutches, staring down the camera as if I might eat it. Next to me is Craig, gentlemanly in a little bow tie and suit jacket, bearing an earnest expression. He's two years old and already the portrait of brotherly watchfulness and responsibility—his arm extended toward mine, his fingers wrapped protectively around my fat wrist.

At the time the photo was taken, we were living across the hall from my dad's parents in Parkway Gardens, an affordable housing project on the South Side made up of modern apartment buildings. It had been built in the 1950s and was meant to ease a post–World War II housing shortage for Black working-class families. Later, it would deteriorate under the grind of poverty and gang violence, becoming one of the city's more dangerous places to live. Long before this, though, when I was still a toddler, my parents—who had met as teenagers and married in their mid-twenties—accepted an offer to move a few miles south to Robbie and Terry's place in a nicer neighborhood.

On Euclid Avenue, we were two households living under one not very big roof. Judging from the layout, the second-floor space had probably been meant for one or two people, but four of us found a way to fit inside. My parents slept in the lone bedroom, while Craig and I shared a bigger area that I assume was intended to be the living room. Later, as we grew, my grandfather—Purnell Shields, my mom's dad, who was an enthusiastic if not deeply skilled carpenter—brought over some cheap wooden paneling and built a makeshift partition to divide the room into two semiprivate spaces. He added a plastic accordion door to each space and created a little common play area in front where we could keep our toys and books.

I loved my room. It was just big enough for a twin bed and a narrow desk. I kept all my stuffed animals on the bed, painstakingly tucking them around my head each night as a form of comfort. On his side of the wall, Craig lived with his own bed pushed up against the paneling, parallel to mine. The partition between us was so flimsy that we could talk as we lay in bed at night, often tossing a balled sock back and forth through the ten-inch gap between the partition and the ceiling as we did.

Aunt Robbie, meanwhile, kept her part of the house like a museum, the furniture swathed in protective plastic that felt cold and sticky on my bare legs when I dared sit on it. Her shelves were loaded with porcelain figurines we weren't allowed to touch. I'd let my hand hover over a set of sweet-faced glass poodles—a delicate-looking mom and three tiny puppies—and then pull it back, fearing Robbie's anger. When piano lessons weren't happening, the first floor was deadly silent. The television was never on, the radio never played. I'm not even sure the two of them talked much down there. Robbie's husband's full name was William Victor Terry, but for some reason we called him only by his last name. Terry was like a shadow, a distinguished-looking man who wore three-piece suits every day of the week and pretty much never said a word.

I came to think of upstairs and downstairs as two different universes. Upstairs, we were noisy and unapologetically so. Craig and I threw balls and chased each other around the apartment. We sprayed Pledge furniture polish on the wood floor of the hallway so we could slide farther and faster in our socks, often crashing into the walls. We held brother-sister boxing matches in the kitchen, using the two sets of gloves my dad had given us for Christmas, along with personalized instructions on how to land a proper jab. At night, as a family, we played board games, told stories and jokes, and cranked Jackson 5 records on the stereo. When it got to be too much for Robbie down below, she'd flick the light switch in our shared stairwell, which also controlled the lightbulb in our upstairs hallway, off and on, again and again—her polite-ish way of telling us to pipe down.

Robbie and Terry were older. They grew up in a different era, with different concerns. They'd seen things our parents hadn't—things that Craig and I, in our childishness, couldn't begin to guess. This was some version of what my mom would say if we got too wound up about the grouchiness downstairs. Even if we didn't know the details, we were instructed to remember that everyone on earth was carrying around an unseen history, and that alone deserved some tolerance. Robbie, I'd learn many years later, had sued Northwestern University for discrimination, having registered for a choral music workshop there in 1943 and been denied a room in the women's dorm. She was instructed to stay instead in a rooming house in town—a place "for coloreds," she was told. Terry, meanwhile, had once been a Pullman porter on one of the overnight passenger rail lines running in and out of Chicago. It was a respectable if not well-paying profession, made up entirely of Black men who kept their uniforms immaculate while also hauling luggage, serving meals, and generally tending to the needs of train passengers, including shining their shoes.

Years after his retirement, Terry still lived in a state of numbed formality—perfectly dressed and never asserting himself in any way, at least that I would see. I'd watch him mow our lawn in the high heat of summer in a pair of wing tips, suspenders, and a thin-brimmed fedora, the sleeves of his dress shirt carefully rolled up. It was as if he'd surrendered a part of himself as a way of coping. Some part of me wanted Terry to talk, to spill whatever secrets he carried. I imagined that he had all sorts of interesting stories about cities he'd visited and how rich people on trains behaved or maybe didn't. But we wouldn't hear any of it. For some reason, he'd never tell.

I WAS ABOUT four when I decided I wanted to learn piano. Craig, who was in the first grade, was already making trips downstairs for weekly lessons on Robbie's upright piano and returning relatively un-harmed. I figured I was ready. I was pretty convinced I already *had* learned piano, almost as if by magic—all those hours spent listening to other kids fumbling through their songs. The music was already in my head. I just wanted to go downstairs and demonstrate to my great-aunt, who had such high expectations, what a gifted girl I was, how it would take no effort at all for me to become her star student.

Robbie's piano sat in a small square room at the rear of the house, close to a window that overlooked the backyard. She kept a potted plant in one corner and a folding table where students could fill out music worksheets in the other. During lessons, she sat straight-spined in an upholstered high-back armchair, tapping out the beat with one finger, her head cocked as she listened keenly for each mistake. Was I afraid of Robbie? Not exactly, but there was a scariness to her; she represented a rigid kind of authority I hadn't yet encountered elsewhere. She demanded excellence from every kid who sat on her piano bench. I saw her as someone to win over, or maybe to somehow conquer. With her, it always felt like there was something to prove.

At my first lesson, my legs dangled from the piano bench, too short to reach the floor. Robbie gave me my own elementary music workbook, which I was thrilled about, and showed me how to position my hands properly over the keys.

"All right, pay attention," she said, scolding me before we'd even begun. "Find middle C."

When you're little, a piano can look like it has a thousand keys. You're staring at an expanse of black and white that stretches farther than two small arms can reach. Middle C, I soon learned, was the anchoring point. It was the dividing line between where the right hand and the left hand traveled, between the treble and the bass clefs. If you could lay your thumb on middle C, everything else automatically fell into place. The keys on Robbie's piano had uneven colors and shapes, places where bits of the ivory had broken off over time, leaving them looking like a set of bad teeth. Helpfully, the middle C key had a full corner missing, a wedge about the size of my fingernail, which got me centered every time.

It turned out I liked the piano. Sitting at it felt natural, like something I was meant to do. My family was loaded with musicians and music lovers, especially on my mom's side. I had an uncle who played in a professional band. Several of my aunts sang in church choirs. I

9

had Robbie, who in addition to her choir and lessons ran a musical theater program for kids, which Craig and I attended every Saturday morning in the basement of her church. The musical center of my family, though, was my grandfather Shields, the carpenter, who was also Robbie's younger brother. He was a carefree, round-bellied man with an infectious laugh and a scraggly salt-and-pepper beard. When I was younger, he'd lived on the West Side of the city and Craig and I had referred to him as Westside. But he moved into our neighborhood the same year I started taking piano lessons, and we'd renamed him Southside.

Southside had separated from my grandmother decades earlier, when my mom was in her teens. He lived with my aunt Carolyn, my mom's oldest sister, and my uncle Steve, her youngest brother, just two blocks from us in a cozy one-story house that he'd wired top to bottom for music, putting speakers in every room, including the bathroom. In the dining room, he built an elaborate cabinet system to hold his stereo equipment, much of it found at yard sales. He had two mismatched turntables and shelves packed with records he'd collected over many years.

There was a lot about the world that Southside didn't trust. He didn't trust dentists, which led to his having almost no teeth. He didn't trust the police, and he didn't always trust white people, either, being the grandson of a Georgia slave and having spent his early childhood in Alabama during the time of Jim Crow segregation before coming north to Chicago in the 1920s. When he had kids of his own, Southside had taken pains to keep them safe—scaring them with real and imagined stories about what might happen to Black kids who crossed into the wrong neighborhood, lecturing them about avoiding the police.

Music seemed to be a cure for his worries, a way to relax and crowd them out. When Southside had a payday for his carpentry work, he'd sometimes splurge and buy himself a new album. He threw regular parties for the family, forcing everyone to talk loudly over whatever he put on the stereo, because the music always dominated. We celebrated most major life events at Southside's house, which meant that over the years we unwrapped Christmas presents listening to the music of Ella Fitzgerald and blew out birthday candles to John Coltrane. According to my mom, as a younger man Southside had made a point of pumping jazz into his seven children, often waking everyone at sunrise by playing one of his records at full blast.

His love for music was passed on to me. Once Southside moved to our neighborhood, I'd spend whole afternoons at his house, pulling albums from the shelf at random and putting them on his stereo, each one its own immersing adventure. Even though I was small, he put no limits on what I could touch. He'd later buy me my first album, Stevie Wonder's *Talking Book,* which I'd keep at his house on a special shelf he gave me for my favorite records. If I was hungry, he'd make me a milk shake or fry us a whole chicken while we listened to Aretha Franklin or Miles Davis or Billie Holiday. To me, Southside was as big as heaven. And heaven, as I envisioned it, had to be a place full of jazz.

AT HOME, I continued to work on my own progress as a musician. Sitting at Robbie's upright piano, I was quick to pick up the scales, and I threw myself into filling out the sight-reading worksheets she gave me. Because we didn't have a piano of our own, I had to do my practicing downstairs on hers, waiting until nobody else was having a lesson, often dragging my mom with me to sit in the upholstered chair and listen to me play. I learned one song in the piano book and then another. I was probably no better than her other students, no less fumbling, but I was driven to succeed. To me, there was magic in the learning. I got a buzzy sort of satisfaction from it. For one thing, I'd picked up on the simple, encouraging connection between how long I practiced and how much I achieved. And I sensed something in Robbie as well—too deeply buried to be outright pleasure, but still, a pulse of something lighter and happier coming from her when I made it through a song without messing up, when my right hand picked out a melody while my left touched down on a chord. I'd notice it out of the corner of my eye: Robbie's lips would unpurse themselves just slightly; her tapping finger would pick up a little bounce.

This, it turns out, was our honeymoon phase. It's possible that we might have continued this way, Robbie and I, had I been less curious and more respectful when it came to her piano method. But the lesson book was thick enough and my progress on the opening few songs slow enough that I got impatient and started peeking ahead—and not just a few pages ahead but deep into the book, checking out the titles of the more advanced songs and beginning, during my practice sessions, to fiddle around with playing them. When I proudly debuted one of my late-in-the-book songs for Robbie, she exploded, slapping down my achievement with a vicious "Good *night*!" I got chewed out the way I'd heard her chewing out plenty of students before me. All I'd done was try to learn more and faster, but Robbie viewed it as a serious crime. She wasn't impressed, not even a little bit.

I didn't care. I was the kind of kid who liked clear answers to my questions, who liked to reason things out to some logical if exhausting end. I was lawyerly and also veered toward dictatorial, as my brother, who often got ordered out of our shared play area, would agree. When I thought I had a good idea about something, I didn't like being told no. Which is how my great-aunt and I ended up in each other's faces, both of us hot and unyielding.

"How could you be mad at me for wanting to learn a new song?"

"You're not ready for it. That's not how you learn piano."

"But I *am* ready. I just played it."

"That's not how it's done."

"But *why*?"

Piano lessons became dramatic and trying, largely due to my refusal to follow Robbie's method and Robbie's refusal to see anything good in my freewheeling approach to her songbook. We went back and forth, week after week, as I remember it. I was stubborn and so was she. I had a point of view and she did, too. In between disputes, I continued to play the piano and she continued to listen, offering a stream of corrections. I gave her little credit for my improvement as a player. She gave me little credit for improving. But still, the lessons went on.

Upstairs, my parents and Craig found it all so very funny. They cracked up at the dinner table as I recounted my battles with Robbie, still seething as I ate my spaghetti and meatballs. Craig, for his part, had no issues with Robbie, being a cheerful kid who followed her rules as a piano student. My parents expressed no sympathy for my woes and none for Robbie's, either. In general, they weren't ones to get involved in matters outside schooling, expecting early on that my brother and I should handle our own business. They seemed to view their job as mostly to listen and bolster us as needed inside the four walls of our home. And where another parent might have scolded a kid for being sassy with an elder as I had been, they also let that be. My mom had lived with Robbie on and off since she was about sixteen, following every old-fashioned rule the woman laid down, and it's possible she was secretly happy to see Robbie's authority challenged. Looking back on it now, I think my parents appreciated my feistiness and I'm glad for it. It was a flame inside me they wanted to keep lit.

ONCE A YEAR, Robbie held a fancy recital so that her students could perform for a live audience. To this day, I'm not sure how she managed it, but she somehow got access to a practice hall at Roosevelt University in downtown Chicago, holding her recitals in a grand stone building on Michigan Avenue, right near where the Chicago Symphony Orchestra played. Just thinking about going there made me nervous. Our apartment on Euclid Avenue was about nine miles south of the Chicago Loop, which with its glittering skyscrapers and crowded sidewalks felt a world away to me. My family made trips into the heart of the city only a handful of times a year, to visit the Art Institute or see a play, the four of us traveling like astronauts in the capsule of my dad's Buick.

My dad loved any excuse to drive. He was devoted to his car, a bronze-colored two-door Buick Electra 225, which he referred to with pride as "the Deuce and a Quarter." He kept it buffed and waxed and was careful about the maintenance schedule, taking it to Sears for tire rotations and oil changes the same way my mom carted us kids to the pediatrician for checkups. We loved the Deuce and a Quarter, too. It had smooth lines and narrow taillights that made it look cool and futuristic. It was roomy enough to feel like a house. I could practically stand up inside it, running my hands over the cloth-covered ceiling. This was back when wearing a seat belt was not required by law, so most of the time Craig and I just flopped around in the rear, draping our bodies over the front seat when we wanted to talk to our parents. Half the time I'd pull myself up on the headrest and jut my chin forward so that my face could be next to my dad's and we'd have the exact same view.

The car provided another form of closeness for my family, a chance to talk and travel at once. In the evenings after dinner, Craig and I would sometimes beg my dad to take us out for an aimless drive. As a treat on summer nights, we'd head to a drive-in theater southwest of our neighborhood to watch Planet of the Apes movies, parking the Buick at dusk and settling in for the show, my mom handing out a dinner of fried chicken and potato chips she'd brought from home, Craig and I eating it on our laps in the backseat, careful to wipe our hands on our napkins and not the seat.

It would be years before I fully understood what driving the car meant to my dad. As a kid, I could only sense it—the freedom he felt behind the wheel, the pleasure he took in having a smooth-running engine and perfectly balanced tires humming beneath him. He'd been in his thirties when a doctor informed him that the odd weakness he'd started to feel in one leg was just the beginning of a long and probably painful slide. The odds were that someday, due to a mysterious disease attacking his brain and spinal cord, he'd find himself unable to walk at all. I don't have the precise dates, but it seems that the Buick came into my dad's life at roughly the same time that multiple sclerosis did. And though he never said it, the car had to provide some sort of sideways relief.

The diagnosis was not something he or my mom dwelled upon. We were decades, still, from a time when a simple Google search would bring up a head-spinning array of charts, statistics, and medical explainers that either gave or took away hope. I doubt he would have wanted to see them anyway. Although my dad was raised in the church, he wouldn't have prayed for God to spare him. He wouldn't have looked for alternative treatments or a guru or some faulty gene to blame. In my family, we have a long-standing habit of blocking out bad news, of trying to forget about it almost the moment it arrives. Nobody knew how long my dad had been feeling poorly before he first took himself to the doctor, but my guess is it had already been months if not years. He didn't like medical appointments. He wasn't interested in complaining. He was the sort of person who accepted what came and just kept moving forward.

I do know that on the day of my big piano recital, he was already walking with a slight limp, his left foot unable to catch up to his right. All my memories of my dad include some reminder of his disability, even if none of us were quite willing to call it that yet. What I knew at the time was that my dad moved a bit more slowly than other dads. I sometimes saw him pausing before walking up a flight of stairs, as if needing to think through the maneuver before actually attempting it. When we went shopping at the mall, he'd park himself on a bench, content to watch the bags or sneak in a nap while the rest of the family roamed freely.

Riding downtown for the piano recital, I sat in the backseat of the Buick wearing a nice dress and patent leather shoes, my hair in pigtails, experiencing the first cold sweat of my life. I was anxious about performing, even though back at home in Robbie's apartment I'd practiced my song practically to death. Craig, too, was in a suit and prepared to play his own song. But the prospect of it wasn't bothering him. He was sound asleep, in fact, knocked out cold in the backseat, his mouth slightly open, his expression blissful and unworried. This was Craig. I'd spend a lifetime admiring him for his ease. He was playing by then in a Biddy Basketball league that had games every weekend and apparently had already tamed his nerves around performing.

My dad would often pick a lot as close to our destination as possible, shelling out more money for parking to minimize how far he'd have to walk on his unsteady legs. That day, we found Roosevelt University with no trouble and made our way up to what seemed like an enormous, echoing hall where the recital would take place. I felt tiny inside it. The room had elegant floor-to-ceiling windows through which you could see the wide lawns of Grant Park and, beyond that, the white-capped swells of Lake Michigan. There were steel-gray chairs arranged in orderly rows, slowly filling with nervous kids and expectant parents. And at the front, on a raised stage, were the first two baby grand pianos I'd ever laid eyes on, their giant hardwood tops propped open like black bird wings. Robbie was there, too, bustling about in a floral-print dress like the belle of the ball, making sure all her students had arrived with sheet music in hand. She shushed the room to silence when it was time for the show to begin.

I don't recall who played in what order that day. I only know that when it was my turn, I got up from my seat and walked with my very best posture to the front of the room, mounting the stairs and finding my seat at one of the gleaming baby grands. The truth is I was ready. As much as I found Robbie to be snippy and stubborn, I'd also fully absorbed her devotion to preparation. I knew my song so well I hardly had to think about it. I just had to start moving my hands.

And yet there was a problem, one I discovered in the split second it took to lift my little fingers to the keys. I was sitting at a perfect piano, it turned out, with its surfaces carefully dusted, its internal wires precisely tuned, its eighty-eight keys laid out in a flawless ribbon of black and white. The issue was that I wasn't used to flawless. In fact, I'd never once in my life encountered it. My experience of the piano came entirely from Robbie's squat little music room with its scraggly potted plant and view of our modest backyard. The only instrument I'd ever played was her less-than-perfect upright, with its honky-tonk patchwork of yellowed keys and its conveniently chipped middle C. To me, that's what a piano was—the same way my neighborhood was my neighborhood, my dad was my dad, my life was my life. It was all I knew.

Now, suddenly, I was aware of people watching me from their chairs as I stared hard at the high gloss of the piano keys, finding nothing there but sameness. I had no clue where to place my hands. With a tight throat and chugging heart, I looked out to the audience, trying not to show my panic, searching for the safe harbor of my mom's face. Instead, I spotted a figure rising from the front row and slowly moving in my direction. It was Robbie. We had brawled plenty by then, to the point where I viewed her a little bit like an enemy. But here in my moment of embarrassment, she arrived at my shoulder almost like an angel. Maybe she understood my shock. Maybe she knew that the inequalities of the world had just quietly shown themselves to me for the first time. It's possible she needed simply to hurry things up. Either way, without a word, Robbie gently laid one finger on middle C so that I would know where to start. Then, turning back with the smallest smile of encouragement, she left me to play my song.

2

I STARTED KINDERGARTEN AT BRYN MAWR ELEMEN-
tary School in the fall of 1969, showing up with the twin advantages
of knowing in advance how to read basic words and having a well-
liked second-grade brother ahead of me. The school, a four-story brick
building with a yard in front, sat just a couple of blocks from our house
on Euclid. Getting there involved a two-minute walk or, if you did it
like Craig, a one-minute run.

I liked school right away. I liked my teacher, a small white lady
named Mrs. Burroughs, who seemed ancient to me. Her classroom
had big sunny windows, a collection of baby dolls to play with, and
a giant cardboard playhouse in the back. I made friends in my class,
drawn to the kids who, like me, seemed eager to be there. I was confident in my ability to read. At home, I'd plowed through the Dick
and Jane books, courtesy of my mom's library card, and was thrilled
to hear that our first job as kindergartners would be learning to read
new sets of words by sight. We were assigned a list of names of colors
to study: "red," "blue," "green," "black," "orange," "purple," "white." In
class, Mrs. Burroughs quizzed us one student at a time, holding up a

series of large manila cards and asking us to read whatever word was printed in black letters on the front. I watched one day as the girls and boys I was just getting to know stood up and worked through the color cards, and were told to sit back down at whatever point they got stumped. It was meant to be something of a game, I think, the way a spelling bee is a game, but you could see a sorting going on and a knowing slump of humiliation in the kids who didn't make it past "red." This, of course, was 1969, in a public school on the South Side of Chicago. If you'd had a head start at home, you were rewarded for it at school. Teachers thought you were "bright" or "gifted," which in turn only increased your confidence. The advantages piled up quickly. The two smartest kids in my kindergarten class were Teddy, a Korean American boy, and Chiaka, an African American girl, who both would remain at the top of the class for years to come.

I was driven to keep up with them. When my turn came to read the words off the teacher's manila cards, I stood up and gave it everything I had, rattling off "red," "green," and "blue" without effort. "Purple" took a second, though, and "orange" was hard. But it wasn't until the letters W-H-I-T-E came up that I froze altogether, my throat instantly dry, my mouth awkward and unable to shape the sound as my brain glitched madly, trying to dig up a color that resembled "wuh-haaa." It was a straight-up choke. I felt a weird airiness in my knees, as if they might buckle. But before they did, Mrs. Burroughs instructed me to sit back down. And that's exactly when the word hit me in its full and easy perfection. *White. Whiiiite.* The word was "white."

Lying in bed that night with my stuffed animals packed around my head, I thought only of "white." I spelled it in my head, forward and backward, angered by my own stupidity. The embarrassment felt like a weight, like something I'd never shake off, even though I knew my parents wouldn't care whether I'd read every card correctly. I just wanted to achieve. Or maybe I didn't want to be dismissed as unable to achieve. I was sure my teacher had now pegged me as someone who couldn't read or, worse, didn't try. I obsessed over the dime-sized gold-foil stars that Mrs. Burroughs had given to Teddy and Chiaka that day to wear on their chests as an emblem of their accomplishment, or maybe a sign that they were marked for greatness when the rest of us weren't. The two of them, after all, had read every last color card without a hitch.

The next morning in class, I asked for a do-over.

When Mrs. Burroughs said no, cheerily adding that we kindergartners had other things to get to, I demanded it.

Pity the kids who then had to watch me face the color cards a second time, going slower now, pausing to breathe after I'd pronounced each word, refusing to let my nerves short-circuit my brain. And it worked, through "black," "orange," "purple," and especially "white." I was practically shouting the word "white" before I'd even seen the letters on the card. I like to imagine now that Mrs. Burroughs was impressed with this little Black girl who'd found the courage to stand up for herself. I didn't know whether Teddy and Chiaka had even noticed. I was quick to claim my trophy, though, heading home that afternoon with my head up and one of those gold-foil stars stuck on my shirt.

AT HOME, I lived in a world of high drama and intrigue, creating an ever-evolving soap opera with my dolls. There were births, feuds, and betrayals. There was hope, hatred, and sometimes love. My preferred way to pass the time between school and dinner was to park myself in the common area outside my room and Craig's and spread my Barbies across the floor, imagining scenes that felt as real to me as life itself, sometimes inserting Craig's G.I. Joe action figures into the plotlines. I kept my dolls' outfits in a child-sized vinyl suitcase covered in a floral print. I assigned every Barbie and every G.I. Joe a personality. I also used the worn-out alphabet blocks my mom had used years earlier to teach us our letters. They, too, were given names and inner lives.

I rarely chose to join the neighborhood kids who played outside after school, nor did I invite school friends home with me, in part because I was an extremely neat and tidy kid and didn't want anyone meddling with my dolls. I'd been to other girls' houses and seen, to my horror, Barbies whose hair had been hacked off or whose faces had been crosshatched with Magic Marker. And one thing I was learning at school was that relationships between kids could be messy. Whatever sweet scenes you might witness on a playground, there were queen bees, bullies, and followers. I wasn't shy, but I also wasn't sure I needed any of that messiness in my life outside school. Instead, I sank my energy into being the only one in charge of my little common-area universe. If Craig showed up and had the nerve to move a single block, I'd start shrieking. I was also not above hitting him when necessary— usually a direct fist blow to the middle of his back. The point was that the dolls and blocks needed me to give them life, and I dutifully gave it to them, imposing one personal crisis after another. Like any good all-powerful ruler, I was there to see them suffer and grow.

Meanwhile, from my bedroom window, I could observe most of the real-world happenings on our block of Euclid Avenue. In the late afternoons, I'd see Mr. Thompson, the tall African American man who owned the building across the street, loading his big bass guitar into the back of his Cadillac, setting off for a gig in one jazz club or another. I'd watch the Mendozas, the Mexican family next door, arriving home in their pickup truck loaded with ladders after a long day of painting houses, greeted at the fence by their yapping dogs.

Our neighborhood was middle-class and racially mixed. Kids found one another based not on the color of their skin but on who was outside and ready to play. My friends included a girl named Rachel, whose mom was white and had a British accent; Susie, a curly-haired redhead; and the Mendozas' granddaughter whenever she was visiting. We were a mix of last names—Kansopant, Abuasef, Yacker, Robinson—and were too young to understand that things around us were changing fast. Fifteen years before my parents moved to South Shore, the neighborhood had been 96 percent white. By the time I'd leave for college decades later, it would be about 96 percent Black.

Craig and I were raised squarely in the middle of the changing times. The blocks surrounding us were home to Jewish families, immigrant families, white and Black families, folks who were thriving and some who were not. In general, people tended to their lawns and kept track of their children. They wrote checks to Robbie so their kids could learn piano. My family, in fact, was probably on the poor side of the neighborhood. We were among the few people we knew who didn't own their own home, stuffed as we were into Robbie and Terry's second floor. South Shore hadn't changed the way other neighborhoods had—with the better-off people long departed for the suburbs and the neighborhood businesses closing one by one. But the change was clearly beginning.

We were starting to feel the effects of this change, especially at school. My second-grade classroom turned out to be a group of unruly kids and flying erasers, which neither Craig nor I had experienced before. All this seemed due to a teacher who couldn't figure out how to assert control—who didn't seem to like children, even. Beyond that, it wasn't clear that anyone was particularly bothered by the fact that the teacher was incompetent. The students used it as an excuse to act out, and she seemed to think only the worst of us. In her eyes, we were a class of "bad kids," though we had no guidance and no structure and had been sentenced to a grim, underlit room in the basement of the school. Every hour there felt hellish and long. I sat miserably at my desk, in my puke-green chair, learning nothing and waiting for the midday lunch break, when I could go home and have a sandwich and complain to my mom.

When I got angry as a kid, I almost always directed it through my mom. As I fumed about my new teacher, she listened, saying things like "Oh, dear" and "Oh, really?" She never indulged my outrage, but she took my frustration seriously. If my mom were somebody different, she might have done the polite thing and said, "Just go and do your best." But she knew the difference. She knew the difference between whining and actual distress. Without telling me, she went over to the school many times to convince them to do something. This led to me and a couple of other high-performing kids getting quietly pulled out of class, given tests, and about a week later promoted into a bright and orderly third-grade class upstairs, governed by a smiling, no-nonsense teacher who knew her stuff.

It was a small but life-changing move. I didn't stop to ask myself then what would happen to all the kids who'd been left in the basement with the teacher who couldn't teach. Now that I'm an adult, I realize that kids know at a very young age when they're not valued, when adults aren't invested enough to help them learn. Their anger over it can manifest itself as unruliness. It's hardly their fault. They aren't "bad kids." They're just trying to survive bad circumstances. At the time, though, I was just happy to have escaped.

AS TIME WENT BY, my mom started nudging me to go outside and play with kids in the neighborhood. She was hoping that I'd learn to glide socially the way my brother had. Craig, as I've mentioned, had a way of making hard things look easy. He was by then a growing sensation on the basketball court, high-spirited and agile and quickly growing tall. My dad pushed him to seek out the toughest competition he could find, which meant that he would later send Craig across town on his own to play with the best kids in the city. But for now, he left him to wrangle the neighborhood talent. Craig would take his ball and carry it across the street to Rosenblum Park, passing the monkey bars and swing set where I liked to play and disappearing through a veil of trees to the far side of the park, where the basketball courts were. I thought of it as a dark forest full of drunks and thugs and criminal goings-on, but Craig, once he started visiting that side of the park, would set me straight, saying that really nobody over there was all that bad.

Basketball, for my brother, seemed to unlock every frontier. It taught him how to approach people he didn't know when he wanted to snag a spot in a pickup game. He learned how to trash-talk his bigger, faster opponents on the court in a friendly way. It helped, too, to prove untrue various myths about who was who and what was what around the neighborhood, reinforcing the possibility—something that had long been my dad's point of view—that most people were good people if you just treated them well. Even the sketchy guys who hung out in front of the corner liquor store lit up when they spotted Craig, calling his name and high-fiving him as we passed by.

"How do you even know them?" I'd ask.

"I don't know. They just know me," he'd say with a shrug.

I was ten when I finally mellowed enough to start heading out myself, a decision driven in large part by boredom. It was summer and school was out. Craig and I rode a bus to Lake Michigan every day to go to a city-run camp, but we'd be back home by four, with many daylight hours still to fill. My dolls were becoming less interesting, and without air-conditioning our apartment got unbearably hot in the late afternoons. And so I started tailing Craig around the neighborhood, meeting the kids I didn't already know from school. Across the alley behind our house, there was a mini housing community called Euclid Parkway, where about fifteen homes had been built around a common green space. It was a kind of paradise, free from cars and full of kids playing softball and jumping double Dutch or sitting on stoops, just hanging out. But before I could find my way into the fold of girls my age who hung out at the Parkway, I faced a test. It came in the form of DeeDee, a girl who went to a nearby Catholic school. DeeDee was athletic and pretty, but she wore her face in a pout and was always ready

24

with an eye roll. She often sat on her family's stoop next to another, more popular girl named Deneen.

Deneen was always friendly, but DeeDee didn't seem to like me. I don't know why. Every time I went over to Euclid Parkway, she'd make quiet, cutting remarks, as if just by showing up I'd managed to ruin everyone's day. As the summer went on, DeeDee's comments only grew louder. I was upset. I understood that I had choices. I could continue on as the picked-on new girl, I could give up on the Parkway and just go back to my toys at home, or I could attempt to earn DeeDee's respect. And inside that last choice lay another one: I could try to win DeeDee over with words, or I could just shut her up.

The next time DeeDee made one of her remarks, I lunged for her, summoning everything my dad had taught me about how to throw a punch. The two of us fell to the ground, fists flailing and legs thrashing, every kid in Euclid Parkway instantly clustered in a tight knot around us, their hollers fueled by excitement. I can't remember who finally pulled us apart, whether it was Deneen or my brother or maybe a parent who'd been called to the scene, but when it was done, something had taken place. I was now officially an accepted member of the neighborhood tribe. DeeDee and I were unharmed, dirt-stained and panting and destined never to be close friends, but at least I'd earned her respect.

MY DAD'S BUICK continued to be our shelter, our window to the world. We took it out on Sundays and summer evenings, cruising for no reason but the fact that we could. Sometimes we'd end up in a neighborhood to the south, an area known as Pill Hill due to an apparently large number of African American doctors living there. It was one of the prettier, richer parts of the South Side, where people kept two cars in the driveway and had abundant beds of flowers blooming along their walkways.

My dad viewed rich people with a shade of suspicion. He didn't like people who were uppity and had mixed feelings about owning a home. There was a short period when he and my mom considered buying a home for sale not far from Robbie's house, driving over one day to inspect the place with a real estate agent, but ultimately deciding against it. At the time, I'd been all for it. In my mind, I thought it would mean something if my family could live in a place with more than one floor. But my dad was naturally cautious, understanding the need to maintain some savings for a rainy day. "You never want to end up house poor," he'd tell us, explaining how some people handed over their savings and borrowed too much, ending up with a nice home but no freedom at all.

My parents talked to us like we were adults. They didn't lecture, but rather indulged every question we asked, no matter how juvenile. They never hurried a discussion for the sake of convenience. Our talks could go on for hours, often because Craig and I took every opportunity to grill my parents about things we didn't understand. When we were little, we'd ask, "Why do people go to the bathroom?" or "Why do you need a job?" and then blitz them with follow-ups. One of my early victories came from a question driven by self-interest: "Why do we have to eat eggs for breakfast?" Which led to a discussion about the necessity of protein, which led me to ask why peanut butter couldn't count as protein, which eventually, after more debate, led to my mom changing her mind about eggs, which I had never liked to eat in the first place. For the next nine years, knowing that I'd earned it, I made myself a fat peanut butter and jelly sandwich for breakfast each morning and never ate a single egg.

As we grew, we spoke more about life choices and race and inequality and politics. My parents didn't expect us to be perfect. They also never sugarcoated what they took to be the harder truths about life. Craig, for example, got a new bike one summer and rode it east to Lake Michigan, to the paved pathway along Rainbow Beach, where

26

you could feel the breeze off the water. He'd been promptly picked up by a police officer who accused him of stealing it, unwilling to accept that a young Black boy would have come across a new bike in an honest way. (The officer, an African American man himself, ultimately got a brutal tongue-lashing from my mom, who made him apologize to Craig.) What had happened, my parents told us, was unjust but also unfortunately common. The color of our skin made us vulnerable. It was a thing we'd always have to navigate.

My dad's habit of driving us through Pill Hill was a bit of an aspirational exercise. It was his chance to show us what a good education could lead to. My parents had spent almost their entire lives living within a couple of square miles in Chicago, but they did not expect that Craig and I would do the same. Before they were married, both of them had briefly attended community colleges, but each had abandoned school long before getting a degree. My mom had been studying to become a teacher but realized she'd rather work as a secretary. My dad had simply run out of money to pay tuition, joining the Army instead. He'd had no one in his family to talk him into returning to school, no model of what that sort of life looked like. Instead, he served two years moving between different military bases. If finishing college and becoming an artist had been a dream for my dad, he quickly redirected his hopes, using his wages to help pay for his younger brother's degree in architecture instead.

In his late thirties, my dad was focused on saving for us kids. Our family was never going to be house poor, because we weren't going to own a house. My dad operated from a practical place, sensing that resources were limited and maybe so, too, was time. When he wasn't driving, he now used a cane to get around. Before I finished elementary school, that cane would become a crutch and soon after that two crutches. Whatever disease was inside my dad, it was withering his muscles and stripping his nerves. My dad viewed it as his own private challenge, as something to silently withstand.

As a family, we allowed ourselves humble luxuries. When Craig and I got our report cards at school, our parents celebrated by ordering in a pizza from Italian Fiesta, our favorite place. During hot weather, we'd buy hand-packed ice cream—a pint each of chocolate, butter pecan, and black cherry—and make it last for days. Every year for the Air and Water Show, we packed a picnic and drove north along Lake Michigan to the fenced-off peninsula where my dad's water filtration plant was located. It was one of the few times a year when employee families were allowed through the gates and onto a grassy lawn overlooking the lake, where the view of fighter jets swooping in formation over the water rivaled that of any penthouse on Lake Shore Drive.

Each July, my dad would take a week off from his job tending boilers at the plant, and we'd pile into the Buick with an aunt and a couple of cousins, seven of us in that two-door car for hours, taking the Skyway out of Chicago, skirting the south end of Lake Michigan, and driving until we landed in White Cloud, Michigan, at a place called Dukes Happy Holiday Resort. It had a game room, a vending machine that sold glass bottles of pop, and most important to us, a big outdoor swimming pool. We rented a cabin with a kitchenette and passed our days jumping in and out of the water.

My parents barbecued, smoked cigarettes, and played cards with my aunt, but my dad also took long breaks to join us kids in the pool. He was handsome, my dad, with a mustache that tipped down the sides of his lips. His chest and arms were thick and roped with muscle. It showed that he had once been an athlete. During those long afternoons in the pool, he paddled and laughed and tossed our small bodies into the air, his weakened legs suddenly less of a problem.

DECLINE CAN BE a hard thing to measure, especially when it's happening all around you. Every September, when Craig and I showed up back at Bryn Mawr Elementary, we'd find fewer white kids on the playground. Some had transferred to a nearby Catholic school, but many had left the neighborhood altogether. At first it felt as if just the white families were leaving, but then that changed, too. It soon seemed that anyone who had the means to go was now going. Much of the time, the departures went unannounced and unexplained. We'd see a "For Sale" sign in front of the Yacker family's house or a moving van in front of Teddy's and know what was coming.

Perhaps the hardest time for my mom came when her friend Velma Stewart announced that she and her husband had put a down payment on a house in a suburb called Park Forest. The Stewarts had two kids and lived down the block on Euclid. Like us, they were apartment dwellers. Mrs. Stewart had a terrific sense of humor and a big laugh, which drew my mom to her. The two of them swapped recipes and kept up with each other, but never fell into the neighborhood's gossip the way other moms did. Mrs. Stewart's son, Donny, was Craig's age and just as athletic, giving the two of them an instant bond. Her daughter, Pamela, was a teenager already and not so interested in me, though I found all teenagers interesting. I don't remember much about Mr. Stewart, except that he drove a delivery truck for one of the big bakery companies in the city and that he and his wife and their kids were the lightest-skinned Black people I'd ever met.

How they afforded a place in the suburbs, I couldn't guess. Park Forest was one of America's first fully planned communities—a full village with shopping malls, churches, schools, parks, and mass-produced houses with cookie-cutter yards. There were also limits on how many Black families could live on a given block, though by the time the Stewarts got there, the limits had apparently been abolished.

Not long after they moved, the Stewarts invited us to come visit them on one of my dad's days off. We were excited. For us, it would be a new kind of outing, a chance to glimpse the suburbs. The four of us took the Buick south on the expressway, following the road out of Chicago, exiting about forty minutes later near a drab shopping plaza.

We were soon winding through a network of quiet streets with houses that all looked the same.

"Now why would anyone want to live all the way out here?" my dad asked, staring over the dashboard. I agreed that it made no sense. As far as I could see, there were no big trees like the giant oak that sat outside my bedroom window at home. Everything in Park Forest was new and wide and uncrowded. There was no corner liquor store with ratty guys hanging out in front of it. There were no cars honking or sirens. There was no music floating from anybody's kitchen. The windows in the houses all looked to be shut.

Craig would remember our visit there as heavenly, namely because he played ball all day long in the wide-open lots under a blue sky with Donny Stewart and his new pack of suburban brothers. My parents had a pleasant enough catch-up with Mr. and Mrs. Stewart, and I followed Pamela around, gaping at her hair, her fair skin, and her teenager jewelry. At some point, we all had lunch.

It was evening when we finally said good-bye. Leaving the Stewarts, we walked in the dusk to the curb where my dad had parked the car. Craig was sweaty, dead on his feet after all the running he'd done. I, too, was fatigued and ready to go home. Something about the place had put me on edge. I wasn't a fan of the suburbs, though I couldn't explain exactly why.

My mom would later make an observation about the Stewarts and their new community, based on the fact that almost all of their neighbors on the street seemed to be white.

"I wonder," she said, "if nobody knew that they're a Black family until we came to visit."

She thought that maybe we'd accidentally outed them, arriving from the South Side with a housewarming gift and our obvious dark skin. Even if the Stewarts weren't trying to hide their race on purpose, they probably didn't speak of it one way or another with their new neighbors. Whatever vibe existed on their block, they hadn't disrupted it. At least not until we came to visit.

Was somebody watching through a window as my dad approached our car that night? Was there a shadow behind some curtain, waiting to see how things would go? I'll never know. I just remember the way my dad's body stiffened slightly when he reached the driver's side door and saw what was there. Someone had scratched a line across the side of his beloved Buick, a thin ugly mark that ran across the door and toward the tail of the car. It had been done with a key or a rock and was in no way accidental.

I've said before that my dad was a man who never complained about small things or big, who cheerily ate liver when it was served to him, who had a doctor give him what amounted to a death sentence and then just carried on. This thing with the car was no different. If there was some way to fight it, if there was some door to pound in response, my dad wouldn't have done it anyway.

"Well, I'll be darned," he said, before unlocking the car.

We rode back to the city that night without much discussion about what had happened. It was too exhausting, maybe, to even think about. In any event, we were done with the suburbs. My dad must have had to drive the car to work the next day looking the way it did, and I'm sure that didn't sit well with him. But the gash in his chrome didn't stay for long. As soon as there was time, he took the car over to the body shop and had it erased.

3

SOMEWHERE ALONG THE WAY, MY NORMALLY LAID-back brother started to sprout worries. I can't say exactly when or why this began, but Craig—the boy who could high-five and what-up his way around the neighborhood, who catnapped anytime he had ten free minutes, regardless of his surroundings—grew more fretful and vigilant at home, convinced that catastrophe was creeping our way. In the evenings at our apartment, he rehearsed for every possible outcome. Worried he'd lose his sight, he took to wearing a blindfold around the house, learning to navigate our living room and kitchen by feel. Worried he might go deaf, he began teaching himself sign language. There was also apparently the threat of amputation, prompting Craig to fumble his way through various meals and homework sessions with his right arm tied behind his back. Because you never did know.

Craig's biggest fear, however, was also probably the most realistic, and that was fire. House fires were a regular occurrence in Chicago, in part due to slumlords who let their buildings slide into disrepair and were all too happy to reap the insurance benefits when a fire tore through. Home smoke detectors were a recent development and still expensive for working-class people to afford. Inside our tight city grid, fire was almost a fact of life, a random but persistent snatcher of homes and hearts. My grandfather Southside had moved to our neighborhood after a fire destroyed his old house on the West Side, though luckily nobody'd been hurt. (According to my mom, Southside stood on the curb outside the burning house, shouting for the firefighters to direct their hoses away from his precious jazz albums.) More recently, in a tragedy almost too giant for my young mind to take in, one of my fifth-grade classmates—a boy with a sweet face and a tall Afro named Lester McCullom, who lived around the corner from us—had died in a fire that also killed his brother and sister, the three of them trapped by flames in bedrooms upstairs.

Theirs was the first wake I ever attended: every kid in the neighborhood sobbing at the funeral parlor as a Jackson 5 album played softly in the background; the adults stunned into silence. There were three closed caskets at the front of the room, each one with a framed photograph of a smiling child on its lid. Mrs. McCullom, who with her husband had managed to survive the fire by jumping out a window, sat before them, so slumped and broken that it hurt to look in her direction.

For days afterward, the skeleton of the McCulloms' burned-out town house continued to hiss and cave in on itself. The smell of smoke lingered heavily in the neighborhood.

As time passed, Craig's anxieties only grew. At school, we'd been put through the paces of teacher-led evacuation drills and taught how to stop, drop, and roll. And as a result, Craig decided that we needed to step it up on safety at home, electing himself the family fire marshal, with me as his lieutenant, ready to clear exit pathways during drills or boss around our parents as needed. If there was ever going to be a fire, we wanted to be ready for it. Preparation mattered. Our family was not just on time; we arrived early to everything, knowing that it made my dad less vulnerable, sparing him from having to worry about finding a parking spot that didn't require him to walk a long way or an accessible seat in the bleachers at one of Craig's basketball games. The lesson being that in life you control what you can.

To this end, as kids, we ran through our possible escape routes, trying to guess whether we could jump from a window to the oak tree in front of the house or to a neighbor's rooftop in the event of a fire. We imagined what would happen if a grease fire broke out in the kitchen, or if an electrical fire started in the basement, or if lightning struck from above. Craig and I had little concern about our mom in an emergency. She was small and agile and one of those people who, if she had to, could probably lift a car off a baby. What was harder to talk about was Dad's disability—the obvious but unstated truth that he couldn't readily leap from a window like the rest of us, and it had been years since we'd seen him run.

If things got scary, we realized, our rescue wouldn't unfold the way rescues did in the after-school movies we watched on TV. It would not be our dad who'd throw us over his shoulder like Hercules and carry us to safety. If anyone, it would have to be Craig, who would eventually tower over my dad but was then still a narrow-shouldered, spindle-legged boy who seemed to understand that any heroics on his part would require practice. Which is why during our family fire drills, he started thinking of the worst-case scenarios, ordering my dad to the floor, instructing him to lie there limp and heavy as a sack, as if he'd passed out from smoke inhalation.

"Oh, good Lord," Dad would say, shaking his head. "You're really going to do this?"

My dad was not used to being helpless. He took care of everything on his own, carefully looking after our car, paying the bills on time, never discussing his advancing multiple sclerosis nor missing a day of work. My dad loved to be the rock for others. What he couldn't do physically, he made up for with guidance and support, which is why he enjoyed his work as a precinct captain for the city's Democratic Party. My dad loved the job, which baffled my mom given the amount of time it demanded. He paid weekend visits to a nearby neighborhood, often dragging me along. We'd park the car and walk from house to house, landing on a doorstep to find a hunched-over widow or a big-bellied factory worker with a can of beer peering through the screen door. Often, these people were delighted by the sight of my dad smiling broadly on their porch, propped up by his cane.

"Well, *Fraser!*" they'd say. "What a surprise. Get on in here."

For me, this was never good news. It meant we were going inside. It meant that my whole Saturday afternoon would now get sucked up as I got parked on a musty sofa or with a 7UP at a kitchen table while my dad fielded complaints that he'd then pass on to an elected official. When somebody had problems with garbage pickup or snow plowing or was irritated by a pothole, my dad was there to listen. His purpose was to help people feel cared for by the Democrats—and to vote accordingly when elections rolled around. To my dismay, he never rushed anyone along. Time, as far as my dad was concerned, was a gift you gave to other people. He clucked approvingly at pictures of cute grandkids, patiently endured gossip and talk of people's health woes, and nodded knowingly at stories about how money was tight. He hugged the old ladies as we finally left their houses, assuring them he'd do his best to get the fixable issues fixed.

My dad had faith in his own ability to be useful. It was a point of pride. Which is why at home during our fire drills he had little interest in being a passive prop, even in a pretend crisis. He had no intention, under any circumstance, of winding up the unconscious guy on the floor. But still, some part of him seemed to understand that this mattered to us—to Craig in particular. When we asked him to lie down, he'd humor us, dropping first to his knees, then to his butt, then spreading himself out obligingly, faceup on the living room carpet. He'd exchange glances with my mom, who found it all a little funny, as if to say, *These darn kids.*

With a sigh, he'd close his eyes, waiting to feel Craig's hands hook themselves solidly beneath his shoulders to start the rescue operation. My mom and I would then watch as, with no small amount of effort and a good deal of awkwardness, my brother managed to drag our 170-pound dad backward through the imaginary fire, hauling him across the floor, rounding the couch, and finally making it to the stairwell.

From here, Craig figured he could probably slide my dad's body down the stairs and out the side door to safety. My dad always refused to let him practice this part, saying gently, "That's enough now," and insisting on getting back to his feet before Craig could try to lug him down the stairs. But between the small man and the grown man, the point had been made. None of this would be easy or comfortable if it came to it, and there were, of course, no guarantees that any of us would survive. But if the very worst happened, we at least had a plan.

SLOWLY, I WAS becoming more outgoing and social, more willing to open myself up to the messes of the wider world. My natural resistance to chaos had been worn down somewhat through all the hours I'd spent trailing my dad through his precinct visits, plus all the other weekend outings we made, dropping in on our dozens of aunts, uncles, and cousins, sitting in thick clouds of barbecue smoke in someone's backyard or running around with neighborhood kids in a neighborhood that wasn't ours.

My mom was one of seven children in her family. My dad was the oldest of five. My mom's relatives tended to gather at Southside's house around the corner—drawn by my grandfather's cooking, the ongoing games of bid whist, and the exuberant blasting of jazz. Southside acted as a magnet for all of us. He was forever mistrustful of the world beyond his own yard and worried about everyone's safety and well-being. As a result, he poured his energy into creating an environment where we were always well fed and entertained, likely with the hope we'd never want to move away from it. He even got me a dog, a cinnamon-colored shepherd mutt we called Rex. Mom didn't allow Rex to live at our house, but I'd visit him all the time at Southside's, lying on the floor with my face buried in his soft fur, listening to his tail *thwap* appreciatively anytime Southside walked past. Southside spoiled the dog the same way he spoiled me, with food and love and tolerance, all of it a silent, earnest plea never to leave him.

My dad's family, meanwhile, sprawled across Chicago's broader South Side and included lots of great-aunts and third cousins. We orbited between all of them. I quietly figured out where we were going by the number of trees I'd see on the street outside. The poorer neighborhoods often had no trees at all. But to my dad, everyone was kin. He lit up when he saw his uncle Calio, and he adored his aunt Verdelle, who lived with her eight children in a neglected apartment building, in a neighborhood where Craig and I understood that the rules of survival were very different.

On Sunday afternoons, all four of us normally drove to Parkway Gardens to eat dinner with my dad's parents, whom we called Dandy and Grandma, and his three youngest siblings, Andrew, Carleton, and Francesca. They'd been born more than a decade after my dad and thus seemed more like sister and brothers to us than aunt and uncles. My dad, I thought, seemed more like a dad and less like a brother with the three of them, offering them advice and slipping them cash when they needed it. Francesca was smart and beautiful and sometimes let me brush her long hair. Andrew and Carleton were in their early twenties and dazzlingly hip. They wore bell-bottoms and turtlenecks. They owned leather jackets, had girlfriends, and talked about things like Malcolm X and "soul power." Craig and I passed hours in their bedroom at the back of the apartment, just trying to sponge up their cool.

My grandfather, also named Fraser Robinson, was decidedly less fun to be around, a cigar-puffing patriarch who'd sit in his recliner with a newspaper open on his lap and the evening news blaring on the television nearby. His personality was nothing like my dad's. For Dandy, everything was annoying. He was outraged by the day's headlines, by the state of the world as shown on TV, by the young Black men—"boo-boos," he called them—whom he believed were hanging uselessly around the neighborhood, giving Black people everywhere a bad name. He shouted at the television. He shouted at my grandmother, a sweet, soft-spoken woman and devout Christian named LaVaughn. (My parents had named me Michelle LaVaughn Robinson, in honor of her.) By day, my grandmother expertly managed a thriving Bible bookstore on the Far South Side, but in her off-hours with Dandy she was reduced to a meekness I found confusing, even as a young girl. She cooked his meals and absorbed his constant flow of complaints and said nothing in her own defense. Even at a young age, there was something about my grandmother's silence and passivity in her relationship with Dandy that got under my skin.

According to my mom, I was the only person in the family to talk back to Dandy when he yelled. I did it regularly because it drove me crazy that my grandmother wouldn't speak up for herself and because everyone else fell silent around him. And lastly I did it because I loved Dandy as much as he was hard for me to understand. His stubbornness was something I recognized in myself. There was also a softness in Dandy, which I caught only in glimmers. He tenderly rubbed my neck sometimes when I sat at the foot of his reclining chair. He smiled when my dad said something funny or one of us kids managed to slip a sophisticated word into a conversation. But then something would set him off and he'd start snarling again.

"Quit shouting at everyone, Dandy," I'd say. Or, "Don't be mean to Grandma." Often, I'd add, "What's got you so mad anyway?"

The answer to that question was both complicated and simple. Dandy himself would leave it unanswered, shrugging crankily and returning to his newspaper. Back at home, though, my parents would try to explain.

Dandy was from the South Carolina Low Country, having grown up in the humid seaport of Georgetown, where thousands of slaves once labored on vast plantations, harvesting crops of rice and indigo and making their owners rich. My grandfather, born in 1912, was the grandson of slaves, the son of a millworker, and the oldest of ten children. A quick-witted and intelligent kid, he'd been nicknamed "the Professor" and set his sights early on the idea of someday going to college. But not only was he Black and from a poor family, he also came of age during the Great Depression. After finishing high school, Dandy went to work at a lumber mill, knowing that if he stayed in Georgetown, his options would never widen. When the mill eventually closed, like many African Americans of his generation he took a chance and moved north to Chicago, joining what became known as the Great Migration, in which six million southern Blacks relocated to big northern cities over the course of five decades, fleeing racial oppression and chasing industrial jobs.

If this were an American Dream story, Dandy, who arrived in Chicago in the early 1930s, would have found a good job and a pathway to college. But the reality was far different. Jobs were hard to come by, limited at least somewhat by the fact that managers at some of the big factories in Chicago regularly hired European immigrants over African American workers. Dandy took what work he could find, setting pins in a bowling alley and working as a handyman. Gradually, he let go of his hopes of going to college, thinking he'd train to become an electrician instead. But this, too, was not possible. If you wanted to work as an electrician (or as a steelworker, carpenter, or plumber) on any of the big job sites in Chicago, you needed a union card. And if you were Black, the overwhelming odds were that you weren't going to get one.

This particular form of discrimination altered the destinies of generations of African Americans, including many of the men in my family. It limited their income, their opportunity, and, eventually, their dreams. As a carpenter, Southside wasn't allowed to work for the larger construction companies that offered steady pay because he couldn't join a labor union. My great-uncle Terry, Robbie's husband, had abandoned a career as a plumber for the same reason, instead becoming a Pullman porter. There was also Uncle Pete, on my mom's side, who'd been unable to join the taxi drivers' union and instead turned to driving an unlicensed cab, picking up customers who lived in the less safe parts of the West Side, where normal cabs didn't like to go. These were highly intelligent, able-bodied men who were denied stable high-paying jobs, which in turn kept them from being able to buy homes, send their kids to college, or save for retirement. It pained them, I know, to be cast aside, to be stuck in jobs that they were overqualified for. They watched white people leapfrog past them at work, sometimes training new employees they knew might one day become their bosses. And it made them feel at least a basic level of resentment and mistrust: You never quite knew what other folks saw you to be.

As for Dandy, life wasn't all bad. He met my grandmother while attending church on the South Side and ultimately found work through the federal government's Works Progress Administration, the relief program that hired unskilled laborers for public construction projects during the Depression. He then went on to spend thirty years as a postal worker before retiring with a pension that helped allow him all that time to yell at the boo-boos on TV from the comfort of his recliner.

In the end, he had five kids who were as smart and disciplined as he was. Nomenee, his second child, would end up with a degree from Harvard Business School. Andrew would go on to become a train conductor, and Carleton became an engineer. Francesca worked as a creative director in advertising for a time and eventually became a grade school teacher. But still, Dandy would remain unable to see his children's accomplishments as any sort of extension of his. As we saw every Sunday arriving at Parkway Gardens for dinner, my grandfather lived with the bitter taste of his own dashed dreams.

. . .

IF MY QUESTIONS for Dandy were hard and unanswerable, I soon learned that many questions are just that way. In my own life, I was starting to encounter questions I couldn't easily answer. One came from a girl whose name I can't remember—one of the distant cousins who played with us in the backyard of one of my great-aunts' houses farther west of us. As the adults drank coffee and laughed in the kitchen, Craig and I would join whatever pack of kids came with those adults. Sometimes it was awkward, all of us managing a forced friendship, but generally it worked out. Craig almost always disappeared into a basketball game. I'd jump double Dutch or try to fall into whatever conversation was going on.

One summer day when I was about ten, I sat on a stoop, chatting with a group of girls my age. We were all in pigtails and shorts and basically just killing time. What were we discussing? It could have been anything—school, our older brothers, an anthill on the ground.

At one point, one of the girls gave me a sideways look and said, just a touch hotly, "How come you talk like a white girl?"

I could tell that she was trying to insult me, or at least challenge me, but that she was also curious to know why the two of us sounded different. We seemed to be related but of two different worlds.

"I don't," I said, looking scandalized that she'd even suggest it and embarrassed by the way the other girls were now staring at me.

But I knew what she was getting at. There was no denying it, even if I just had. I *did* speak differently than some of my relatives, and so did Craig. Our parents had drilled into us the importance of using proper diction, of saying "going" instead of "goin'" and "isn't" instead of "ain't." We were taught to finish off our words. They bought us a dictionary and a full *Encyclopaedia Britannica* set, which lived on a shelf in the stairwell to our apartment, its titles etched in gold. Any time we had a question about a word, or a concept, or some piece of

41

history, they directed us toward those books. Dandy, too, was an influence, correcting our grammar or ordering us to enunciate our words when we went over for dinner. Dandy and my parents wanted us to have more opportunities than they had. They'd planned for it. They encouraged it. We were expected not just to be smart but to own our smartness—to inhabit it with pride—and this filtered down to how we spoke.

Yet it also could be a problem. Speaking a certain way—the "white" way, as some would have it—was seen as a betrayal, as being uppity, as somehow denying our culture. Years later, after I'd met and married my husband—a man who is light-skinned to some and dark-skinned to others, who speaks like an Ivy League–educated Black Hawaiian raised by white middle-class Kansans—I'd see this confusion play out on the national stage among whites and Blacks alike. I'd see the need people have to define others by their ethnicity or the color of their skin. America would bring to Barack Obama the same questions my cousin was unconsciously putting to me that day on the stoop: Are you what you appear to be? Do I trust you or not?

I passed the rest of that day trying to say less to my cousin, feeling put off by her hostility, but also wanting her to see me as genuine—not trying to show off some advantage. It was hard to know what to do. All the while, I could hear the sound of conversation going on between the adults in the kitchen nearby, my parents' laughter ringing easy and loud over the yard. I watched my brother in the flow of a sweaty game with a group of boys on the street corner. Everyone seemed to fit in, except for me. I look back on the discomfort of that moment now and recognize the more universal challenge of figuring out how who you are fits with where you come from and where you want to go. I also realize that I was a long way, still, from finding my voice.

4

AT SCHOOL, WE WERE GIVEN AN HOUR-LONG BREAK for lunch each day. I usually marched home with four or five other girls, all of us talking nonstop, ready to play games on the kitchen floor and watch TV while my mom handed out sandwiches. This began a habit that has sustained me for life, keeping a close and high-spirited group of girlfriends whose wisdom I can rely on. In my lunch group, we talked about whatever had gone on that morning at school, any differences we had with teachers, any assignments we thought were useless. We loved the Jackson 5 and weren't sure how we felt about the Osmonds. The Watergate scandal had happened, but none of us understood it. It seemed like a lot of old guys talking into microphones in Washington, D.C., which to us was just a faraway city filled with a lot of white buildings and white men.

My mom was happy to serve us. It gave her an easy window into our world. As my friends and I ate and gossiped, she often stood by quietly, doing some household chore, not hiding the fact that she was listening to every word. In my family, with four of us packed into a small apartment, we'd never had any privacy anyway. It only mattered sometimes. Craig, who was suddenly interested in girls, had started taking his phone calls in the bathroom.

As Chicago schools went, Bryn Mawr fell somewhere between being a bad school and a good school. The student population only grew Blacker and poorer with each year. There was, for a time, a city-wide movement to bus kids to new schools, but Bryn Mawr parents had fought it off, arguing that the money was better spent improving the school itself. As a kid, I had no opinion on whether the facilities were run-down or whether it mattered that there were hardly any white kids left. The school ran from kindergarten all the way through eighth grade, which meant that by the time I'd reached the upper grades, I knew every light switch, every chalkboard and cracked patch of hallway. I knew nearly every teacher and most of the kids. For me, Bryn Mawr was practically an extension of home.

As I was entering seventh grade, the *Chicago Defender,* a weekly newspaper that was popular with African American readers, ran a mean-spirited opinion piece that claimed Bryn Mawr had gone from being one of the city's best public schools to a "run-down slum" governed by a "ghetto mentality." Our school principal, Dr. Lavizzo, defended his community of parents and students, calling the newspaper piece "an outrageous lie, which seems designed to incite only feelings of failure and flight."

Dr. Lavizzo was a round, cheery man who had an Afro that puffed out on either side of his bald spot. He understood precisely what he was up against. Failure is a feeling long before it becomes an actual result. It's a feeling of vulnerability mixed in with self-doubt and made even stronger by fear. Those "feelings of failure" he mentioned were everywhere already in my neighborhood, in the form of parents who couldn't get ahead financially, of kids who were starting to suspect that their lives would be no different, of families who watched their better-off neighbors leave for the suburbs or transfer their children to Catholic schools. Real estate agents made things worse by whispering

44

to homeowners that they should sell before it was too late. The comments pushed people to feel that failure was coming, that it had already half arrived. You could get caught up in the ruin or you could escape it. They used the word everyone was most afraid of—"ghetto"—dropping it like a lit match.

My mom bought into none of this. She'd lived in South Shore for ten years already and would end up staying another forty. She didn't buy into fearmongering or pie-in-the-sky idealism. She was a straight-down-the-line realist, controlling what she could.

At Bryn Mawr, she became one of the most active members of the PTA, helping raise money for new classroom equipment and throwing appreciation dinners for the teachers. She also helped convince the school to create a special multigrade classroom for higher-performing students. The class was Dr. Lavizzo's idea. It brought the brighter kids together so they could learn at a faster pace.

The idea was controversial, as all "gifted and talented" programs are. But for my last three years at Bryn Mawr, I benefited. I joined a group of about twenty students from different grades, set off in a self-contained classroom apart from the rest of the school. We had our own recess, lunch, music, and gym schedules. We were also given special opportunities, including weekly trips to a community college to attend an advanced writing workshop or dissect a rat in the biology lab. Back in the classroom, we did a lot of independent work, setting our own goals and moving at whatever speed best suited us.

We were given dedicated teachers, first Mr. Martinez and then Mr. Bennett, both gentle and friendly African American men who cared a lot about what their students had to say. We could tell that the school had invested in us, which made us all try harder and feel better about ourselves. Being allowed to learn independently made me even more competitive. I tore through the lessons, quietly aware of where I stood among my peers as we moved from long division to pre-algebra, from writing single paragraphs to turning in full research papers. For me, it was like a game. And as with any game, like most any kid, I was happiest when I was ahead.

I TOLD MY mom everything that happened at school. I'd update her in a rush as I walked through the door in the afternoon, slinging my book bag on the floor and hunting for a snack. I realize I don't know exactly what my mom did during the hours we were at school, mainly because I never asked. I don't know what she thought about, how she felt about being a traditional homemaker as opposed to working a different job. I only knew that when I showed up at home, there'd be food in the fridge, not just for me, but for my friends. I knew that when my class was going on a trip, my mom would almost always volunteer to chaperone, arriving in a nice dress and dark lipstick to ride the bus with us to the community college or the zoo.

In our house, we lived on a budget but didn't often discuss its limits. My mom did her own nails, dyed her own hair (one time accidentally turning it green), and got new clothes only when my dad bought them for her as a birthday gift. She'd never be rich, but she was always crafty. When we were young, she magically turned old socks into puppets that looked exactly like the Muppets. She sewed a lot of my clothes, at least until middle school, when I insisted she stop.

Every so often, she'd change the layout of our living room, putting a new slipcover on the sofa, swapping out the photos and framed prints that hung on our walls. Every year, when the weather turned warm, she did a spring cleaning—vacuuming furniture, laundering curtains, and removing every storm window so she could Windex the glass and wipe down the sills before replacing them with screens to allow the spring air into our tiny, stuffy apartment. She'd then often go downstairs to Robbie and Terry's, particularly as they got older and less able, to clean for them as well. It's because of my mom that whenever I catch the scent of Pine-Sol, I automatically feel better about life.

At Christmastime, she got especially creative. One year, she figured out how to cover our radiator with cardboard printed to look like red bricks, so that we'd have our own chimney and fireplace. She then asked my dad—the family's resident artist—to paint orange flames on pieces of very thin paper, which, when backlit with a lightbulb, made for a half-convincing fire. On New Year's Eve, as a matter of tradition, she'd buy a special food basket, the kind that came filled with blocks of cheese, smoked oysters in a tin, and different kinds of salami. She'd invite my dad's sister Francesca over to play board games. We'd order a pizza for dinner and then snack our way elegantly through the rest of the evening, my mom passing around trays of pigs in a blanket, fried shrimp, and a special cheese spread baked on Ritz crackers. As midnight drew close, we'd each have a tiny glass of champagne.

My mom was always calm. I had friends whose moms rode their highs and lows as if they were their own, and I knew plenty of other kids whose parents were too overwhelmed by their own challenges to be much of a presence at all. My mom was simply even-keeled. She wasn't quick to judge and she wasn't quick to meddle. Instead, she monitored our moods and bore kindhearted witness to whatever problems or triumphs a day might bring. When things were bad, she gave us only a small amount of pity. When we'd done something great, we received just enough praise to know she was happy with us, but never so much that it became the reason we did what we did.

Advice, when she offered it, tended to be practical. "You don't have to *like* your teacher," she told me one day after I came home full of complaints. "But that woman's got the kind of math in her head that you need in yours. Focus on that and ignore the rest."

She loved us consistently, Craig and me, but we were not overmanaged. Her goal was to push us out into the world. "I'm not raising babies," she'd tell us. "I'm raising adults." She and my dad offered guidelines rather than rules. It meant that as teenagers we'd never have a curfew. Instead, they'd ask, "What's a reasonable time for you to be home?" and then trust us to stick to our word.

One day when Craig was in eighth grade, a girl he liked asked him to come by her house, letting him know that her parents wouldn't be home and they'd be left alone. My brother had agonized over whether to go or not—excited by the opportunity but knowing it was sneaky and dishonorable, the sort of behavior my parents would never approve of. This didn't, however, stop him from telling my mom a half-truth, letting her know about the girl but saying they were going to meet in the public park.

Guilt-ridden before he'd even done it, guilt-ridden for even thinking about it, Craig finally confessed the whole home-alone scheme, expecting or maybe just hoping that my mom would blow a gasket and forbid him to go.

But she didn't. She wouldn't. It wasn't how she operated.

She listened, but she made him responsible for his own choice. "Handle it how you think best," she said, before turning back to the dishes in the sink or the pile of laundry she had to fold.

It was another small push out into the world. I'm sure that in her heart my mom knew already that he'd make the right choice. Every move she made, I realize now, was rooted in the quiet confidence that she'd raised us to be adults. Our decisions were on us. It was our life, not hers, and always would be.

BY THE TIME I was fourteen, I thought of myself as half a grown-up anyway—maybe even as two-thirds of a grown-up. I'd gotten my period, which I announced immediately and with huge excitement to everyone in the house, because that was just the kind of household we had. I'd graduated from a training bra to one that looked slightly more womanly, which also thrilled me. Instead of coming home for lunch, I now ate with my classmates in Mr. Bennett's room at school. Instead of dropping in at Southside's house on Saturdays to listen to his jazz records and play with Rex, I rode my bike right past, headed east to the house on Oglesby Avenue where the Gore sisters lived.

The Gore sisters were my best friends and also a little bit my idols. Diane was in my grade, and Pam a grade behind. Both were beautiful girls—Diane was fair-skinned, and Pam was darker—each with a kind of self-possessed grace that seemed to come naturally. Their little sister, Gina, was a few years younger. Theirs was a home with few men. Their dad didn't live there and was rarely discussed. There was one much older brother who was not often present. Mrs. Gore was an upbeat, attractive woman who worked full-time. She had a makeup table full of perfume bottles and face powder compacts, which seemed as exotic as jewels to me. I loved spending time at their house. Pam, Diane, and I talked endlessly about which boys we liked. We put on lip gloss and took turns trying on one another's clothes, suddenly aware that certain pairs of pants made our hips look curvier. Much of my energy in those days was spent inside my own head, sitting alone in my room listening to music, daydreaming about a slow dance with a cute boy, or glancing out the window, hoping for a crush to ride his bike down the block. So it was a blessing to have found some sisters to ride through these years with together.

Boys weren't allowed inside the Gore house, but they buzzed around it like flies. They rode their bikes back and forth on the sidewalk. They sat on the front stoop, hoping Diane or Pam might come out to flirt. Everywhere I looked, bodies were changing. Boys from school were suddenly man-sized and awkward, their energy twitchy and their voices deep. Some of my girlfriends, meanwhile, looked like they were eighteen, walking around in short-shorts and halter tops, their expressions cool and confident as if they knew some secret, as if they now lived on a different plane, while the rest of us remained uncertain, waiting for our call-up to the adult world.

Like a lot of girls, I became aware of my body early, long before I began to even look like a woman. I moved around the neighborhood now with more independence, less tied to my parents. I'd catch a city bus to go to late-afternoon dance classes at Mayfair Academy, where I was taking jazz and acrobatics. I ran errands for my mom sometimes. With the new freedoms came new challenges. I learned to keep my gaze fixed firmly ahead anytime I passed a group of men clustered on a street corner. I knew to ignore the catcalls when they came. I learned which blocks in our neighborhood were thought to be more danger-ous than others. I knew never to walk alone at night.

At home, my parents gave in to the fact they were housing two growing teenagers, turning the back porch off our kitchen into a bed-room for Craig, who was now a sophomore in high school. The flimsy partition that Southside had built for us years earlier came down. I moved into what had been my parents' room, they moved into what had been the kids' room, and for the first time my brother and I had actual space for ourselves. My new bedroom was dreamy, complete with a blue-and-white floral bed skirt and pillow shams, a crisp navy-blue rug, and a white princess-style bed with a matching dresser and lamp. Each of us was given our own phone extension, too—my phone was a light blue to match my new decor, while Craig's was a manly black.

I arranged my first real kiss over the phone. It was with a boy named Ronnell. Ronnell didn't go to my school or live in my neighbor-hood, but he sang in the Chicago Children's Choir with my classmate Chiaka. With Chiaka acting as the go-between, we somehow had de-cided we liked each other. Our phone calls were a little awkward, but I didn't care. I liked the feeling of being liked. I don't remember which one of us suggested that we meet outside my house one afternoon to give kissing a try, but I remember that we were both excited.

There was nothing earth-shattering or especially inspiring about our kiss, but it was fun. Being around boys, I was slowly coming to realize, was fun. The hours I passed watching Craig's games from the bleachers of one gym or another began to feel less like a sisterly obligation, because what was a basketball game if not a showcase of boys? I'd wear my snuggest jeans and put on some extra bracelets and sometimes bring one of the Gore sisters along so I would be more noticeable in the stands. When a boy on the JV team smiled at me as he left the court one evening, I smiled right back. It felt like my future was just beginning to arrive.

I was slowly separating from my parents, gradually less eager to blurt every last thought in my head. I rode in silence behind them in the backseat of the Buick as we drove home from those basketball games, my feelings too deep or too jumbled to share. I was caught up in the lonely thrill of being a teenager now, convinced that the adults around me had never been there themselves.

Sometimes in the evenings I'd emerge from brushing my teeth in the bathroom and find the apartment dark, the lights in the living room and kitchen turned off for the night, everyone settled into their own sphere. I'd see a glow beneath the door to Craig's room and know he was doing homework. I'd catch the flicker of television light coming from my parents' room and hear them talking quietly, laughing to themselves. Just as I never wondered what it was like for my mom to be a full-time, at-home mom, I never wondered then what it meant to be married. But I understand now that even a happy marriage can be challenging, that it's a relationship that needs to be renewed again and again. I took my parents' union for granted. It was the simple solid fact upon which all four of our lives were built.

Much later, my mom would tell me that every year when spring came and the air warmed up in Chicago, she considered the idea of leaving my dad. For her it was an active fantasy, something that felt healthy and maybe even energizing to ponder, almost a springtime ritual.

If you've never passed a winter in Chicago, let me describe it: You can live for a hundred straight days beneath an iron-gray sky that claps itself like a lid over the city. Frigid, biting winds blow in off the lake. Snow falls in dozens of ways, in heavy overnight dumps and daytime, sideways squalls, in demoralizing sloppy sleet and fairy-tale billows of fluff. There's ice, usually, lots of it, that shellacs the sidewalks and windshields that then need to be scraped. There's the sound of that scraping in the early mornings—the *hack hack hack* of it—as people clear their cars to go to work. Your neighbors, unrecognizable in the thick layers they wear against the cold, keep their faces down to avoid the wind. City snowplows thunder through the streets as the white snow gets piled up and sooty, until nothing is pristine.

Eventually, however, something happens. A slow reversal begins. It can be subtle, a whiff of humidity in the air, a slight lifting of the sky. You feel it first in your heart, the possibility that winter might have passed. You may not trust it at the beginning, but then you do. Because now the sun is out and there are little nubby buds on the trees and your neighbors have taken off their heavy coats. And maybe there's a new airiness to your thoughts on the morning you decide to pull out every window in your apartment so you can spray the glass and wipe down the sills. It allows you to think, to wonder if you've missed out on other possibilities by becoming a wife to this man in this house with these children.

Maybe you spend the whole day considering new ways to live before finally you fit every window back into its frame and empty your bucket of Pine-Sol into the sink. And maybe now all your certainty returns, because yes, truly, it's spring and once again you've made the choice to stay.

5

MY MOM WENT BACK TO WORK WHEN I BEGAN HIGH
school, finding a job as an executive assistant at a bank in the dense,
skyscrapered heart of Chicago. She bought new clothes for work and
began commuting each morning, catching the bus north on Jeffery
Boulevard or riding along with my dad in the Buick, if their start
times happened to line up. The job was a welcome change in routine,
and our family needed the money. My parents had been paying tuition
for Craig to go to Catholic school. He was starting to think about college, with me coming up right behind him.

My brother was now full grown, a graceful giant with a spring in
his legs, and considered one of the best basketball players in the city.
At home, he ate a lot. He drank gallons of milk, devoured entire large
pizzas in one sitting, and often snacked from dinner to bedtime. He
managed, as he'd always done, to be both easygoing and deeply focused, maintaining lots of friends and good grades while also turning
heads as an athlete. He'd traveled around the Midwest on a summer rec-league team that featured a future superstar named Isiah
Thomas, who would later go on to a Hall of Fame career in the NBA.
As he approached high school, Craig had been sought after by some

of Chicago's top public school coaches looking to fill gaps in their rosters. These teams pulled in big crowds as well as college scouts, but my parents didn't want Craig to sacrifice his education for the short-lived glory of being a high school phenom.

Mount Carmel, with its strong Catholic-league basketball team and a challenging curriculum, had seemed like the best solution—worth the thousands of dollars the school was costing my parents. Craig's teachers were brown-robed priests who went by "Father." Most of his classmates were white, many of them Irish Catholic kids who came from working-class white neighborhoods. By the end of his junior year, he was already being courted by Division I college teams, a couple of which would probably offer him a free ride. Still, my parents wanted him to keep all his options open and aim for the best college possible. They would figure out how to manage the costs.

My high school experience thankfully cost us nothing except for bus fare. I was lucky enough to test into Chicago's first magnet high school, Whitney M. Young High School, which was in a run-down area just west of the Loop but was on its way to becoming a top public school in the city. Whitney Young was named for a civil rights activist and had been opened a few years earlier as an alternative to busing and a means of integrating students across race and class. Located squarely on the dividing line between the North and the South Sides of the city, the school was designed to draw high-performing students of all colors. The student body was meant to be 40 percent Black, 40 percent white, and 20 percent Hispanic or other. But when I attended, about 80 percent of the students were nonwhite.

Just getting to school for my first day of ninth grade was a whole new experience, involving ninety minutes of complicated travel on two different city bus routes as well as a transfer downtown. I got out of bed at five o'clock that morning, putting on new clothes and a pair of nice earrings. I ate breakfast, having no idea where lunch would be. I said good-bye to my parents, unclear on whether I'd even still be myself at the end of the day. High school was meant to be a time of change. And Whitney Young was where it would all happen for me.

The school was striking and modern, like no school I'd ever seen. There was a whole building dedicated to the arts, with special rooms for the choir to sing and bands to play, and other rooms for photography and pottery. The whole place was built like a temple for learning. Students streamed through the main entryway, with a sense of purpose already on day one.

There were about 1,900 kids at Whitney Young, and to me they all seemed older and more confident than I would ever be. I'd been one of the older kids at Bryn Mawr and was now among the youngest of the high schoolers. Getting off the bus, I'd noticed that along with their book bags a lot of the girls carried actual purses.

My biggest worry about high school was, *Am I good enough?* It was a question that dogged me through my first month, even as I got used to the extra-early wake-ups and moving between buildings for class. Whitney Young was subdivided into five "houses," each one serving as a home base for its members and meant to add a friendly feeling to the big-school experience. I was in the Gold House, led by an assistant principal named Mr. Smith, who happened to live a few doors down from my family on Euclid Avenue. I'd been doing odd jobs for Mr. Smith and his family for years, everything from babysitting his kids and giving them piano lessons to attempting to train their untrainable puppy. Seeing Mr. Smith at school was a small comfort, a bridge between Whitney Young and my neighborhood, but it didn't take away my anxiety.

Just a few kids from my neighborhood had come to Whitney Young. My neighbor and friend Terri Johnson had gotten in, and so had my classmate Chiaka, whom I'd known and been in friendly competition with since kindergarten, as well as one or two boys. Some of us rode the bus together in the mornings and back home at the end of the day, but at school we were mostly on our own. I was also operating, for the first time ever, without the protection of my older brother. At Bryn Mawr, Craig had softened up the teachers with his sweetness and earned a certain cool-kid respect on the playground. He'd created sunshine that I could then just step into. I had always, pretty much everywhere I'd gone, been known as Craig Robinson's little sister.

Now, though, I was just Michelle Robinson, with no Craig attached. At Whitney Young, I had to figure out who I was on my own. At first my strategy involved keeping quiet and trying to observe my new classmates. Who were these kids anyway? All I knew was that they were smart. The smartest kids in the city, apparently. But wasn't I as well? Hadn't all of us—me and Terri and Chiaka—landed here because we were smart like them?

The truth is I didn't know. I had no idea whether we were smart like them.

I knew only that we were the best students coming out of what was thought to be a not so great, mostly Black school in a not so great, mostly Black neighborhood. But what if that wasn't enough? What if we were just the best of the worst?

This was the doubt that sat in my mind through student orientation, through my first high school biology and English lessons, through my awkward get-to-know-you conversations in the cafeteria with new friends. *Not enough. Not enough.* It was doubt about where I came from and what I'd believed about myself until now. I knew it would grow stronger unless I could find some way to stop it.

CHICAGO, I WAS LEARNING, was a much bigger city than I'd ever imagined it to be. This was a new understanding formed in part over the three hours I now spent on the bus every day, often forced to stand because it was too crowded to find a seat.

Through the window, I got a long slow view of the South Side in what felt like its entirety, its corner stores and barbecue joints still shuttered in the gray light of early morning, its basketball courts and paved playgrounds lying empty. We'd go north and then west, then north again, zagging and stopping every two blocks to collect more people. We crossed Jackson Park Highlands and Hyde Park, where the University of Chicago campus sat hidden behind a massive wrought-iron gate. After what felt like an eternity, we'd finally accelerate onto Lake Shore Drive, following the curve of Lake Michigan north toward downtown.

There's no hurrying a bus ride. You get on and you endure. Every morning, I'd switch buses downtown at the height of rush hour. Through the window, I watched men and women in fancy suits and skirts and clicking heels carrying their coffee to work with a bustle of self-importance. I didn't yet know that people like this were called professionals. I hadn't yet tracked the college degrees they must have earned to be entering the tall corporate castles downtown. But I did like how determined they looked.

Meanwhile, at school I was quietly collecting information, trying to sort out where I fit among all these smart kids. Until now, my experiences with kids from other neighborhoods had been limited to visits with my cousins and a few summers of city-run day camp at Rainbow Beach, where every camper still came from some part of the South Side and nobody was well-off. At Whitney Young, I met white kids who lived on the North Side—a part of Chicago that felt like the dark side of the moon, a place I'd never thought about nor had reason to go to. I also learned that there was such a thing as an African American elite. Most of my new high school friends were Black, but that didn't necessarily mean that our experiences had been the same. Many of them had parents who were lawyers or doctors and seemed to know one another through an African American social club called Jack and Jill. They'd been on ski vacations and trips that required passports. They talked about things that were unknown to me, like summer internships and historically Black colleges. One of my Black classmates, a nerdy boy who was always kind to everyone, had parents who'd founded a big beauty-supply company. They lived in one of the ritziest high-rises downtown.

This was my new world. It's not to say that everyone at the school was rich or overly sophisticated. There were plenty of kids who came from neighborhoods just like mine, who struggled with far more than I ever would. But my first months at Whitney Young showed me something that had previously been invisible—the way connections and privilege give some people an advantage over others.

MY FIRST ROUND of grades at school turned out to be pretty good, and so did my second. During my freshman and sophomore years, I began to build the same kind of confidence I'd had at Bryn Mawr. With each little accomplishment, with every high school screwup I managed to avoid, my doubts slowly faded. I liked most of my teachers. I wasn't afraid to raise my hand in class. At Whitney Young, it was safe to be smart. The belief was that everyone was working toward college, which meant that you never hid your intelligence for fear of someone saying you talked like a white girl.

I loved any subject that involved writing and worked hard in precalc. I was a half-decent French student. I had classmates who were always a step or two ahead of me, whose achievements seemed effortless, but I tried not to let that get to me. I was beginning to understand that if I put in extra hours of studying, I could often close the gap. I wasn't a straight-A student, but I was always trying, and there were semesters when I got close.

Craig, meanwhile, had enrolled at Princeton University, leaving a six-foot-six, two-hundred-pound gap in our daily lives. Our fridge was less loaded with meat and milk, the phone line no longer tied up by girls calling to talk to him. He'd been recruited by big universities offering him a basketball scholarship, which would have made him a celebrity at college, but with my parents' encouragement he'd chosen Princeton, which cost more but, as they saw it, promised more as well.

My dad burst with pride when Craig became a starter on Princeton's basketball team as a sophomore. Wobbly on his feet and using two canes to walk, he still enjoyed a long drive. He'd traded in his old Buick for a new Buick, this one a shimmering deep maroon. When he could get time off work, he'd drive twelve hours across Indiana, Ohio, Pennsylvania, and New Jersey to catch one of Craig's games.

Because of my long commute to Whitney Young, I saw less of my parents. Looking back at it, I'd guess that it was a lonely time for them, or at least required some adjustment. I was now gone more than I was home. In the evenings, I dragged myself back through the door around six or seven o'clock, in time for a quick dinner and a chance to talk to my parents about whatever had gone on that day. But once the dishes had been washed, I disappeared into homework, often taking my books downstairs to the encyclopedia nook off the stairwell next to Robbie and Terry's apartment for privacy and quiet.

My parents never once spoke of the stress of having to pay for college, but I knew that it was there. When my French teacher announced that she'd be leading an optional class trip to Paris over one of our breaks for those who could come up with the money to do it, I didn't even bother to mention this at home. This was the difference between me and the Jack and Jill kids, many of whom were now my close friends. I had a loving and orderly home, bus fare to get me across town to school, and a hot meal to come home to at night. Beyond that, I wasn't going to ask my parents for a thing.

Yet one evening my parents sat me down, looking puzzled. My mom had learned about the France trip through Terri Johnson's mom.

"Why didn't you tell us?" she said.

"Because it's too much money."

"That's actually not for you to decide, Miche," my dad said gently, almost offended. "And how are we supposed to decide, if we don't even know about it?"

I looked at them both, unsure of what to say. My mom glanced at me, her eyes soft. My dad had changed out of his work uniform and into a clean white shirt. They were in their early forties then, married nearly twenty years. Neither one of them had ever vacationed in Europe. They never took beach trips or went out to dinner. They didn't own a house. We were their investment, me and Craig. Everything went into us.

A few months later, I boarded a flight to Paris with my teacher and a dozen or so of my classmates from Whitney Young. We would tour the Louvre and the Eiffel Tower. We'd buy *crêpes* from stands on the street. We'd speak French like a bunch of high school kids from Chicago, but we'd at least speak French. As the plane pulled away from its gate that day, I looked out my window and back at the airport, knowing that my mom stood somewhere behind its black-glass windows, dressed in her winter coat and waving me on.

IN THE MANNER of all high schoolers everywhere, my friends and I liked to hang out. On days when school got out early or when homework was light, we all went downtown to the eight-story mall at Water Tower Place. Once there, we rode the escalators up and down, spent our money on gourmet popcorn from Garrett's, and took over tables at McDonald's for hours. We browsed the designer jeans and the purses at department stores, often silently tailed by security guards who didn't like the look of us. Sometimes we went to a movie.

We were happy—happy with our freedom, happy with one another, happy with the way the city seemed to glitter more on days when we weren't thinking about school. We were city kids learning how to range.

I spent a lot of my time with a classmate named Santita Jackson, who in the mornings boarded the Jeffery bus a few stops after I did and who became one of my best friends in high school. Santita had beautiful dark eyes, full cheeks, and the bearing of a wise woman, even at sixteen. At school, she was one of those kids who signed up for every AP class available and seemed to ace them all. She wore skirts when everyone else wore jeans and had a singing voice so clear and powerful that she'd end up touring years later as a backup singer for Roberta Flack. She was also deep. It's what I loved most about Santita. Like me, she could be goofy when we were with a larger group, but on our own we'd get thoughtful and intense, two girl-philosophers together trying to sort out life's issues, big and small. We passed hours on the floor of Santita's room on the second floor of her family's white Tudor house in Jackson Park Highlands, a wealthier section of South Shore, talking about things that annoyed us and where our lives were headed and what we did and didn't understand about the world. As a friend, she was a good listener and helpful, and I tried to be the same.

Santita's dad was famous. This was an impossible-to-get-around fact in her life. She was the oldest child of the Reverend Jesse Jackson, a fiery Baptist preacher and powerful political leader. Jackson had worked closely with Martin Luther King Jr. and founded a political organization called Operation PUSH, which fought for the rights of African Americans. By the time we were in high school, he'd become a celebrity. He toured the country calling for Black people to shake off negative stereotypes and claim their long-denied political power. He had schoolkids sign pledges to turn off the TV and devote two hours to their homework each night. He made parents promise to stay involved. He pushed back against the feelings of failure that had grown in so many African American communities, urging people to take charge of their own destiny. "Nobody, but nobody," he'd yell, "is too poor to turn off the TV two hours a night!"

Hanging around Santita's house could be exciting. The place was roomy and a little chaotic, home to the family's five children and stuffed with heavy Victorian furniture and antique glassware that Santita's mom, Jacqueline, liked to collect. Mrs. Jackson, as I called her, had a big spirit and a big laugh. She wore colorful, billowy clothes and served meals at a massive table in the dining room, hosting anyone who turned up, mostly people who belonged to what she called "the movement." This included business leaders, politicians, and poets, plus a group of famous people, from singers to athletes.

Unlike at my apartment on Euclid, where life ran at an orderly and predictable pace, where my parents' concerns hardly ever extended beyond keeping our family happy and on track for success, the Jacksons seemed caught up in something larger, messier, and seemingly more important. Santita and her siblings were being raised to be politically active. They knew how and what to boycott. They marched for their dad's causes. They went on his work trips, visiting places like Israel and Cuba, New York and Atlanta. They'd stood on stages in front of big crowds and were learning to absorb the anxiety and uncertainty that came with having a dad, maybe especially a Black dad, in public life. Reverend Jackson had bodyguards—large, silent men who traveled with him. At the time, it only half registered with me that there had been threats against his life.

Santita adored her dad and was proud of his work, but she was also trying to live her own life. She and I were all for strengthening the character of Black youth across America, but we also needed to get to Water Tower Place before the sneaker sale ended. We often found ourselves looking for rides or to borrow a car. Sometimes we'd hitch rides with the various staff members or visitors who buzzed in and out of the Jackson house. What we gave up was control. This would become one of my early, unwitting lessons about life in politics: Schedules and plans never seemed to stick. Santita and I were often stuck waiting out some delay that related to her dad—a meeting that was running long or a plane that was still circling the airport—or detouring through a series of last-minute stops. We'd think we were getting a ride home from school or going to the mall, but instead, we'd end up at a political rally on the West Side or stranded for hours at the Operation PUSH headquarters.

One day we found ourselves marching with a crowd of Jesse Jackson supporters in the Bud Billiken Day Parade. The parade is one of the South Side's grandest traditions, an extravaganza of marching bands and floats that runs for almost two miles along Martin Luther King Jr. Drive. It was all about African American pride. If you were any sort of community leader or politician, it was—and still is, to this day—more or less required that you show up and walk the route.

I didn't know it at the time, but in a few years, Santita's dad would run for president. In 1984, Jesse Jackson became the second African American ever to run a serious campaign for the presidency, after Congresswoman Shirley Chisholm, who ran in 1972. (Among his fellow Democrats, he came in third place.)

What I did know was that I didn't love the feeling of being in the parade, under a baking sun with balloons and bullhorns, trombones and cheering people all around me. The fanfare was fun, but there was something about it, and about politics in general, that made me uncomfortable. For one thing, I was someone who liked things to be neat and planned in advance, and from what I could tell, there seemed to be nothing especially neat about a life in politics. The parade had not been part of my plan. But I loved Santita, and I was also a polite kid who for the most part went along with what adults told me to do, and so when I was asked to join the parade, I'd agreed.

I arrived home at Euclid Avenue that evening to find my mom laughing. "I just saw you on TV," she said. She'd been watching the news and spotted me marching alongside Santita, waving and smiling. What made her laugh, I'd guess, is that she also picked up on the discomfort—the fact that maybe I'd been caught up in something I'd rather not do.

WHEN IT CAME time to look at colleges, Santita and I both were interested in schools on the East Coast. She went to check out Harvard but was upset when an admissions officer was hostile with her about her dad's politics, when all she wanted was to be seen for who she was. I spent a weekend visiting Craig at Princeton, where he seemed to have slipped into a productive rhythm of playing basketball, taking classes, and hanging out at a campus center designed for minority students. The campus was large and pretty—an Ivy League school covered with ivy—and Craig's friends seemed nice enough. I didn't overthink it from there. No one in my immediate family had much in the way of direct experience with college, so there was little, anyway, to talk about or explore. As had always been the case, I figured that whatever Craig liked, I would like, too, and that whatever he could accomplish, I could as well. And with that, Princeton became my top choice for school.

Early in my senior year at Whitney Young, I went for my first appointment with the school college counselor to whom I'd been assigned. I can't tell you much about the counselor, because I almost instantly blocked this experience out. I don't remember her age or race or how she happened to look at me that day when I turned up in her office doorway, full of pride at the fact that I was on track to graduate in the top 10 percent of my class at Whitney Young, that I'd been elected treasurer of the senior class, made the National Honor Society, and managed to overcome pretty much every doubt I'd arrived with as a nervous ninth grader. I don't remember whether she looked at my transcript before or after I announced my interest in joining my brother at Princeton the following fall.

It's possible, in fact, that during our short meeting the college counselor said things to me that might have been positive and helpful, but I recall none of it. Because rightly or wrongly, I got stuck on one single sentence the woman uttered.

"I'm not sure," she said, giving me a fake smile, "that you're Princeton material."

Her judgment was as swift as it was dismissive, probably based on a glance at my grades and test scores. I imagine she did this all day long, telling seniors where they did and didn't belong. I'm sure she figured she was only being realistic. I doubt that she gave our conversation another thought.

But as I've said, failure is a feeling long before it's an actual result. And for me, it felt like that's exactly what she was planting—a suggestion of failure long before I'd even tried to succeed. She was telling me to lower my sights, which was the absolute reverse of every last thing my parents had ever told me.

Had I decided to believe her, her judgment would have toppled my confidence all over again, reviving my old doubt that I was *not enough, not enough.*

But three years of keeping up with the ambitious kids at Whitney Young had taught me that I was something more. I wasn't going to let one person's opinion change everything I thought I knew about myself. I would apply to Princeton and some other schools, but without any more input from the college counselor. Instead, I sought help from someone who actually knew me. Mr. Smith, my assistant principal and neighbor, had seen my strengths as a student and furthermore trusted me with his own kids. He agreed to write me a recommendation letter.

I've been lucky enough now in my life to meet all sorts of extraordinary and accomplished people—world leaders, inventors, musicians, astronauts, athletes, professors, entrepreneurs, artists and writers, pioneering doctors and researchers. Some (though not enough) of them are women. Some (though not enough) are Black or of color. Some were born poor or have lived lives with a lot of struggle, and yet still they seem to operate as if they've had every advantage in the world. What I've learned is this: All of them have had doubters. Some continue to have lots of critics and naysayers who will shout *I told you so* at every little mistake. But the most successful people I know have figured out how to live with criticism, to lean on the people who believe in them, and to push onward with their goals.

That day I left the college counselor's office at Whitney Young, I was furious, my ego bruised more than anything. My only thought was *I'll show you.*

But then I settled down and got back to work. I never thought getting into college would be easy, but I was learning to focus and have faith in my own story. I tried to tell the whole thing in my college essay. I wrote about my dad's MS and my family's lack of experience with higher education. I knew I wouldn't be a student who instantly fit in at Princeton. I owned the fact that I was reaching. Given my background, reaching was really all I could do.

And ultimately, I did show that college counselor, because six or seven months later, a letter arrived in our mailbox on Euclid Avenue, offering me admission to Princeton. My parents and I celebrated that night by having pizza delivered from Italian Fiesta. I called Craig and shouted the good news. The next day I knocked on Mr. Smith's door to tell him about my acceptance, thanking him for his help. I never did stop in on the college counselor to tell her she'd been wrong—that I was Princeton material after all. It would have done nothing for either of us. And in the end, I hadn't needed to show her anything. I was only showing myself.

6

MY DAD DROVE ME TO PRINCETON IN THE SUMMER OF 1981, across the flat highways connecting Illinois to New Jersey. But it was more than a simple dad-daughter road trip. My boyfriend, David, came along for the ride. I'd been invited to attend a special three-week summer orientation program giving certain incoming freshmen extra time and help settling into college. Craig had done it two years earlier, and it seemed like an opportunity. So I packed up my stuff, said good-bye to my mom—neither of us teary or sentimental—and climbed into the car.

I was eager to leave town, in part because I'd spent the last couple of months working an assembly-line job at a small bookbinding factory in downtown Chicago—a boring routine that went on for eight hours a day, five days a week, and served as a great reminder that going to college was a good idea. David's mom worked at the bookbindery and had helped get the two of us jobs there. David was smart and gentle, a tall, good-looking guy who was two years older than I was. He'd first befriended Craig on the neighborhood basketball court a few years earlier. Eventually, he started hanging around with me. During the school year, David went away to college out of state, which kept him from being any sort of distraction from my studies. During holiday breaks and over the summer, though, he came home to stay with his mom on the far southwest side of the city and drove over almost every day to pick me up in his car.

David was easygoing and also more of an adult than any boyfriend I'd had. He sat on the couch and watched ball games with my dad. He joked around with Craig and made polite conversation with my mom. We went on real dates, going for dinners at Red Lobster and to the movies. By day at the bookbindery, we used glue guns and made wise-cracks until there was nothing left to say. Neither of us was particu-larly interested in the job, beyond trying to save up money for school. I'd be leaving town soon. In some ways, I was already gone—my mind flown off in the direction of Princeton.

Which is to say that on the early August evening when our dad-daughter-boyfriend trio finally pulled off Route 1 and turned onto the wide leafy avenue leading to campus, I was fully ready to get on with things. I was ready to cart my two suitcases into the summer-session dorm, ready to shake the hands of the other kids who'd come (mi-nority and low-income students primarily, with a few athletes mixed in). I was ready to taste the dining-hall food, memorize the campus map, and conquer whatever assignments anyone wanted to throw my way. I was there. I had landed. I was seventeen years old, and my life was under way.

There was only one problem, and that was David, who as soon as we crossed the state line from Pennsylvania had begun to look sad. As we wrestled my luggage out of the back of my dad's car, I could tell he was feeling lonely already. We'd been dating for over a year. We'd even said "I love you." While my dad took his customary extra minute to get out of the driver's seat and steady himself on his canes, David and I stood wordlessly in the dusk, looking at the perfect diamond of green lawn outside my dorm. Were we going to visit? Write love letters? Was this a temporary farewell or a breakup? I realized we had never discussed these important things.

David held my hand in a serious way. It was confusing. I knew what I wanted but couldn't find the words. I hoped that someday my feelings for a man would knock me sideways, that I'd get swept off my feet the way I read about in all the best love stories. My parents had fallen in love as teenagers. My dad took my mom to her high school prom, even. I knew that teenage relationships were sometimes real and lasting. I wanted to believe that there was a guy who'd come into my life and become everything to me.

It just wasn't the guy standing in front of me right now.

My dad finally broke the silence between me and David, saying that it was time for us to get my stuff up to the dorm. He'd booked a motel room in town for the two of them. They planned to take off the next day, headed back to Chicago.

In the parking lot, I hugged my dad tight. His arms had always been strong from his youthful devotion to boxing and swimming and were now further strengthened by the effort required to move around by cane.

"Be good, Miche," he said, releasing me, his face showing no emotion other than pride. He then got into the car, kindly giving me and David some privacy.

We stood together on the pavement, both of us shy and stalling. My heart burst with affection as he leaned in to kiss me. This part always felt good.

I had my arms around a good-hearted Chicago guy who genuinely cared about me. But in a matter of minutes, I would be living in a new world. I was nervous about living away from home for the first time, about leaving the only life I'd ever known. But some part of me understood it was better to make a clean, quick break. Our good-bye that night was for real and forever. I probably should have told David directly that our relationship was over, but I chickened out, knowing it would hurt, both to say and to hear. Instead, I just let him go.

IT TURNED OUT there were a lot of things I had yet to learn about life, or at least life at Princeton in the early 1980s. After I spent several exciting weeks as a summer student, surrounded by a few dozen other kids who seemed both easy to get to know and familiar to me, the fall semester officially began. I moved my belongings into a new dorm room and then watched through my third-floor window as several thousand mostly white students poured onto campus, carting stereos and racks of clothes. Some kids arrived in limos. One girl brought two limos—stretch limos—to accommodate all her stuff.

Princeton was extremely white and very male. There was no avoiding the facts. Men on campus outnumbered women almost two to one. Black students made up less than 9 percent of my freshman class. If during the orientation program we'd begun to feel some ownership of the space, we now stood out like poppy seeds in a bowl of rice. I'd never been part of a mostly white community before. I'd never stood out in a crowd or a classroom because of the color of my skin. It was uncomfortable, at least at first.

With time, I learned to adapt. Some of the adjustment was easy. For one thing, nobody seemed much concerned about crime. Students left their rooms unlocked, their bikes casually kickstanded outside buildings, their gold earrings unattended on the sink in the dorm bathrooms. Their trust in the world seemed infinite. For me, it was something to get used to. I'd spent years quietly guarding my possessions on the bus ride to and from Whitney Young. Walking home to Euclid Avenue in the evenings, I carried my house key wedged between two knuckles and pointed outward, in case I needed it to defend myself.

At Princeton, it seemed the only thing I needed to be concerned about was my studies. Everything otherwise was designed to take care of our well-being as students. The dining halls served five different kinds of breakfast. There were enormous spreading oak trees to sit under and open lawns where we could throw Frisbees to relieve our stress. The main library was like a cathedral, with high ceilings and glossy hardwood tables where we could lay out our textbooks and study in silence. We were protected, cocooned, catered to. A lot of kids, I was coming to realize, had never in their lifetimes known anything different.

Attached to all of this was a new vocabulary, one I needed to master. What was a precept? What was a reading period? Nobody had explained to me the meaning of "extra-long" bedsheets on the school packing list, which meant that I bought myself too-short bedsheets and would thus spend my freshman year sleeping with my feet resting on the exposed plastic of the dorm mattress. There was an especially big learning curve when it came to sports. I'd been raised watching football, basketball, and baseball, but it turned out that East Coast prep schoolers did more. Lacrosse was a thing. Field hockey was a thing. Squash, even, was a thing. For a kid from the South Side, it could be a little dizzying. "You row crew?" What does that even mean?

I had only one advantage, the same one I'd had when starting kindergarten: I was still Craig Robinson's little sister. Craig was now a junior and a top player on the varsity basketball team. He was, as he'd always been, a man with fans. Even the campus security guards greeted him by name. Craig had a life, and I managed to slip into it. I got to know his teammates and their friends.

Craig was living rent-free as a caretaker in an upstairs bedroom at the Third World Center, an organization that supported students of color.

The Third World Center—or TWC, as most of us called it—quickly became a kind of home base for me. It hosted parties and meals. There were volunteer tutors to help with homework and spaces just to hang out. I'd made a handful of instant friends during the summer program, and many of us spent our free time at the center. Among them was Suzanne Alele. Suzanne was tall and thin with thick eyebrows and luxurious dark hair that fell in a shiny wave down her back. She had been born in Nigeria and raised in Kingston, Jamaica, though her family had moved to Maryland when she was a teenager. Perhaps as a result, she seemed free from any single cultural identity. People were drawn to Suzanne. It was hard not to be. She carried herself with what I think of as a Caribbean breeziness, a lightness of spirit that caused her to stand out among Princeton's students. She was unafraid to go to parties where she didn't know anyone. Even though she was studying to become a doctor, she made a point of taking pottery and dance classes for the simple reason that they made her happy.

Later, during our sophomore year, Suzanne joined an eating club, which was Princeton's version of a sorority or fraternity. I loved the stories Suzanne brought back from the eating-club banquets and parties she went to, but I had no interest in joining myself. I was happy with the community of Black and Latino students I'd found through the TWC, happy to remain at the edges of Princeton's larger social scene. Our group was small but tight. We threw parties and danced half the night. At meals, we often packed ten or more around a table, casual and laughing. Our dinners could stretch into hours, not unlike the meals my family used to have around the table at Southside's house.

I imagine that the administrators at Princeton didn't love the fact that students of color largely stuck together. The hope was that all students of different races and ethnicities would mix easily, deepening the quality of student life across the board. It's a worthy goal. I understand that when it comes to campus diversity, the ideal would be to achieve something resembling what's often shown on college brochures—smiling students working and socializing in neat, ethnically blended groups. But even today, with white students continuing to outnumber students of color on college campuses, the burden of fitting in is put largely on the shoulders of minority students. In my experience, it's a lot to ask.

At Princeton, I needed my Black friends. We provided one another relief and support. So many of us arrived at college not even aware of what our disadvantages were. You learn only slowly that your fellow students had been given SAT tutoring or college-level teaching in high school or had gone to boarding school and weren't dealing with the difficulties of being away from home for the first time. It was like stepping onstage at your first piano recital and realizing that you'd never played anything but an instrument with broken keys. Your world shifts, but you're asked to adjust and overcome, to play your music the same as everyone else.

This is doable, of course—minority and underprivileged students rise to the challenge all the time—but it takes energy. It takes energy to be the only Black person in a lecture hall or one of a few nonwhite people trying out for a play or joining an intramural team. It requires effort, an extra level of confidence, to speak in those settings and own your presence in the room. Which is why when my friends and I found one another at dinner each night, it was with a sense of relief. It's why we stayed a long time and laughed as much as we could.

My two white roommates in Pyne Hall were both perfectly nice, but I wasn't around the dorm enough to strike up any sort of deep friendship. I didn't, in fact, have many white friends at all. I realize it was my fault as much as anyone's. I was cautious. I stuck to what I knew. It's hard to put into words what sometimes you pick up in the air, the quiet, cruel nuances of not belonging—the subtle hints that tell you to not risk anything, to find your people and just stay put.

Cathy, one of my roommates, would surface in the news many years later, describing with embarrassment something I hadn't known when we lived together: Her mom, a schoolteacher from New Orleans, had been so upset that her daughter had been given a Black roommate that she'd badgered the university to separate us. Her mom also gave an interview, confirming the story and providing more context. She had been raised in a home where the *n*-word was a part of the family vocabulary and had a grandfather who'd been a sheriff and used to brag about chasing Black people out of his town. She'd been "horrified," as she put it, by my closeness to her daughter.

All I knew at the time is that midway through our freshman year, Cathy moved out of our triple and into a single room. I'm happy to say that I had no idea why.

MY FINANCIAL AID package at Princeton required me to get a work-study job, and I ended up with a good one. I was hired as an assistant to the director of the TWC. I helped out about ten hours a week when I wasn't in class, sitting at a desk alongside Loretta, the full-time secretary, typing memos, answering the phone, and helping students who came in with questions. I loved the feeling of being there, of having office work to do. I loved the little ping of satisfaction I got anytime I finished off some small organizational job. But more than anything, I loved my boss, Czerny Brasuell.

Czerny was a smart, lively, and beautiful Black woman who wore flared jeans and wedge sandals and seemed always to be having four or five ideas at once. For students of color at Princeton, she was a mentor and defender, working to make the university more inclusive for us. It was an incredible experience, being around her—as close-up as I'd ever been to an independent woman with a job that thrilled her. She was also a single mom raising a sweet, intelligent boy named Jonathan, whom I often babysat.

Czerny saw potential in me, though I was also clearly short on life experience. She treated me like an adult, asking for my thoughts, listening as I described the various worries and administrative tangles students had brought in. She seemed determined to make me more bold. A good number of her questions began with "Have you ever . . . ?" Had I ever, for example, read the work of James Cone? Had I ever questioned Princeton's investments in South Africa or whether more could be done to recruit minority students? Most of the time the answer was no, but once she mentioned a topic, I became immediately interested.

"Have you ever been to New York?" she asked me one day.

The answer was no, but Czerny soon changed that. One Saturday morning, we piled into her car—me and young Jonathan and another friend who also worked at the TWC—and rode along as Czerny drove full speed toward Manhattan, talking all the way. New York was home for Czerny, the same way Chicago was home for me. You don't really know how attached you are until you move away.

Before I knew it, we were in the heart of New York City, locked into a flow of yellow taxis and blaring car horns as Czerny floored it between stoplights, hitting her brakes at the absolute last second before a red light caught her short. I don't remember exactly what we did that day: I know we had pizza. We saw Rockefeller Center, drove through Central Park, and caught sight of the Statue of Liberty with her hopeful torch. Czerny had things to pick up, things to drop off. She double-parked on busy cross streets as she dashed in and out of buildings. The rest of us sat helplessly in the car as drivers around us honked angrily. New York overwhelmed me. It was fast and noisy, a less patient place than Chicago. But Czerny was full of life there.

She was about to double-park again when she sized up the traffic in her rearview and suddenly seemed to think better of it. Instead, she waved to me in the passenger seat, indicating that I should slide over and take her place behind the steering wheel.

"You have a license, right?" she asked. When I nodded, she said, "Great. Take the wheel. Just do a slow loop around the block. Or maybe two. Then come back around. I'll be five minutes or less, I promise."

I looked at her like she was nuts. She *was* nuts, in my opinion, for thinking I could drive in Manhattan—me being just a teenager, a stranger in this crazy city, inexperienced and fully incapable, as I saw it, of taking not just her car but her young son for an uncertain, time-killing spin in the late-afternoon traffic. But my reluctance only triggered something in Czerny that I will forever associate with New Yorkers—an immediate pushback against thinking small. She climbed out of the car, giving me no choice but to drive. *Get over it and just live a little* was her message.

I WAS LEARNING all the time now. I was holding my own in classes, doing most of my studying in a quiet room at the Third World Center or at the library. I was learning how to write efficiently, how to think critically. When I accidentally signed up for a class that was supposed to be for more advanced students, I struggled through it and ended up doing okay. I found it encouraging, proof that I could work my way out of just about any hole. Whatever shortcomings I might have arrived with, coming from an inner-city high school, it seemed that I could make up for them by putting in extra time, asking for help when I needed it, and learning to pace myself and not put things off.

Still, it was impossible to be a Black kid at a mostly white school and not feel that certain students and even some professors were watching me closely, wondering whether I'd only gotten into Princeton because I was Black. These moments could be upsetting, even if I'm sure I was just imagining some of it. It planted a seed of doubt. Was I here merely as part of a social experiment?

Slowly, though, I began to understand that there were many kinds of people who got an extra boost when they applied to college. As minorities, we were the most visible, but it became clear that special allowances were made to admit all kinds of students whose grades or accomplishments might not be the best, but who had other qualities that the school wanted. There were the athletes, for example. There

← This is my family dressed up for a celebration—my dad, Fraser; my mom, Marian; and my protective big brother, Craig.

→ Me as a baby with my great-aunt and piano teacher, Robbie.

← My dad, Fraser Robinson, worked for more than twenty years in the city of Chicago, tending boilers at a water filtration plant on the lakeshore. Even as his multiple sclerosis made it increasingly difficult for him to walk, he never missed a day of work.

Me and my
parents.
➜

I was always more
cautious than my
brother, Craig, seen
here hanging upside
down on a swing set.

My dad's beloved car was a Buick Electra 225—we called it the Deuce and a Quarter.

Each summer we drove to Dukes Happy Holiday Resort in Michigan, which is where this picture of Craig and me was taken.
→

My kindergarten class; I'm third row, second from the right.

My fifth-grade class; I'm third row, center. You can see how my class changed a lot in five years, as many better-off families moved away from the South Side to the suburbs while Black families stayed. This phenomenon is called white flight. ↓

My mom and dad made this special holiday display by hand using cardboard and rice paper, transforming our simple radiator into a festive Christmas fireplace.
→

Here I am at Princeton.
←

I was nervous about heading off to college but found many close friends there, including Suzanne Alele, who taught me a lot about living joyfully.
↓

Barack and me in the second-floor apartment on Euclid Avenue, where I'd been raised and where we lived as young lawyers.
←

Barack took this photo of me in Lamu, Kenya, on our first trip there together.
→

Our wedding was one of the happiest days of my life. Standing in for my dad, Craig walked me down the aisle.
←

Barack's always loved children, and I knew he would be a great dad. Our lives changed forever when Malia, pictured here, was born.
→

Sasha was born about three years after Malia, completing our family. Here are all four of us on one of our yearly trips to Barack's home state of Hawaii at Christmastime.
←

Malia and Sasha's bond has always been tight. And their cuteness still melts my heart.
→

were the legacy kids, whose dads and grandfathers had been Tigers or whose families had funded the building of a dorm or a library. I also learned that being rich didn't protect you from failure. Around me, I saw students struggling—white, Black, privileged or not. Some partied too much, some were crushed by stress, and others were just plain lazy or so overwhelmed they needed to run away. My job, as I saw it, was to hold steady, earn the best grades I could, and get myself through.

By sophomore year, when Suzanne and I moved into a double room together, I'd figured out how to better manage. I was used to being one of a few students of color in a packed lecture hall. I tried not to feel intimidated when male students talked so much in class that it was hard for anyone else to participate. Hearing them, I realized that they weren't smarter than the rest of us. They were simply more confident, floating on an ancient tide of superiority, buoyed by the fact that history had never told them anything different.

Some of my peers felt more out of place than I did. My friend Derrick remembers white students refusing to share the sidewalk with him. Another girl we knew was surprised when her white roommate complained to school officials after she'd invited some Black friends to her dorm room to celebrate her birthday. There were so few of us minority kids at Princeton, I suppose, that our presence was always noticeable. I responded by doing everything I possibly could to keep up with or do better than the more privileged people around me. Just as it had been at Whitney Young, my intensity was inspired at least in part by a feeling of *I'll show you*. If in high school I'd felt as if I were representing my neighborhood, now at Princeton I was representing my race. Anytime I found my voice in class or nailed an exam, I quietly hoped it helped make a larger point.

Suzanne, I was learning, was not an overthinker. I nicknamed her Screwzy, for her impractical ways. She based most of her decisions—who she'd date, what classes she took—mainly on how fun it was likely to be. And when things weren't fun, she quickly changed direction. While I joined the Organization for Black Unity and generally stuck close to the Third World Center, Suzanne ran track and managed the lightweight football team, enjoying the fact that it kept her close to cute, athletic men. Through the eating club, she had friends who were white and wealthy, including a teenage movie star and a European student rumored to be a princess. Suzanne had felt some pressure from her parents to pursue medicine though eventually gave up on it, finding that it messed with her joy. At some point, she was put on academic probation, but even that didn't seem to bother her much. She was the Ernie to my Bert. Our shared room resembled a battlefield, with Suzanne living in a wrecked landscape of tossed clothing and strewn papers on her side and me perched on my bed, surrounded by my carefully arranged possessions.

"You really gotta do that?" I'd say, watching Suzanne arrive back from track practice and head to the shower, dropping her sweaty clothes on the floor where they would live, mixed with clean clothes and unfinished school assignments, for the next week.

"Do what?" she'd say back, flashing her smile.

I sometimes had to block out Suzanne's chaos so I could think straight. I sometimes wanted to yell at her, but I never did. Suzanne was who she was. She wasn't going to change. When it got to be too much, I'd scoop up her junk and pile it on her bed.

I see now that she challenged me in a good way, introducing me to the idea that not everyone needs to have their file folders labeled and alphabetized, or even to have files at all. Years later, I'd fall in love with a guy who, like Suzanne, stored his belongings in heaps and felt no need to ever fold his clothes. But I was able to live with it, thanks to Suzanne. I am still living with that guy to this day. This is what a control freak learns at college, maybe above all else: There are simply other ways of being.

"HAVE YOU EVER thought about starting a little after-school program for kids?" Czerny asked me one day.

She was asking out of kindness. Over time, I'd grown so dedicated to her son, Jonathan, who was now in elementary school, that a good number of my afternoons were spent wandering around Princeton with him as my sidekick, or at the Third World Center, the two of us playing duets on its poorly tuned piano or reading on a saggy couch. Czerny paid me for my time but seemed to think it wasn't enough.

"I'm serious," she said. "I know plenty of faculty members who're always looking for after-school care. You could run it out of the center. Just try it and see how it goes."

With Czerny's word-of-mouth advertising, it wasn't long before I had three or four children to look after. These were the kids of Black administrators and professors at Princeton, who themselves were a minority and like the rest of us were drawn to the TWC. Several afternoons a week, after public elementary school let out, I fed them healthy snacks and ran around with them on the lawn. If they had homework, we worked on it together.

For me, the hours flew. Being around children had a wonderful effect, wiping out school stress, forcing me out of my head and into the moment. As a girl, I'd passed whole days playing "mommy" to my dolls, pretending that I knew how to dress and feed them, brushing their hair, and tenderly putting Band-Aids on their plastic knees. Now I was doing it for real, finding the after-school program a lot messier but no less satisfying than what I'd imagined. I'd go back to my dorm after a few hours with the kids, drained but happy.

Once a week or so, if I found a quiet moment, I'd pick up the phone and dial the number for our apartment on Euclid. If my dad was working early shifts, I could catch him in the late afternoon, sitting—or so

I imagined—with his legs up in his reclining chair in our living room, watching TV and waiting for my mom to get home from work. In the evenings, it was usually my mom who picked up the phone. I shared my college life with both my parents in detail—from how I didn't like my French professor to the antics of the little kids in my after-school program to the fact that Suzanne and I had a mutual crush on an African American engineering student with gorgeous green eyes who, even though we carefully shadowed his every move, seemed to barely know we were alive.

My dad chuckled at my stories. "Is that right?" he'd say. And, "How about that?" And, "Maybe that engineer-boy doesn't deserve either one of you girls."

When I was done talking, he ran through the news from home. Dandy and Grandma had moved back to Dandy's hometown of Georgetown, South Carolina, and Grandma, he reported, was finding herself a bit lonely. He described how my mom was working overtime trying to care for Robbie, who was now in her seventies, widowed, and struggling with health issues. He never mentioned his own struggles, but I knew they were there. At one point when Craig had a home basketball game on a Saturday, my parents drove all the way to Princeton to see it, and I got my first look at their changing life—at what never got said on the phone. After pulling into the vast parking lot outside Jadwin Gym, my dad reluctantly slid into a wheelchair and allowed my mom to push him inside.

I almost didn't want to see what was happening to my dad. I couldn't bear it. I'd done some research on multiple sclerosis in the Princeton library, photocopying medical journal articles to send to my parents. I'd tried to insist that they call a specialist or sign Dad up for some physical therapy, but he didn't want to hear any of it. For all the hours we spent talking on the phone while I was at college, his health was the one topic he wouldn't touch.

If I asked how he was feeling, the answer was always "I feel good." And that would be that.

I let his voice comfort me. It had no trace of pain or self-pity, only good humor and softness and just the tiniest hint of jazz. I lived on it as if it were oxygen. It was full of love, and it was always enough. Before hanging up, he always asked if I needed anything—money, for instance—but I never said yes.

7

HOME BEGAN TO FEEL MORE DISTANT, ALMOST LIKE A place in my imagination. While I was in college, I kept up with a few of my high school friends, most especially Santita, who'd landed at Howard University in Washington, D.C. I went to visit her there over a long weekend and we laughed and had deep conversations, same as we always had. Howard's campus was urban—"Girl, you're still in the *hood*!" I teased, after a giant rat charged past us outside her dorm— and its student population was almost entirely Black. I envied Santita for the fact she was not isolated by her race—she didn't have to feel that everyday pressure of being one of the only students of color—but still, I was content returning to the emerald lawns and stone archways of Princeton, even if few people there could relate to my background.

I was majoring in sociology, pulling good grades. I started dating a football player who was smart and liked to have fun. Suzanne and I were now rooming with another friend, Angela Kennedy, a fast-talking kid from Washington, D.C. Angela had a quick, wacky sense of humor and made a game of making us laugh. Despite being an urban Black girl, she dressed like a preppy, wearing saddle shoes and pink sweaters. She somehow managed to pull off the look.

I was from one world but now lived fully in another, one in which people were nervous about getting into law school and their squash games. It was a tension that never quite went away. At school, when anyone asked where I was from, I answered, "Chicago." To make it clear that I wasn't one of those kids from the wealthy suburbs, I would add, with a touch of pride, "the South Side." I knew that for some those words called up stereotypes of a Black ghetto, given that gang battles and violence in housing projects were what most often showed up in the news. But again, I was trying to represent the opposite. I belonged at Princeton, as much as anybody. And I came from the South Side of Chicago. It felt important to say out loud.

For me, the South Side was different from what got shown on TV. It was home. And home was our apartment on Euclid Avenue, with its fading carpet and low ceilings, my dad kicked back in his easy chair. It was our tiny yard with Robbie's blooming flowers and the stone bench where I'd kissed that boy Ronnell. Home was my past, connected by threads to where I was now.

We did have one relative in Princeton, Dandy's younger sister, Aunt Sis. She was a simple, bright woman who lived in a simple, bright house on the edge of town. I don't know what brought Aunt Sis to Princeton originally, but she'd been there for a long time, doing housekeeping for local families and never losing her Southern accent. Like Dandy, Aunt Sis had been raised in Georgetown, South Carolina, which I remembered from a couple of summer visits we'd made with my parents when I was a kid. I remembered the thick heat of the place, the live oaks covered with Spanish moss, the cypress trees rising from the swamps and the old men fishing on the muddy creeks. There were also alarming numbers of insects that buzzed and whirred in the evening air like little helicopters.

We stayed with my great-uncle Thomas during our visits, another brother of Dandy's. He was a cheerful high school principal who'd take me over to his school and let me sit at his desk, who generously bought me a tub of peanut butter when I turned my nose up at the enormous breakfasts of bacon, biscuits, and yellow grits that Aunt Dot, his wife, served every morning. I both loved and hated being in the South, for the simple reason that it was so different from what I knew. On the roads outside town, we'd drive past the gateways to what were once slave plantations, though they were enough of a fact of life that nobody ever bothered to remark on them. Down a lonely dirt road deep in the woods, we ate deer meat in a falling-down country shack belonging to some more distant cousins. One of the distant cousins took Craig out back and showed him how to shoot a gun. Late at night, both of us had a hard time sleeping, given the deep silence, which was punctuated only by cicadas throbbing in the trees.

The hum of those insects and the twisting limbs of the live oaks stayed with us long after we'd gone north again, beating in us almost like a second heart. Even as a kid, I understood that the South was part of me and my heritage. It was meaningful enough for my dad to make return visits to see his people there. It was powerful enough that Dandy wanted to move back to Georgetown, even though as a young man he'd needed to escape it. When he did return, it wasn't to some idyllic little river cottage with a white fence and tidy backyard but rather (as I saw when Craig and I made a trip to visit) a bland, cookie-cutter home near a teeming strip mall.

The South wasn't paradise, but it meant something to us. It was part of our history, even if that history included an ugly legacy of racism. Many of the people I knew in Chicago—the kids I'd gone to Bryn Mawr with, many of my friends at Whitney Young—had similar family histories. Kids simply went "down south" every summer to run around with their second cousins back in Georgia, or Louisiana, or Mississippi. They probably had grandparents or other relatives who'd joined the Great Migration, a time when Black families moved from the South to the North hoping to find jobs and escape racism. Dandy had moved to Chicago from South Carolina, and Southside's mom was from Alabama. Like most people who made the Great Migration, they were probably descended from slaves.

That meant that I was, too, and so were many of my friends at Princeton. But I was also coming to understand that there were other ways of being Black in America. I was meeting kids from East Coast cities whose roots were Puerto Rican, Cuban, and Dominican. One of my good friends, David Maynard, had been born into a wealthy Bahamian family. And there was Suzanne, with her Nigerian birth certificate and her collection of beloved aunties in Jamaica. We were all different. We didn't talk about our ancestry. Why would we? We were young, focused only on the future—though of course we knew nothing of what lay ahead.

Once or twice a year, Aunt Sis invited me and Craig to dinner at her house on the other side of Princeton. She piled our plates with juicy ribs and steaming collard greens and passed around a basket with neatly cut squares of corn bread, which we slathered with butter. She refilled our glasses with impossibly sweet tea and urged us to go for seconds and then thirds. As I remember it, we never discussed anything big with Aunt Sis. It was an hour or so of polite, go-nowhere small talk, accompanied by a hot, hearty South Carolina meal. I saw Aunt Sis simply as a sweet older lady, but she was giving us a gift we were still too young to recognize. She was filling us up with the past— ours, hers, our dad's and grandfather's—without once needing to comment on it. We just ate, helped clean the dishes, and then walked our full bellies back to campus.

HERE'S A MEMORY, which like most memories is imperfect and personal. It's from sophomore year of college and involves Kevin, my football-player boyfriend.

Kevin is from Ohio and is a near-impossible combination of tall, sweet, and rugged. He's a safety for the Tigers, fast on his feet and fearless with his tackles, and at the same time studying to be a doctor. He's two years ahead of me at school, in the same class as my brother, and soon to graduate. He's got a cute gap in his smile and makes me feel special. We're both busy and have different sets of friends, but we like being together. We get pizza and go out on weekends. He's always restless and has a hard time sitting still.

"Let's go driving," Kevin says one day. We're soon in his car driving across campus and turning down an almost-hidden dirt road. It's spring in New Jersey, a warm clear day with open sky all around us.

Are we talking? Holding hands? I don't recall, but the feeling is easy and light, and after a minute Kevin hits the brakes, rolling us to a stop. He's halted alongside a wide field, its high grass stunted and strawlike after the winter but shot through with tiny early-blooming wildflowers. He's getting out of the car.

"Come on," he says, motioning for me to follow.

"What are we doing?"

He looks at me as if I should know. "We're going to run through this field."

We dash from one end of the field to the other, waving our arms like little kids, cheerfully shouting to break the silence. We plow through the dry grass and leap over the flowers. *We're supposed to run through this field! Of course we are!*

Plopping ourselves back in the car, Kevin and I are panting and giddy.

It's a small moment, seemingly unimportant in the end. It's still with me for no reason but the silliness, for how it opened me up just briefly from my more serious every day. Because while I was a social student who continued to hang out through group mealtimes and had no problem trying to own the dance floor at Third World Center parties, I was still at all times focused on the future. Beneath my laid-back college-kid demeanor, I lived quietly but unswervingly focused on achievement, bent on checking every box. My to-do list lived in my head and went with me everywhere. I kept track of my goals and my wins. If there was a challenge to meet, I'd meet it. Such is the life of a girl who can't stop wondering, *Am I good enough?* and is still trying to show herself the answer.

Kevin, meanwhile, was someone who swerved. He took chances and did the unexpected. And he enjoyed it. He and Craig graduated from Princeton at the end of my sophomore year. Craig moved to Manchester, England, to play basketball professionally. Kevin, I'd thought, was headed to medical school, but then he swerved, deciding to put off school and instead try to become a sports mascot.

Yes, that's right. He'd set his sights on trying out for the Cleveland Browns—not to be a player, but rather to be a goofy dog named Chomps. It was what he wanted. It was a dream—another field to run through, because why not? That summer, Kevin even came up to Chicago from his family's home outside Cleveland, supposedly to visit me but also so he could find the right kind of furry animal suit for his upcoming audition. We spent a whole afternoon shopping for the perfect animal suit for him. I'm not sure whether he landed the mascot job in the end, though he did finally become a doctor, and a very good one at that.

At the time I judged him unfairly for making a swerve. I could not understand why someone would not immediately use their expensive Princeton degree to help them get ahead in the world. Why, when you could be in medical school, would you be a dog who does handsprings?

But that was me. I was a box checker, marching to the beat of effort/ result, effort/result. I was a devoted follower of the established path, if only because nobody in my family (aside from Craig) had ever set foot on the path before. I wasn't particularly imaginative in how I thought about the future. I was already thinking about law school.

Life on Euclid Avenue had taught me to be careful and practical about both time and money. The biggest swerve I'd ever made was a decision to spend the first part of the summer after sophomore year working as a camp counselor in New York's Hudson Valley. I looked after urban kids who were having their first experiences in the woods. I'd loved the job, but it didn't pay well. I came out of it nearly broke, more dependent on my parents financially than I wanted to be. Though they never once complained, I'd feel guilty about it for years to come.

This was the same summer, too, when people I loved started to die. My great-aunt Robbie, my piano teacher, passed away in June. She left her house on Euclid to my parents, allowing them to become homeowners for the first time. Southside died a month later from lung cancer. His belief that doctors were untrustworthy had kept him from getting medical help until it was too late. After Southside's funeral, my mom's enormous family piled into his snug little home, along with friends and neighbors. I felt the warm tug of the past and sadness. I had gotten used to my life in the world of college, surrounded by young people and far from home. Now I felt something deeper than what I normally felt at school, the way my family was experiencing a generational change. My kid cousins were full grown; my aunts had grown old. There were new babies and new spouses. A jazz album roared from the home-built stereo shelves in the dining room, and we dined on a potluck brought by loved ones—baked ham, Jell-O molds, and casseroles. But Southside himself was gone. It was painful, but time pushed us all forward.

Each spring, companies came to the Princeton campus to look for graduating seniors they could hire. You'd see a classmate who normally dressed in jeans and an untucked shirt crossing campus in a pin-striped suit and know that he or she was hoping to get a job in a Manhattan skyscraper. It happened quickly—the bankers, lawyers, doctors, and executives of tomorrow moving toward their next launchpad, whether it was graduate school or a high-paying job. I'm certain there were some who followed their hearts into education, the arts, and nonprofit work or who went off on Peace Corps missions or to serve in the military, but I knew very few of them. I was busy climbing my ladder to success.

Maybe if I'd stopped to think about it, I might have realized that I was burned out by school. Probably I would have benefited from doing something different. Instead, I took the law school exams and reached for the next rung, applying to the best law schools in the country. I saw myself as smart, thoughtful, and ambitious. I'd been raised on energetic dinner-table debates with my parents. I could make a strong argument and prided myself on never rolling over in a conflict. Was this not the stuff lawyers were made of? I figured it was.

I can see now that my wanting to become a lawyer was driven in part by my wish for other people's approval. When I was a kid, anytime I announced to a teacher, a neighbor, or one of Robbie's church-choir friends that I wanted to be a pediatrician, their expressions would say, *My, isn't that impressive?* Their reaction always made me feel good. Years later, it was really no different. Professors, relatives, random people I met, asked what was next for me, and when I mentioned I was bound for Harvard Law School, the approval I received was over-whelming. I was applauded just for getting in, even if the truth was I'd somehow squeaked in off the wait list. But I was in. People looked at me as if already I'd made my mark on the world.

This may be the biggest problem with caring a lot about what others think: It can put you on the established path—the *my-isn't-that-impressive* path—and keep you there for a long time. Maybe it stops you from swerving, from ever taking chances, because risking other people's good opinion of you can feel too costly. I ended up spending three years in Massachusetts, studying constitutional law and complicated legal issues. For some, this might be truly interesting, but for me it was not. During those three years, I made friends I'd love and respect forever, people who really loved studying the law. But that wasn't me. Even though I wasn't passionate, I didn't want to fail. I wasn't willing to swerve. I had to keep achieving in order to finally answer that important question. *Am I good enough? Yes, in fact I am.*

That was when the rewards seemed to get real. I got a job with a salary in the Chicago offices of a fancy law firm called Sidley & Austin. I was back in the city where I was born, only now I went to work on the forty-seventh floor in a downtown building. I used to pass by it as a South Side kid riding the bus to high school, peering silently out the window at the people who walked like giants to their jobs. Now I was one of them. I'd made it. At the age of twenty-five, I had an assistant. I made more money than my parents ever had. My coworkers were polite, educated, and mostly white. I wore expensive designer suits. I made monthly payments on my law school loans and went to step aerobics after work. Because I could, I bought myself an expensive car.

Is there anything to question? It doesn't seem that way. You're a lawyer now. You've taken everything ever given to you—the love of your parents, the faith of your teachers, the music from Southside and Robbie, the meals from Aunt Sis, the vocabulary words drilled into you by Dandy—all of it had brought you to this place. You've climbed the mountain. Most of your job is pretty boring, but there is one part of it that you like, which is helping the company recruit new young lawyers. A senior partner asks if you'll mentor an incoming summer associate, and the answer is easy: Of course you will. You do not know yet how the simple act of saying yes could change your life forever. Next to your name on the assignment sheet is another name, that of some hotshot law student who's busy climbing his own ladder. Like you, he's Black and from Harvard. Other than that, you know nothing—just the name, and it's an odd one.

8

BARACK OBAMA WAS LATE ON DAY ONE. I SAT IN MY office on the forty-seventh floor, waiting for him to arrive. Like most first-year lawyers, I was busy. I worked long hours at Sidley & Austin, often eating at my desk while trying to deal with a continuous flow of documents, all of them written in precise lawyer language. At this point, I thought of myself basically as knowing three languages. I knew the relaxed way we talked on the South Side, and the formal speech of the Ivy League, and now I spoke Lawyer, too. I'd been hired into the firm's marketing and intellectual property practice group, which was considered more creative than other groups because we dealt at least some of the time with advertising. Part of my job involved carefully reading scripts for our clients' TV and radio ads, making sure they didn't violate government rules. I would later be assigned to look after the legal concerns of Barney the Dinosaur. (Yes, this is what passes for creative in a law firm.)

The problem for me was that as a junior lawyer, my work didn't involve much direct interaction with people. I was a Robinson, raised in the busy social world of my extended family, molded by my dad's natural love of a crowd. To deal with the loneliness, I joked around with Lorraine, my assistant, a totally organized, good-humored African American woman several years older than me who sat just outside my office and answered my phone. I had friendly professional relationships with colleagues, but in general everyone was overloaded with work and careful not to waste time. Which put me back at my desk, alone with my documents.

If I had to spend seventy hours a week somewhere, my office was a pleasant enough place. I could look out the window overlooking the city and see Lake Michigan, which in summertime was dotted with bright sailboats. If I angled myself a certain way, I could glimpse a narrow part of the South Side. From where I sat, the neighborhoods appeared still and almost toylike, but the reality was in many cases far different. Parts of the South Side had become lifeless as businesses shut down and families continued to move out. The drug epidemic, which had destroyed African American communities in places like Detroit and New York, was only just reaching Chicago, but the problems were no less destructive. Gangs battled for territory and were reaching out to young boys to run their street-corner business. The kids realized that selling and dealing paid more than going to school. The city's murder rate was starting to tick upward—a sign of even more trouble to come.

Since finishing law school, I'd been living back in my old South Shore neighborhood, which was still relatively unchanged by gangs and drugs. My parents had moved downstairs into Robbie and Terry's old space. They invited me to take over the upstairs apartment, where we'd lived when I was a kid. I decorated it with a new couch and framed prints on the walls. I wrote my parents an occasional check to cover part of my share of the bills. It hardly counted as paying rent, but they insisted it was plenty. Though my apartment had a private entrance, I most often passed through the downstairs kitchen as I came and went from work—in part because my parents' back door opened directly to the garage and in part because I was still and always would be a Robinson. Even if I now thought of myself as the independent young professional I'd always dreamed of being, I didn't much like being alone. I still enjoyed daily check-ins with my mom and dad. I'd hugged them that very morning, before dashing out the door and driving through a heavy rainstorm to get to work. To get to work, I might add, *on time*.

I looked at my watch.

"Any sign of this guy?" I called to Lorraine.

"Girl, no," she called back. She was amused, I could tell. She knew how tardiness drove me nuts.

Barack Obama had already created a stir at the firm. For one thing, he'd just finished his first year of law school, and normally we only hired second-year students for summer positions. But rumor had it he was exceptional. Word had spread that one of his professors at Harvard claimed he was the most gifted law student she'd ever had. Some of the secretaries who'd seen the guy come in for his interview were saying that on top of this reputation for brilliance, he was also cute.

I was skeptical. In my experience, you put a suit on any half-intelligent Black man and white people tended to go bonkers. I was doubtful he'd earned the hype. I'd checked out his photo in the summer edition of our staff directory and had been unimpressed. He had a big smile and looked kind of geeky. His bio said he was originally from Hawaii, which at least made him an exotic geek. Otherwise, nothing stood out. The only surprise had come weeks earlier when I made a quick phone call to introduce myself. I'd been pleasantly startled by the voice on the other end of the line—a rich baritone that didn't seem to match his photo one bit.

It was another ten minutes before he checked in at the reception area on our floor. I walked out to meet him. He was seated on a couch—one Barack Obama, dressed in a dark suit and still a little damp from the rain. He grinned sheepishly and apologized for his lateness as he shook my hand. He had a wide smile and was taller and thinner than I'd imagined he'd be. He looked like he didn't eat much and was not used to wearing a business suit. If he knew he was arriving with a whiz-kid reputation, it didn't show. As I walked him through the office, showing him where everything was, he was quiet and respectful, listening attentively. After about twenty minutes, I delivered him to the senior partner who'd be his actual supervisor for the summer and went back to my desk.

Later that day, I took Barack to lunch at the fancy restaurant on the first floor of our office building. This was the benefit of having a summer associate to advise: It was an excuse to eat out and have the company pay for it. As Barack's adviser, my assignment was to make sure he was happy in the job, that he had someone to come to if he needed advice, and that he felt connected to the larger team. The idea with all summer associates was that the firm might want to offer them full-time jobs once they had their law degrees.

Very quickly, I realized that Barack would not need much advice. He was three years older than I was—about to turn twenty-eight. Unlike me, he'd worked for several years after finishing college at Columbia before moving on to law school. What struck me was how confident he seemed of his own direction in life. He was oddly free from doubt, though at first glance it was hard to understand why. Compared with my own march toward success, Barack's path was an unplanned zigzag through different worlds. I learned over lunch that he was the son of a Black Kenyan dad and a white mom from Kansas whose marriage had been both youthful and short-lived. He'd been born and raised in Honolulu, Hawaii, but had spent four years of his childhood flying kites and catching crickets in Indonesia. After high school, he'd spent two years as a student at Occidental College in Los Angeles before changing to Columbia University in New York. There, as he told it, he'd behaved nothing like a college boy set loose in the big city and instead he had lived like a mountain hermit, reading serious works of literature and philosophy, writing bad poetry, and fasting on Sundays.

We laughed about all of it, swapping stories about our backgrounds and what led us to the law. Barack was serious without being full of himself. He was breezy in his manner but powerful in his mind. It was a strange, exciting combination. Surprising to me, too, was how well he knew Chicago.

Barack was the first person I'd met at Sidley who had spent time in the barbershops, barbecue joints, and Bible-thumping Black parishes of the Far South Side. Before going to law school, he'd worked in Chicago for three years as a community organizer, earning very little money from a nonprofit that served local churches. His job was to help rebuild neighborhoods and bring back jobs. The work had been rewarding but also frustrating. His efforts were criticized by union leaders and picked apart by Black folks and white folks alike. Yet over time, he'd won a few victories, and this seemed to encourage him. He was in law school, he explained, because community organizing had shown him that meaningful change for society required not just the work of the people on the ground but stronger policies and governmental action, too.

Despite my resistance to the hype about him, I found myself admiring Barack for both his self-assuredness and his earnestness. He was refreshing, unusual, and weirdly elegant. Not once, though, did I think about him as someone I'd want to date. For one thing, I was his mentor at the firm. I'd also recently decided not to date, being too busy with work to put any effort into it. And finally, to my horror, at the end of lunch Barack lit a cigarette, which would have been enough to turn off any interest, if I'd had any to begin with.

He would be a good summer mentee, I thought to myself.

OVER THE NEXT couple of weeks, we fell into a casual routine. In the late afternoon, Barack would wander down the hall and flop onto one of the chairs in my office, as if he'd known me for years.

Sometimes it felt as if he had. Our conversation was easy, our mind-sets alike. We gave each other sideways glances when people around us got stressed to the point of seeming crazy, when partners made comments that seemed belittling or out of touch. What was unspoken but obvious was that he was a brother, and in our office, which employed more than four hundred lawyers, only about five full-time attorneys were African American. Our pull toward each other was easy to understand.

Barack was unlike the typical eager summer associate (as I myself had been two years earlier at Sidley), networking furiously and anxiously wondering whether a golden-ticket job offer was coming. He strolled around, remaining calm and cool, which seemed only to increase his appeal. Inside the firm, his reputation was continuing to grow. Already, he was being asked to give input on complicated legal issues. At some point early in the summer, he wrote a thirty-page memo about corporate governance that was so thorough and convincing it became instantly legendary. Who was this guy? Everyone seemed intrigued.

"I brought you a copy," Barack said one day, sliding his memo across my desk with a smile.

"Thanks," I said, taking the file. "Looking forward to it."

After he left, I tucked it into a drawer.

Did he know I'd never read it? I think he probably did. He'd given it to me half as a joke. We were in different specialty groups, so there was no overlap in our work anyway. I had plenty of my own documents to handle. And I didn't need to be wowed. We were friends now, Barack and I. We ate lunch out at least once a week and sometimes more often than that. Gradually, we learned more about each other. He knew that I lived in the same house as my parents, that my happiest memories of Harvard Law School involved the work I'd done in the Legal Aid Bureau. I knew that he devoured volumes of political philosophy as if it were beach reading, that he spent all his spare money on books. I knew that his dad had died in a car crash in Kenya and that he'd made a trip there to try to understand more about the man. I knew he loved basketball, went for long runs on the weekends, and spoke with emotion of his friends and family on Oahu. I knew he'd had plenty of girlfriends in the past, but didn't have one now.

This last bit was something I thought I could fix. My life in Chicago was full of successful, single Black women. Even though I worked long hours, I liked to socialize. I had friends from work, friends from high school, friends developed through professional networking, and friends I'd met through Craig, who was newly married and making his living as an investment banker in town. We were a merry crew, gathering when we could and catching up over long, lavish meals on weekends. I'd gone out with a couple of guys in law school but hadn't met anyone special upon returning to Chicago, and had little interest anyway. I'd announced to everyone that my career was my priority. I did, though, have plenty of girlfriends who were looking for someone to date.

One evening early in the summer, I brought Barack along with me to a gathering at a meeting place downtown, which served as an unofficial monthly mixer for Black professionals and was where I often met up with friends.

There was no arguing with the fact that Barack was a catch. He was good-looking, poised, and successful. He was athletic, interesting, and kind. What more could anyone want? I sailed into the restaurant, certain I was doing everyone a favor—Barack and all the ladies. Almost immediately, he was approached by an acquaintance of mine, a beautiful and high-powered woman who worked in finance. She perked up instantly, I could see, talking to Barack. Pleased with this, I moved on toward others I knew in the crowd.

Twenty minutes later, I caught sight of Barack across the room, in the grips of an endless conversation with the woman, who was doing a large portion of the talking. He shot me a look. It seemed that he'd like to be rescued. But he was a grown man. I let him rescue himself.

"Do you know what she asked me?" he said the next day, turning up in my office, still slightly surprised. "She asked if I liked to go *riding*. She meant on horseback." He said they'd discussed their favorite movies, which also hadn't gone well.

Barack was a thinker, probably too brainy for most people to put up with, and maybe I should have realized that earlier. My world was filled with hopeful, hardworking people who had new cars and were buying their first condos and liked to talk about it. Barack was more content to spend an evening alone, reading up on urban housing policy. As a community organizer, he'd spent weeks and months listening to poor people describe their challenges. His belief in hope and the possibility of improving people's lives set him apart.

There was a time, he told me, when he'd been less serious and more wild. He'd spent the first twenty years of his life going by the nickname Barry. Somewhere along the way, though, he'd stepped into the fullness of his birth name—Barack Hussein Obama—and his complicated identity. He was white and Black, African and American. He was humble and lived simply, yet knew the richness of his own mind and the world of privilege that would open up to him as a result. He took it all seriously, I could tell. He could be lighthearted and jokey, but he never strayed far from a larger sense of duty. He was on some sort of quest, though he didn't yet know where it would lead. All I knew was that it didn't translate to casual conversation. Next time my friends were gathering, I left him at the office.

WHEN I WAS a kid, my parents smoked. They lit cigarettes in the evenings as they sat in the kitchen, talking through their workdays. They smoked while they cleaned the dinner dishes later at night, sometimes opening a window to let in some fresh air. They weren't heavy smokers, but they were daily smokers, and stubborn ones, too. They smoked long after the research made clear that it was bad for you.

The whole thing drove me crazy, and Craig as well. We made an elaborate show of coughing when they lit up. When Craig and I were very young, we pulled a brand-new carton of Newport cigarettes from a shelf and set about destroying them, snapping them like beans over the kitchen sink. Another time, we dipped the ends of their cigarettes in hot sauce and returned them to the pack. We lectured our parents about lung cancer, explaining the horrors that had been shown to us during health class at school—images of smokers' lungs, as black as charcoal, death right inside your chest. For contrast, we'd been shown pictures of healthy pink lungs, uncontaminated by smoke. The clear information about the dangers of smoking was simple enough to make their behavior frustrating: Good/Bad. Healthy/Sick. You choose your own future. It was everything our parents had ever taught us. And yet it would be years before they finally quit.

Barack smoked the way my parents did—after meals, walking down a city block, or when he was feeling anxious and needed to do something with his hands. In 1989, smoking was more common than it is now. Research on the effects of secondhand smoke was relatively new. People smoked in restaurants, offices, and airports. But still, I'd seen the research. To me, and to every sensible person I knew, smoking was pure self-destruction.

Barack knew exactly how I felt about it. Our friendship was built on a plainspoken honesty that I think we both enjoyed.

"Why would someone as smart as you do something as dumb as that?" I'd blurted on the very first day we met, watching him end our lunch with a smoke. It was an honest question.

As I recall, he just shrugged, admitting that I was right. Smoking was the one topic where Barack's logic seemed to leave him altogether.

Whether I was going to admit it or not, though, something between

99

us had started to change. On days when we were too busy to check in face-to-face, I found myself wondering what he'd been up to. I talked myself out of being disappointed when he didn't surface in my office doorway. I talked myself out of being too excited when he did. I had feelings for the guy, but they were buried deep beneath my decision to keep my life and career focused on the future and free from any drama. I was on track to become a partner at Sidley & Austin. It was everything I wanted—or so I was trying to convince myself.

I might have been ignoring whatever was growing between us, but he wasn't.

"I think we should go out," Barack announced one afternoon as we sat finishing a meal.

"What, you and me?" I pretended to be shocked that he even considered it a possibility. "I told you, I don't date. And I'm your adviser."

He laughed. "Like that counts for anything. You're not my boss," he said. "And you're pretty cute."

Barack had a smile that seemed to stretch the whole width of his face. And he was so smooth and reasonable. More than once, he laid out the evidence for why we should be going out. We got along well. We made each other laugh. We were both single, and we confessed to being almost immediately uninterested in anyone else we met. Nobody at the firm, he argued, would care if we dated. In fact, maybe it would be seen as a positive. He figured that the partners wanted him to come work for them eventually. If he and I were dating, it would improve the odds of his committing.

"You mean I'm like some sort of bait?" I said, laughing. "You flatter yourself."

Over the course of the summer, the firm organized a series of events and outings for its associates, sending around sign-up sheets for anyone who wanted to go. One was a weeknight performance at a theater not far from the office. I put us on the list for two tickets.

We sat side by side in the theater, both of us worn out after a long day of work. The curtain went up and the singing began.

When the lights went up for intermission, I stole a glance at Barack. He was slumped down, with his right elbow on the armrest and index finger resting on his forehead, his expression unreadable.

"What'd you think?" I said.

He gave me a sideways look. "Horrible, right?"

I laughed, glad that he felt the same way.

Barack sat up in his seat. "What if we got out of here?" he said. "We could just leave."

Under normal circumstances, I wouldn't leave. I wasn't that sort of person. I cared too much about what the other lawyers thought of me—what they'd think if they spotted our empty seats. I cared too much, in general, about finishing what I'd started, about seeing every last little thing through to the absolute end. This, unfortunately, was the box checker in me. I endured misery for the sake of appearances. But now, it seemed, I'd joined up with someone who did not.

Avoiding everyone we knew from work, we slipped out of the theater. The last light was draining from a purple sky. I exhaled, my relief so obvious that it caused Barack to laugh.

"Where are we going now?" I asked.

"How 'bout we grab something to eat?"

We walked to a nearby place in the same manner we always seemed to walk, with me a step forward and him a step back. Barack moved with a Hawaiian casualness and didn't hurry, even and especially when instructed to hurry. I, on the other hand, had a hard time slowing down. But I remember how that night I told myself to slow down, just a little—just enough so that I could hear what he was saying, because I was beginning to realize that I cared about hearing everything he said.

Until now, I'd built my life carefully, as if folding a tight and airless piece of origami. I was proud of how it looked. But it was delicate. If one corner came untucked, I might discover that I was restless. If another popped loose, it might reveal that I was uncertain about the professional path I'd put myself on, about all the things I told myself I wanted. I think now it's why I guarded myself so carefully, why I still wasn't ready to let him in. He was like a wind that threatened to unsettle everything.

A day or two later, Barack asked if I could give him a ride to a barbecue for summer associates, which was happening that weekend at a senior partner's home in one of the wealthy lakefront suburbs north of the city. The weather was clear that day, the lake sparkling at the edge of a well-tended lawn. The party was a reminder of the rewards we would get if we continued to work at the law firm. Barack, I knew, wrestled with what he wanted to do with his life, which direction his career would take. Like me, he'd never been wealthy, and he didn't aspire to it, either. He wanted to be effective far more than he wanted to be rich, but he was still trying to figure out how.

We walked through the party not quite like a couple but still mostly together, drifting between clusters of colleagues, drinking lemonade, eating hamburgers and potato salad from plastic plates. We'd get separated and then find each other again. It all felt natural. He was quietly flirty with me and I was flirty back. Some of the men started playing pickup basketball, and I watched as Barack strolled over to the court in his flip-flops to join. He got along well with everyone at the firm, from the older, stuffier lawyers to the secretaries to the ambitious young guys who were now playing basketball. *He's a good person*, I thought to myself, watching him pass the ball to another lawyer.

Having sat through dozens of high school and college games, I recognized a good player when I saw one. Barack quickly passed the test. He was athletic, moving quickly and gracefully, showing power I hadn't noticed before. I couldn't stop watching him.

As we drove back to the city in the early evening, I felt a new ache.

It was July. Barack would be leaving in August, disappearing into law school and whatever else life held for him there. We were kidding around, as we always did, gossiping about who'd said what at the barbecue, but I felt a certain kind of longing. As we followed the southward curve of Lake Shore Drive, I was arguing silently with myself. Was there a way to date him casually? How badly could it hurt my job? Would it matter if other people found out? I didn't feel clear about anything, but I suddenly realized that I was done waiting for clarity.

He was living in Hyde Park, subletting an apartment from a friend. By the time we pulled into Barack's neighborhood, there was a tension in the air between us. It felt like something was finally about to happen. Or was I imagining it? Maybe I'd shut him down too many times. Maybe he'd given up and now just saw me as a good friend—a girl with an air-conditioned car who'd drive him around when he needed it.

I halted the car in front of his building. We let an awkward moment pass, each waiting for the other to begin to say a good-bye. Barack cocked his head at me.

"Should we get some ice cream?" he said.

This is when I knew something was happening between us. For once, I decided to stop thinking and just live. It was a warm summer evening in the city that I loved. We went to an ice cream store on the block near Barack's apartment. We got ourselves two cones, taking them outside to eat, finding ourselves a spot on the curb. We sat close together with our knees pulled up, pleasantly tired after a day spent outdoors, eating our ice cream quickly and wordlessly, trying to stay ahead of the melt. Maybe Barack read it on my face or sensed that I was beginning to loosen up.

He was looking at me curiously, with the trace of a smile.

"Can I kiss you?" he asked.

And with that, I leaned in and everything felt clear.

Becoming Us

9

AS SOON AS I ALLOWED MYSELF TO HAVE FEELINGS FOR Barack, they came rushing. I felt a sense of gratitude and wonder. Any worries I'd felt about my life and career and even about Barack seemed to fall away with that first kiss. I wanted to know him better, to explore and experience everything about him as fast as I could.

Maybe because he was due back at Harvard in a month, we wasted no time being casual. I began spending time at Barack's apartment, a cramped, second-floor walk-up above a storefront on a noisy street. There was a small table, a couple of rickety chairs, and a queen-sized mattress on the floor. Piles of Barack's books and newspapers covered the open surfaces and a good deal of the floor. He hung his suit jackets on the backs of the kitchen chairs and kept very little in the fridge. It wasn't homey, but now that we were together, it felt like home.

Barack was not like anyone I'd dated before. He seemed so secure. He was openly affectionate. He told me I was beautiful. He made me feel good. To me, he was sort of like a unicorn—unusual to the point of seeming almost unreal. He never talked about buying a house or a car or even new shoes. He read late into the night, often long after I'd fallen asleep, plowing through history and biographies and Toni

Morrison, too. He read several newspapers daily. He was aware of the latest book reviews, the American League standings, and what the South Side elected officials were up to. He could speak with equal passion about the Polish elections and the latest movies.

With no air-conditioning, we had little choice but to keep the windows open at night, trying to cool the sweltering apartment. Barack's neighborhood was busy and loud. Almost hourly, a police siren would blare outside the window or someone would start shouting and startle me awake. If I found it unsettling, Barack did not. I sensed already that he was more at home with the messiness of the world than I was. I woke one night to find him staring at the ceiling, his profile lit by the glow of streetlights outside. He looked vaguely troubled, as if he were pondering something deeply personal. Was it our relationship? The loss of his dad?

"Hey, what're you thinking about over there?" I whispered.

He turned to look at me, his smile a little sheepish. "Oh," he said. "I was just thinking about income inequality."

This, I was learning, was how Barack's mind worked. He thought a lot about big and abstract issues, and had a crazy sense that he might be able to do something about them. It was new to me. Until now, I'd hung around with good people who cared about important enough things but who were focused on building their careers and providing for their families. Barack was just different. He was dialed into the day-to-day demands of his life, but at the same time, especially at night, his thoughts seemed to roam toward bigger questions.

Most of our time was still spent at work, in the office. Every morning I shook off any dreaminess and zipped myself back into my junior-associate existence, returning to my stack of documents. Barack worked on his own documents in a shared office down the hall and continued to impress the partners.

Still concerned about what others would think, I insisted we keep our relationship out of sight of our colleagues. But it hardly worked.

Lorraine, my assistant, gave Barack a knowing smile each time he surfaced in my office.

Work, during this time, felt like the thing we had to do before we could spend time together again. Away from the office, Barack and I talked endlessly, over leisurely walks and meals that seemed short to us but in reality went on for hours. We talked about musicians we loved, Stevie Wonder and Marvin Gaye. I was smitten. I loved the slow roll of his voice and the way his eyes softened when I told a funny story. I was coming to appreciate how he never hurried, never worried about time.

Each day brought small discoveries: I was a Cubs fan, while he liked the White Sox. I loved mac and cheese, and he couldn't stand it. He liked dark, dramatic movies, while I went all-in for romantic comedies. He was a lefty with perfect handwriting; I had a heavy right-hand scrawl. In the month before he went back to Harvard, we shared what felt like every memory and thought, running through our childhood stories, teenage blunders, and past romances. Barack was especially curious about my upbringing—the year-to-year, decade-to-decade sameness of life on Euclid Avenue, with me and Craig and Mom and Dad making up four corners of a sturdy square. Barack had spent a lot of time in churches during his time as a community organizer, which had left him with an appreciation for organized religion, but at the same time he remained less traditional. Marriage, he told me early on, seemed unnecessary.

I don't remember introducing Barack to my family that summer, though Craig tells me I did. He says that the two of us walked up to the house on Euclid Avenue one evening. Craig was over for a visit, sitting on the front porch with my parents. Barack, he reminded me, was friendly and confident and made a couple of minutes of easy small talk before we ran up to my apartment to pick something up.

My dad appreciated Barack instantly, but still didn't like his odds. He'd seen me dump my high school boyfriend David at the gates of

Princeton. He'd watched me dismiss Kevin the college football player as soon as I'd seen him in a furry mascot outfit. My parents knew better than to get too attached to any of my boyfriends. They'd raised me to run my own life, and that's basically what I did. I was too focused and too busy, I'd told my parents plenty of times, to make room for any man.

According to Craig, my dad shook his head and laughed as he watched me and Barack walk away.

"Nice guy," he said. "Too bad he won't last."

IF MY FAMILY was a square, then Barack's was a more elaborate shape. His family reached across oceans, and he'd spent years trying to make sense of it. His mom, Ann Dunham, had been a seventeen-year-old college student in Hawaii when she fell for a Kenyan student named Barack Obama. Their marriage was brief. Her new husband, it turned out, already had a wife in Nairobi. After Ann got a divorce, she went on to marry a Javanese geologist named Lolo Soetoro. They moved to Jakarta, Indonesia, bringing along the junior Barack Obama—*my* Barack Obama—who was then six years old.

As Barack described it to me, he'd been happy in Indonesia and got along well with his new stepfather, but his mom had concerns about the quality of his schooling. She sent him back to Oahu, Hawaii, to attend private school and live with her parents. She was a free spirit who would go on to spend years moving between Hawaii and Indonesia. Aside from making one long trip back to Hawaii when Barack was ten, his dad—a man who had both a powerful mind and a powerful drinking problem—remained absent.

And yet Barack was loved deeply. His grandparents on Oahu spoiled him and his younger half sister Maya. His mom, though still living in Jakarta, was warm and supportive from afar. Barack also spoke affectionately of another half sister in Nairobi, named Auma. He'd grown up with far less stability than I had, but he didn't complain. His story was his story. His family life had left him self-reliant and optimistic. The fact he'd navigated his unusual upbringing so successfully seemed only to reinforce the idea that he was ready to take on more.

On a humid evening, I went with him as he did a favor for an old friend. A former community-organizer co-worker had asked if he could lead a training at a Black parish in Roseland, on the Far South Side. This was a place that had been crippled by steel mill closings. For Barack, it was a welcome one-night return to his old job and the part of Chicago where he'd once worked. It occurred to me as we walked into the church, both of us still dressed in our office clothes, that I'd never thought much about what a community organizer actually did. We followed a stairwell down to a low-ceilinged, fluorescent-lit basement area, where fifteen or so parishioners—mostly women—were sitting in folding chairs, fanning themselves in the heat. I took a seat in the back as Barack walked to the front of the room and said hello.

To them, he must have seemed young and lawyerly. I could see that they were sizing him up, trying to figure out whether he was some sort of outsider or had something of value to offer. The atmosphere was plenty familiar to me. I'd grown up attending my great-aunt Robbie's weekly music workshop in a church not unlike this one. The women in the room were no different from the ladies who sang in Robbie's choir or who'd turned up with casseroles after Southside died. They were well-intentioned, community-minded women, often single moms or grandmothers, the type who stepped in to help when no one else would volunteer.

After introducing himself, Barack started a conversation that would last about an hour. He asked people to share their stories and describe their concerns about life in the neighborhood. Barack shared his own story, tying it to the idea of community organizing. He was there to convince them that our stories connected us to one another, and that our stories could help create meaningful change. Even they,

he said—a tiny group inside a small church, in what felt like a forgotten neighborhood—could build real political power. It took effort, he
cautioned. It required listening to your neighbors and building trust
in communities where trust was often lacking. It meant asking people
you'd never met to give you a bit of their time or a tiny piece of their
paycheck. It involved being told no in a dozen or a hundred different
ways before hearing the "yes" that would make all the difference. But
he assured them they could have influence. They could make change.
He'd seen the process work, if not always smoothly, in a local public-
housing project, where a group just like this one had managed to register new voters, get residents to meet with city officials about asbestos
contamination, and persuade the mayor's office to fund a neighborhood job-training center.

The heavyset woman sitting next to me bounced a toddler on her
knee and did nothing to hide that she hardly believed him. She inspected Barack with her chin lifted and her bottom lip stuck out, as if
to say, *Who are you to be telling us what to do?*

But her attitude didn't bother him. Barack was a unicorn, after all,
with his unusual name, heritage, and ethnicity. He was used to having
to prove himself, pretty much anywhere he went.

The idea he was presenting wasn't an easy sell. Roseland had taken
one hit after another, from the departure of white families and the
failure of the steel industry to the deterioration of its schools and
the growth of the drug trade. As an organizer working in urban communities, Barack had told me, he most often had to deal with a deep
weariness in people—especially Black people—a cynicism bred from a
thousand small disappointments over time. I understood it. I'd seen it
in my own neighborhood, in my own family. A bitterness and a loss of
faith. It lived in both of my grandfathers because of every goal they'd
abandoned and every compromise they'd had to make. It was inside
the second-grade teacher who'd basically given up trying to teach us
at Bryn Mawr. It was inside the neighbor who'd stopped mowing her

lawn or keeping track of where her kids went after school. It lived in every piece of trash tossed carelessly in the grass at our local park. It lived in every last thing we deemed unfixable, including ourselves.

Barack didn't talk down to the people of Roseland, and he wasn't trying to win them over, either, by hiding his privilege and acting more "Black." Amid the parishioners' fears and frustrations, their disenfranchisement and sinking helplessness, he was somewhat brashly pointing an arrow in the opposite direction.

I'd never been someone who dwelled on the more negative parts of being African American. I'd been raised to think positively. I'd absorbed my family's love and my parents' commitment to seeing us succeed. I'd stood with Santita Jackson at rallies, listening to her dad call for Black people to remember their pride. My purpose had always been to see past my neighborhood—to look ahead and overcome. And I had. I'd scored myself two Ivy League degrees. I had a seat at the table at an important law firm. I'd made my parents and grandparents proud. But listening to Barack, I began to understand that his version of hope reached far beyond mine: It was one thing to get yourself out of a stuck place, I realized. It was another thing entirely to try and get the place itself unstuck.

I was gripped all over again by a sense of how special he was. All around me, too, the church ladies began nodding their approval, punctuating his sentences with calls of "Mmmm-hmm" and "That's right!"

His voice climbed in intensity. He wasn't a preacher, but he was definitely preaching something—a vision. The choice, as he saw it, was this: You give up or you work for change. "What's better for us?" Barack called to the people gathered in the room. "Do we settle for the world as it is, or do we work for the world as it should be?"

It was a phrase borrowed from a book he'd read when he first started out as an organizer, and it would stay with me for years. It was as close as I'd come to understanding what motivated Barack. *The world as it should be.*

Next to me, the woman with the toddler on her lap all but exploded. "That's right!" she bellowed, finally convinced. "Amen!"

Amen, I thought to myself. Because I was convinced, too.

BEFORE HE RETURNED to law school, sometime in the middle of August, Barack told me he loved me. Our feelings had caught us by surprise. Even though we'd known each other only a couple of months, even though it was kind of impractical, we were in love.

But now, with Barack returning to law school, we'd be more than nine hundred miles apart. Barack had two years of school left and said he hoped to settle in Chicago when he was done. There was no expectation that I would leave my life there in the meantime. As a still-newish associate at my law firm, I understood that the next phase of my career was important. My accomplishments would determine whether I was promoted or not. Having been through law school myself, I also knew how busy Barack would be. He'd been chosen as an editor on the *Harvard Law Review,* a monthly student-run journal that was considered one of the top legal publications in the country. It was an honor to be picked for the editorial team, but it was also like tacking a full-time job onto the already-heavy load of being a law student.

What did this leave us with? It left us with the phone. This was 1989, when cell phones didn't live in our pockets. Texting wasn't a thing; no emoji could sub for a kiss. The phone required both time and availability. Personal calls happened usually at home, at night, when you were dog tired and in need of sleep.

Barack told me, ahead of leaving, that he preferred letter writing.

"I'm not much of a phone guy" was how he put it. As if that settled it.

But it settled nothing. We'd just spent the whole summer talking. I didn't want to wait for letters to arrive in the mail. This was another small difference between us: Barack could pour his heart out through a pen. He'd been raised on letters, in the form of wispy airmail envelopes from his mom in Indonesia. But I was an in-your-face sort of person—brought up on Sunday dinners at Southside's, where you sometimes had to shout to be heard.

In my family, we talked. My dad, who'd recently traded in his car for a specialized van to accommodate his disability, still made a point of showing up in his cousins' doorways as often as possible for in-person visits. Friends, neighbors, and cousins of cousins also regularly turned up on Euclid Avenue and planted themselves in the living room next to my dad in his recliner to tell stories and ask for advice. My dad had no problem with the phone, either. For years, I'd seen him call my grandmother in South Carolina almost daily, asking for her news.

I informed Barack that if our relationship was going to work, he'd better get comfortable with the phone. "If I'm not talking to you," I announced, "I might have to find another guy who'll listen." I was joking, but only a little.

And so it was that Barack became a phone guy. Over the course of that fall, we spoke as often as we could manage, both of us locked into our separate worlds and schedules but still sharing the little details of our days. As months passed, our feelings stayed steady and reliable.

At my law firm, I was part of the Chicago office's recruiting team. As a recruiter, my goal was to bring in law students who were not just smart and hard-driving but also something other than male and white. There was exactly one other African American woman on the recruiting team, a senior associate named Mercedes Laing. Mercedes was about ten years older than I was and became a dear friend and mentor. Like me, she had two Ivy League degrees and routinely sat at tables where nobody looked like her. The struggle, we agreed, was not to get used to it or accept it. In meetings on recruitment, I argued insistently that the firm cast a wider net when it came to finding young talent. The long-held practice was to engage students from a select group of law schools—Harvard, Stanford, Yale, Northwestern, the

University of Chicago, and the University of Illinois, primarily—the places where most of the firm's lawyers had earned their degrees. Recruiting was usually a circular process: one generation of lawyers hiring new lawyers whose life experience and educational backgrounds mirrored their own, leaving little room for diversity of any sort.

To help fix the issue at my firm, I pushed for us to consider law students coming from state schools and from historically Black colleges like Howard University. When the recruiting team gathered to review student résumés, I objected anytime a student was automatically dismissed for having a B on a transcript or for having gone to a less prestigious college. If we were serious about bringing in minority lawyers, we'd need to think about how they'd used whatever opportunities life had afforded them rather than measuring them simply by their academic performance at an elite school. The point wasn't to lower the firm's high standards. It was to realize that by sticking with the most rigid and old-school way of evaluating a new lawyer's potential, we were overlooking all sorts of people who could contribute to the firm's success. We needed to interview more students before writing them off.

I loved making recruiting trips to Harvard because I could choose to meet with a diverse group of students. It also gave me an excuse to see Barack. The first time I visited, he picked me up in his car, a snub-nosed, banana-yellow car he'd bought used on his tight student budget. When he turned the key, the engine revved and the car spasmed violently before settling into a loud, sustained growling that shook us in our seats. I looked at Barack in disbelief.

"You drive this thing?" I said, raising my voice over the noise.

He flashed me an impish, I-got-this-covered grin. "Just give it a minute or two," he said, shifting the car into gear. "It goes away." After another few minutes, having steered us onto a busy road, he added, "Also, maybe don't look down."

I'd already spotted what he wanted me to avoid—a rusted-out, four-inch hole in the floor of his car, through which I could see the pavement rushing beneath us.

Life with Barack would never be dull. I knew it even then. It would be some version of banana yellow and slightly hair-raising. It occurred to me, too, that quite possibly the man would never make any money.

At Christmastime that year, we flew to Honolulu. I'd never been to Hawaii before but was pretty certain I'd like it. I was coming from Chicago, after all, where winter stretched through April. For me, getting away from winter had always felt like a joyride.

During college, my friend Suzanne had taken me to powdery white beaches in Kingston, Jamaica, where we dodged waves in water that looked like jade. She'd piloted us expertly through a chaotic market, jabbering with street vendors.

"Try dis!" she'd shouted at me, handing me pieces of grilled fish to taste, handing me fried yams, stalks of sugarcane, and cut-up pieces of mango. She demanded I try everything, intent on getting me to see how much there was to love.

It was no different visiting Oahu with Barack. He'd spent more than a decade on the mainland, but Hawaii still mattered to him deeply. He wanted me to take it all in, from the palm trees that lined the streets of Honolulu and the crescent arc of Waikiki Beach to the green hills surrounding the city. We stayed in a borrowed apartment belonging to family friends and made trips every day to the ocean, to swim and laze about in the sun. I met Barack's half sister Maya, who at nineteen was kind and smart and getting a degree at Barnard College in New York. She had round cheeks and wide brown eyes and dark hair that curled in a rich tangle around her shoulders. I met his grandparents Madelyn and Stanley Dunham, or Toot and Gramps, as he called them. They lived in the same high-rise where they'd raised Barack, in a small apartment decorated with Indonesian textiles that Ann had sent home over the years.

And I met Ann herself, a plump, lively woman with dark frizzy hair and the same angular chin as Barack. She wore chunky silver jewelry, a bright batik dress, and sturdy sandals. She was friendly toward me and curious about my background and my career. It was clear she adored her son. She was eager to sit down and talk with him, describing her work as an anthropologist and swapping book recommendations as if catching up with an old friend.

Everyone in the family still called him Barry. Though they'd left their home state of Kansas a long time ago, his grandparents seemed to me like the misplaced midwesterners Barack had always described them as. Gramps was big and bearlike and told silly jokes. Toot, a stout, gray-haired woman who'd worked her way up to becoming the vice president of a local bank, made us tuna salad sandwiches for lunch. In the evenings, she served Ritz crackers piled with sardines for appetizers and put dinner on TV trays so that everyone could watch the news or play a heated game of Scrabble. They were a modest, middle-class family, in many ways not at all unlike my own.

There was something comforting in this, for both me and Barack. As different as we were, we fit together in an interesting way. It was as if the reason for the ease and attraction between us was now explained by how similar our families were.

In Hawaii, Barack was laid-back. He was at home. And home was where he didn't feel the need to prove anything to anyone. We were late for everything we did, but it didn't matter—not even to me. Barack's high school buddy Bobby, who was a commercial fisherman, took us out on his boat one day for some snorkeling and an aimless cruise. It was then that I saw Barack as relaxed as I'd ever seen him, lounging under a blue sky with an old friend, no longer obsessed with the day's news or law school reading or what should be done about income inequality. The sun-bleached mellowness of the island opened up space for the two of us, in part by giving us time we'd never before had.

So many of my friends judged potential mates from the outside in, focusing first on their looks and financial prospects instead of their character. If it turned out the person they'd chosen wasn't a good communicator or was uncomfortable with being vulnerable, they seemed to think time or marriage vows would fix the problem. But from our very first conversation, Barack had shown me that he wasn't afraid of expressing fear or weakness. He valued being truthful. At work, I'd witnessed his willingness to sacrifice his own needs and wants for a bigger purpose.

And now in Hawaii, I could see his character reflected in other small ways. His long-lasting friendships with his high school buddies showed his consistency in relationships. In his devotion to his strong-willed mom, I saw a deep respect for women and their independence. I knew he could handle a partner like me who had her own passions and voice. These were things you couldn't teach in a relationship, things that not even love could really build or change. In opening up his world to me, Barack was showing me everything I'd ever need to know about the kind of life partner he'd be.

One afternoon, we sat on a ribbon of soft beach and watched surfers rip across enormous waves. We stayed for hours, just talking, as the sun dropped toward the horizon and the other beachgoers packed up to go home. If I'd come to Hawaii to sample something of Barack's past, we were now sitting at the edge of a giant ocean, imagining our future together, discussing what kind of house we'd want to live in someday, what kind of parents we wanted to be. It felt a little daring to talk like this, but it was also reassuring, because it seemed as if maybe this conversation between us could go on for life.

BACK IN CHICAGO, separated again from Barack, I rarely went to parties or stayed out late. I was now content to spend a Saturday night reading a good novel on the couch.

When I got bored, I called up old friends. Even now that I had a serious boyfriend, my girlfriends were the ones who held me steady.

Santita Jackson was now traveling the country as a singer, but we spoke when we could. A year or so earlier, I'd sat with my parents in their living room, bursting with pride as we watched Santita and her siblings introduce their dad at the 1988 Democratic National Convention. Reverend Jackson had made a respectable run for the presidency, even winning about a dozen primaries. Along the way, he'd filled households like ours with a new and profound level of hope and excitement, even if in our hearts we understood that he was a long shot's long shot.

I spoke regularly with Verna Williams, a close friend from law school. She'd met Barack a couple of times and liked him a lot but teased me that I'd let my insanely high standards slip, having allowed a smoker into my life. Angela Kennedy and I still laughed hard together, even though she was working as a teacher in New Jersey while also parenting a young son and trying to hold herself steady as her marriage slowly fell apart. We'd known each other as goofy, half-mature college girls, and now we were adults, with adult lives and adult concerns. That idea alone sometimes struck us as hilarious.

Suzanne was the same free spirit she'd been when we roomed together at Princeton—flitting in and out of my life, continuing to measure the value of her days purely by whether they were pleasurable or not. We'd go long stretches without talking but then pick up the thread of our friendship with ease. As always, I called her Screwzy and she called me Miche. Our worlds continued to be as different as they'd been at school. Even then, Suzanne was like a sister whose life I could only track from afar, across the gulf of our inherent differences. She was maddening, charming, and always important to me. She'd ask my advice and then willfully ignore it. Would it be bad to date a womanizing semi-famous pop star? Why, yes it would, but she'd do it anyway, because *why not?* Most galling to me was when she turned down an opportunity to go to an Ivy League business school after college, deciding that it would be too much work and therefore no fun.

Instead, she got her MBA from a not-so-stressful program at a state school, which I viewed as kind of a lazy move.

Suzanne's choices sometimes seemed like the opposite of my way of doing things, a vote in favor of easing up and striving less. I can say now that I judged her unfairly for them. At the time, though, I just thought I was right.

Not long after I'd started dating Barack, I called Suzanne to gush about my feelings for him. She'd been thrilled to hear me so happy. She also had news of her own: She was ditching her job as a computer specialist and going traveling—not for weeks, but for months. Suzanne and her mom were soon to head off on some round-the-world-style adventure. Because *why not?*

I could never guess whether Suzanne knew unconsciously that something strange was happening in the cells of her body, that a silent hijacking was already under way. What I did know was that during the fall of 1989, while I wore patent leather pumps and sat through long, dull conference-room meetings at the law firm, Suzanne and her mom were trying not to spill curry on their sundresses in Cambodia and dancing at dawn on the grand walkways of the Taj Mahal. As I balanced my checkbook, picked up my dry cleaning, and watched the leaves wither and drop from the trees along Euclid Avenue, I imagined Suzanne was careening through hot, humid Bangkok, full of joy. I don't know what any of her travels actually looked like or where she went, because she didn't keep in touch. She was too busy living, stuffing herself full of what the world had to give.

When she got home to Maryland and found a moment to reach out to me, her news was so shocking that I could hardly take it in.

"I have cancer," Suzanne told me, her voice husky with emotion. "A lot of it."

Her doctors had just diagnosed it. She described a plan for treatment, but I was too overwhelmed to note the details. Before hanging up, she told me that in a cruel twist of fate, her mom had fallen gravely ill as well.

I'm not sure that I ever believed that life was fair, but I had always thought that you could work your way out of just about any problem. Suzanne's cancer was the first real challenge to my way of seeing the world. Because even if I didn't have the specifics nailed down yet, I did have ideas about what my future would be. I had that agenda I'd been following since freshman year of college, a neat line of boxes I was meant to check.

For me and Suzanne, it was supposed to go like this: We'd be the maids of honor at each other's weddings. Our husbands would be really different, of course, but they'd like each other a lot. We'd have babies at the same time, take family beach trips to Jamaica, and be favorite fun aunties to each other's kids as they grew. I'd get her kids books for their birthdays; she'd get mine pogo sticks. We'd laugh and share secrets and roll our eyes at the other person's ridiculous habits, until one day we'd realize we were two old ladies who'd been best friends forever, surprised by where the time had gone.

That, for me, was the world as it should be.

WHAT I FIND remarkable as I look back was that I just continued to do my job. I was a lawyer, and lawyers worked. We worked all the time. There was no choice, I told myself. The work was important, I told myself. And so I kept showing up every morning at the office.

Back in Maryland, Suzanne was living with her disease. She was coping with medical appointments and surgeries and at the same time trying to care for her mom, who was also fighting cancer that was completely unrelated to Suzanne's. It was bad luck, bad fortune, freakish to the point of being too scary to think about. The rest of Suzanne's family was not particularly close-knit, except for two of her favorite female cousins who helped her out as much as they could. Our friend Angela drove down from New Jersey to visit sometimes, but she was juggling both a toddler and a job. I enlisted Verna, my law school friend, to go by when she could, as I was unable to do because of work. Verna had met Suzanne a couple of times while we were at Harvard and by sheer coincidence was now living in Silver Spring, in a building near Suzanne's.

It was a lot to ask of Verna, who'd recently lost her dad and was wrestling with her own grief. But she was a true friend, a compassionate person. She phoned my office one day in May to relay the details of a visit.

"I combed her hair," she said.

That Suzanne needed to have her hair combed should have told me everything, but I'd walled myself off from the truth. Some part of me still insisted this wasn't happening. I held on to the idea that Suzanne would get better.

It was Angela, finally, who called me in June and got right to the point. "If you're going to come, Miche," she said, "you'd better get to it."

By then, Suzanne had been moved to a hospital. She was too weak to talk, and I realized the end was soon. I hung up the phone and bought a plane ticket. When I arrived at the hospital, I found her there, lying in bed as Angela and her cousin watched over her, everyone silent. Suzanne's mom, it turned out, had died just a few days earlier, and now Suzanne was in a coma. Angela made room for me to perch on the side of her bed.

I stared hard at Suzanne, at her perfect heart-shaped face and reddish-brown skin. She seemed oddly undiminished by the illness. Her dark hair was still lustrous and long; someone had put it in two ropy braids that reached almost to her waist. Her track runner's legs lay hidden beneath the blankets. She looked young, like a sweet, beautiful twenty-six-year-old who was maybe in the middle of a nap.

I regretted not coming earlier. I regretted the many times, over the course of our long friendship, that I'd insisted she was making a wrong move, when possibly she'd been doing it right. I was suddenly glad for all the times she'd ignored my advice. I was glad that she hadn't overworked herself to get some fancy business school degree. That she'd gone off for a weekend with a semi-famous pop star, just for fun. I was happy that she'd made it to the Taj Mahal to watch the sunrise with her mom. Suzanne had lived in ways that I had not.

That day, I held her limp hand and watched as her breathing grew ragged. At some point, the nurse gave us a knowing nod. It was happening. Suzanne was leaving. My mind went dark. I had no deep thoughts. I had no revelations about life or loss. If anything, I was mad.

To say that it was unfair that Suzanne got sick and died at twenty-six seems too simple a thing. But it was a fact, as cold and ugly as they come. What I was thinking as I finally left her body in that hospital room was this: *She's gone and I'm still here.* Outside in the hallway, there were people wandering in hospital gowns who were far older and sicker-looking than Suzanne, and they were still here. I would take a packed flight back to Chicago, drive along a busy highway, and ride an elevator up to my office. I'd see all these people looking happy in their cars, walking the sidewalk in their summer clothes, sitting idly in cafés, and working at their desks, all of them oblivious to what happened to Suzanne—apparently unaware that they, too, could die at any moment. It didn't feel right, but the world just carried on. Everyone was still here, except for my Suzanne.

10

THAT SUMMER, I STARTED KEEPING A JOURNAL. I bought myself a clothbound black book with purple flowers on the cover and kept it next to my bed. I took it with me when I went on business trips. I was not a daily writer, or even a weekly writer: I picked up a pen only when I had the time and energy to sort through my jumbled feelings. I'd write a few entries in a single week and then lay the journal down for a month or sometimes more. The whole exercise of recording one's thoughts was new to me—a habit I'd picked up in part from Barack, who had kept journals on and off over the years.

He'd come back to Chicago over his summer break from Harvard, moving directly into my apartment on Euclid Avenue. This meant that Barack got to know my family. He'd talk sports with my dad as he headed out for a shift at the water plant. He sometimes helped my mom carry her groceries in from the garage. It was a good feeling. Craig had already tested Barack's character by including him in a weekend basketball game with a bunch of his buddies. He'd done this, actually, at my request. Craig's opinion of Barack mattered to me. My brother knew how to read people, especially in the way a person played a game. Barack had passed the test. He was smooth on the floor, my brother said, and knew when to make the right pass, but he also wasn't afraid to shoot when he was open. "He's no ball hog," Craig said. "But he's got guts."

Barack had accepted a summer job with a downtown firm whose offices were close to where I worked, but his time in Chicago was short. He'd been elected president of the *Harvard Law Review* for the coming school year, and he would need to get back to Harvard early in order to get started. The competition to lead the *Review* was ferocious every year, so being picked for the position was an enormous achievement for anyone. Barack was the first African American in the publication's 103-year history to be selected—a milestone so huge that it had been written about in the *New York Times*, along with a photo of Barack, smiling in a scarf and winter coat.

My boyfriend was a big deal. He could have landed any number of fat-salaried law firm jobs, but instead he was thinking about practicing civil rights law once he got his degree, even if it would take twice as long to pay off his student loans. Everyone he knew was urging him to follow the lead of many previous *Review* editors and apply for a clerkship with the Supreme Court. But Barack wasn't interested. He wanted to live in Chicago. He had ideas for writing a book about race in America and planned to find work that connected with his values. He wouldn't end up in corporate law. He steered himself with a certainty I found astounding.

All this confidence was admirable, but honestly, try living with it. Barack's strong sense of purpose was something I had to adjust to. In the presence of his certainty that he could make a difference in the world, I couldn't help but feel a little bit lost. His sense of purpose seemed like a challenge to my own.

So began my journaling. On the very first page, in careful handwriting, I spelled out my reasons for starting it:

One, I feel very confused about where I want my life to go. What kind of person do I want to be? How do I want to contribute to the world?

Two, I am getting very serious in my relationship with Barack and I feel that I need to get a better handle on myself.

This little flowered book has now survived a couple of decades and moves. It sat on a shelf in my dressing room at the White House for eight years, until very recently, when I pulled it out from a box in my new home to try to remember who I'd been as a young lawyer. I read those lines today and see exactly what I was trying to tell myself—what a no-nonsense female mentor might have said to me. Really, it was simple: The first thing was that I hated being a lawyer. I wasn't suited to the work. I felt empty doing it, even if I was plenty good at it. This was a distressing thing to admit, given how hard I'd worked and how in debt I was. In my need to excel and do things perfectly, I'd missed the signs and taken the wrong road.

The second was that I was deeply in love with a guy whose forceful intellect and ambition could possibly end up swallowing mine. I saw it coming already, like a wave ready to pull me under. I wasn't going to get out of its path—I was too committed to Barack by then, too in love—but I did need to quickly anchor myself on two feet.

This meant finding a new profession, and what shook me most was that I had no specific ideas about what I wanted to do. Somehow, in all my years of schooling, I hadn't managed to think through my own passions and how they might match up with work I found meaningful. As a young person, I'd explored exactly nothing. Barack, on the other hand, had tried out different jobs, gotten to know all sorts of people, and learned his own priorities along the way. These experiences had given him a sense of maturity. I, meanwhile, had been so afraid of losing my way, so eager for respectability and a way to pay the bills, that I'd marched myself unthinkingly into the law.

In one year, I'd gained Barack and lost Suzanne, and the power of those two things together had left me spinning. Suzanne's sudden death had awakened me to the idea that I wanted more joy and meaning in my life. I both credited and blamed Barack for the confusion. "If there were not a man in my life constantly questioning me about what drives me and what pains me," I wrote in my journal, "would I be doing it on my own?"

I thought about what I might do, what skills I might have. Could I be a teacher? A college administrator? Could I run some sort of after-school program? I was interested in possibly working for a foundation or a nonprofit. I was interested in helping underprivileged kids. I wondered if I could find a job that satisfied me and still left me enough time to do volunteer work, or appreciate art, or have children. I wanted to feel whole. I made a list of issues that interested me: education, teen pregnancy, Black self-esteem. A more meaningful job, I knew, would involve a pay cut. More serious was my next list, this one of my essential expenses—what was left after I let go of the luxuries I'd allowed myself on a lawyer's salary, things like my health-club membership. I had a big monthly payment on my student loans, a car payment, money spent on food, gas, and insurance, plus the money I'd need for rent if I ever moved out of my parents' house.

Nothing was impossible, but nothing looked simple. I started asking around about opportunities in entertainment law, thinking perhaps that it might be interesting and would also spare me the loss of a big salary. But in my heart, I felt a slow-growing certainty of my own: I wasn't built to practice law. One day I made note of an article I'd read about how many lawyers felt tired, stressed, and unhappy—especially female ones. "How depressing," I wrote in my journal.

I SPENT A GOOD chunk of that August working in a rented conference room at a hotel in Washington, D.C., having been dispatched to help prepare a case. Even though I was too busy to see much of the city, the change of scenery and routine distracted me just enough from the bigger questions beginning to bubble up in my mind.

On the evening I flew home to Chicago, I felt a heavy dread settling over me, knowing that I was about to step back into my everyday routine and the fog of my confusion.

My mom was kind enough to meet my flight at O'Hare. Just seeing her gave me comfort. She was in her early fifties now, working full-time as an executive assistant at a downtown bank filled with men who had gone into the business because their dads had been bankers before them. My mom was a force. She had little tolerance for fools. She kept her hair short and wore practical, unfussy clothes. She was competent and calm. As it had been when Craig and I were kids, she didn't get involved with our private lives. Her love came in the form of always being there for us. She showed up when your flight came in. She drove you home and offered food if you were hungry. Her even temper was like shelter to me, a place to feel safe.

As we drove downtown toward the city, I heaved a big sigh.

"You okay?" my mom asked.

I looked at her. "I don't know," I began. "It's just . . ."

And with that, I unloaded my feelings. I told her that I wasn't happy with my job, or even with my chosen profession—that I was seriously *unhappy*. I told her how I was desperate to make a major change but worried about not making enough money if I did. My emotions were raw. I let out another sigh. "I'm just not fulfilled," I said.

I see now how this must have come across to my mom, who was then in the ninth year of a job she'd taken primarily so she could help pay for my college education. This was after years of *not* having a job so that she'd be free to sew my school clothes, cook my meals, and do laundry for my dad. As for my dad, for the sake of our family he spent eight hours a day watching gauges on a boiler at the filtration plant. My mom, who'd just driven an hour to fetch me from the airport, who was letting me live rent-free in the upstairs of her house, and who would have to get herself up at dawn the next morning in order to help my disabled dad get ready for work, was hardly ready to feel sorry for my feelings about how I needed more meaning in my life.

Fulfillment, I'm sure, struck her as a rich person's wish. I doubt that my parents, in their thirty years together, had even once discussed it.

My mom didn't judge me. She wasn't one to give lectures or draw attention to her own sacrifices. She'd quietly supported every choice I'd ever made. This time, though, she gave me a sideways look, hit her turn signal to get us off the highway and back to our neighborhood, and chuckled just a little. "If you're asking me," she said, "I say make the money first and worry about your happiness later."

I SPENT THE next six months quietly trying to feel better about my work without making any sort of sudden change. I met with the partner in charge of my division, asking to be given more challenging assignments. I tried to focus on the projects I found most meaningful, including my efforts to recruit a new and more diverse group of summer associates. At the same time, I kept an eye on job listings and did my best to get to know more people who weren't lawyers. One way or another, I figured I'd work myself toward feeling whole.

At home on Euclid Avenue, I felt powerless in the face of a new reality. My dad's feet had started to swell for no obvious reason. His skin looked strange. Anytime I asked how he was feeling, though, he gave me the same answer that he'd given me for years.

"I'm fine," he'd say, as if the question were never worth asking. He'd then change the subject.

It was winter again in Chicago. I woke in the mornings to the sound of the neighbors chipping ice from their windshields on the street. The wind blew, and the snow piled up. The sunlight was weak. Through my office window on the forty-seventh floor, I looked out at a tundra of ice on Lake Michigan and a gray sky above. I wore my wool and hoped for a thaw. In the Midwest, winter is an exercise in waiting—for relief, for a bird to sing, for the first flowers to push up through the snow. You have no choice in the meantime but to pep-talk yourself through.

My dad hadn't lost his good humor. Craig came by for family dinners once in a while, and we sat around the table and laughed the same as always, though we were now joined by Janis, Craig's wife. Janis was happy and hard-driving, a telecommunications analyst who worked downtown and, like everyone else, adored my dad. Craig, meanwhile, was a great example of professional success. He was getting an MBA and had a job as a vice president at a bank, and he and Janis had bought a nice home in Hyde Park. He wore tailored suits and had driven over for dinner in his red sportscar. I didn't know it then, but none of this made him happy. Like me, he had his own crisis brewing, and in coming years he would struggle with questions about whether his work was meaningful and truly rewarding. Knowing how thrilled our dad was by what his kids had managed to accomplish, neither of us ever brought up our unhappiness over dinner.

Saying good-bye at the end of a visit, Craig would give my dad a final, concerned look and ask the usual question about his health, only to be given the merry brush-off of "I'm fine."

We accepted this because it was steadying, and steady was how we liked to be. Dad had lived with MS for years and had managed always to be fine. We wanted to believe him, even as we saw he was declining. He was fine, we told each other, because he still got up and went to work every day. He was fine because we'd watched him have a second helping of meat loaf that night. He was fine, especially if you didn't look too hard at his feet.

I had several tense conversations with my mom, asking why it was that Dad wouldn't go to the doctor. But like me, she'd all but given up, having asked him and been shut down enough times already. For my dad, doctors had never brought good news and therefore were to be avoided. As much as he loved to talk, he didn't want to talk about his problems. He wanted to get by in his own way. To manage his bulging feet, he'd simply asked my mom to buy him a bigger pair of work boots.

The silence over a doctor's visit continued through January and into February that year. My dad moved with a pained slowness, using an aluminum walker to get himself around the house, pausing often to catch his breath. It took longer in the mornings now for him to get from bed to bathroom, bathroom to kitchen, and finally to the back door and down the three stairs to the garage so that he could drive himself to work. Despite what was happening at home, he insisted that all was well at the filtration plant. He used a motorized scooter to pilot himself from boiler to boiler and took pride in being needed at work. In twenty-six years, he hadn't missed a single shift. If a boiler happened to overheat, my dad claimed to be one of only a few workers with enough experience to quickly contain a disaster. He was optimistic and had recently put his name in for a promotion.

Even though my dad was telling us he was fine, my mom and I could see that he wasn't. At home in the evenings, my dad spent much of his time watching basketball and hockey games on TV. He looked weak and exhausted in his chair. In addition to his feet, there seemed to be something swelling in his neck now, we'd noticed. It put an odd rattle in his voice.

We finally decided we had to do something. Craig was never one to be the bad cop, and my mom stuck to her decision not to discuss my dad's health. In a conversation like this, the role of tough talker almost always fell to me. I told my dad that he owed it to us to get some help and that I planned to call his doctor in the morning. He promised that if I made the appointment, he would go. I urged him to let himself sleep late the next morning, to give his body a rest.

We went to bed that night, my mom and I, feeling relieved that we'd finally gained some control.

MY DAD, HOWEVER, felt that resting was a form of giving in. I came downstairs in the morning to find him sitting at the kitchen table with his walker parked next to him. He was dressed in his navy-blue city uniform. He was struggling to put on his shoes. He was going to work.

"Dad," I said, "I thought you were going to rest. We're getting you that doctor's appointment . . ."

He shrugged. "I know, sweetie," he said, his voice gravelly from whatever new thing was wrong in his neck. "But right now, I'm fine."

His stubbornness was packed beneath so many layers of pride that it was impossible for me to be angry. There was no stopping him. My parents had raised us to handle our own business, which meant that I had to trust him to handle his, even if he could barely put on his shoes. So I let him handle it. I stuffed down my worries, gave my dad a kiss, and took myself back upstairs to get ready for my own workday. I figured I'd call my mom later at her office, telling her we'd need to come up with a plan about how to force the man to take some time off.

I heard the back door click shut. A few minutes later, I returned to the kitchen to find it empty. My dad's walker sat by the back door. I went over and looked through the little glass peephole in the door, just to confirm that his van was gone.

But the van was there, and so, too, was my dad. He was dressed in a cap and his winter jacket and had his back to me. He'd made it only partway down the stairs before needing to sit down. I could see his exhaustion in the sideways droop of his head and the half-collapsed heaviness with which he was resting against the wooden railing. He wasn't in a crisis so much as he looked just too weary to carry on. It seemed clear he was trying to summon enough strength to turn around and come back inside.

I realized I was seeing him in a moment of pure defeat.

How lonely it must have been to live twenty-some years with such a disease, to keep going without complaint as your body is slowly being consumed. Seeing my dad on the stoop, I ached in a way I never had. My instinct was to rush outside and help him back into the warm house, but I fought it, knowing it would be just another blow to his dignity. I took a breath and turned away from the door.

I'd see him when he came back in, I thought. I'd help take off his work boots, get him some water, and get him to his chair, with the silent understanding between us that now without question he would need to accept some help.

I sat listening for the sound of the back door. I waited for five minutes and then five minutes more, before finally I went back to the peephole to make sure he'd made it to his feet. But the stoop was empty now. Somehow my dad, in defiance of everything that was swollen and off-kilter in his body, had willed himself down those stairs and across the icy walkway and into his van, which was now probably almost halfway to the filtration plant. He was not giving in.

FOR MONTHS NOW, Barack and I had talked about the idea of marriage. We'd been together a year and a half and remained totally in love. He was in his final semester at Harvard and busy with his *Law Review* work but would soon head back to take the Illinois bar exam and look for a job. The plan was that he'd move back to Euclid Avenue, this time more permanently. For me, it was another reason why winter couldn't end soon enough.

We'd talked about how each of us viewed marriage, and it worried me sometimes how different those views seemed to be. For me, getting married had been a given, something I'd grown up expecting to do someday—the same way having children had always been a given, dating back to the attention I'd heaped on my baby dolls as a girl. Barack wasn't opposed to getting married, but he was in no rush. For him, our love meant everything already. It was foundation enough for a full and happy life together—with or without rings.

We were both products of how we'd been raised. Barack's mom had married twice and been divorced twice, but had succeeded in keeping her life, career, and young children intact. My parents had stayed together and had made every decision and effort jointly. In thirty years, they'd hardly spent a night apart.

Barack saw marriage as two people being joined together by love but keeping their independent lives, dreams, and ambitions. I saw marriage as a complete joining of two people, with the well-being of a family being more important than any individual interest or goal. I didn't exactly want a life like my parents had. I didn't want to live in the same house forever or work the same job. But I did want the steadiness they had.

We'd work out our feelings, I figured, when Barack came back to Chicago, when the weather warmed up. I just had to wait, though waiting was hard. I craved permanence. From my apartment, I could hear my parents talking on the floor below, my mom laughing as my dad told some sort of story. I heard them shutting off the TV to get ready for bed. I was twenty-seven years old now, and there were days when all I wanted was to feel complete. I wanted to grab every last thing I loved and stake it ruthlessly to the ground. I'd known just enough loss by then to know that there was more coming.

I HAD MADE the appointment for my dad to see a doctor, but it was my mom who got him there—by ambulance, as it turned out. His feet had ballooned and grown tender to the point that he finally admitted that walking on them felt like walking on needles. When it was time to go, he couldn't stand on them at all. I was at work that day, but my mom described it to me later—Dad being carried out of the house by paramedics, trying to joke with them as they went.

He was taken directly to the hospital at the University of Chicago. As days passed, my dad continued to swell. His face puffed up, his neck got thicker, his voice grew weak. Cushing's syndrome was the official diagnosis, possibly related to his MS and possibly not. Either way, his condition was bad. A scan showed that he had a growth in his throat that had become so enlarged he was practically choking on it.

"I don't know how I missed that," my dad said to the doctor, sounding genuinely surprised, as if he hadn't felt a single symptom leading up to this point, as if he hadn't spent weeks and months, if not years, ignoring his pain.

We took turns visiting him—my mom, Craig, Janis, and me. We came and went over days as the doctors blasted him with medicine, as tubes were added and machines were hooked up. We tried to understand what the specialists were telling us but could make little sense of it. We rearranged my dad's pillows and talked uselessly about college basketball and the weather outside, knowing that he was listening, though it exhausted him now to speak. We were a family of planners, but now everything seemed unplanned. Slowly, my dad was sinking away from us. We called him back with old memories, seeing how they put a little brightness in his eyes. Remember the Deuce and a Quarter and how we used to roll around in that giant backseat on our summer outings to the drive-in? Remember the boxing gloves you gave us, and the swimming pool at Dukes Happy Holiday Resort? What about how you used to build the props for Robbie's music workshop? What about dinners at Dandy's house? Remember when Mom made us fried shrimp on New Year's Eve?

One evening I stopped by and found my dad alone. My mom had gone home for the night. The room was quiet. The whole floor of the hospital was quiet. It was the first week of March, the winter snow having just melted, leaving the city damp. My dad had been in the hospital about ten days then. He was fifty-five years old, but he looked like an old man, with yellowed eyes and arms too heavy to move. He was awake but unable to speak, whether due to the swelling or due to emotion, I'll never know.

I sat in a chair next to his bed and watched him struggling to breathe. When I put my hand in his, he gave it a comforting squeeze. We looked at each other silently. There was too much to say, and at the same time it felt as if we'd said everything. What was left was only one truth. We were reaching the end. He would not recover. He was going to miss the whole rest of my life. I was losing his steadiness, his comfort, his everyday joy. I felt tears spilling down my cheeks.

Keeping his gaze on me, my dad lifted the back of my hand to his lips and kissed it again and again and again. It was his way of saying, *Hush now, don't cry.* He was expressing sorrow, but also something calmer and deeper, a message he wanted to make clear. With those kisses, he was saying that he loved me with his whole heart, that he was proud of the woman I'd become. He was saying that he knew he should have gone to the doctor a lot sooner. He was asking for forgiveness. He was saying good-bye.

I stayed with him until he fell asleep that night, leaving the hospital in icy darkness and driving back home to Euclid Avenue, where my mom had already turned off the lights. We were alone in the house now, just me and my mom and whatever future we were now meant to have. Because by the time the sun came up, he'd be gone. My dad—Fraser Robinson III—had a heart attack and passed away that night, having given us absolutely everything.

11

IT HURTS TO LIVE AFTER SOMEONE HAS DIED. IT JUST does. It can hurt to walk down a hallway or open the fridge. It hurts to put on a pair of socks, to brush your teeth. Food tastes like nothing. Colors look dull. Music hurts, and so do memories. You look at something you'd otherwise find beautiful—a purple sky at sunset or a playground full of kids—and it only somehow deepens the loss. Grief is so lonely this way.

The day after my dad died, we drove to a South Side funeral parlor—me, my mom, and Craig—to pick out a casket and plan a service. *To make arrangements,* as they say in funeral parlors. I don't remember much about our visit there, except for how stunned we were, each of us trying to cope with our private grief. Still, as we went through the ritual of shopping for the right box in which to bury our dad, Craig and I managed to have our first and only fight as adult siblings.

I wanted to buy the fanciest, most expensive casket in the place, complete with every extra handle and cushion a casket could possibly have. I had no particular reason for wanting this. It was something to do when there was nothing else to do. The practical part of our upbringing wouldn't allow me to put much stock in the gentle, well-intentioned words of sympathy people would heap on us a few days later at the funeral. I couldn't be easily comforted by the suggestion that my dad had gone to a better place or was sitting with angels. As I saw it, he just deserved a nice casket.

Craig insisted that Dad would want something basic—modest and practical and nothing more. It suited our dad's personality, he said. Anything else would be too showy.

We started quiet, but soon exploded, as the kindly funeral director pretended not to listen and our mom just stared at us silently, through the fog of her own pain.

We were yelling for reasons that had nothing to do with the casket. We were having a bizarre and inappropriate argument because in the wake of death, every single thing on earth feels that way. In the end, we'd bury our dad in a not too fancy, not too plain casket and never once discuss it again.

We drove Mom back to Euclid Avenue. The three of us sat downstairs at the kitchen table, feeling sad all over again at the sight of the fourth empty chair. Soon, we were weeping. We sat for what felt like a long time, blubbering until we were exhausted and out of tears. My mom, who hadn't said much all day, finally offered a comment.

"Look at us," she said sadly.

And yet there was a touch of lightness in how she said it. She was pointing out that we Robinsons had been reduced to a true and ridiculous mess—with our swollen eyelids and dripping noses, our hurt and strange helplessness here in our own kitchen. Who were we? Didn't we know? Hadn't Dad shown us? She was calling us back from our loneliness with three blunt words, as only our mom could do.

Mom looked at me and I looked at Craig, and suddenly the moment seemed a little funny. The first chuckle, we knew, would normally have come from that empty chair. Slowly, we started to crack up, collapsing finally into full-blown fits of laughter. I realize that might seem strange, but we were so much better at this than we were at crying. The point was he would have liked it, and so we let ourselves laugh.

LOSING MY DAD made me feel that there was no time to sit around and wonder how my life should go. My dad was just fifty-five when he died. Suzanne had been twenty-six. The lesson there was simple: Life is short and not to be wasted. If I died, I didn't want people remembering me for the stacks of legal briefs I'd written or the corporate trademarks I'd helped defend. I felt certain that I had something more to offer the world. It was time to make a move.

Still unsure of where I hoped to land, I typed up letters of introduction and sent them to people all over the city of Chicago. Thankfully, some people did respond, inviting me to have lunch or come in for a meeting, even if they had no job to offer. I put myself in front of anyone I thought might be able to give me advice. The point was less to find a new job than to widen my understanding of what was possible and how others had gone about it. I was realizing that the next phase of my journey would not simply unfold on its own, that my fancy academic degrees weren't going to automatically lead me to fulfilling work. Finding a career as opposed to a job wouldn't just come from perusing the contact pages of an alumni directory; it required deeper thought and effort. I would need to hustle and learn. And so, again and again, I laid out my professional dilemma for the people I met, quizzing them on what they did and whom they knew. I asked everybody I could think of what kind of work might be available to a lawyer who didn't, in fact, want to practice law.

Many people offered to talk to me, and one afternoon, I visited the office of a friendly, thoughtful man named Art Sussman, who was a lawyer for the University of Chicago. It turned out that my mom had spent about a year working for him as a secretary when I was a sophomore in high school, before she'd taken her job at the bank. Art was surprised to learn that I hadn't ever visited her at work—that I'd never actually set foot on the university's campus before now, despite having grown up just a few miles away.

If I was honest, there'd been no reason for me to visit the campus. My neighborhood school didn't run field trips there. If there were cultural events open to the community when I was a kid, my family hadn't known about them. We had no friends—no acquaintances, even—who were students or graduates. The University of Chicago was an elite school, and to most everyone I knew growing up, elite meant *not for us*. Its gray stone buildings almost literally had their backs turned to the streets surrounding campus. Driving past, my dad used to roll his eyes at the flocks of students haplessly jaywalking across Ellis Avenue, wondering how it was that such smart people had never learned how to properly cross a street.

Like many South Siders, my family maintained what was a limited view of the university, even if my mom had passed a year happily working there. When it came time for me and Craig to think about college, we didn't even consider applying to the University of Chicago. Princeton, for some reason, had struck us as more accessible.

Hearing all this, Art was incredulous. "You've really never been here?" he said. "Never?"

"Nope, not once."

There was an odd power in saying it out loud. I hadn't given the idea much thought before now, but it occurred to me that I'd have made a perfectly fine University of Chicago student, if only I'd known about the school and the school had known about me. I realized there was something I could contribute. Being Black and from the South Side, I suddenly saw, helped me recognize problems that a man like Art Sussman didn't even realize existed.

In several years, I'd get my chance to work for the university and

141

reckon with some of these community-relations problems directly, but right now Art was just kindly offering to pass around my résumé.

Art didn't have a job for me, but he introduced me to some friends of his, beginning a fateful chain of events that led me to a very important person in my life: Valerie Jarrett. Like me, she was from the South Side and was someone who would end up altering my life, not once, but repeatedly.

Valerie Jarrett was the newly appointed deputy chief of staff to the mayor of Chicago and had deep connections across the city's African American community. She'd been smart enough to land herself a job in a well-known firm after law school and had then been self-aware enough to realize that she didn't like that job. She'd moved to city hall largely because she was inspired by Harold Washington, who'd been elected mayor in 1983 when I was away at college. He was the first African American to hold the office. My parents loved him for how he could connect with everyday people, for his ability to quote Shakespeare in his speeches, and for the famous enthusiasm with which he ate fried chicken at community events on the South Side. Most important, he didn't like the Democratic leaders who had long governed Chicago. These politicians gave major city contracts to donors and generally kept Blacks in service to the party but rarely allowed them to advance into official elected roles.

Building his campaign around reforming the city's political system and better tending to its neglected neighborhoods, Washington won the election by a hair. He was a Black, brainy superhero. He clashed regularly and fearlessly with the mostly white members of the city council and was viewed as something of a walking legend, especially among the city's Black citizens. His vision had been an early inspiration for Barack, who arrived in Chicago to work as an organizer shortly after Washington was elected.

Valerie, too, was drawn by Washington. She joined his staff at the start of his second term. She was also the mom of a young daughter and soon to be divorced. Even though it was difficult for her, she took a big pay cut when she left her fancy law firm to work in city government. And within months of her starting the job, tragedy struck: Harold Washington abruptly had a heart attack and died. In the aftermath, a Black official was appointed by the city council to take Washington's place, but he didn't last long. In the next election, voters went on to elect Richard M. Daley, the son of a previous mayor who was broadly considered the godfather of Chicago's famous only-help-your-own system. For African Americans, this was a sad return to the old white ways of Chicago politics.

Though she had concerns about the new administration, Valerie had decided to stay on at city hall, moving out of the legal department and directly into Mayor Daley's office. She was glad to be there. She described to me how moving from corporate law into government felt like a relief, and how she was energized by working in what felt like the real world.

Chicago's City Hall and County Building is a flat-roofed, eleven-story, gray-granite monolith that occupies an entire city block. City hall, as I learned on the summer day I showed up to meet Valerie for a job interview, was packed with people.

There were couples getting married and people registering cars. There were people lodging complaints about potholes, their landlords, their sewer lines, and everything else they felt the city could improve. There were babies in strollers and old ladies in wheelchairs. There were journalists and lobbyists, and also homeless people just looking to get out of the heat. Out on the sidewalk in front of the building, a group of activists waved signs and shouted chants, though I can't remember what it was they were angry about. What I do know is that I was both taken aback and completely enthralled by the clunky, controlled chaos of the place. City hall belonged to the people. It was noisy and lively, unlike my law firm.

Valerie had reserved twenty minutes on her schedule to talk to me that day, but our conversation ended up stretching for an hour and a half. A thin, light-skinned African American woman dressed in a beautifully tailored suit, she was soft-spoken and calm, with a steady brown-eyed gaze and an impressive grasp of how the city functioned. She enjoyed her job but didn't avoid talking about how hard government work could be. Something about her caused me instantly to relax. Years later, Valerie would tell me that to her surprise I'd managed to reverse the standard interview process on her that day—that I'd given her some basic, helpful information about myself, but otherwise I'd grilled her, wanting to understand every last feeling she had about the work she did and how responsive the mayor was to his employees. I was testing the suitability of the work for me as much as she was testing the suitability of me for the work.

I asked Valerie lots of questions, taking advantage of what felt like a rare opportunity to speak with a woman whose background mirrored mine but who was a few years ahead of me in her career. Valerie was calm, bold, and wise in ways that few people I'd met before were. She was someone to learn from, to stick close to. I saw this right away.

Before I left, she offered me a job, inviting me to join her staff as an assistant to Mayor Daley, beginning as soon as I was ready. I would no longer be practicing law. My salary would be about half of what I was currently making. She told me I should take some time and think about whether I was truly prepared to make this sort of change. It was my leap to consider, my leap to make.

I had never been one to hold city hall in high regard. Having grown up Black and on the South Side, I had little faith in politics. Politics had traditionally been used against Black folks, as a means to keep us isolated and excluded, leaving us undereducated, unemployed, and underpaid. I had grandparents who'd lived through the horror of Jim Crow laws and the humiliation of housing discrimination and basically mistrusted authority of any sort. (Southside, as you may recall, thought that even the dentist was out to get him.) My dad, who was a city employee most of his life, had essentially been conscripted into service as a Democratic precinct captain in order to even be considered for promotions at his job. He relished the social aspect of his precinct duties but had always been put off by city hall cronyism.

But I was suddenly considering a city hall job. I'd winced at the pay cut, but I was feeling drawn toward the opportunity Valerie had offered me. It was a whole different future from the one I'd planned for. I was almost ready to leap, but for one thing. It wasn't just about me anymore. When Valerie called me a few days later to follow up, I told her I was still thinking the offer over. I then asked a final and probably strange question. "Could I please," I said, "also introduce you to my fiancé?"

I SUPPOSE I should back up here. Barack had flown back to Chicago to be with me for as long as he could around my dad's funeral before returning to finish at Harvard. After graduation in late May, he packed up his things, sold his banana-yellow car, and flew back to Chicago, delivering himself to 7436 South Euclid Avenue and to me. I loved him. I felt loved by him. We'd made it almost two years as a long-distance couple, and now, finally, we could be a short-distance couple. We could have Monday night dinners and Tuesday, Wednesday, and Thursday night dinners, too. We could shop for groceries and fold laundry in front of the TV. On the many evenings when I still got weepy over the loss of my dad, Barack was now there to comfort me.

Barack was relieved to be done with law school and eager to start working. He'd also sold his idea for a nonfiction book about race and identity to a New York publisher, which for someone who worshipped books as he did felt like an enormous and humbling accomplishment. He'd been paid in advance and had about a year to write the book.

Barack had plenty of choices. His reputation—the complimentary reports by his law school professors, the *New York Times* story about his selection as president of the *Law Review*—seemed to bring a flood of opportunity. He was offered teaching jobs, corporate law jobs, and civil rights law jobs.

There's something deeply encouraging about a person who sees his opportunities as endless. Barack had worked hard for everything he was now being given, but he wasn't measuring his progress against that of others, as so many people I knew did—as I sometimes did myself. He seemed not to even see the giant rat race of life and all the material things a young lawyer was supposed to be going after, like fancy cars and houses. I'd observed this quality in him before, but now that we were together and I was considering making the first real swerve of my life, I came to value it even more.

Barack believed and trusted when others did not. He had a simple, inspiring faith that if you stuck to your principles, things would work out. I'd had so many careful, sensible conversations at this point, with so many people, about how to change my career. I'd read the caution and concern on so many faces when I spoke of having loans to pay off, of not yet having managed to buy a house. I couldn't help but think about how my dad avoided every risk in order to give us stability at home. I still walked around with my mom's advice ringing in my ear: *Make the money first and worry about your happiness later.* Adding to my anxiety was one deep longing bigger than any other wish: I knew I wanted to have children, sooner rather than later. And how would that work if I started over in a brand-new job?

Barack, when he showed up back in Chicago, absorbed my worries, listened as I told him about every financial obligation I had, and told me that he, too, was excited to have children. He said that there was no way we could predict how exactly we'd manage things, given that neither of us wanted to be locked into the predictability of a lawyer's life. But we were far from poor and our future was promising—maybe even more promising because it couldn't easily be planned.

He was the only one telling me to just go for it, to overcome my worries and go toward whatever I thought would make me happy. It was okay to make my leap into the unknown, because—and this would count as startling news to most every member of my extended family, going back all the way to Dandy and Southside—the unknown wasn't going to kill me.

Don't worry, Barack was saying. *You can do this. We'll figure it out.*

A WORD NOW about the bar exam. It's necessary for any lawyer wishing to practice, and it's a very difficult two-day, twelve-hour exam meant to prove your knowledge of everything involved with practicing law. Just as Barack was intending to, I had sat for the Illinois bar exam three years earlier, the summer after finishing up at Harvard.

Though I had intended to spend two months working through fat books of practice tests, Craig was getting married to Janis that summer. Janis asked me to be one of her bridesmaids, and I hurled myself eagerly into the role. I oohed and aahed at wedding dresses and helped plan the bachelorette activities. I was far more excited about my brother's wedding than I was about studying for the test.

That fall, with both the bar exam and the wedding behind me, I called my dad from work one day and asked if he'd check to see if the mail had come in. It had. I asked if there was an envelope in there for me. There was. Was it a letter from the Illinois State Bar Association? Why, yes, that's what it said on the envelope. I next asked if he'd open it for me, which is when I heard some rustling and then a long pause on the other end of the line.

I had failed.

I had never in my entire life failed a test, unless you want to count the moment in kindergarten when I stood up in class and couldn't read the word "white" off the manila card held by my teacher. But I'd blown it with the bar. I was ashamed, sure that I'd let down every person who'd ever taught, encouraged, or employed me. I wasn't used to making mistakes. If anything, I generally overdid things, especially when it came to preparing for a big moment or test, but this one I'd let slip by. I think now that it was because of the disinterest I'd felt all through law school, burned out as I was on being a student and bored by subjects that struck me as removed from real life. I wanted to be around people and not books, which is why the best part of law school for me had been volunteering at the school's Legal Aid Bureau, where I could help someone get a Social Security check or stand up to an out-of-line landlord.

But still, I didn't like to fail. The sting of it would stay with me for months, even as plenty of my colleagues at the law firm confessed that they, too, hadn't passed the bar exam the first time. Later that fall, I buckled down and studied for a do-over test, going on to pass it easily. In the end, aside from hurting my pride, my screwup would make no difference at all.

Several years later, the memory of failure the first time was causing me to regard Barack with extra curiosity. He was attending bar review classes and carrying around his own bar review books, and yet didn't seem to be studying them as often as I thought maybe he should. But I wasn't going to nag him or even offer myself as an example of what could go wrong. Barack's head was an overpacked suitcase of information. I called him "the fact guy," for how he seemed to have a statistic to match every little twist in a conversation. His memory seemed almost photographic. The truth was, I wasn't worried about whether he'd pass the bar and, somewhat annoyingly, neither was he.

So we celebrated early, on the very same day he finished the exam—booking ourselves a table at a restaurant downtown. It was one of our favorite places, a special-occasion kind of joint. It was the height of summer and we were happy.

As we were reaching the end of the meal, Barack smiled at me and raised the subject of marriage. He reached for my hand and said that as much as he loved me with his whole being, he still didn't really see the point. I felt the blood rise in my cheeks. It was like pushing a button in me—the kind of big blinking red button you might find in some sort of nuclear facility surrounded by warning signs and evacuation maps. Really? We were going to do this now?

In fact, we were. We'd had the hypothetical marriage discussion plenty of times already, and nothing much ever changed. I was a traditionalist and Barack was not. It seemed clear that neither one of us could be swayed. But still, this didn't stop us—two lawyers, after all—from taking up the topic with hot gusto. Surrounded by men in sport coats and women in nice dresses enjoying their fancy meals, I did what I could to keep my voice calm.

"If we're committed," I said, as evenly as I could muster, "why wouldn't we formalize that commitment? What part of your dignity would be sacrificed by that?"

From here, we had the old argument. Did marriage matter? Why did it matter? What was wrong with him? What was wrong with me? What kind of future did we have if we couldn't sort this out? We were going back and forth, lawyer-style. I was more inflamed, and it was I who was doing most of the talking.

Eventually, our waiter came around holding a dessert plate, covered by a silver lid. He slid it in front of me and lifted the cover. I was almost too annoyed to even look down, but when I did, I saw a dark velvet box where the chocolate cake was supposed to be. Inside it was a diamond ring.

Barack looked at me playfully. He'd tricked me. It had all been a ruse. It took me a second to get over my anger and slide into joyful shock. He'd riled me up because this was the very last time he would argue against marriage, ever again, as long as we both should live. The case was closed. He dropped to one knee then, and with an emotional hitch in his voice asked sincerely if I'd please do him the honor of marrying him. Later, I'd learn that he'd already gone to both my mom and my brother to ask for their approval ahead of time. When I said yes, it seemed that every person in the whole restaurant started to clap.

For a full minute or two, I stared dumbfounded at the ring on my finger. I looked at Barack to confirm that this was all real. He was smiling. He'd completely surprised me. In a way, we'd both won. "Well," he said lightly, "that should shut you up."

I SAID YES TO BARACK, and shortly after that I said yes to Valerie Jarrett, accepting her offer to come work at city hall. Before committing, I made a point of following through on my request to introduce Barack and Valerie, scheduling a dinner during which the three of us could talk.

I did this for a couple of reasons. For one, I liked Valerie. I was impressed by her, and whether or not I ended up taking the job, I was excited to get to know her better. I knew that Barack would be impressed, too. More important, though, I wanted him to hear Valerie's story. Like Barack, she'd spent part of her childhood in a different country—in her case, Iran, where her dad had been a doctor at a hospital—and returned to the United States for her schooling, giving her the same kind of clear-eyed perspective I saw in Barack. Barack had concerns about my working at city hall. Like Valerie, he'd been inspired by the leadership of Harold Washington when he was mayor, but felt much less enthusiastic about the old-school politicians currently represented by Richard M. Daley. It was the community organizer in him: Even while Washington was in office, he'd had to battle with the city in order to get even the smallest bit of support for grassroots projects. Though he'd been nothing but encouraging about my job prospects, I think he was quietly worried I might end up unhappy.

Valerie was the right person to address any concerns. She'd rearranged her entire life in order to work for Washington and then lost him almost immediately. The emptiness that followed Washington's death offered a kind of cautionary tale for the future. In Chicago, we'd made the mistake of putting all our hopes on the shoulders of one person without building the political network to support his vision. Voters, especially liberal and Black voters, viewed Washington as a kind of golden savior, a symbol, the man who could change everything. He'd carried the load, inspiring people like Barack and Valerie to move out of the private sector and into community work and public service. But when Harold Washington died, most of the energy he'd generated did, too.

Valerie's decision to stay on with the mayor's office had required some thought, but she explained to us why she felt it was the right choice. She described feeling supported by Daley and knowing that she was being useful to the city. Her loyalty, she said, had been to Harold Washington's principles more than to the man himself. Inspiration on its own was shallow; you had to back it up with hard work. This idea inspired both me and Barack. Inside that one dinner I felt as if something had been cemented: Valerie Jarrett was now a part of our lives. Without our ever discussing it, it seemed almost as if the three of us had somehow agreed to carry one another a good long way.

THERE WAS ONE last thing to do, now that we were engaged, now that I'd taken a new job and Barack had made a commitment to a public interest law firm. We took a vacation. More accurately, we went on a pilgrimage. We flew out of Chicago on a Wednesday in late August, had a long wait in the airport in Frankfurt, Germany, and then flew another eight hours to arrive in Nairobi, Kenya, just before dawn, stepping outside in the Kenyan moonlight and into what felt like a different world altogether.

I had been to Jamaica and the Bahamas, and to Europe a few times, but this was my first time being this far from home. I felt

Nairobi's foreignness—or really, my own foreignness in relation to it—immediately, even in the first strains of morning. It's a sensation I've come to love as I've traveled more, the way a new place signals itself instantly. The air has a different weight from what you're used to; it carries smells you can't quite identify, a faint whiff of wood smoke or diesel fuel, maybe, or the sweetness of something blooming in the trees. The same sun comes up, but looking slightly different from what you know.

Barack's half sister Auma met us at the airport, greeting us both warmly. The two of them had met only a handful of times, beginning six years earlier when Auma had visited Chicago, but they had a close bond. Auma is a year older than Barack. Her mom, Grace Kezia, had been pregnant with Auma when Barack Obama Sr. left Nairobi to study in Hawaii, where he met Barack's mom.

Auma had ebony skin and brilliant white teeth and a strong British accent. Her smile was enormous and comforting. I was so tired from the travel I could barely make conversation, but I took note of how the quickness of Auma's smile was just like Barack's. Auma also clearly had inherited the family brains: She'd been raised in Kenya and returned there often, but she'd gone to college in Germany and was still living there, studying for a PhD. She was fluent in English, German, Swahili, and her family's local language, called Luo. Like us, she was just here for a visit.

Auma had arranged for me and Barack to stay in a friend's empty apartment, a spartan one-bedroom in a nondescript cinder-block building that had been painted bright pink. For the first couple of days, we were so zonked by jet lag it felt as if we were moving at half speed. Or maybe it was just the pace of Nairobi, which ran on an entirely different logic than Chicago. Its roads were clogged by a mix of pedestrians, bikers, cars, and *matatus*—the tottering, informal jitney-like buses that could be seen everywhere, painted brightly with murals and tributes to God, their roofs piled high with strapped-on luggage, so crowded that passengers sometimes just rode along, clinging dangerously to the exterior.

I was in Africa now. It was heady, draining, and new to me. Auma's sky-blue car was so old that it often needed to be pushed in order to get the engine into gear. I'd bought new white sneakers to wear on the trip, and within a day, after all the pushing we did, they'd turned reddish brown, stained with the cinnamon-hued dust of Nairobi.

Barack was more at home in Nairobi than I was, having been there once before. I moved with the awkwardness of a tourist, aware that we were outsiders, even with our Black skin. People sometimes stared at us on the street. I hadn't been expecting to fit right in, but I think I arrived there believing I'd feel some immediate connection to the continent I'd grown up thinking of as a motherland. But Africa, of course, owed us nothing. It's a curious thing to realize, the in-betweenness one feels being African American in Africa. It gave me a hard-to-explain feeling of sadness, a sense of being unrooted in both lands.

Days later, I was still feeling dislocated, and we both had sore throats. Barack and I got into a fight—about what exactly, I can't remember. For every bit of awe we felt in Kenya, we were also tired, which led to quibbling, which led finally, for whatever reason, to rage. "I'm so angry at Barack," I wrote in my journal. "I don't think we have anything in common." My thoughts trailed off there. To express my frustration, I drew a long emphatic gash across the rest of the page.

Like any newish couple, we were learning how to fight. We didn't fight often, and when we did, it was typically over petty things. But we did fight. And for better or worse, I sometimes begin to yell when I'm angry. Barack, meanwhile, tends to remain cool and rational, which sometimes annoys me even more. It's taken us years to understand that we are just built differently, but over time, we have figured out how to express and overcome our irritations. We still argue sometimes, but always with our love for each other, no matter how strained, still in sight.

We woke the next morning in Nairobi to blue skies and fresh energy, feeling like our happy, regular selves. We met Auma at a downtown train station, and the three of us boarded a passenger train to head west out of the city and toward the Obama family's ancestral home. Sitting by a window in a cabin packed with Kenyans, some of whom were traveling with live chickens in baskets, others with pieces of furniture they'd bought in the city, I was again struck by how strange my life had suddenly become—how this man sitting next to me had shown up at my office one day with his weird name and quick smile and changed everything. I sat glued to the window as the community of Kibera, the largest urban slum in Africa, streamed past, showing us its low-slung shanties with tin roofs, its muddy roads and open sewers, and a kind of poverty I'd never seen before nor could hardly have imagined.

We were on the train for several hours. Barack finally opened a book, but I continued to stare out the window as the Nairobi slums gave way to jewel-green countryside. The train rattled north to the town of Kisumu, where Auma, Barack, and I got off into the broiling equatorial heat. From there we took a last bumpy ride through the maize fields to their grandmother's village of Kogelo.

I will always remember the deep red clay of the earth in that part of Kenya. Its dust caked the dark skin and hair of the children who shouted greetings to us from the side of the road. I remember being sweaty and thirsty as we walked the last bit of the way to Barack's grandmother's well-kept concrete home, where she'd lived for years. She farmed an adjacent vegetable patch and tended several cows. Granny Sarah, they called her. She was a short, wide-built lady with wise eyes and a crinkling smile. She spoke no English, only Luo, and expressed delight that we'd come all this way to see her. Next to her, I felt very tall. She studied me with curiosity, as if trying to place where I came from and how I'd landed on her doorstep. One of her first questions for me was, "Which one of your parents is white?"

I laughed and explained, with Auma's help, that I was Black through and through, basically as Black as we come in America.

Granny Sarah found this funny. She seemed to find everything funny, teasing Barack for not being able to speak her language. I adored her easy joy. As evening fell, she butchered us a chicken and made us a stew, which she served with a cornmeal mush called *ugali*. All the while, neighbors and relatives popped in to say hello to the younger Obamas and to congratulate us on our engagement. I gobbled the food gratefully as the sun dropped and night settled over the village, which had no electricity. There was a bright spray of stars overhead. That I was in this place seemed like a little miracle. I listened to the sound of crickets in the cornfields all around us, the rustle of animals we couldn't see. I remember feeling awed by the scope of land and sky around me and at the same time snug and protected inside that tiny home. I had a new job, a fiancé, and an expanded family—an approving Kenyan granny, even. It was true: I'd been flung out of my world, and for the moment it was all good.

12

BARACK AND I GOT MARRIED ON A SUNNY OCTOBER Saturday, the two of us standing before hundreds of our friends and family at Trinity United Church of Christ on the South Side. It was a big wedding, and big was how it needed to be. Having the wedding in Chicago, there was no trimming the guest list. My roots went too deep. I had not just cousins but also cousins of cousins, and those cousins of cousins had kids, none of whom I'd ever leave out. Everyone made the day more meaningful and merry.

My dad's younger siblings were there, and so was my mom's entire family. I had old school friends and neighbors who came, people from Princeton, people from Whitney Young. Mrs. Smith, the wife of my high school assistant principal who still lived down the street from us on Euclid Avenue, helped organize the wedding, while our neighbors Mr. and Mrs. Thompson and their jazz band played later that day at our reception. Santita Jackson was my maid of honor. I'd invited old colleagues from the law firm and new colleagues from city hall. The law partners from Barack's firm were there, as were his old organizer friends. Barack's fun-loving Hawaiian high school friends mingled happily with a handful of his Kenyan relatives, who wore brightly colored East African hats. Sadly, we'd lost Gramps—Barack's grandfather—the previous winter, but his mom and grandmother had made the trip to Chicago, as had Auma and Maya, half sisters from different continents. It was the first time our two families had met, and the feeling was joyful.

We were surrounded by love—a mixture of the multicultural Obama kind and the anchoring Robinsons-from-the-South-Side kind. It was now interwoven inside the church. I held tightly to Craig's elbow as he walked me down the aisle. As we reached the front, I caught my mom's gaze. She was sitting in the first row, looking regal in a floor-length black-and-white sequined dress we'd picked out together. Her chin was lifted high, and her eyes were proud. We still ached for my dad every day, though as he would've wanted, we were continuing on.

Barack had woken up that morning with a nasty head cold, but it had miraculously cleared as soon as he arrived at the church. He was now smiling at me, bright-eyed, from his place at the altar, dressed in a rented tux and a buffed pair of new shoes. Marriage was still more mysterious to him than it was to me, but in the fourteen months we'd been engaged, he'd been nothing but all in. We'd chosen everything about this day carefully. Barack, having at first declared he was not interested in wedding details, had ended up lovingly—and predictably—giving his opinion on everything from the flower arrangements to the food for the reception. We'd picked our wedding song, which Santita would sing with her stunning voice.

It was a Stevie Wonder tune called "You and I (We Can Conquer the World)." I'd first heard it as a kid, in third or fourth grade, when Southside gave me the *Talking Book* album as a gift—my first record album, utterly precious to me. I kept it at his house and was allowed to play it anytime I came to visit. He'd taught me how to care for the vinyl, how to wipe the record's grooves clean of dust, how to lift the needle from the turntable and set it down delicately in the right spot. Usually he'd left me alone with the music, making himself scarce so that I could learn, in privacy, everything that album had to teach, mostly by belting out the lyrics again and again with my little-girl lungs. *Well, in my mind, we can conquer the world / In love you and I, you and I, you and I . . .*

I was nine years old at the time. I knew nothing about love and commitment or conquering the world. All I could do was imagine for myself shimmery ideas about what love might be like and who might come along someday to make me feel that strong. Would it be Michael Jackson? Someone like my dad? I couldn't even begin to imagine the person who would become the "you" to my "I."

But now here we were.

Trinity Church had a dynamic and soulful reputation. The church's pastor, the Reverend Jeremiah Wright, was known as a sensational preacher with a passion for social justice and was now officiating at our wedding. He welcomed our friends and family and then held up our wedding bands for all to see. He spoke powerfully about what it meant to form a union and have it witnessed by a caring community, these people who knew Barack and me so well.

I felt the power of what we were doing. We stood there with our future still unwritten, just gripping each other's hands as we said our vows.

Whatever was out there, we'd step into it together. I'd poured myself into planning this day, but I understood now that what really mattered, what I'd remember forever, was the feeling of Barack gripping my hand. It settled me like nothing else ever had. I had faith in this union, faith in this man. To declare it was the easiest thing in the world. Looking at Barack's face, I knew for sure that he felt the same. Neither one of us cried that day. If anything, we were a little giddy. From here, we'd gather up all several hundred of our witnesses and roll on over to the reception. We'd eat and drink and dance until we'd exhausted ourselves with our joy.

. . .

OUR HONEYMOON WAS a road trip in Northern California. The day after the wedding, we flew to San Francisco, spent several days in vineyards, and then drove down the coast to read books, stare at the blue bowl of ocean, and clear our minds. It was glorious, despite the fact that Barack's head cold managed to return in full force, and also despite the mud baths, which we deemed to be unsoothing and kind of icky.

After a busy year, we were more than ready to kick back. Barack had originally planned to spend the months leading up to our wedding finishing his book and working at his new law firm, but he'd ended up putting most of it on an abrupt hold. He'd been approached by the leaders of a national nonpartisan organization called Project VOTE!, which spearheaded efforts to register new voters in states where minority turnout was traditionally low. They asked if Barack would open an office in Chicago to enroll Black voters ahead of the November elections. It was estimated that about 400,000 African Americans in the state were eligible to vote but still unregistered.

The pay was low, but the job appealed to Barack's beliefs. That year, an African American candidate, Carol Moseley Braun, had surprised everyone by narrowly winning the Democratic nomination for the U.S. Senate race. Bill Clinton would be running against George H. W. Bush for president. It was no time for minority voters to be sitting out.

To say that Barack threw himself into the job would be an understatement. The goal of Project VOTE! was to sign up new Illinois voters at a staggering pace of ten thousand per week. The work was similar to what he'd done as a grassroots organizer: Over the course of the spring and summer, he and his staff had visited church basements, gone house to house to talk with unregistered voters. He met regularly with community leaders and made his pitch countless times to wealthy donors, helping to fund the production of radio ads and informational brochures that could be handed out in Black neighborhoods and public-housing projects. The organization's message was unwavering and clear: There was power in voting. If you wanted change, you couldn't stay home on Election Day.

In the evenings, Barack came home to our place on Euclid Avenue and often flopped on the couch, reeking of the cigarettes he still smoked when he was out of my sight. He appeared tired but never worn out. He kept careful track of the registration tallies: They were averaging an impressive seven thousand registrations a week but were still falling short of the goal. He strategized about how to get the message across, how to wrangle more volunteers and find pockets of people who remained unfound. He seemed to view the challenges as a Rubik's Cube–like puzzle that could be solved if only he could swivel the right blocks in the right order. The hardest people to reach, he told me, were the younger folks, the eighteen- to thirty-year-olds who seemed to have no faith in government at all.

I'd spent a year now working with Valerie in the mayor's office. The job was broad and people-oriented enough to be almost always interesting. Whereas I'd once spent my days writing briefs in a quiet, plush-carpeted office with a view of the lake, I now worked in a windowless room on one of the top floors of city hall, with citizens streaming noisily through the building every hour of the day.

I shuttled between meetings with various department heads, worked with the staffs of city commissioners, and was dispatched sometimes to different neighborhoods around Chicago. I went on missions to inspect fallen trees that needed removing, talked to neighborhood pastors who were upset about traffic or garbage collection, and often represented the mayor's office at community functions. I once had to break up a shoving match at a senior citizens' picnic on the North Side. None of this was what a corporate lawyer did, and for this reason I found it a terrific change. I was experiencing Chicago in a way I never had before.

I was learning something else of value, too, spending much of my time in the presence of Valerie Jarrett and Susan Sher, a lawyer for the Chicago city government who had originally introduced me to Valerie. They were two women who—I was seeing—managed to be both tremendously confident and tremendously human at the same time.

I saw more of Valerie than I did of Susan, but I took careful note of everything each of them did. It was what I had done when I'd observed Czerny, my college mentor. These were women who knew their own voices and were unafraid to use them. They could be humorous and humble when the moment called for it, but they believed in their own points of view and weren't afraid to speak their minds in rooms full of opinionated men. Also, importantly, they were working moms. I watched them closely, knowing that I wanted someday to be one myself. Valerie never hesitated to step out of a big meeting when a call came in from her daughter's school. Susan dashed out in the middle of the day if one of her sons spiked a fever or was performing in a preschool music show. They never apologized for putting the needs of their children first, even if it meant occasionally disrupting the flow at work. They didn't try to separate work and home the way I'd noticed male partners at the law firm seemed to do. I'm not sure there even was a choice for Valerie and Susan. They were juggling the unique expectations of being moms. They were also both divorced, and that came with its own emotional and financial challenges. They weren't striving for perfect, but managed somehow to be always excellent, the two of them connected by a deep, helpful friendship. This also made a real impression on me. They were just wonderfully, powerfully, and instructively themselves.

·   ·   ·

BARACK AND I came back from our honeymoon to both good and bad news. The good news came in the form of the November election, which brought what felt like a tide of encouraging change. Bill Clinton won overwhelmingly in Illinois and across the country, moving President Bush out of office after only one term. Carol Moseley Braun also won her election, becoming the first African American woman ever to hold a Senate seat. What was even more exciting to Barack was that the Election Day turnout had been nothing short of epic: Project VOTE! had directly registered 110,000 new voters, and its broader get-out-the-vote campaign had likely boosted overall turnout as well.

For the first time in a decade, over half a million Black voters in Chicago went to the polls, proving that they had the power to shape political outcomes. This sent a clear message to lawmakers and future politicians: The African American vote mattered. It would be costly politically for anyone to ignore or discount Black people's needs and concerns. Inside of this, too, was a message to the Black community itself, a reminder that progress was possible, that our worth was measurable. All this was heartening for Barack. As tiring as it was, he'd collaborated with grassroots leaders, everyday citizens, and elected officials, and it had brought results. Several media outlets noted the impressive impact of Project VOTE! A writer for *Chicago* magazine described Barack as "a tall, affable workaholic," suggesting that he should someday run for office, an idea that he simply shrugged off.

And here was the bad news: That tall, likable workaholic I'd just married had not finished his book, having been so caught up in registering voters. He'd managed to turn in only a partial manuscript. We got home from California to learn that the publisher had canceled his contract, and that Barack was now supposed to pay back the money they had given him.

If he panicked, he didn't do it in front of me. I had started a new job after our honeymoon. I was still at city hall, but now I was working for Valerie Jarrett on the planning and economic development commission. I was busy in my new job, and the city's everyday frenzy left me tired in the evenings, ready to switch my brain off and watch TV on the couch. If I'd learned anything from Barack's deep involvement with Project VOTE!, it was that it wasn't helpful for me to worry about his worries. I seemed to find them more overwhelming than he ever did. Barack was like a circus performer who liked to set plates spinning: If things got too calm, he took it as a sign that there was more to do. I was coming to understand that he was someone who would take on new projects without regard for the limits of his time and energy. He'd said yes to serving on the boards of a couple of non-profits while also saying yes to a part-time teaching job at the University of Chicago while also planning to work full-time at the law firm.

And then there was the book. Barack's agent felt sure she could resell the idea to a different publisher, though he'd have to get a draft finished soon. With the approval of the law firm that had waited a year already for him to start full-time, he came up with a solution that seemed to suit him perfectly: He'd write the book in isolation, removing his everyday distractions by renting a little cabin somewhere and working to complete it. He told me his plan about six weeks after our wedding. His mom had even found him the perfect cabin. She'd already rented it for him. It was cheap, quiet, and on the beach. In Sanur. Which was on the Indonesian island of Bali, some nine thousand miles away from me.

IT SOUNDS LIKE a bad joke, doesn't it? What happens when a solitude-loving individualist marries an outgoing family woman who does not love solitude one bit?

The answer is probably the best answer to nearly every question arising inside a marriage, no matter who you are or what the issue is: You find ways to adapt. If you're in it forever, there's really no choice.

Barack flew to Bali and spent about five weeks living alone with his thoughts while working on his book *Dreams from My Father,* filling yellow legal pads with his neat handwriting, thinking through his ideas during daily walks amid the coconut palms and lapping ocean tide. I stayed home on Euclid Avenue, living upstairs from my mom as another Chicago winter hit. I kept myself busy, seeing friends and hitting workout classes in the evenings. In my regular interactions at work or around town, I'd find myself casually saying this strange new term "my husband." *My husband and I are hoping to buy a home. My husband is a writer finishing a book.* I missed Barack terribly, but I convinced myself that, even if we were newlyweds, this time apart was probably for the best.

Barack had shipped himself out to finish his book. Possibly he had done this out of kindness to me. I'd married an outside-the-box thinker, I had to remind myself. He was handling his business in what struck him as the most sensible and efficient way, even if it appeared to be a beach vacation right after his honeymoon with me.

You and I, you and I, you and I. We were learning to adapt, to knit ourselves into a solid and forever form of *us.* Even if we were the same two people we'd always been, we now had new labels, a second set of identities. He was my husband. I was his wife. It did feel as if we owed each other new things.

For many women, including myself, "wife" can feel like a loaded word. It carries a history. If you grew up in the 1960s and 1970s, as I did, the word "wife" seemed to refer to the kind of cheerful, carefully groomed white women who lived inside television sitcoms. They stayed at home, fussed over the children, and had dinner ready on the stove. Never mind that I used to watch those shows in our living room on Euclid Avenue while my own stay-at-home mom fixed dinner and my own clean-cut dad recovered from a day at work. My parents' arrangement was as traditional as anything we saw on TV. Barack sometimes jokes that my upbringing was like a Black version of *Leave It to Beaver,* with the South Side Robinsons as steady and fresh-faced as the Cleaver family of Mayfield, U.S.A., though of course we were a poorer version of the Cleavers, with my dad's blue city worker's uniform subbing for Mr. Cleaver's suit. Barack makes this comparison with a touch of envy, because his own childhood was so different, but also as a way to push back on the idea that African American families are somehow incapable of living out the same stable, middle-class dream as our white neighbors.

Personally, as a kid, I loved *The Mary Tyler Moore Show*. Mary had a job, a snappy wardrobe, and really great hair. She was independent and funny, and unlike those of the other ladies on TV, her problems were interesting. She had conversations that weren't about children or homemaking. She didn't let her boss push her around, and she wasn't only worried about finding a husband. She was youthful and at the same time grown-up. In the pre-pre-pre-internet landscape, when the world came packaged almost exclusively through three channels of network TV, this stuff mattered. If you were a girl with a brain and a sense that you wanted to grow into something more than a wife, Mary Tyler Moore was your goddess.

And here I was now, sitting in the same apartment where I'd watched all that TV and consumed all those meals dished up by my patient and selfless mom, Marian Robinson. I had so much—an education, a healthy sense of self, a deep sense of ambition—and I was wise enough to credit my mom, in particular, with instilling it in me. She'd taught me how to read before I started kindergarten, helping me sound out words as I sat curled like a kitten in her lap, studying a library copy of *Dick and Jane*. She'd cooked for us with care, putting broccoli and Brussels sprouts on our plates and requiring that we eat them. She'd hand sewn my prom dress. The point was, she'd given everything. She'd let our family define her. I was old enough now to realize that all the hours she gave to me and Craig were hours she didn't spend on herself.

My many blessings in life were now causing a kind of whiplash.

I'd been raised to be confident and see no limits, to believe I could go after and get absolutely anything I wanted. And I wanted everything. Because, as Suzanne would say, *why not?* I wanted the excitement of having a career and being independent, like Mary Tyler Moore, and at the same time I was drawn toward being a wife and mom, even with the sacrifices that involved. I wanted to have a work life and a home life, but with some promise that one would never fully take over the other. I hoped to be exactly like my own mom and at the same time nothing like her at all. It was an odd and confusing thing to ponder. Could I have everything? Would I have everything? I had no idea.

Barack came home from Bali looking tanned and carrying a bag stuffed with legal pads filled with his writing. The book was basically finished. Within a matter of months, his agent had resold it to a new publisher, paying off his debt and making sure it would be published. More important to me was the fact that within a matter of hours we'd returned to the easy rhythm of our newlywed life. Barack landed back in my world. *My husband.* He was smiling at the jokes I made, wanting to hear about my day, happy to see me at night.

As the months went by, we cooked, worked, laughed, and planned. Later that spring, we moved out of 7436 South Euclid Avenue and into a pretty, railroad-style apartment, a new launchpad for our life. With Barack's encouragement, I took another risk and switched jobs again. I said good-bye to Valerie and Susan at city hall in order to finally explore the kind of nonprofit work that had always intrigued me. I found a leadership role that would give me a chance to grow. There was still plenty I hadn't figured out about my life—I still wasn't sure how to be both a Mary and a Marian, how to be both a career woman and a stay-at-home wife and mom. Any worries could wait, I figured, because we were an *us* now, and we were happy. And happy seemed like a starting place for everything.

13

MY NEW JOB MADE ME NERVOUS. I'D BEEN HIRED TO BE the executive director for the brand-new Chicago chapter of an organization called Public Allies. It was something like a start-up inside a start-up, and in a field in which I had no professional experience.

Public Allies recruited talented young people and gave them training and mentorship. These young people were then placed in paid apprentice positions inside community organizations and public agencies. The hope was that they'd flourish and contribute in meaningful ways, and that these opportunities would give the recruits—Allies, we called them—both the experience and the drive to continue working in the nonprofit or public sector for years to come. We were trying to build a new generation of community leaders.

For me, the idea resonated in a big way. At Princeton, most of my friends and I hadn't even stopped to think about careers in public service. Public Allies wanted to change that.

Public Allies was all about promise—finding it, nurturing it, and putting it to use. You didn't need a college degree to become an Ally. You needed only a high school diploma or GED, to be older than seventeen and younger than thirty, and to have shown some leadership capability, even if so far in life it had gone largely untapped. It was their goal to seek out young people whose best qualities might otherwise be overlooked and to give them a chance to do something meaningful. To me, the job felt like an invitation, finally, to use what I knew. I had a sense of how much promise sat undiscovered in neighborhoods like my own, and I was pretty sure I'd know how to find it.

Thinking about my new job, my mind often traveled back to childhood, and in particular to the month or so I'd spent in the pencil-flying chaos of that second-grade class, before my mom had me plucked out. In the moment, I'd felt nothing but joy at my own good fortune. My luck in life seemed only to snowball from there. Now I thought more about the twenty or so kids who'd been left behind with an uncaring teacher. I knew I was no smarter than any of them—I just had the advantage of my mom standing up for me. I thought about this more often now that I was an adult, especially when people applauded me for my achievements. I had been lucky. Through no fault of their own, those second graders had lost a year of learning. I'd seen enough at this point to understand how quickly even small disadvantages can snowball, too.

Back in Washington, D.C., the Public Allies founders had recruited a class of fifteen Allies who were working in various organizations around the city. They'd raised enough money to launch a new chapter in Chicago. This is where I came into the picture, thrilled and anxious in equal parts about the opportunity.

It hit me hard that as much as I wanted to do good, I had to think about my obligations first. I was initially offered a salary so small that I simply couldn't afford to say yes because it was so far below what I was making working for the city of Chicago, which was already half of what I'd been earning as a lawyer. I'd never forgotten what my mom had said concerning money and happiness: *Make the money first and worry about your happiness later.* I was aware that there were others who didn't have loans to pay off, or had some other monetary safety net provided by more privileged families or a working spouse. These people could afford to work at nonprofits, while people like me, equally big-hearted and passionate people who could have done the job just as well, had to consider their income and make a tough choice.

It became clear that if I wanted to join the nonprofit world, I'd have to ask for exactly what I needed in terms of salary. What I needed was more than Public Allies had expected to pay. This was simply my reality. I couldn't be shy or embarrassed about my needs. I still had student debt to pay off each month on top of my regular expenses, and I was married to a man with his own load of law school loans to cover. But the organization's leaders went out and secured new funding that enabled me to come on board.

And with that, I was off and running, eager to make good on the opportunity I'd been handed. This was my first chance ever to build something from the ground up: Success or failure would depend almost entirely on my work, not my boss's or anyone else's. I spent the spring working furiously to set up an office and hire a small staff so that we could have a class of Allies in place by the fall.

Meanwhile, I reached out to every connection Barack and I'd ever made in Chicago, seeking donors who could provide Public Allies with financial support and anyone in the public service field who'd be willing to host an Ally in their organization. Valerie Jarrett helped me arrange placements in the mayor's office and the city health department. Barack's network of community organizers connected us with legal aid, advocacy, and teaching opportunities for Allies. Partners from my old law firm wrote checks and helped introduce me to donors.

Finding the Allies was my favorite part of the job. My team and I visited community colleges and some of the big urban high schools around Chicago. We knocked on doors in the housing projects, went to community meetings, and canvassed programs that worked with single moms. We quizzed everyone we met, from pastors to professors to the manager of the neighborhood McDonald's, asking them to identify the most interesting young people they knew. Who were the leaders? Who was ready for something bigger than what he or she had? These were the people we wanted to encourage to apply, urging them to forget for a minute whatever obstacles normally made such things impossible. We promised we'd do what we could—whether it was supplying a bus pass or money for child care—to help cover their needs.

By fall, we had twenty-seven Allies working all over Chicago, holding internships everywhere from city hall to a South Side community assistance agency to Latino Youth high school. The Allies together were a spirited group, loaded with idealism and dreams. They came from a wide variety of backgrounds. Among them we had a former gang member, a Latina woman who'd grown up in the southwest part of Chicago and had gone to Harvard, another woman who lived in the projects and was raising a child while also trying to save money for college, and a twenty-six-year-old who'd left high school but had kept up his education with library books and later gone back to earn his diploma.

Each Friday, the whole group of Allies gathered to go through a series of professional development workshops. I loved these days more than anything. I loved how the room got noisy as the Allies piled in, dumping their backpacks in the corner and peeling off layers of winter wear as they settled into a circle. I loved helping them, whether it was mastering Excel, figuring out how to dress for an office job, or finding the courage to voice their ideas in a roomful of better-educated, more confident people. If I'd heard reports of Allies being late to work or not taking their duties seriously, I let them know that we expected better. When Allies grew frustrated, I counseled them to keep perspective, reminding them of their own relative good fortune.

We celebrated each new bit of learning or progress. And there was lots of it. Not all the Allies would go on to work in the nonprofit or public sectors and not everyone would manage to overcome the hurdles of coming from a less-privileged background, but I've been amazed over time to see how many of our recruits did succeed and commit themselves long term to serving a larger public good. Twenty-five years after it began, Public Allies is still going strong. There are chapters in Chicago and two dozen other cities and thousands of alumni around the country. To know that I played some small part in that, helping to create something that's endured, is one of the most gratifying feelings I've had in my professional life.

I think of it as the best job I ever had, for how wonderfully on the edge I felt while I was doing it and for how even a small victory— whether it was finding a good placement for a native Spanish speaker or sorting through someone's fears about working in an unfamiliar neighborhood—had to be thoroughly earned.

For the first time in my life, I felt I was doing something meaningful, directly impacting the lives of others. It felt good to stay connected to both my city and my culture. It also gave me a better understanding of how Barack had felt when he'd worked as an organizer and on Project VOTE! This type of work is a draining uphill battle, but it gives you everything you'll ever need.

WHILE I WAS focused on Public Allies, Barack had settled into what was, for him, a relatively tame and predictable period. He was teaching a class on racism and the law at the University of Chicago Law School and working by day at his law firm. Most of his cases involved voting rights and employment discrimination. He still sometimes ran community-organizing workshops as well. It seemed like a perfect existence for a smart, civic-minded guy who'd turned down many higher-paying options in favor of his principles. He'd found a noble balance. He was a lawyer, a teacher, and also an organizer. And he was soon to be a published author, too.

After returning from Bali, Barack had spent more than a year writing a second draft of his book during the hours he wasn't at one of his jobs. He worked late at night in a small room we'd converted to a study—a messy bunker full of books. I referred to it lovingly as the Hole. I'd sometimes go in, stepping over his piles of paper while he worked, trying to get his attention with a joke and a smile. He was good-humored about my interruptions, but only if I didn't stay too long.

Barack, I've come to understand, is the sort of person who needs a hole, a closed-off place where he can read and write undisturbed. Time spent there seems to fuel him. Recognizing this, we've managed to create some version of a hole inside every home we've ever lived in. To this day, when we arrive at a rental house in Hawaii or on Martha's Vineyard, Barack goes off looking for an empty room that can serve as the vacation Hole. There, he can flip between the six or seven books he's reading at the same time and toss his newspapers on the floor. For him, the Hole is a kind of sacred place, where his deepest thoughts are born. For me, it's an off-putting and disorderly mess. One requirement has always been that the Hole, wherever it is, have a door so that I can shut it.

Dreams from My Father was finally published. It got good reviews yet didn't sell that many copies, but that was okay. The important thing was that Barack had managed to make sense of his life story. He snapped together the pieces of his Afro-Kansan-Indonesian-Hawaiian-Chicagoan identity, writing himself into a sort of wholeness. I was proud of him. Through the writing, he'd made a kind of peace with his dad, who had been absent for most of his life. All alone, Barack had tried to understand every mystery the senior Obama had ever created. But this was how he'd always done it anyway. Since the time he was a boy, I realized, he'd tried to carry everything all on his own.

· · ·

↑
I worked hard to connect South Side communities with local hospitals and find residents affordable health care in my job at the University of Chicago Medical Center.

It was difficult, but important for me, to balance the needs of my family with the demands of my job.
←

From time to time our kids came out to visit Barack on the campaign trail. Here's Malia, watching through the campaign bus window as her dad gives a speech.

Barack announced his candidacy for president in Springfield, Illinois, on a freezing cold day. I'd bought Sasha a too-big pink hat for the occasion and kept worrying it was going to slip off her head, but miraculously she managed to keep it on.

→

Campaigning was exciting, but the pace could be exhausting. I stole moments of rest when I could.

Malia and Sasha goof off backstage before a campaign appearance.
←

I shared my story with a massive audience for the first time at the Democratic National Convention in Denver. Afterward, Sasha and Malia joined me onstage to say hello to Barack via video.
→

On November 4, 2008—election night—my mom, Marian Robinson, sat next to Barack, the two of them quietly watching as the results came in.
←

↑

Malia was ten years old and Sasha just seven in January 2009 when their dad was sworn in as president. Sasha was so small, she had to stand on a special platform in order to be visible during the ceremony.

My husband, and my
gorgeous gown by
Jason Wu, energized
me and inspired me
to make it through
ten inaugural balls
after a day already
full of festivities.

First Lady Laura Bush and her daughters, Jenna and Barbara, showed us the fun parts of living in the White House, including how to use this hallway as a slide. →

Barack and I loved getting to meet young people around the world, like this group of girls from El Salvador. ←

Seeing Sasha's little face peering through this bullet-proof car window on her way to her first day of school made me worry about what this experience would do to our kids. →

I wanted the White House to be a place where all kids could feel at home and be themselves, and maybe even have a chance to jump double Dutch with the First Lady.

Our Let's Move! initiative encouraged kids to get active, and whenever I could, I loved to participate and be active with them.

We promised Malia and Sasha we'd get a dog if Barack became president. Our first dog, Bo, always kept us on our toes.
→

Barack and I developed a special fondness for Queen Elizabeth, who reminded Barack of his no-nonsense grandmother. Over the course of many visits, she showed me that humanity is more important than protocol or formality.
←

Meeting Nelson Mandela, the former South African president and civil rights icon, reminded me that real change happens slowly, over lifetimes instead of months and years.
→

WITH THE BOOK FINISHED, there was new space in his life. As usual, Barack felt a need to fill it immediately. He'd been coping with difficult news: His mom, Ann, had been diagnosed with cancer and had moved from Jakarta back to Honolulu for treatment. Both Maya and Toot were helping look after her in Hawaii, and Barack checked in often. But her diagnosis had come late, after the cancer had advanced, and it was difficult to know what would happen. I knew this weighed heavily on Barack's mind.

In Chicago, the political chatter was starting to kick up again. The state senator who represented my South Side neighborhood was running for the U.S. Congress, leaving her state senate seat open. This meant that Barack could run for it.

Was he interested? Would he run?

I couldn't have known it then, but these questions would come to dominate the next decade of our lives. *Would he? Could he? Was he? Should he?* But ahead of these always came another question about running for office of any sort, posed by Barack himself: "What do you think about it, Miche?"

For me, the answer was never all that tough to come up with. I didn't think it was a great idea for Barack to run for office. My reasons might have varied slightly each time the question came back around, but my larger opinion never changed.

I didn't much like politicians, and therefore didn't like the idea of my husband becoming one. Most of what I knew about state politics came from what I read in the newspaper, and none of it seemed especially good. My friendship with Santita Jackson had given me a sense that politicians were often required to be away from home. In general, I thought of lawmakers almost like armored tortoises, leather-skinned, slow-moving. Barack was too sincere and full of bold plans to become one of those self-interested politicians.

In my heart, I just believed there were better ways for a good person to have an impact. I thought he'd get eaten alive by politics.

However, if Barack believed he could do something in politics, who was I to get in his way? Who was I to stomp on the idea before he'd even tried it? After all, he was the only person who had waved me forward when I wanted to leave my law career. He'd had his concerns about my going to city hall but supported me anyway. He was even working multiple jobs to help make up for the pay cut I'd taken to become a full-time do-gooder at Public Allies. In our six years together, he hadn't once doubted me. He'd always say: *Don't worry. You can do this. We'll figure it out.*

And so I gave my approval to his first run for office, adding a bit of wifely caution. "I think you'll be frustrated," I warned. "If you end up getting elected, you're gonna go down to Springfield and nothing will get accomplished, no matter how hard you try. It'll drive you crazy."

"Maybe," Barack said with a shrug. "But maybe I can do some good. Who knows?"

"That's right," I said, shrugging back. It wasn't my job to get in the way of his optimism. "Who knows?"

AS MOST PEOPLE know by now, my husband did become a politician. He was a good person who wanted to have an impact in the world, and despite my doubts, he decided this was the best way to go about it.

Barack was elected to the Illinois senate in November 1996 and sworn in two months later, at the start of the following year. To my surprise, I'd enjoyed watching the campaign unfold. I'd helped collect signatures to put him on the ballot, knocking on doors in my old neighborhood on Saturdays, listening to what residents had to say about all the things they thought needed fixing. This reminded me of the weekends I'd spent as a child trailing my dad as he climbed up all those porch steps, going about his duties as a precinct captain. Beyond this, I wasn't much needed, and that suited me perfectly. I could treat campaigning like a hobby, picking it up when it was convenient, having some fun with it, and then getting back to my own work.

Barack's mom had passed away in Honolulu shortly after he announced he would run for office. Her decline had been so swift that he hadn't made it there to say good-bye. This crushed him. It was Ann Dunham who'd introduced him to the richness of literature and the power of a well-reasoned argument. Without her, he might never have learned to appreciate how easy and thrilling it was to jump from one continent to another, or how to embrace the unfamiliar. She was an explorer, a fearless follower of her own heart. I saw her spirit in Barack in big and small ways. The pain of losing her sat right alongside the pain that had been embedded in my family when we'd lost my dad.

Now that it was winter and the legislature was in session, we were separated for a good part of every week. Barack drove four hours to Springfield on Monday nights and checked into a cheap hotel where a lot of the other legislators stayed, usually returning late on Thursday. He had a small office in the statehouse and a part-time staffer in Chicago. He'd scaled back his work at the law firm, but to keep up with our debts, he'd added more courses to his teaching load at the law school. We spoke on the phone every night he was away, comparing notes and swapping tales about our days. On Fridays, back in Chicago, we had a standing date night, usually meeting downtown at a restaurant after we'd both finished up work.

I remember these nights with a deep fondness now. With my devotion to punctuality, I'd always be the first to show up. I'd wait for Barack, and because it was the end of the workweek, and because I was accustomed to it at this point, it didn't bother me that he was late. I knew he'd get there eventually and that my heart would leap as it always did, seeing him walk through the door and hand his winter coat off to the hostess before threading his way through the tables, grinning when his eyes finally landed on mine. *My husband.* The routine settled me. We ordered the same thing pretty much every Friday—pot roast, Brussels sprouts, and mashed potatoes—and when it came, we ate every bite.

This was a golden time for us, with our marriage feeling balanced as Barack worked to fulfill his purpose and I worked to fulfill mine. During a single, early week of senate business in Springfield, Barack had introduced seventeen new bills—possibly a record, and a sign of his eagerness to get something done. Some would ultimately pass, but most would get quickly shut down in the Republican-controlled chamber. I saw in those early months how, just as I'd predicted, politics would be a wearying fight involving standoffs and betrayals, dirty dealmakers and painful compromises. But I saw, too, that Barack's own forecast had been correct as well. He was strangely suited to the tussle of lawmaking, calm and accustomed to being an outsider, taking defeats in his easy Hawaiian stride. He stayed hopeful, convinced that some part of his vision would someday prevail. He was getting battered already, but it wasn't bothering him. It did seem he was built for this.

I, too, was in the midst of a transition. I'd taken a new job, surprising myself by deciding to leave the organization I'd put together and grown with such care. For three years, I'd given myself to it fully, taking responsibility for the largest and the smallest of tasks, right down to restocking paper in the printer. With Public Allies thriving, I felt that I could now step away. And a new opportunity had cropped up almost out of nowhere.

The University of Chicago was looking for an associate dean to focus on community relations and help the school do a better job of integrating with the city. This person would be reaching out to local communities, especially the South Side neighborhood that surrounded the school, and creating a community service program to connect students to volunteer opportunities in the neighborhood. Like the position at Public Allies, this new job spoke to a reality I'd lived personally. The University of Chicago had always felt less interested in me than the fancy East Coast schools I'd attended. The chance to try to change that, to get more students involved with the city and more city residents with the university, was one I found inspiring.

There were also practical reasons for taking the job. My pay was better, my hours would be more reasonable, and there were other people who would keep paper in the printer. I was starting to think more about what kind of life I wanted to have. On our date nights, Barack and I often continued a conversation we'd been having for years about how and where each one of us could make a difference.

For me, some of the old questions about who I was and what I wanted to be in life had returned to my mind. I'd taken the new job in part to create more room in our life, and also because the health-care benefits were better than anything I'd ever had. And this would end up being important. As Barack and I sat holding hands across the table in the candle glow of another Friday date night, there was one big piece missing in our happiness. We wanted to start a family, but we were having difficulty getting pregnant.

IF I WERE to start a file on things nobody tells you about until you're going through them yourself, I might begin with having trouble having a baby. Barack and I were excited when I finally did get pregnant. But sadly, that time I did not carry the baby to full term. Miscarriage, which is what that loss is called, is a deeply lonely and painful experience. If you have one, you will likely mistake it for a personal failure, which it is not. Or a tragedy, which it also is not, even if it feels utterly devastating in the moment. What nobody tells you is that miscarriage happens to many women when they're trying to start a family. I learned this only after I mentioned that I'd miscarried to a couple of friends, and they responded by sharing overwhelming love and support and also their own miscarriage stories. It didn't take away the pain, but in revealing their own struggles, they steadied me during mine. They helped me see that what I'd been through was not uncommon.

Eventually, Barack and I went to see a doctor to help us. With the help of medical technology, we explored how to deal with our issues. I so wanted a baby. It was a need that had been there forever. As a girl, when I'd grown tired of kissing the vinyl skin of my baby dolls, I'd begged my mom to have another baby, a real one, just for me. I promised I'd do all the work.

Now it felt like I was. The state legislature had returned for its fall session, meaning Barack had to be away for work much of the time and I had to go to many medical appointments and tests alone. Sometimes it felt unfair that as the woman, I had to go through this and Barack didn't. I'd been waiting a long time. We both wanted a family. But I was the one who had to endure the treatment alone, hoping we'd have our dream of having a family come true.

It was maybe then that I felt a first flicker of resentment involving politics and Barack's unshakable commitment to the work that kept him away so much. Barack was doting and cared deeply about our having a baby, but he got to go about his regular business while I had to interrupt my routine with daily visits to the doctor's office. He didn't have to go get his blood drawn like I did. He didn't have to cancel meetings to go see doctors. None of this was his fault, but it wasn't equal, either. For any woman who believes that equality is important, this can be a little confusing. It was me who'd put my individual passions and career dreams on hold, to fulfill this shared piece of our dream. Did I want it? Yes, I wanted it so much.

I FINALLY HEARD a sound that erased any traces of resentment: a heartbeat picked up on ultrasound. We were finally going to have a baby. It was for real. Suddenly the responsibility and challenge of the medical treatments felt worth it, and the world took on new colors. I walked around with a secret inside me. This was my privilege, the gift of being female. I felt bright with the promise of what I carried.

We had our outward lives, but now there was something inward happening, a baby growing, a tiny girl. We couldn't see her, but she was there, gaining in size and spirit as fall became winter and then became spring. Even though before I had been upset about the treatment affecting me more than Barack, now I felt that I was so lucky to be the one who got to be with the baby constantly. I was never alone, never lonely. She was there, always, while I was driving to work, or chopping vegetables for a salad, or lying in bed at night. What a feeling this was after the overwhelming sense of loneliness after my miscarriage and the isolation I felt during the medical treatment. But it was all behind me now.

Summers in Chicago are special to me. I love how the sky stays light right into evening, how Lake Michigan gets busy with sailboats and the heat ratchets up to the point that it's almost impossible to recall the struggles of winter. I love how in summer the business of politics slowly starts to go quiet and life tilts more toward fun.

Though really we'd had no control over anything, somehow in the end it felt as if we'd timed it all perfectly. Very early in the morning on July 4, 1998, I felt the first twinges of labor. Barack and I checked into the University of Chicago hospital, bringing both Barack's sister Maya—who'd flown in from Hawaii to be there the week I was due—and my mom for support. It was still hours before the barbecue coals would start to blaze across the city and people would spread their blankets on the grass along the lakeshore, waving flags and waiting for the city fireworks to bloom over the water. We'd miss all of it that year anyway, lost in a whole new blaze and bloom. We were thinking not about country but about family as Malia Ann Obama, one of the two most perfect babies ever to be born to anyone, anywhere, dropped into our world.

14

MOTHERHOOD BECAME MY MOTIVATOR. IT TOOK NO
time for me to be fully wrapped up in my new role as a mom. Barack
and I studied little Malia, taking in the mystery of her rosebud lips, her
dark fuzzy head and unfocused gaze, the herky-jerky way she moved
her tiny limbs. We bathed and swaddled her and kept her pressed to
our chests. We tracked her eating, her hours of sleep, her every gurgle.

She was a tiny person, a person entrusted to us. I could lose an hour
just watching her breathe. When there's a baby in the house, none of
the regular rules apply. Barack and I laughed about what parenthood
had done to us. If we'd once spent the dinner hour talking about big
ideas, we now debated whether Malia was too dependent on her paci-
fier and compared our methods for getting her to sleep. Nothing made
us happier. We even hauled little Malia in her baby carrier with us to
our Friday-night dates.

Several months after Malia was born, I'd returned to work at the
University of Chicago. I worked out that I would come back only half-
time, figuring this would be a win-win arrangement—I could now be
both career woman and perfect mom. We'd found a babysitter, Glorina
Casabal, a doting, expert caregiver. Born in the Philippines, she was

trained as a nurse and had raised two kids of her own. Glorina—"Glo," as we called her—was a short, bustling woman with a short, practical haircut and gold wire-rimmed glasses who could change a diaper in twelve seconds flat. She had a nurse's hyper-competent, do-anything energy and would become a vital and cherished member of our family for the next few years. Her most important quality was that she loved my baby passionately.

What I didn't realize is that a part-time job, especially when it's meant to be a scaled-down version of your previously full-time job, can be something of a trap. At work, I was still attending all the meetings I always had while also dealing with most of the same responsibilities. The only difference was that I now made half my original salary and was trying to cram everything into a twenty-hour week. It was hard to keep my sanity. I felt guilty when I had to take work calls at home and when I was distracted by thoughts of Malia when I was at work. Part-time work was meant to give me more freedom, but mostly it left me feeling as if I were only half doing everything.

Meanwhile, it seemed that Barack had hardly missed a stride. A few months after Malia's birth, he'd been reelected to a four-year term in the state senate, winning with 89 percent of the vote. He was popular and successful. He was also starting to think about bigger things—like running for the U.S. Congress. He was hoping to unseat a four-term Democrat named Bobby Rush. Did I think it was a good idea for him to run for Congress? No, I did not. It struck me as unlikely that he'd win because he was still unknown to many people. But he was a politician now, and some of his advisers were urging him to give it a shot. And this I know for sure about my husband: You don't dangle an opportunity in front of Barack, something that could help him make a bigger difference, and expect him just to walk away. Because he doesn't. He won't.

. . .

WHEN MALIA WAS almost eighteen months old, we took her to Hawaii at Christmastime to visit her great-grandmother Toot, who was now seventy-seven years old. Toot lived in the same small apartment she'd been in for decades. It was meant to be a family visit—the one time each year Toot could see her grandson and great-granddaughter. We'd booked a modest hotel room near Waikiki Beach and started counting down the days until our trip. But then politics got in the way.

The Illinois senate was debating a major crime bill. Barack called me from Springfield, saying we'd need to delay our trip by a few days while they debated the bill. This wasn't great news, but I understood it was out of his hands. All I cared was that we eventually got there. I didn't want Toot spending Christmas alone, and Barack and I needed some time away to relax.

He was now officially running for Congress, which meant that he rarely switched off, and he rarely spent time at home with me and Malia. This was the painful reality of campaigning. On top of his other responsibilities, Barack was under pressure to spend all his time on the campaign trail to improve his chances of winning. What I was learning, too, was that in the eyes of his campaign staff, any minutes or hours Barack spent privately with his family were basically a waste of that valuable time.

I knew enough by now to try to keep myself from thinking about the daily ups and downs of the race. I had okayed Barack's decision to run with a let's-just-get-this-out-of-the-way attitude, but I wanted the campaign to be over. I thought maybe he'd try and fail to get into national politics and that this would then motivate him to want to try something entirely different. In my ideal world, Barack would take a job where he could have an impact on issues that mattered and also make it home for dinner at night.

We flew to Hawaii on December 23, after the state senate finally paused for the holiday, though it still hadn't voted on the crime bill. But to my relief, we'd made it. Waikiki Beach was a revelation for young Malia. She tootled up and down the shoreline, kicking at the waves and exhausting herself with joy. We spent a merry, uneventful Christmas with Toot in her apartment, opening gifts and marveling at her devotion to the five-thousand-piece jigsaw puzzle she had going. As it always had, Oahu's green waters and cheery people helped us forget our everyday concerns, leaving us happy and caught up in the warm weather and our daughter's delight at absolutely everything.

All was going fine until Barack got a call from someone back in Illinois, letting him know that the senate was going back into session to finish work on the crime bill. If he intended to vote, he had to get back to Springfield quickly. With a sinking heart, I watched as Barack jumped into action, rebooking our flights to leave the following day. We had to go. We had no choice. I wasn't happy with the idea of leaving, but I understood, again, this was the way of politics. The vote was an important one—the bill included new gun-control measures, which Barack had strongly supported—and it had also proven difficult enough that a single absent senator could potentially prevent the bill from passing. We were going home.

But then something unexpected happened. Overnight, Malia got a high fever. She'd ended the day happy but was now wailing in pain, and she was still too young to tell us anything specific about it. We gave her Tylenol, but it didn't help much. She was tugging at one ear, which made me suspect it was infected. We were supposed to fly home in a few hours. I saw the worry deepening on Barack's face, caught as he was between his responsibilities to his work and to his family.

"She can't fly," I said, "obviously."

"I know."

"We have to switch the flights again."

"I know."

Unspoken was the fact that he could walk out the door and catch a cab to the airport and still make it to Springfield in time to vote. He could leave his sick daughter and worried wife halfway across the

Pacific and go join his colleagues. It was a possibility, but not one I was going to suggest because I was worried about Malia. What if Malia's fever got worse? What if she needed a hospital? Was he really thinking about leaving?

It turns out he wasn't. He didn't. He would never.

He called his legislative aide to explain that he'd miss the crime-bill vote. I didn't care. I was just focused on our girl. And as soon as Barack got off that call, he was, too. She was our little human. We owed everything to her first.

After a couple of days of rest and some antibiotics, Malia's ear infection cleared up, returning our toddler to her normal bouncy state. Life would go on. It always did. On another perfect blue-sky day in Honolulu, we boarded a plane and flew home to Chicago, back into the chill of winter and into what for Barack was shaping up to be a political disaster.

THE CRIME BILL had failed to pass, losing by five votes. There was no math to do: Even if Barack had made it back from Hawaii in time, his vote almost certainly wouldn't have changed the outcome. Still, he paid a price for his absence. His opponents in the congressional race pounced on the opportunity to depict Barack as someone who'd rather be on vacation in Hawaii and hadn't cared enough to come back to vote on something as significant as gun control.

Nobody seemed to know that he was from Hawaii and had been visiting his widowed grandmother. No one cared that his daughter had fallen ill. All that mattered was the vote. The press went after him for weeks, and one of his opponents took his own shots, telling a reporter that "to use your child as an excuse for not going to work also shows poorly on the individual's character."

I wasn't accustomed to any of this. I wasn't used to having opponents or seeing my family life examined in the news. Never before had

I heard my husband's character questioned like that. It hurt to think that a good decision—the right decision, as far as I was concerned—seemed to be costing him so much. Barack calmly defended his choice to stay with me and Malia in Hawaii. "We hear a lot of talk from politicians about the importance of family values," he wrote in our neighborhood's paper. "Hopefully, you will understand when your state senator tries to live up to those values as best he can."

It seemed that Barack's three years of work in the state senate had been all but wiped away. He'd earned the trust of legislators from all parts of the state, Republican and Democrat alike. But none of the real stuff seemed to matter now. The race had turned into a series of low blows.

From the start of the campaign, Barack's opponents and their supporters had been attacking him to create fear and mistrust among African American voters, suggesting that Barack was part of an agenda cooked up by wealthy white residents to push their preferred candidate on the South Side. Bobby Rush, Barack's opponent for the congressional race, said, "He went to Harvard and became an educated fool. We're not impressed with these folks with these eastern elite degrees." He's not one of us, in other words. Barack wasn't a real Black man, like them—someone who spoke like that, looked like that, and read that many books could never be.

What bothered me most was that Barack exemplified everything parents on the South Side often said they wanted for their kids. He was everything so many Black leaders had talked about for years: He'd gotten an education, and rather than abandoning the African American community, he was now trying to serve it. Barack was being attacked for all the wrong things. I was astonished to see how our leaders treated him only as a threat to their power, stirring up mistrust by playing on backward ideas about race and class.

It made me sick.

Barack, for his part, took it more in stride than I did, having already seen in Springfield how nasty politics could get. Bruised but unwilling to give up, he continued to campaign through the winter, trying earnestly to make progress, even as more and more support went to Bobby Rush. With the clock ticking down to the primary, Malia and I hardly saw him at all, though he called us every evening to say good night.

I was more grateful than ever for those few days we'd had on the beach. I knew that in his heart Barack was, too. I caught a trace of pain in his voice nearly every time he hung up the phone before spending another night away from us. It was almost as if every day he were forced to cast another vote, between family and politics, politics and family.

In March, Barack lost the Democratic primary to Bobby Rush, and it wasn't close.

All the while, I just kept hugging our girl.

AND THEN CAME our second girl. Natasha Marian Obama was born on June 10, 2001. Malia, now almost three, waited at home with my mom. Our new baby was beautiful, a little lamb-child with a full head of dark hair and alert brown eyes—the fourth corner to our square. Barack and I were over the moon.

Sasha, we planned to call her. I'd chosen the name because I thought it had a sassy ring. A girl named Sasha would suffer no fools. Like all parents, I found myself wanting so much for our children, praying that nothing would ever hurt them. My hope was that they'd grow up to be bright and energetic, optimistic like their dad and hard-driving like their mom. More than anything, I wanted them to be strong, and keep moving forward, no matter what. I didn't know a thing about how our family's life would unfold—whether everything would go well or everything would go poorly, or whether, like most people, we'd get a solid mix of both. My job was just to make sure they were ready for it.

My job at the university had left me feeling worn out, and our finances were strained by the high cost of childcare. After Sasha was born, I debated whether I even wanted to return to my job at all, thinking that maybe our family would be better served if I stayed home full-time. Our babysitter loved our kids as if they were her own, but she couldn't turn down a high-paying nursing job that had been offered to her. I couldn't blame her, but I'd wept and wept the night she told me, knowing how hard it would be for us to balance without her. I knew how fortunate we were to have the money to hire her in the first place. But now that she was gone, it felt like losing an arm.

I loved being with my little daughters. I recognized the value of every minute and hour put in at home, especially with Barack's irregular schedule. I thought once again of my mom's decision to stay home with me and Craig. Surely, that choice had also come with negatives, but compared with the way I'd been living, it seemed manageable, and possibly worth trying. I liked the idea of being in charge of one thing rather than two, of not having my brain scrambled by the constant switching between home and work.

But then came a call from Susan Sher, my former mentor and colleague at city hall who now had a big job at the University of Chicago Medical Center. The center had made improving community outreach a top priority. They were looking to hire an executive director for community affairs, a job that seemed almost custom-made for me. Was I interested in interviewing?

At first I wasn't sure. Life with a new baby is tiring and stressful. I was up several times a night to nurse Sasha, which put me behind on sleep and therefore sanity. Even as I was still fanatically devoted to neatness, I was losing the battle. Our home was strewn with baby toys, toddler books, and packages of diaper wipes. Any trip outside the house involved a giant stroller and an unfashionable diaper bag full of the essentials: a Ziploc of Cheerios, a few everyday toys, and an extra change of clothes—for everyone.

But motherhood had also brought with it a wonderful group of friends. Most of us were working in all sorts of careers. Many of our children were the same age. The more children we had, the closer we grew. We saw one another nearly every weekend. We looked after each other's babies, went on group outings to the zoo, and saw Disney on Ice together. Sometimes on a Saturday afternoon, we just set the whole pack of kids loose in somebody's playroom and sat together eating and talking.

Each one of these women was educated, ambitious, dedicated to her kids, and as bewildered as I was about how to balance the demands of a career with the demands of being a mom. When it came to working and parenting, we were doing it every sort of way. Some of us worked full-time, some part-time, some stayed at home with their kids. Some allowed their toddlers to eat hot dogs and corn chips; others served whole-grain everything. A few had husbands who were super involved with parenting; others had husbands like mine, who were overly busy and away a lot. Some of my friends were incredibly happy; others were trying to make changes to achieve more balance. Most of us lived in a state of constant adjustment, tweaking one area of life in hopes of bringing more steadiness to another.

Our afternoons together taught me that there was no one way to be a good mom. No single approach could be deemed right or wrong. Every small child in that playroom was cherished and growing just fine. I felt it every time we gathered, the collective force of all these women trying to do right by their kids. In the end, no matter what, I knew we'd help one another and we'd all be okay.

After talking it through with both Barack and my friends, I decided to interview for the university hospital job. My feeling was I'd be perfect for the job. I knew I had the right skills and plenty of passion. But I knew I'd also need to make it work for my family.

I was done with part-time work. I wanted a full-time job, with a competitive salary to match so that we could better afford child care and housekeeping help. I wasn't going to try to hide the messiness of my existence, from the breastfeeding baby and the three-year-old in preschool to the fact that with my husband's topsy-turvy political schedule, I was in charge of more or less every aspect of life at home.

I laid all this out in my interview with the hospital's new president. I even brought three-month-old Sasha along with me, too. Sasha was little and still needed a lot from me. She was a fact of my life. *Here is me,* I was saying, *and here also is my baby.*

It seemed a miracle that my would-be boss appeared to get it. I walked out of the interview feeling pleased and fairly certain I'd be offered the job. But no matter what happened, I knew I'd at least done something good for myself in speaking up about my needs. There was power, I felt, in just saying it out loud. With a clear mind and a baby who was starting to fuss, I rushed us both back home.

THIS WAS THE new math in our family: We had two kids, three jobs, two cars, one condo, and what felt like no free time. I accepted the new position at the hospital; Barack continued teaching and legislating. And as much as he'd been stung by his defeat in the congressional primary, Barack still had ideas about trying to run for a higher office. George W. Bush was now president. As a country, we'd endured the shock and tragedy of the terror attacks of 9/11. There was a war going on in Afghanistan, and Osama bin Laden was apparently hiding somewhere in a cave. Barack was absorbing every bit of news carefully, going about his regular business while quietly developing his own thoughts about it all.

I don't recall exactly when it was that he first raised the possibility of running for a seat in the U.S. Senate. What I do remember is my response, which was just to look at him in disbelief as if to say, *Don't you think we're busy enough?*

My distaste for politics was only getting stronger, mainly because

Barack's overloaded schedule was starting to really bother me. As Sasha and Malia grew, I found that the pace only got faster and the to-do lists only got longer. Barack and I did all we could to keep the girls' lives calm and manageable. We had a new babysitter helping out at home. Malia was happy at her preschool, making friends and loading up her own little calendar with birthday parties and swim classes on weekends. Sasha was now about a year old, wobbling on two feet and beginning to say words and crack us up with her megawatt smiles. She was madly curious and eager to keep up with Malia and her four-year-old buddies. My hospital job was going well, though I was getting up at 5:00 a.m. and putting in a couple of hours on the computer before anyone else woke up.

This left me a little tired in the evenings and sometimes put me in direct conflict with my night-owl husband. He turned up on Thursday nights from Springfield wanting to dive headfirst into family life, making up for all the time he'd lost. But Barack's lack of punctuality, which before I'd gently teased him about, was now a straight-up frustration. I knew that Thursdays made him happy. I'd hear his excitement when he called to report that he was done with work and finally headed home. He'd say "I'm on my way!" or "Almost home!" For a while, I believed those words. I'd give the girls their nightly bath but delay bedtime so that they could wait up to give their dad a hug. Or I'd feed them dinner and put them to bed but hold off on eating myself, lighting a few candles and looking forward to sharing a meal with Barack.

And then I'd wait. I'd wait so long that Sasha's and Malia's eyelids would start to droop and I'd have to carry them to bed. Or I'd wait alone, hungry and increasingly angry as my own eyes got heavy and candle wax pooled on the table. Saying "On my way" or "Almost home," I was learning, was the product of Barack's eternal optimism and his eagerness to be home, but it did not mean he would actually arrive soon. Sometimes he was on his way but needed to stop in to have one last conversation with a colleague before he got into the car. Other times, he was almost home but forgot to mention that he was first going to fit in a quick workout at the gym.

As a working full-time mom with a half-time husband and a pre-dawn wake-up time, I felt my patience slipping away. When Barack finally made it home, he'd find me angry or unavailable, having flipped off every light in the house and gone to sleep.

WE LIVE BY the examples we know. In Barack's childhood, his dad disappeared and his mom came and went. As far as he was concerned, there was nothing wrong in this approach. He'd had hills, beaches, and his own mind to keep him company. Independence mattered in Barack's world. But I had been raised inside the tight weave of my own family, in our South Side neighborhood, with my grandparents and aunts and uncles all around, everyone jammed at one table for our regular Sunday-night meals. After thirteen years in love, we needed to think through what this meant for how our own family worked.

I felt vulnerable when he was away. Not because he wasn't fully devoted to our marriage, but because having been brought up in a family where everyone always showed up, I could be extra let down when someone didn't show. I was lonely and felt fierce about sticking up for the girls' needs, too. We wanted him close. We missed him when he was gone. I worried that he didn't understand what that felt like for us. I feared that the path he'd chosen for himself would end up steamrolling our every need. When he'd first approached me about running for state senate years earlier, there had been only two of us to think about. But now we had two children, and I had learned that politics was never especially kind to families. I'd had a glimpse of it back in high school, through my friendship with Santita Jackson, and had seen it again when Barack's political opponents had used his decision to stay with Malia in Hawaii when she was sick against him.

Sometimes, watching the news or reading the paper, I found myself staring at images of people who'd committed themselves to political life—the Clintons, the Gores, the Bushes, old photos of the Kennedys—and wondering what the backstories were. Was everyone normal? Happy? Were those smiles real?

Barack and I loved each other deeply, but now we were having disagreements because of our stresses and wildly different schedules.

Barack didn't want to try couples counseling at first. He was used to solving complicated problems on his own, and felt uncomfortable with sitting down in front of a stranger. But I wanted to really talk, and to really listen. The few people I knew who'd tried couples counseling and were open enough to talk about it said that it had done them some good. And so I booked us an appointment with a psychologist who came recommended by a friend, and Barack and I went to see him a handful of times.

Our counselor was a soft-spoken white man. I thought he would hear what Barack and I had to say and then instantly agree with all my complaints. I'm going to guess that Barack might have felt the same way about his own complaints.

This turned out to be the big surprise for me about counseling: No sides were taken. When it came to our disagreements, the counselor would never be the deciding vote. Instead, he was a patient listener, and slowly, he helped us to talk about our feelings and issues together. Over hours of talking, the knot between Barack and me began to loosen. Each time Barack and I left his office, we felt a bit more connected.

I began to see that there were ways I could be happier and that they didn't need to come from Barack's quitting politics. Our counseling sessions had shown me that this was an unrealistic expectation. I began to see how I'd been caught up in the notion that everything was unfair and then, like a Harvard-trained lawyer, collecting evidence to support my side. Now I saw that it was possible that I was more in charge of my happiness than I was allowing myself to be. I was too busy resenting Barack for managing to fit workouts into his schedule, for example, to even begin figuring out how to exercise regularly myself. I spent so much energy stewing over whether or not he'd make it home for dinner that dinners, with or without him, were no longer fun.

This was a turning point for me. That isn't to say that Barack didn't make his own adjustments—counseling helped him to see the gaps in how we communicated, and he worked to be better at it—but I made mine, and they helped me, which then helped us. For starters, I'd worked out with a trainer for a couple of years, but having children had changed my regular routine. I missed exercising and being healthy. My fix for this came in the form of my ever-giving mom. She still worked full-time but volunteered to start coming over to our house at 4:45 in the morning several days a week so that I could run out for a 5:00 a.m. workout and then be home by 6:30 to get the girls up and ready for their days. This new regimen changed everything: Calmness and strength, two things I feared I was losing, were back.

When it came to dinners at home, I set new boundaries, ones that worked better for me and the girls. We made our schedule and stuck to it. Dinner each night was at 6:30. Baths were at 7:00, followed by books, cuddling, and lights-out at 8:00 sharp. The routine put the weight of responsibility on Barack to either make it on time or not. For me, this made so much more sense than holding off dinner or having the girls wait up sleepily for a hug. It went back to my wishes for them to grow up strong and centered. I didn't want them ever to believe that life began when the man of the house arrived home. We didn't wait for Dad. It was his job now to catch up with us.

15

ON CLYBOURN AVENUE IN CHICAGO, JUST NORTH OF downtown, there was a strange paradise, seemingly built for the working parent, seemingly built for me: a standard, supremely American, got-it-all strip mall. It had a BabyGap, a Best Buy, a Gymboree, and a CVS, plus a handful of other chains, small and large, meant to take care of any urgent consumer need, be it a toilet plunger, or a ripe avocado, or a child-sized bathing cap. There was also a nearby Container Store and a Chipotle, which made things even better. This was my place. I could park the car, whip through two or three stores as needed, pick up a burrito bowl, and be back at my desk inside sixty minutes. I excelled at the lunchtime blitz—the replacing of lost socks, the purchasing of gifts for whatever five-year-old was having a birthday party on Saturday, the stocking and restocking of juice boxes and single-serving applesauce cups.

Sasha and Malia were three and six years old now, feisty, smart, and growing fast. Their energy left me breathless. There were times when I'd sit in my parked car after running errands and eat my fast food alone with the car radio playing, overcome with relief, impressed with my efficiency. This was life with little kids. I had the applesauce. I was eating a meal. Everyone was still alive.

Look how I'm managing, I wanted to say in those moments, to my audience of no one. *Does everyone see that I'm pulling this off?*

This was me at the age of forty as a working mom. On my better days, I gave myself credit for making it happen—there was at least something there that resembled balance. The hospital job had turned out to be a good one, challenging and satisfying and in line with my beliefs. It astonished me that so many university medical center employees seemed to find the neighborhood around them so scary that they wouldn't even cross an off-campus street. For me, that fear was motivating.

I'd spent most of my life living alongside these kinds of divisions—noting the nervousness of white people in my neighborhood, and all the ways people with influence seemed to veer away from my community. My job was an invitation to undo some of that, to knock down barriers where I could—mostly by encouraging people to get to know one another, and creating a stronger relationship between the hospital and its neighboring community. I started with one person working for me but eventually led a team of twenty-two. We took hospital staff and trustees out into neighborhoods around the South Side, having them visit community centers and schools, signing them up to be tutors, mentors, and science-fair judges, getting them to try the local barbecue joints. We brought local kids in to learn about the jobs hospital employees did, set up a program to increase the number of neighborhood people volunteering in the hospital, and encouraged students in the community to consider medicine as a career. After realizing that the hospital system could be better about hiring minority- and women-owned businesses, I helped set up the Office of Business Diversity as well.

Finally, there was the issue of people desperately needing medical care. The South Side had a population that had high rates of the kinds of chronic conditions that tend to afflict the poor—asthma, diabetes, hypertension, heart disease—and not enough medical providers to care for them all. Because many people were uninsured or dependent on Medicaid, they often avoided going to the doctor until they were so sick that they showed up at the emergency room. The problem was glaring, expensive, inefficient, and stressful for everyone involved. ER visits did little to improve anyone's long-term health, either. Trying to address this problem became an important focus for me. Among other things, we began hiring and training patient advocates—friendly, helpful local people, generally—who could sit with patients in the ER, helping them set up follow-up appointments at community health centers and educating them on where they could go to get decent and affordable regular care.

My work was interesting and rewarding, but still I had to be careful not to let it overwhelm me. I felt I owed that to my girls. Our decision to let Barack's career grow—to give him the freedom to shape and pursue his dreams—led me to hold back my own efforts at work. Almost deliberately, I'd numbed myself somewhat to my ambition, stepping back in moments when I'd normally step forward. I'm not sure anyone around me would have said I wasn't doing enough, but I was always aware of everything I could have followed through on and didn't. There were certain projects I chose not to take on, and young employees I wanted to mentor who I didn't spend enough time with. People talk all the time about the trade-offs of being a working mom. These were mine. If I'd once been someone who threw herself completely into every task, I was now more cautious, protective of my time, knowing I had to maintain enough energy for life at home.

. . .

MY GOALS MOSTLY involved maintaining normalcy and stability, but those would never be Barack's goals. We'd grown better about recognizing this and letting it be. One yin, one yang. I craved routine and order, and he did not. He could live in the ocean; I needed the boat. When he was present at home, he was at least impressively present, playing on the floor with the girls, reading *Harry Potter* out loud with Malia at night, laughing at my jokes and hugging me, reminding us of his love and steadiness before vanishing again for another half a week or more. We made the most of the gaps in his schedule, having meals and seeing friends. He indulged me (sometimes) by watching my favorite television shows. I indulged him (sometimes) by watching his favorite television shows. I'd given myself over to the idea that being away was just part of his job. I didn't like it, but for the most part I'd stopped fighting it. Barack could happily end a day in a faraway hotel with all sorts of political battles brewing and loose ends floating. I, meanwhile, lived for the shelter of home—for the sense of completeness I felt each night, with Sasha and Malia tucked into their beds and the dishwasher humming in the kitchen.

I had no choice but to adjust to Barack's absences, anyway. They weren't going to end. On top of his regular work, he was once again campaigning, this time for a seat in the U.S. Senate.

He'd been slowly growing restless in Springfield, frustrated by the slow pace of state government. He was confident that he could accomplish more and better in Washington. Knowing that I had plenty of reasons to be against the idea of Barack running for the Senate and that he had many arguments for why he should, we'd gathered some friends to see what they thought. We met with them over brunch at the home of Valerie Jarrett, who was equally my friend and Barack's. She was warm and wise, like a big sister to each of us. She saw us clearly, saw our goals clearly, and was protective of us both.

She'd also told me privately ahead of time that she wasn't convinced

Barack should run for the Senate, so I'd walked into brunch that morning figuring I had the argument sewn up.

But I'd been wrong.

This Senate race presented a unique opportunity, Barack explained that day. He felt he had a real shot at winning. When I asked how we'd afford living expenses if we were going to have homes in both D.C. and Chicago, he'd said, "Well, I'll write another book and it'll be a big book, one that makes money."

This made me laugh. Barack was the only person I knew who thought that writing a book could solve any problem. He was like the little boy from "Jack and the Beanstalk," I teased, who trades his family's livelihood for a handful of magic beans, believing with his whole heart that they will yield something, even if no one else does.

On all other fronts, Barack's logic was solid. I watched Valerie's face as he spoke, realizing that he was quickly convincing her that he should run. He had an answer for every "but what about?" question we could throw his way. I knew he was making sense, even as I fought off the urge to tally up all the additional hours he'd spend away from us if he won the race.

Though we'd argued about the impact of his political career on our family for years now, I did love and trust Barack. His attention was already divided between me and the girls and his 200,000 or so South Side constituents. Would sharing him with the state of Illinois really be all that different? I couldn't know one way or another, but I also couldn't bring myself to stand in the way of his dream, that thing always tugging at him to try for more.

And so, with the support of our friends, we'd made a deal. Valerie Jarrett agreed to be the finance chair for Barack's Senate campaign. A number of our friends agreed to donate time and money to the effort. I signed off on all of it, with one condition, repeated out loud so that everyone could hear it: If he lost, he'd move on from politics altogether and find a different sort of job. If it didn't work out on Election Day, this would be the end.

Really and for real, this would be the end.

What came next for Barack, though, was a lucky turn of events. The current senator decided not to run for re-election, and then two leading candidates dropped out of the race due to personal scandals. With just a few months remaining before the election, he didn't even have a Republican opponent.

To be sure, he'd been running an excellent campaign, having learned plenty from his failed congressional run. He'd beaten out seven Democratic opponents and earned more than half the vote to win the nomination. Traveling the state and interacting with potential voters, he was the same man I knew at home—funny and charming, smart and prepared, proving he belonged on the Senate floor. But still, Barack's path to the Senate seemed paved in four-leaf clover.

All this was before John Kerry invited Barack to give the keynote address at the 2004 Democratic National Convention. Kerry, then a senator from Massachusetts, was locked in a back-and-forth fight for the presidency with George W. Bush.

My husband was still a complete nobody. He was a humble state legislator who'd never stood before a crowd like the one of fifteen thousand that would be gathered at the Democratic Convention. He'd never been live on prime-time television. He was a Black man in what was historically a white man's business, with a weird name and odd backstory, hoping to strike a chord with the common Democrat.

And yet he seemed destined for exactly this moment. I knew because I'd seen up close how his mind worked nonstop. Over years, I'd watched him inhale books, newspapers, and ideas, sparking to life anytime he spoke with someone who shared new experience or knowledge. He'd been quietly working at building his vision as long as I'd known him. I'd created room for that vision in our shared life, even if reluctantly. And now maybe the size of the audience would finally match the scope of what he believed to be possible. He'd been ready for that call. All he had to do was speak.

"MUST'VE BEEN A good speech" became my refrain afterward. It was a joke between me and Barack, one I repeated often following that night—July 27, 2004.

I'd left the girls at home with my mom and flown to be with Barack at the convention. Barack stepped into the hot glare of the stage lights and into view of all those millions of people. He was a little nervous and so was I, though we were both determined not to show it. This was how Barack operated anyway. The more pressure he was under, the calmer he seemed to get. He'd written his speech over the course of a couple of weeks. He memorized his words and rehearsed them carefully. Barack looked out at the audience and into the TV cameras, and as if kick-starting some engine inside of him, he just smiled and began to roll.

He spoke for seventeen minutes that night, explaining who he was and where he came from—his grandfather a GI who'd joined Patton's Army, his grandmother who'd worked on an assembly line during the war, his dad who'd grown up herding goats in Kenya, his parents' love, their faith in what a good education could do for a son who wasn't born rich or well connected. He cast himself not as an outsider but rather as a living example of the American story. He reminded the audience that a country couldn't be carved up simply into Republican red and Democratic blue, that we were united by a common humanity and needed to care for each other. He called for hope over cynicism. He spoke with hope, projected hope, almost sang with it, really.

It was seventeen minutes of Barack's easy way with words, seventeen minutes of his deep, dazzling optimism on display. By the time he finished, the crowd was on its feet and roaring, the applause booming in the rafters. I walked out onto the stage, stepping into the blinding lights wearing heels and a white suit, to give Barack a hug before turning to wave with him at the cheering crowd.

The energy was electric, the sound absolutely deafening. That Barack was a good person with a big mind and serious faith in democracy was no longer any sort of secret. I was proud of what he'd done, though it didn't surprise me. This was the guy I'd married. I'd known his abilities all along. Looking back, I think it was then that I quietly began to let go of the idea that there was any reversing his path, that he'd ever belong only to me and the girls. I could hear it almost in the pulse of the applause. *More, more, more.*

The media response to Barack's speech was explosive. "I've just seen the first Black president," one television commentator declared. A front-page headline in the *Chicago Tribune* the next day read simply, "The Phenom." Barack's cell phone began to ring nonstop. The media was calling him a "rock star" and an "overnight success," as if he hadn't spent years working up to that moment onstage, as if the speech had created him instead of the other way around. Still, the speech was the beginning of something new, not just for him, but for our whole family. We were swept into a more public life, where other people's expectations could quickly come to define us.

It was surreal, the whole thing. All I could do, really, was joke about it.

"Must've been a good speech," I'd say with a shrug as people began stopping Barack on the street to ask for his autograph or to tell him they'd loved what he'd said. "Must've been a good speech," I said when we walked out of a restaurant in Chicago to find that a crowd had gathered on the sidewalk to wait for him. I said the same thing when journalists started asking for Barack's thoughts on important national issues, and when nine years after publication, Barack's book *Dreams from My Father* landed on the *New York Times* bestseller list.

"Must've been a good speech," I said when a beaming, bustling

Oprah Winfrey showed up at our house to spend a day interviewing us for her magazine.

What was happening to us? I almost couldn't track it. In November, Barack was elected to the U.S. Senate, winning 70 percent of the vote statewide, the largest margin in Illinois history and the biggest in any Senate race in the country that year. He'd won among Blacks, whites, and Latinos; men and women; rich and poor; urban, suburban, and rural. At one point, we went to Arizona for a quick trip, and he was mobbed by well-wishers there. This for me felt like a true and odd measure of his fame: Even white people were recognizing him now.

I HELD ON tight to whatever remained normal in my life. When we were at home with our kids, everything was the same. When we were with our friends and family, everything was the same. But outside, things were different. Barack was flying back and forth to Washington, D.C., all the time now. He had a Senate office and a little one-bedroom apartment in a building on Capitol Hill that was already cluttered with books and papers, his Hole away from home.

I stuck to my routine in Chicago. Gym, work, home, repeat. Dishes in the dishwasher. Swim lessons, soccer, ballet. I kept pace as I always had. Barack had a life in Washington now, operating with some of the seriousness that came with being a senator, but I was still me, living my same normal life. I was sitting one day in my parked car at the shopping plaza on Clybourn Avenue, having some Chipotle and a little me-time after a dash through BabyGap, when my secretary called. A woman in D.C.—someone I'd never met, the wife of a fellow senator—wanted to talk to me.

"Sure, put her through," I said.

And on came the voice of this senator's wife, pleasant and warm. "Well, hello!" she said. "I'm so glad to finally talk to you!"

I told her that I was excited to talk to her, too.

"I'm just calling to welcome you," she said, "and to let you know that we'd like to invite you to join something very special."

She'd called to ask me to be in some sort of private organization, a club that was made up primarily of the wives of important people in Washington. They got together regularly for luncheons and to discuss issues of the day. "It's a nice way to meet people, and I know that's not always easy when you're new to town," she said.

In my whole life, I'd never been asked to join a club. I'd watched friends in high school go off on ski trips. At Princeton, I'd waited up sometimes for Suzanne to come home from her eating-club parties. Half the lawyers at my old law firm belonged to country clubs. I'd visited plenty of those clubs over time, raising money for Public Allies, raising money for Barack's campaigns. You learned early on that clubs, in general, were expensive and full of wealthy people. Belonging signified more than just belonging.

It was a kind offer she was making, coming from a genuine place, and yet I was all too happy to turn it down.

"Thank you," I said. "It's so nice of you to think of me. But actually, we've made the decision I won't be moving to Washington." I let her know that we had two little girls in school in Chicago and that I was attached to my job. I explained that Barack was settling into life in D.C., commuting home when he could.

"That can be very hard on a marriage, you know," she said gently. "Families fall apart."

I felt her judgment then. Her comment implied that by choosing to stay in Chicago, I was making a dangerous choice, that there was only one correct way to be a senator's wife and I was choosing wrong.

I thanked her again, hung up, and sighed. None of this had been my choice in the first place. None of this was my choice at all. I was now, like her, the wife of a U.S. senator—Mrs. Obama, she'd called me throughout the conversation—but that didn't mean I had to drop everything to support him. Truly, I didn't want to drop a thing.

I knew there were other senators with spouses who chose to live in their hometowns rather than in D.C. I knew that the Senate, with fourteen of its one hundred members being female, was not quite as antiquated as it had once been. But still, I found it presumptuous that another woman would tell me I was wrong to want to keep my kids in school and remain in my job. A few weeks after the election, I'd gone with Barack to Washington for a daylong orientation offered to newly elected senators and their spouses. There'd been only a few of us attending that year, and after a quick introduction the politicians went one way, while spouses were led into another room. I'd come with questions, knowing that politicians and their families were expected to adhere to strict standards dictating everything from whom they could receive gifts from to how they paid for travel to and from Washington. I thought maybe we'd discuss how to navigate social situations with lobbyists or the legalities of raising money for a future campaign.

What we got, however, was a lecture on the history and architecture of the Capitol and a look at the official china patterns produced for the Senate, followed by a polite and chitchatty lunch. The whole thing had gone on for hours. It would have been funny, maybe, if I hadn't taken a day off from work and left our kids with my mom in order to be there. If I was going to be a political spouse, I wanted to treat it seriously. I didn't care about the politics, but I also didn't want to make mistakes.

The truth was that Washington confused me, with its old-fashioned traditions and self-importance, its whiteness and maleness, its ladies having lunch off to one side. I was afraid that as much as I hadn't chosen to be involved, I was getting sucked in. I'd been Mrs. Obama for the last twelve years, but it was starting to mean something different. I was now Mrs. Obama in a way that could feel diminishing, a woman defined by her man. I was the wife of Barack Obama, the political rock star, the only Black person in the Senate—the man who'd spoken of hope and tolerance so powerfully that he now had a hornet buzz of expectation following him.

My husband was a newly elected senator, but everyone was already keen to know whether he would make a run for president in 2008. There was no shaking the question. Every reporter asked it. Nearly every person who approached him on the street asked it. My colleagues at the hospital asked it. Even Malia, who was six and a half on the day she put on a pink velvet dress and stood next to Barack as he was sworn in to the Senate, wanted to know. Unlike many of the others, though, our first grader was wise enough to sense how premature it all seemed.

"Daddy, are you gonna try to be president?" she'd asked. "Don't you think maybe you should be vice president or something first?"

I was with Malia on this matter. As a practical person for my entire life, I would always advise a slow approach, the methodical checking of boxes. I was a natural-born fan of the long and thoughtful wait for well-earned rewards. In this regard, I felt better anytime I heard Barack pushing back at the people who asked him with an aw-shucks kind of modesty, batting away questions about the presidency, saying that the only thing he was planning was to put his head down and work hard in the Senate. And, he would sometimes add, he had two kids he needed to raise.

But the drum was already beating. It was hard to make it stop. Barack was writing his second book, *The Audacity of Hope*—putting his beliefs and his vision for the country into words on his legal pads late at night. He really was content, he told me, to stay where he was, building his influence in the Senate over time, but then a storm arrived.

Hurricane Katrina blasted the Gulf Coast of the United States late in August 2005, swamping and flooding New Orleans, stranding people—Black people, mostly—on the rooftops of their destroyed homes. The aftermath was horrific. Hospitals were without backup power. Families who'd lost everything were herded into the Super-dome football stadium. Emergency workers lacked supplies. Eighteen hundred people died, and more than half a million others were displaced. The tragedy was made worse by the federal government's slow response, which was especially devastating in poor areas. Katrina is a heartbreaking example of how African Americans and poor people of all races in our country were most vulnerable to harm when things got rough.

Where was hope now?

I watched the Katrina coverage with a knot in my stomach, knowing that if a disaster hit Chicago, many of my aunts and uncles, cousins and neighbors, would have suffered a similar fate. Barack's reaction was no less emotional. A week after the hurricane, he flew to Houston to join former president George H. W. Bush, along with Bill and Hillary Clinton, to spend time with the tens of thousands of New Orleans evacuees who'd sought shelter in the Astrodome there. The experience awakened something in him, that nagging sense he wasn't yet doing enough.

THIS WAS THE thought I returned to a year or so later, when the drumbeat truly got loud, when the pressure on both of us felt immense. We went about our regular business, but the question of whether Barack would run for president unsettled the air around us. *Could he? Will he? Should he?* By fall, thanks in part to the publication of *The Audacity of Hope* and media appearances afforded by the book tour, polls showed that voters considered him a strong presidential candidate. This was hard evidence of his potential. I was aware that he'd been having private conversations with friends and advisers, signaling to everyone that he was thinking over the idea. But there was one conversation he avoided having, and that was with me.

He knew, of course, how I felt. We'd discussed it, around the edges of other topics. We'd lived with other people's expectations of Barack's potential for so long that they were almost part of every conversation we had. It was there even when we didn't want it to be there, adding a strange energy to everything. From my point of view, my husband was doing plenty already. If he was going to even think about running for president, I hoped he'd take the cautious path, preparing slowly, waiting until the girls were older.

Since I'd known him, it seemed to me that Barack had always had his eyes on some far-off horizon, on his idea of the world as it should be. Just for once, I wanted him to be content with life as it was. I didn't understand how he could look at Sasha and Malia, now five and eight, with their pigtailed hair and giggly joy, and feel any other way. It hurt me sometimes to think that he did.

We were riding a seesaw, the two of us, him on one side and me on the other. We lived in a nice house now, on a quiet street, with a wide porch and tall trees in the yard—exactly the kind of place Craig and I used to stare at during Sunday drives in my dad's Buick. I thought often of my dad and all he'd invested in us. I wished desperately for him to be alive, to see how things were playing out. Craig was so happy now, having finally made a swerve, leaving his career in investment banking and returning to his first love—basketball. After a few years as an assistant at Northwestern, he was now head coach at Brown University in Rhode Island. He was getting married again, to Kelly McCrum, a beautiful, down-to-earth college dean of admissions from the East Coast. His two children had grown tall and confident, vibrant advertisements for what the next generation could do.

I was a senator's wife, but more important, I had a career that mattered to me. I'd gotten a promotion at work and spent the past couple of years developing a program called the South Side Healthcare Collaborative. The program had already connected more than fifteen hundred patients who'd turned up in our Emergency Department with care providers they could see regularly, regardless of whether they could pay. My work felt personal. I saw Black folks streaming into the ER with medical issues that had long been neglected. I couldn't help but think of every medical appointment my own dad had failed to make for himself, every symptom of his MS he'd downplayed in order not to make a fuss, or cost anyone money, or to spare himself the feeling of being talked down to by a wealthy white doctor.

I liked my job, and while it wasn't perfect, I also liked my life. With Sasha about to move into elementary school, I felt as though I was on the brink of being able to fire up my ambition again and consider a new set of goals. I knew a presidential campaign would interfere with those plans. Barack and I had been through five campaigns already, and each one had forced me to fight a bit harder to hang on to my own priorities. Each one had put a little dent in my soul and also in our marriage. A presidential run, I feared, would change everything. Barack would be gone for more time than ever, months at a time. What would that do to our family? What would the publicity do to our girls?

I did what I could to ignore the whirlwind around Barack, even if it showed no sign of dying down. He was recognized nearly everywhere he went now, but I still had the blessing of invisibility. Standing in line at a convenience store one day in October, I spotted the cover of *Time* magazine and had to turn my head away: It was an extreme close-up of my husband's face, next to the headline "Why Barack Obama Could Be the Next President."

What I hoped was that Barack himself would put an end to the rumors and declare that he would not run for president. But he didn't do this. He wanted to run. He wanted it and I didn't.

Anytime a reporter asked whether he'd join the race for president, Barack would say simply, "I'm still thinking about it. It's a family decision." Which was code for "Only if Michelle says I can."

On nights when Barack was in Washington, I lay alone in bed, feeling as if it were me against the world. I wanted Barack for our family. Everyone else seemed to want him for our country. He had his council of advisers, his chief of staff, and Valerie supporting him. They'd also made clear that there was no half doing a presidential campaign. Barack and I both would need to be fully on board. The demands on him would be unimaginable. Without missing a beat in his Senate duties, he'd have to build and maintain a coast-to-coast campaign, develop his ideas for the country, and raise an astonishing amount of money. My job would be not just to quietly support the campaign but to participate in it. I'd be expected to make myself and our children available for viewing, to smile approvingly and shake a lot of hands. Everything would be about him now, I realized, in support of this larger cause.

Even Craig, who'd protected me since the day I was born, had gotten swept up in the excitement of a potential run. He called me one evening to make a plug. "Listen, Miche," he said, speaking as he often did, in basketball terms. "I know you're worried about this, but if Barack's got a shot, he's got to take it. You can see that, right?"

It was on me. It was all on me. Was I afraid or just tired?

For better or worse, I'd fallen in love with a man with a vision who was optimistic without being unrealistic, not afraid of conflict, and intrigued by how complicated the world was. Barack was strangely unintimidated by how much work there was to be done. He dreaded the thought of leaving me and the girls for long stretches, he said, but he also kept reminding me of how secure our love was. "We can handle this, right?" he said, holding my hand one night as we sat in his upstairs study and finally began to really talk about it. "We're strong and we're smart, and so are our kids. We'll be just fine. We can afford this."

What he meant was, yes, a campaign would impact our family. There were things we'd give up—time, togetherness, our privacy. It was too early to predict exactly how much would be required, but it would be a lot. For me, it was like spending money without knowing your bank balance. How much would we be able to bounce back from the demands a campaign would make on all of us? The uncertainty felt like a threat, a thing that could drown us. Growing up in a working-class community and with a disabled parent, I'd learned that planning and vigilance mattered a lot. It could mean the difference between stability and poverty. One missed paycheck could leave you without electricity; one missed homework assignment could put you behind and possibly out of college.

Having lost a fifth-grade classmate to a house fire, having watched Suzanne die before she'd had a chance to really be an adult, I'd learned that the world could be brutal and random, that hard work didn't always lead to positive outcomes. Sitting in our quiet brick home on our quiet street, I couldn't help but want to protect what we had—to look after our girls and forget the rest, at least until they'd grown up a bit more.

And yet there was another side to this, and Barack and I both knew it well. We'd watched the devastation of Katrina from our place of privilege, safely away from harm. We'd seen parents lifting their babies above floodwaters and African American families trying to hold themselves together in horrendous conditions. My various jobs—from city hall to Public Allies to the university—had helped me see how hard it could be for some people to secure things like basic health care and housing. I'd seen the flimsy line that separated getting by and going under. Barack had spent plenty of time listening to laid-off factory workers, young military veterans trying to manage lifelong disabilities, moms fed up with sending their kids to poorly functioning schools. We understood how ridiculously fortunate we were, and we both felt a need to do something for others.

Knowing that I really had no choice, I finally allowed myself to consider the possibility of Barack running for president. Barack and I talked the idea through, not once, but many times, right up to and through our Christmas trip to visit his grandmother Toot in Hawaii. Some of our conversations were angry and tearful, some of them positive. We were continuing a conversation we had been having for years: *Who were we? What mattered to us? What could we do?*

In the end, I said yes because I believed that Barack could be a great president. He was self-assured in ways that few people are. He had the smarts and discipline to do the job, the character to endure everything that would make it hard, and the rare degree of understanding that would keep him tuned to the country's needs. He was surrounded by good, smart people who were ready to help. Who was I to stop him? How could I put my own needs, and even those of our girls, in front of the possibility that Barack could be the kind of president who helped make life better for millions of people?

I said yes because I loved him and had faith in what he could do.

I said yes, though I was at the same time hiding a painful thought, one I wasn't ready to share: I supported him in campaigning, but I also felt certain he wouldn't make it all the way. He spoke so often and so passionately of healing our country's divisions, believing that most people had higher ideals. But I'd seen enough of the divisions to not get my own hopes up. Barack was a Black man in America, after all. I didn't really think he could win.

16

ALMOST FROM THE MINUTE WE AGREED IT WOULD BE okay for him to run, Barack became a kind of human blur, a man who quite suddenly had to be everywhere all at once. There was not quite a year until the primary contests got started, when voters in each state would decide who they wanted to be the Democratic nominee for president, beginning with Iowa. Barack had to hire staff, woo donors who could write big checks, and figure out how to introduce his candidacy in the most powerful way possible. The goal was to get on people's radar and stay there right through Election Day.

The plan was that Barack would formally announce his candidacy in Springfield, Illinois. Everyone agreed that it would be a fitting backdrop for what we hoped would be a different kind of campaign—one led from the ground up, largely by people new to the political process. This was the foundation of Barack's hope. His years as a community organizer had shown him how many people felt unheard and powerless within our democracy. Project VOTE! had helped him see what was possible if those people were empowered to participate. His run for president would be an even bigger test of that idea. Would his message work on a larger scale? Would enough people come out to help?

Barack knew he was an unusual candidate. He wanted to run an unusual campaign.

Barack was to announce his candidacy from the steps of the Old State Capitol in Illinois, in the middle of February, when temperatures were often below freezing. I thought the idea was impractical, and it did little to build my confidence in the campaign team that now more or less ran our lives. I was unhappy about it, imagining the girls and me trying to smile through blowing snow or frigid winds, Barack trying to appear energized instead of chilled. I thought about all the people who would decide to stay home that day rather than stand out in the cold for hours. I was a midwesterner: I knew the weather could ruin everything. I knew also that Barack couldn't afford an early flop.

About a month earlier, Hillary Clinton had declared her own candidacy, brimming with confidence. John Edwards had launched his campaign a month before that, speaking in front of a New Orleans home that had been ravaged by Hurricane Katrina. A total of nine Democrats would throw their hats into the ring. There would be fierce competition.

Barack's team was gambling with an outdoor announcement, but it wasn't my place to doubt them, so I held my tongue. I had little control anymore. Rallies were being planned, strategies mapped, volunteers mustered. The campaign was under way, and there was no stopping it now.

I shifted my focus toward something I could control, which was finding acceptable headwear for Malia and Sasha for the announcement. I'd found new winter coats for them, but I'd forgotten all about hats until it was nearly too late.

As the announcement day neared, I began making anxious after-work trips to department stores, hunting the clearance racks of winter wear in vain. It wasn't long before I became less concerned with making sure Malia and Sasha looked like the daughters of a future president than making sure they looked like they at least had a mom.

Finally, I found some—two knit hats, white for Malia and pink for Sasha, both in a women's size small, which ended up fitting snugly on Malia's head but drooping loosely around Sasha's little five-year-old face. They weren't high fashion, but they looked cute enough, and more important, they'd keep the girls warm. It was a small triumph, but it was mine.

ANNOUNCEMENT DAY—February 10, 2007—turned out to be a bright, cloudless morning, the kind of sparkling midwinter Saturday that looks a lot better than it actually feels. The air temperature sat at about twelve degrees, with a light breeze blowing. Our family had arrived in Springfield the previous day.

Already, we were beginning to experience the pressures of a national campaign. But I was surprised that the first shots fired at us came from within the Black community. The campaign was criticized for scheduling Barack's announcement on the same day as the State of the Black Union, a forum put on by famous African American broadcaster Tavis Smiley. Then, just a day ahead of the announcement, a magazine published a story about Barack that quoted from an angry and inflammatory sermon the Reverend Jeremiah Wright had delivered many years earlier. In his sermon, the Reverend criticized the treatment of Blacks in our country.

It was a disaster in the making, especially because Reverend Wright was scheduled to speak to the crowd ahead of Barack's speech. Barack had to make a difficult call, asking the pastor whether he'd be willing to simply give us a private backstage blessing instead. Reverend Wright's feelings were hurt, Barack said, but he also seemed to understand.

That morning, it hit me that we'd reached the no-turning-back moment. We were literally now putting our family in front of the American people. The day was meant to be a massive kickoff party for the campaign, but I couldn't shake the fear that no one would show up. Unlike Barack, I could be a doubter. I still held on to the worries I'd had since childhood. What if we're not good enough? Maybe everything we'd been told was an exaggeration. Maybe Barack was less popular than his people believed. Maybe it just wasn't yet his time. I tried to shove all doubts aside as we arrived through a side entrance to the old capitol, still unable to see what was going on out front. So that I could get a briefing from the staff, I handed Sasha and Malia off to my mom and Kaye Wilson—"Mama Kaye"—a former mentor of Barack's who had in recent years stepped into the role of second grandmother to our girls.

The crowd was looking good, I was told. People had started gathering before dawn. The plan was for Barack to walk out first, and then the girls and I would join him a few moments later on the platform. I'd made it clear already that we would not stay onstage for his entire speech. It was too much to ask two little kids to sit still and pretend to be interested. If they looked at all bored, if either one sneezed or started fidgeting, it would do nothing for Barack's cause. The same went for me. I knew there was a stereotype about politicians' wives, that we were meant to look like perfectly groomed dolls with painted-on smiles, gazing bright-eyed at our husbands, as if hanging on their every word. This was not me and never would be. I could be supportive, but I couldn't be a robot.

Barack walked out to greet the audience, his appearance met with a roar I could hear from inside the capitol. I went back to find Sasha and Malia, beginning to feel truly nervous. "Are you girls ready?" I said.

"Mommy, I'm hot," Sasha said, tearing off her pink hat.

"Oh, sweetie, you've got to keep that on. It's freezing outside." I grabbed the hat and fitted it back on her head.

"But we're not outside, we're inside," she said.

This was Sasha, our round-faced little truth teller. I couldn't argue with her logic. Instead, I tried to send a mental message to one of the staffers nearby: *If we don't get this thing started now, we're going to lose these two.*

She nodded and motioned us toward the entrance. It was time.

I'd been to many of Barack's political events by now—campaign kickoffs, fund-raisers, and election-night parties. I'd seen audiences filled with old friends and longtime supporters. But Springfield was something else entirely.

My nerves left me the moment we stepped onstage. I was focused completely on Sasha, making sure she was smiling and not about to trip over her own booted feet. "Look up, sweetie," I said, holding her hand. "Smile!" Malia was out ahead of us already, her chin high and her smile giant as she caught up with her dad and waved. It wasn't until we were up the stairs that I was finally able to take in the crowd, or at least try to. The rush was enormous. More than fifteen thousand people had come that day. They were spilling out from the capitol, enveloping us with their enthusiasm.

I'd never been one who'd choose to spend a Saturday at a political rally. The appeal of standing in an open gym or high school auditorium to hear politicians make promises never made much sense to me. Why, I wondered, were all these people here? Why would they layer on extra socks and stand for hours in the cold? I could imagine people bundling up and waiting to hear a band whose every lyric they could sing or enduring a snowy Super Bowl for a team they'd followed since childhood. But politics? This was unlike anything I'd experienced before.

It began dawning on me that we were the band. We were the team about to take the field. What I felt more than anything was a sudden sense of responsibility. We owed something to each one of these people. We were asking for an investment of their faith, and now we had to deliver by carrying that enthusiasm through twenty months and fifty states and right into the White House. I hadn't believed it was possible, but maybe now I did. This was how democracy worked, I realized. *You show up for us, and we'll show up for you.* I had fifteen thousand more reasons to want Barack to win.

I was fully committed now. Our whole family was committed, even if it felt a little scary. I couldn't yet begin to imagine what lay ahead. But there we were—out there—the four of us standing before the crowd and the cameras, in our coats and a slightly too big pink hat on a tiny head.

HILLARY CLINTON WAS a serious and impressive opponent. In poll after poll, she led, with Barack lagging ten or twenty points behind. Democratic voters knew the Clintons, and they were hungry for a win. Far fewer people could even pronounce my husband's name. All of us—Barack and I as well as the campaign team—understood long before his announcement that regardless of his political gifts a Black man named Barack Hussein Obama would always be a long shot.

It was a hurdle we faced within the Black community, too. Similar to how I'd initially felt about Barack's candidacy, plenty of Black folks couldn't bring themselves to believe that my husband had a real chance of winning. Many had yet to believe that a Black man could win in predominantly white areas, which meant they'd often go for the safer bet, the next-best thing. One facet of the challenge for Barack was to shift Black voters away from their long-standing allegiance to Bill Clinton, who'd shown unusual ease with the African American community and formed many connections there as a result. Barack had already built goodwill with a diverse range of voters throughout Illinois, including in the rural white farm areas. He'd already proven that he could appeal to people of all backgrounds, but many people didn't yet understand this about him.

The scrutiny of Barack would be extra intense, the lens always magnified. We knew that as a Black candidate he couldn't afford any sort of stumble. He'd have to do everything twice as well. The hope was that a strong performance in the earliest primaries would give Barack's campaign enough momentum to beat the powerful and well-known Clintons.

Our hopes were pinned on Iowa. We had to win it or otherwise stand down. Mostly rural and more than 90 percent white, it was maybe not the most obvious place for a Black guy based in Chicago to try to define himself. But this was the reality. Iowa went first in presidential primaries and had since 1972, and the whole nation paid attention. We knew that if we made a good showing in Iowa, it would send a message to people all over the country. Black voters especially would know that it was okay to start believing if Barack could win in an overwhelmingly white state.

I would be flying to Iowa almost weekly, making three or four campaign stops in a day. I told Barack's campaign manager early on that part of the deal had to be that they'd get me back to Chicago in time to put the girls to bed at night. My mom had agreed to cut down her hours at work so that she could be around for the kids more when I was traveling. Barack, too, would be logging many hours in Iowa, but the needs of the campaign meant that we'd rarely show up there—or anywhere—together.

Barack now traveled with a swarm of aides, and I was provided funds to hire a two-person staff of my own. I had no idea what kind of support I needed. Melissa Winter, who was my first hire and would later become my chief of staff, had been recommended by Barack's scheduler. I interviewed Melissa—who was blond and bespectacled—in our living room in Chicago and was impressed by her wit and devotion to detail. I knew this would be important as I tried to integrate campaigning into my already-busy schedule at the hospital. She was sharp, highly efficient, and quick moving. She'd also been around politics enough to be unfazed by its intensity and pace. Just a few years younger than I was, Melissa also felt more like a peer and an ally than the much younger campaign workers. She would become someone I trusted—as I do still, to this day—with literally every part of my life.

Katie McCormick Lelyveld rounded out our little trio by coming on board as my communications director. She'd already worked on a presidential campaign and also for Hillary Clinton when she was First Lady. Spunky, intelligent, and always perfectly dressed, Katie would be in charge of handling reporters and TV crews, making sure our events were well covered and also—thanks to the leather briefcase she kept packed with stain remover, breath mints, a sewing kit, and an extra pair of nylons—that I didn't make a mess of myself as we sprinted between airplanes and events.

Barack's advisers had explained that my mission was primarily to spend time with Democrats in every corner of the state, addressing small groups, energizing volunteers, and trying to win over leaders in the community. Iowans, they said, took their voting seriously. They did their homework on candidates and asked serious questions, and they were not likely to be won over with a smile and a handshake. What they didn't tell me was what my message in Iowa was supposed to be. I was given no script, no advice. I figured I'd just work it out for myself.

My first solo campaign event took place in early April inside a modest home in Des Moines. A few dozen people had collected in the living room, sitting on couches and folding chairs, while others sat on the floor. As I looked around the room, what I saw shouldn't have surprised me, but it did. Laid out on the end tables were the same sorts of white crocheted doilies that my grandmother Shields used to have at her house. I spotted porcelain figurines that looked just like the ones Robbie had kept on her shelves downstairs. A man in the front row was smiling at me warmly. I was in Iowa, but I had the distinct feeling of being at home. Iowans, I was realizing, were like my own family. They didn't suffer fools. They didn't trust people who put on airs. They could sniff out a phony a mile away.

My job, I realized, was to be myself, to speak as myself. And so I did.

"Let me tell you about me. I'm Michelle Obama, raised on the South Side of Chicago, in a little apartment on the top floor of a two-story house that felt a lot like this one. My dad was a water-pump operator for the city. My mom stayed at home to raise my brother and me."

I talked about everything—about my brother and the values we were raised with, about this hotshot lawyer I met at work, the level-headed guy who'd stolen my heart with his vision for the world, but who also left his socks lying around the house and sometimes snored in his sleep. I told them about how I was keeping my job at the hospital, about how my mom was picking our girls up from school that day.

I didn't sugarcoat my feelings about politics. The political world was no place for good people, I said, explaining how I'd been conflicted about whether Barack should run at all, worried about what the spotlight might do to our family. But I was standing before them because I believed in my husband and what he could do. I knew how much he read and how deeply he thought about things. I said that he was exactly the kind of smart, decent president I would choose for this country, even if selfishly I'd have rather kept him closer to home all these years.

As weeks went by, I'd tell my story to people all over Iowa, in bookstores, union halls, a home for aging military veterans, and, as the weather warmed up, on front porches and in public parks. The more I told my story, the more my voice settled into itself. I liked my story. I was comfortable telling it. And I was telling it to people who despite the difference in skin color reminded me of my family—postal workers who had bigger dreams just as Dandy once had; civic-minded piano teachers like Robbie; stay-at-home moms who were active in the PTA like my mom; blue-collar workers who'd do anything for their families, just like my dad. I didn't need to practice or use notes. I said only what I sincerely felt.

Along the way, reporters started asking me the same question: What was it like to be a five-foot-eleven, Ivy League–educated Black woman speaking to roomfuls of mostly white Iowans? How odd did that feel? I never liked this question because it focused only on our differences, and assumed the differences were all anyone saw.

This was the opposite of what I was experiencing and what the people I was meeting seemed to be experiencing, too, whether they were farmers, college students, or retirees. These people found me after my talks, seeming eager to talk about what we shared—to say that their dad had lived with MS, too, or that they'd had grandparents just like mine. Many said they'd never gotten involved with politics before but something about our campaign made them feel it would be worth it. Now they were planning to volunteer at the local office, and they'd persuade a spouse or neighbor to come along, too.

These interactions felt natural, genuine. I found myself hugging people and getting hugged tightly back.

IT WAS AROUND this time that I took Malia to our pediatrician for a well-child visit. We wanted keep tabs on the asthma she'd had since she was a baby. The asthma was under control, but the doctor alerted me to something else—Malia's body mass index, a measure of health that combines height, weight, and age, was beginning to creep up. It wasn't a crisis, he said, but if we didn't change some habits, it could become a problem over time, increasing her risk for high blood pressure and type 2 diabetes. Seeing the scared look on my face, he assured me that the problem was both common and solvable. The rate of child-hood obesity was rising all around the country. He'd seen many ex-amples in his practice, which was made up mostly of working-class African Americans.

The news landed like a rock through a stained-glass window. I'd worked so hard to make sure my daughters were happy and whole. What had I done wrong? What kind of mom was I if I hadn't even noticed a change?

Talking further with the doctor, I began to see the pattern we were in. With Barack gone all the time, convenience had become the single most important factor in my choices at home. We'd been eating out more. With less time to cook, I often picked up takeout on my way home from work. In the mornings, I packed the girls' lunch boxes with Lunchables and Capri Suns. Weekends usually meant a trip to the McDonald's drive-through window after ballet and before soccer. None of this, our doctor said, was out of the ordinary, or even all that terrible in isolation. Too much of it, though, was a problem.

Something had to change. But every solution seemed to demand more time—time at the grocery store, time in the kitchen, time spent chopping vegetables—all this coming right when we had so little time.

I then remembered that a few weeks earlier I'd bumped into a friend who'd mentioned that she and her husband had hired a young man named Sam Kass to cook regular healthy meals at her house. It turned out Barack and I had met Sam years earlier through a different set of friends.

I never expected to be the sort of person who hired someone to prepare meals for my family. It felt a little like the kind of thing that my South Side relatives would side-eye. Barack wasn't hot on the idea, either; it didn't fit with his frugality, nor the image he wanted to pro-mote as a presidential candidate. But to me, it felt like the only sane choice. Something had to give. No one else could run my programs at the hospital. No one else could campaign as Barack Obama's wife. No one could fill in as Malia and Sasha's mom at bedtime. But maybe Sam Kass could cook for us.

I hired Sam to come to our house a couple of times a week, making a meal we could eat that night and another that I could heat up the next evening. He was a bit of an outlier in the Obama household— a white twenty-six-year-old with a shiny shaved head—but the girls took to his corny jokes as quickly as they took to his cooking. He showed them how to chop carrots and blanch greens, shifting our family away from the year-round sameness of the grocery store and toward the rhythm of the seasons. He was excited about the arrival of fresh peas in springtime or the moment raspberries came ripe in June. He waited until peaches were rich and plump before serving them to the girls, knowing that then they might actually compete with candy. Sam also knew about food and health issues, understanding how the food industry marketed processed foods to families in the name of convenience and how that was having severe public health consequences. I realized that it tied in to some of what I'd seen while working for the hospital, and to the compromises I'd made myself as a working mom trying to feed her family.

One evening Sam and I spent a couple of hours talking in my kitchen, the two of us batting around ideas about how, if Barack ever managed to win the presidency, I might use my role as First Lady to try to address some of these issues. What if we grew vegetables at the White House and helped advocate for fresh food? What if we started a whole children's health initiative that might help parents avoid some of the challenges I'd experienced?

We talked until it was late. I looked at Sam and let out a sigh. "The only problem is our guy is down by thirty points in the polls," I said as the two of us began to crack up. "He's never gonna win."

It was a dream, but I liked it.

·   ·   ·

WHEN IT CAME to campaigning, each day was another race to be run. I was still trying to cling to some form of normalcy and stability, not just for the girls, but for me. My personal life and political obligations were now, for better or worse, deeply connected. My daily phone calls with Barack tended to be short—*Where are you? How's it going? How are the kids?*—both of us accustomed now to not speaking of fatigue or our personal needs. Life was all about the ticking clock of the campaign.

At work, I was doing what I could to keep up. Several months after Barack's announcement in Springfield and with the support of my colleagues, I'd decided to scale back to part-time hours. On the road two or three days a week together, Melissa, Katie, and I had become a family, meeting up at the airport in the mornings and hustling through security, where the guards all knew my name. I was recognized more often now, mostly by African American women who'd call out "Michelle! Michelle!" as I walked past them to the gate.

Something was changing, so gradually that at first I didn't notice. I sometimes felt as if I were floating through a strange universe, waving at strangers who acted as if they knew me, boarding planes that lifted me out of my normal world. I was becoming *known*. And I was becoming known for being someone's wife and as someone involved with politics, which made it doubly and triply weird.

Working a rope line during campaign events had become like trying to stay upright inside a hurricane, with well-meaning, deeply enthusiastic strangers reaching for my hands and touching my hair, people trying to thrust pens, cameras, and babies at me without warning. I'd smile, shake hands, and hear stories, all the while trying to move forward down the line. By the end, I'd look like I'd just stepped out of a wind tunnel.

Quietly, I worried that as my visibility as Barack Obama's wife rose, the other parts of me were disappearing from view. When I spoke to reporters, they rarely asked about my work. They inserted

"Harvard-educated" in their description of me, but generally left it at that. A couple of news outlets had published stories hinting that I'd been promoted at the hospital not due to my own hard work and merit but because of my husband's growing political stature, which was painful to read. A female journalist for a national newspaper wrote a snarky column in which she referred to me as a "princess of South Chicago," suggesting that I was making Barack look weak when I spoke publicly about how he didn't pick up his socks or put the butter back in the fridge. For me, it had always been important that people see Barack as human and not as some otherworldly savior. I found it odd and sad that such a harsh critique would come from another professional woman, someone who had not bothered to get to know me but was now trying to shape my story in a cynical way.

I tried not to take this stuff personally, but sometimes it was hard not to.

With every campaign event, every article published, every sign we might be gaining ground, we became slightly more exposed, more open to attack. Crazy rumors swirled about Barack: That he was a Muslim. That he refused to recite the Pledge of Allegiance. That he wouldn't put his hand over his heart during the national anthem. That he had a close friend who had once been a terrorist. Even when reporters corrected these lies about him, people still kept repeating them.

Barack's safety was something I didn't want to think about, let alone discuss. So many of us had been brought up with assassinations on the news at night. The Kennedys had been shot. Martin Luther King Jr. had been shot. John Lennon had been shot. Ronald Reagan had been shot and was lucky to survive. If you drew too much heat, you bore a certain risk. But then again, Barack was a Black man. The risk, for him, was nothing new. "He could get shot just going to the gas station," I sometimes tried to remind people when they brought it up.

Beginning in May, Barack had been assigned Secret Service protection. It was the earliest a presidential candidate had been given a protective detail ever, which said something about the seriousness of the threats against him. Barack now traveled in black SUVs provided by the government and was trailed by a team of suited, earpieced men and women with guns. At home, an agent stood guard on our front porch.

I rarely felt unsafe. As I continued to travel, I was managing to pull in bigger crowds. If I'd once met with twenty people at a time at low-key house parties, I was now speaking to hundreds in a high school gym. The campaign staff reported that my talks tended to yield a lot of pledges of support, and they began referring to me as "the Closer" for the way I helped make up minds.

Each day brought a new lesson about how to move more efficiently, how not to get slowed down by illness or mess of any kind. After being served some questionable food at otherwise charming roadside diners, I learned to value the bland certainty of a McDonald's cheeseburger. On bumpy drives between small towns, I learned how to protect my clothing from spills by seeking out snacks that would crumble rather than drip. I learned to sleep through the sound of long-haul trucks barreling down the Iowa interstate after midnight.

As up and down as I sometimes felt, that first year of campaigning was filled primarily with warm memories and bursts of laughter. As often as I could, I brought Sasha and Malia along with me out on the trail. They were hardy, happy travelers. On a busy day at an outdoor fair in New Hampshire, I'd gone off to meet voters, leaving the girls with a campaign staffer to explore the booths and rides before we regrouped for a magazine photo shoot. An hour or so later, I spotted Sasha and panicked. Her cheeks, nose, and forehead had been covered in black and white face paint. She'd been transformed into a panda bear, and she was thrilled about it. My mind went instantly to the magazine crew waiting for us, the schedule that would now be thrown off. But then I looked back at her little panda face. My daughter was cute and content. All I could do was laugh and find the nearest rest-room to scrub off the paint.

From time to time, we'd travel together as a family, all four of us. The campaign rented an RV for a few days in Iowa, so that we could do quick tours of small towns, punctuated by exciting games of Uno between stops. We passed an afternoon at the Iowa State Fair, riding bumper cars and shooting water soakers to win stuffed animals, as photographers shoved their lenses in our faces. The real fun started after Barack got swept off to his next destination, leaving the girls and me free. Once he'd left, we got to explore the midway on our own, the air rushing past us as we rocketed down a giant yellow slide on burlap sacks.

Week after week, I returned to Iowa, watching through the plane window as the seasons changed, as the earth slowly greened and the soybean and corn crops grew in ruler-straight lines. I had come to love the state, even if despite all our work it was looking like we might not be able to win there.

For the better part of a year now, Barack and his team had poured resources into Iowa, but according to most polls he was still running second or third behind Hillary Clinton and John Edwards. The race looked to be close, but he was losing—a reality I was hit with anytime I passed by the cable news blaring in airports or at campaign-stop restaurants.

Months earlier, I'd become so fed up with the constant commen-tary on CNN, MSNBC, and Fox News that I'd decided never to watch those channels during my evenings at home, treating myself instead to a more steadying diet of my favorite reality shows. At the end of a busy day, I will tell you, there is nothing better than watching a young couple find their dream home in Nashville or some young bride-to-be saying yes to the dress.

I didn't believe the television commentators, and I wasn't sure about the polls, either. In my heart, I was convinced they were wrong. What they described from their television studios was not what I was seeing in the church halls and recreation centers of Iowa. The commentators weren't meeting teams of high school "Barack Stars," who volunteered after football practice or drama club. They weren't holding hands with a white grandmother who imagined a better future for her mixed-race grandchildren. They also didn't seem aware of the rapidly growing size of our organization. We were in the process of building a massive grassroots campaign network, the largest in the history of the Iowa caucuses.

We had youth on our side. Our organization was powered by the idealism and energy of young people who had dropped everything and driven themselves to Iowa to join the campaign, each one sharing the same spirit that had compelled Barack to become a community organizer in Chicago all those years ago. They had a spirit and skill that hadn't yet been accounted for in the polls. I felt it every time I visited, a surge of hope that came from interacting with true believers who were spending hours every evening knocking on doors and calling voters, building networks of supporters in even the tiniest and most conservative towns.

To me, the young people managing our field offices represented the promise of the coming generation of leaders. They'd been energized and united. They were connecting voters more directly to their democracy, whether through the field office down the street or a website through which they could organize their own meetings and phone banks. As Barack often said, what we were doing wasn't just about a single election. It was about making politics better for the future—less money-driven, more accessible, and ultimately more hopeful. Even if we didn't end up winning, we were making progress that mattered. One way or another, their work would count.

.   .   .

AS THE WEATHER began to turn cold again, Barack knew he had one last chance to change up the race in Iowa. There was a big public event to be held before Democratic voters across the state would meet to choose their candidate in a process known as the Iowa caucuses. Every candidate gave a speech and also tried to bring along as many supporters as possible. It was basically a giant and competitive pep rally.

For months, the cable news commentators had doubted that Iowans would support Barack at caucus time. But about three thousand of our supporters had driven in from all over the state to attend this last speech, showing that we were both organized and active—stronger than anyone thought.

Onstage that night, each of the other candidates criticized their opponents, trying to make them look weak or untrustworthy. Barack was the last to speak, delivering a passionate defense of his central message—that our country had arrived at a defining moment. We had a chance to step beyond the bitter politics that had long divided us into "Red Americans"—Republicans—and "Blue Americans"— Democrats. "I don't want to pit Red America against Blue America," he said. "I want to be the president of the United States of America."

The auditorium thundered. I watched from the floor with huge pride.

"America, our moment is now," Barack said. "Our moment is now."

His performance that night gave the campaign exactly what it needed. He took the lead in about half the Iowa polls and was only gaining steam as the caucuses approached.

In the days after Christmas, with just a week or so left in the Iowa campaign, it seemed as if half of Chicago's South Side had migrated to the deep freeze of Des Moines. My mom and Mama Kaye showed up. My brother and his wife, Kelly, came, bringing their kids. Sam Kass was there. Valerie Jarrett, who'd joined the campaign earlier in the fall as one of Barack's advisers, was there, along with Susan Sher and my girlfriends and their families. I was touched when colleagues from the hospital showed up, friends of ours from the law firm, law professors who'd taught with Barack. And, in step with the use-every-moment spirit of the campaign, they all signed on to help make the final push, reporting to a local field office, knocking on doors in zero-degree weather, talking up Barack, and reminding people to caucus. The campaign was further reinforced by hundreds of others who'd traveled to Iowa from around the country for the final week, staying in the spare bedrooms of local supporters, heading out each day into even the smallest towns and down the most tucked away of gravel roads.

I was barely present in Des Moines, doing five or six events a day that kept me moving back and forth across the state, traveling in a rented van with Melissa and Katie, driven by a rotating crew of volunteers. Barack was out doing the same, his voice beginning to grow hoarse.

Regardless of how many miles we had to cover, I made sure to be back at our home-base hotel each night in time for Malia and Sasha's eight o'clock bedtime. They, of course, barely seemed to notice I wasn't around, having been surrounded by cousins and friends and baby-sitters all day long, playing games in the hotel room and going on short trips around town. One night, I opened the door, hoping to flop on the bed for a few moments of silence, only to find our room strewn with kitchen utensils. There were rolling pins on the bedspread, dirty cutting boards on the small table, kitchen shears on the floor. The lamp shades and the television screen were covered with a light dusting of . . . was that *flour*?

"Sam taught us to make pasta!" Malia announced. "We got a little carried away."

I laughed. I'd been worried about how the girls would handle their first Christmas break away from their great-grandmother in Hawaii.

But blessedly, a bag of flour in Des Moines appeared to be a fine substitute for a beach towel in Waikiki.

Several days later, the caucuses arrived. Barack and I greeted as many voters as we could. Late that evening, we joined a group of friends and family at dinner, thanking them for their support during what had been a nutty eleven months since the announcement in Springfield. I left the meal early to return to my hotel room in time to prepare, win or lose, for Barack's speech later that night. Within moments, Katie and Melissa burst in with fresh news: "We won!"

We were wild with joy, shouting so loudly that the Secret Service rapped on our door to make sure something wasn't wrong.

On one of the coldest nights of the year, a record number of Iowans had fanned out to their local caucuses, almost double the turnout from four years earlier. Barack had won among whites, Blacks, and young people. More than half of the attendees had never participated in a caucus before, and that group likely helped secure Barack's victory. The cable news anchors had finally made their way to Iowa and were now singing the praises of this political whiz who'd comfortably beaten all the other candidates.

That night at Barack's victory speech, as the four of us—Barack, me, Malia, Sasha—stood onstage, I felt great, even a little chastened. Maybe, I thought to myself, everything Barack had been talking about for all those years really was possible. All those drives to Springfield, all his frustrations about not making a big enough impact, all his idealism, his unusual and sincere belief that people were capable of moving past the things that divided them, that in the end politics could work—maybe he'd been right all along.

We'd accomplished something historic, something monumental—not just Barack, not just me, but every staffer, every volunteer, every teacher and farmer and retiree and high schooler who stood up that night for something new.

Iowa had changed us all. Iowa had given me, in particular, real faith. Our mission now was to share it with the rest of the country. Barack was heading to New Hampshire next, where the state primary election was a week away. In the coming days, our Iowa field organizers would fan out to other states—to Nevada and South Carolina, to New Mexico, Minnesota, and California—to continue spreading the message that had now been proven, that change was really possible.

17

WHEN I WAS IN FIRST GRADE, A BOY IN MY CLASS punched me in the face one day, his fist coming like a comet, full force and out of nowhere. We'd been lining up to go to lunch, all of us discussing whatever felt urgent just then to six- and seven-year-olds—who was the fastest runner or why crayon colors had such weird names—when *blam*, I got whacked. I don't know why. I've forgotten the boy's name, but I remember staring at him dumbfounded and in pain, my lower lip already swelling, my eyes hot with tears. Too shocked to be angry, I ran home to my mom.

The boy got a talking-to from our teacher. My mom went over to school to see for herself what kind of threat he posed. My grandfather Southside, who must have been over at our house that day, insisted on going over with her as well. Some sort of conversation between adults took place. Some type of punishment was given. I received a shame-faced apology from the boy and was instructed not to worry about him further.

"That boy was just scared and angry about things that had nothing to do with you," my mom told me later in our kitchen as she stirred dinner on the stove. She shook her head as if to suggest she knew more than she was willing to share. "He's dealing with a whole lot of problems of his own."

This was how we talked about bullies. When I was a kid, it was easy to grasp: Bullies were scared people hiding inside scary people. I'd see it in DeeDee, the tough girl on my neighborhood block, and even in Dandy, my own grandfather, who could be rude and pushy even with his own wife. They lashed out because they felt overwhelmed. You avoided them if you could and stood up to them if you had to. According to my mom, the key was never to let a bully's insults or aggression get to you personally.

If you did—well, then, you could really get hurt.

Only later in life would this become a real challenge for me. Only when I was trying to help get my husband elected president would I think back to that day in the lunch line in first grade, remembering how confusing it was and how much it hurt to get socked in the face with no warning at all.

In 2008, I spent plenty of time trying not to worry about the punches directed at me.

I'LL BEGIN BY jumping ahead to a happy memory from that year, because I do have many of them. We visited Butte, Montana, on the Fourth of July, which happened to be Malia's tenth birthday and about four months ahead of the general election. Montana had gone for George W. Bush, a Republican, in the last election but had also elected a Democratic governor. It seemed like a good place for Barack to visit.

More than ever, Barack spent every minute of every day being watched, measured, evaluated. People took note of which states he visited, which diner he showed up at for breakfast, what kind of meat he ordered to go with his eggs. About twenty-five members of the press traveled with him continuously now, filling the back of the campaign plane, filling the halls and breakfast rooms of small-town hotels, trailing him from stop to stop. If a presidential candidate caught a cold, it got reported. If someone got an expensive haircut or asked for Dijon mustard at a TGI Fridays, it would get reported and examined a hundred ways on the internet. Was the candidate weak? Was he a snob? A phony? A true American?

This was part of the process—a test to see who had the capacity to hold up as both a leader and a symbol for the country. It was like having your soul X-rayed every day, scanned and re-scanned for any sign of weakness. You didn't get elected if you didn't first submit to having your entire life closely examined by the American people. We were just coming into an age where clicks on the internet were being measured and monetized. Facebook had only recently become popular. Twitter was relatively new. Most American adults owned a cell phone, and most cell phones had a camera. We were standing at the edge of something I'm not sure any of us yet fully understood.

Barack was no longer just trying to win the support of Democratic voters; he was now courting all of America. Following the Iowa caucuses, Barack and Hillary Clinton had spent the winter and spring of 2008 slogging it out in every state and territory, battling vote by hard-earned vote for the privilege of becoming a boundary-breaking candidate—Barack as a Black man, and Hillary as a woman. (The other contenders had all dropped out by the end of January.) The two candidates had tested each other mightily, with Barack opening up a small but ultimately decisive lead midway through February.

"Is he president now?" Malia would ask me sometimes over the months that followed as we stood on one stage or another, with celebratory music blasting around us, her young mind unable to grasp anything but the larger purpose.

"Okay, *now* is he president?"

"No, honey, not yet."

It wasn't until June that Hillary acknowledged that she lacked the delegate count to win. Only then could Barack focus on his Republican opponent, John McCain, a longtime Arizona senator who had become the Republican Party's nominee.

We were in Butte on the Fourth of July with two purposes. Barack had spent the previous four days campaigning in four different states. There was little time to waste by having him come off the campaign trail to celebrate Malia's birthday, and he couldn't slip out of voters' view on what was the country's most symbolic holiday. So instead we flew to him, in an attempt to have a family day together even if it would mostly be in full view of the public. Barack's half sister Maya and her husband, Konrad, came with us, along with their daughter Suhaila, a cute little four-year-old.

Anyone born on a major holiday knows that it's a tough thing to set birthday festivities apart from the holiday celebration. The good people of Butte, Montana, seemed to get it. There were "Happy Birthday Malia!" signs taped inside the windows of storefronts along Main Street. Bystanders shouted out their good wishes to Malia over the pounding of bass drums and flutes piping "Yankee Doodle" as our family watched the town's Fourth of July parade from a set of bleachers.

Later that day, we hosted a picnic in an open field, which was meant to be a rally for several hundred of our local supporters as well as a kind of casual birthday celebration for Malia. I was moved by all the people who'd turned out to meet us. I was struck that day by the tenderness that comes with being a parent, the way time passes so quickly that you notice suddenly that your babies are half-grown, their limbs going from pudgy to lean, their eyes getting wise.

So much of the last decade since Malia had been born had been about trying to strike a balance between my family and my work. I was figuring out how to be loving and present for Malia and Sasha while trying to do well at my job. But things had changed: I was now trying to balance parenting with something different and more confusing. The significance of what was happening in Barack's life, the demands of the campaign, the spotlight on our family, all seemed to be growing quickly. After the Iowa caucuses, I'd decided to take a leave of absence from my position at the hospital. I'd been too busy after Iowa to even go over and box up the things in my office or say any sort of proper good-bye. I was a full-time mom and wife now, even if I was a wife with a cause and a mom who wanted to guard her kids against getting swallowed by that cause. It had been painful to step away from my work, but there was no choice: My family needed me, and that mattered more.

And so here I was at a campaign picnic in Montana, leading a group of mostly strangers in singing "Happy Birthday" to Malia, who sat smiling on the grass with a hamburger on her plate. Voters saw our daughters as sweet, I knew, and our family's closeness as charming. But I did think often of how all this appeared to our daughters. I tried to push aside any guilt. We had a real birthday party planned for the next weekend, one involving a heap of Malia's friends sleeping over at our house in Chicago and no politics whatsoever. And that evening, we'd hold a more private gathering back at our hotel. Still, as the afternoon went on and our girls ran around the picnic grounds while Barack and I shook hands and hugged potential voters, I found myself wondering if the two of them would remember this outing as fun.

I watched Sasha and Malia these days with a new fierceness in my heart. Like me, they now had strangers calling their names, people wanting to touch them and take their pictures. Over the winter, the government had assigned me and the girls Secret Service protection, which meant that when Sasha and Malia went to school or their summer day camp, usually driven by my mom, it was with the Secret Service tailing them in a second car.

At the picnic, each one of us had our own agent flanking us, looking out for any sign of threat. Thankfully, the girls seemed to see the agents less as guards and more as grown-up friends, new additions to the growing knot of friendly people we traveled with, identifiable only by their earpieces and quiet watchfulness. Sasha generally referred to them as "the secret people."

The girls made campaigning more relaxing. For both me and Barack, they were a relief to be around—a reminder that in the end our family meant more than anything else. Neither daughter cared much about the hubbub surrounding their dad. All they really wanted (really, really wanted) was a puppy. They loved playing tag or card games with staff during the quieter moments and made a point of finding an ice cream shop in every new place they went. Everything else was just noise.

To this day, Malia and I still crack up about the fact that she'd been eight years old when Barack, clearly feeling some sense of responsibility, posed the question one night while he was tucking her into bed. "How would you feel if Daddy ran for president?" he'd asked. "Do you think that's a good idea?"

"Sure, Daddy!" she'd replied, pecking him on the cheek. His decision to run would change nearly everything about her life after that, but how was she to know? She'd just rolled over then and drifted off to sleep.

That day in Butte, we visited the local mining museum, had a water-pistol battle, and kicked a soccer ball around in the grass. Barack gave a speech and shook voters' hands, but he also got to hang out with us. Sasha and Malia climbed all over him, giggling and entertaining him with their thoughts. I saw the lightness in his smile, admiring him for his ability to block out all the distractions and just be a dad when he had the chance. He chatted with Maya and Konrad and kept an arm hooked around my shoulder as we walked from place to place.

We were never alone. We had staff around us, agents guarding us, members of the press waiting for interviews, onlookers snapping pictures from a distance. But this was now our normal. During the campaign, our days had become so programmed that our privacy and sense of freedom had slowly slipped away. Both Barack and I had handed nearly every minute of our daily lives and schedules over to a bunch of twentysomethings who were highly intelligent and capable but still couldn't know how painful it could feel to give up control over my own life. If I needed something at the store, I had to ask someone to get it for me. If I wanted to speak to Barack, I usually had to send a request through one of his young staffers. Events and activities I didn't know about would sometimes show up on my calendar.

But slowly, as a matter of survival, we were learning to live our lives more publicly, accepting the reality for what it was.

Before the afternoon ended in Butte, we gave a TV interview, all four of us—me, Barack, and the girls—which was something we'd never done before. Usually, we insisted on keeping the journalists at a distance from our kids, limiting them to photos at public campaign events. I'm not sure why we said yes this time. As I recall, the campaign staff thought it would be nice to give the public a closer glimpse of Barack as a parent. In the moment I saw no harm in this. He loved our children, after all. He loved all children. It was precisely why he'd make a great president.

We sat down for about fifteen minutes with Maria Menounos of *Access Hollywood,* the four of us speaking to her while sitting together on a park bench. Malia had her hair braided and Sasha wore a red tank dress. As always, they were disarmingly cute. Menounos was gracious and kept the conversation light as Malia, the family's junior professor, earnestly considered every question. She said that her dad embarrassed her sometimes when he tried to shake hands with her friends and also that it bothered all of us when he left his campaign luggage blocking the door at home. Sasha did her best to sit still and stay focused, interrupting the interview only once, turning to me to ask, "Hey, when are we getting ice cream?" Otherwise, she listened to her sister, adding at times whatever detail popped into her head. "Daddy had an Afro once!" she squealed at one point toward the end, and we all started to laugh.

Days later, the interview aired on ABC and was met with a wildly enthusiastic response. It was covered by other news outlets with headlines like "Curtain Rises on Obama's Girls in TV Interview" and "The Obamas' Two Little Girls Tell All." Suddenly Malia's and Sasha's little-kid comments were in newspapers around the world.

Immediately, Barack and I regretted what we'd done. We felt like we'd made a wrong choice, putting the girls' voices in front of the public long before they could really understand what any of it meant. Nothing in the video would hurt Sasha or Malia. But it was out in the world and would live forever on the internet. We'd taken two young girls who hadn't chosen this life, and without thinking it through, we'd fed them into the spotlight.

BY NOW, I knew something about living in the spotlight. I had Oprah Winfrey sending me encouraging texts. Stevie Wonder, my childhood idol, was showing up to play at campaign events, joking and calling me by my first name as if we'd known each other forever. The amount of attention felt odd to me, especially because I felt as if we hadn't really done much to deserve it. We were being lifted by the strength of Barack's message, but also, I knew, by what he symbolized. If America elected its first Black president, it would say something not just about Barack but also about the country. For so many people, and for so many reasons, this mattered a lot.

Barack, of course, got most of the public adoration, as well as the criticism that came with it. The more popular you became, the more haters you got. It seemed almost like an unwritten rule, especially in politics, where opponents put money and effort into looking for anything resembling dirt on a candidate.

We are built differently, my husband and I, which is why one of us chose politics and the other did not. He was aware of rumors and false impressions that got pumped into the campaign, but rarely let any of it bother him. Barack had lived through other campaigns. And in general, he's just not someone who's easily rattled or thrown off course by doubts or hurt.

I, on the other hand, was still learning about public life. I considered myself a confident, successful woman, but I was also the same kid who used to tell people she planned to be a pediatrician and devoted herself to setting perfect attendance records at school. I cared what people thought. I'd spent my young life seeking approval, collecting gold stars and avoiding messy social situations. Over time, I'd gotten better about not measuring my self-worth only in terms of achievement, but I did tend to believe that if I worked carefully and honestly, I'd avoid the bullies and always be seen as myself.

This belief, though, was about to come undone.

After Barack's victory in Iowa, my message on the campaign trail grew only more passionate. I'd gone from meeting hundreds of people at a gathering to a thousand or more. I remember pulling up to an event with Melissa and Katie and seeing a line of people five-deep and stretching around the block, waiting to get inside an already-jammed auditorium. It stunned me in the happiest of ways. I said this to every crowd: I was amazed by what people were bringing to Barack's campaign in terms of enthusiasm and effort. I was humbled by the work I saw everyday people doing to help get him elected.

When it came to my stump speech, based on what had worked so well for me in Iowa, I'd developed a loose structure for it, though I didn't use a teleprompter or worry if I didn't say it word-for-word. My words weren't polished, and I'd never be as eloquent as my husband, but I spoke from the heart. I described how my initial doubts about politics had faded week by week, replaced by something more encouraging and hopeful. So many of us, I was realizing, had the same struggles, the same concerns for our kids and worries about the future. And so many believed as I did that Barack was the only candidate who could deliver real change.

For example, Barack wanted to get American troops out of Iraq. He wanted to roll back the tax cuts George W. Bush had pushed through for the super-wealthy. He wanted affordable health care for all Americans. It was an ambitious vision, but every time I walked into an auditorium of revved-up supporters, it seemed as if the nation was ready to look past our differences and make it happen. There was pride in those rooms, a united spirit that went well beyond skin color. The optimism was big and it was energizing. "Hope is making a comeback!" I would declare at every stop.

I'd been in Wisconsin one day in February when Katie got a call from someone on Barack's communications team, saying that there seemed to be a problem. Apparently, I'd said something controversial in a speech a few hours earlier. Katie was confused, as was I. What had I said that was any different from what I'd been saying to every crowd for months? There'd never been an issue before. Why would there be one now?

It turned out someone had taken video of my roughly forty-minute talk and cut it down to a single ten-second clip, changing the meaning of my words.

The original version of what I'd said that day went like this: "What we've learned over this year is that hope is making a comeback! And let me tell you something, for the first time in my adult lifetime, I'm really proud of my country. Not just because Barack has done well, but because I think people are hungry for change. I have been desperate to see our country moving in that direction, and just not feeling so alone in my frustration and disappointment. I've seen people who are hungry to be unified around some basic common issues, and it's made me proud. I feel privileged to be a part of even witnessing this."

But nearly all of that had been cut out, including my references

242

to hope and unity and how moved I was. The important details were gone. What was in the clip—and now being played on conservative radio and TV talk shows—was this: "For the first time in my adult lifetime, I'm really proud of my country."

I didn't need to watch the news to know how it was being spun. *She's not a patriot. She's always hated America. This is who she really is. The rest is just a show.*

In trying to speak casually, I'd forgotten how easily your words could be used against you. By accident, I'd given the haters a fourteen-word feast. Just like that boy's punch in first grade, I hadn't seen it coming.

I flew home to Chicago that night, feeling guilty and dispirited. Melissa, Katie, and I had worked together for a year at this point, logging more miles than any of us could count, always racing the clock so I could get back home to my kids at night. While Barack and his campaign team traveled in chartered planes and cushy tour buses, we were still taking off our shoes in slow-moving airport security lines, sitting in economy class, relying on the goodwill of volunteers to shuttle us to and from events that were sometimes a hundred miles apart.

I felt as if overall we'd been doing a pretty excellent job. I'd seen Katie stand on a chair to shout marching orders at photographers twice her age and dress down reporters who asked out-of-line questions. I'd watched Melissa mastermind every detail of my schedule, expertly coordinating multiple campaign events in a day, quickly addressing potential problems, while also making sure I never missed a school play, an old friend's birthday, or a chance to get myself to the gym. The two of them had given everything over to this effort, sacrificing their own personal lives so that I could try to preserve a little of mine.

I sat under the dome light of the airplane, worried that I'd somehow blown it with those fourteen stupid words.

At home, after I'd put the girls to bed and sent my mom back to Euclid Avenue to get some rest, I called Barack. It was the eve of the Wisconsin primaries, and polls there were showing a tight race. Barack's campaign couldn't afford a letdown. I apologized for what was happening with my speech. "I had no idea I was doing something wrong," I said. "I've been saying the same thing for months."

I could almost hear him shrugging on the other end of the line. "Look, it's because your crowds are so big," he said. "You've become a force in the campaign, which means people are going to come after you a little. This is just the nature of things."

As he did pretty much every time we spoke, he thanked me for the time I was putting in, adding that he was sorry I had to deal with any fallout at all. "I love you, honey," he told me, before hanging up. "I know this stuff is rough, but it'll blow over. It always does."

HE WAS BOTH right and wrong about this. Barack won the Wisconsin primary by a good margin, which seemed to suggest I'd done him no damage there. That same day, Cindy McCain took a potshot at me while speaking at a rally, saying, "I am proud of my country. I don't know about you, if you heard those words earlier— I am very proud of my country." She was taking my words out of context to make me look bad. CNN ran headlines saying we were in a "patriotism flap," and the bloggers did what bloggers do. Within about a week, it seemed that most of the commotion about my speech had died down. Barack and I both made comments to the press, stating clearly that I felt a pride in seeing so many Americans getting involved in the campaign, talking to their neighbors, and gaining confidence about their power inside our democracy, which to me did feel like a first. And then we moved on. In my campaign speeches, I tried to be more careful about how the words came out of my mouth, but my message remained the same. I was still proud and still encouraged. Nothing there had changed.

And yet a sinister seed had been planted—a view of me as sullen and hostile, lacking grace. The rumors and one-sided commentary almost always carried less-than-subtle messaging about race, meant to stir up the deepest and ugliest kind of fear within the voting public. *Don't let the Black folks take over. They're not like you. Their vision is not yours.*

This wasn't helped by the fact that the media was attacking Reverend Jeremiah Wright again. ABC News had combed through hours of his sermons, putting together a jarring highlight reel that showed the preacher resentful and raging against white America, as if white people were to blame for every problem.

Barack and I were sad to see this, a reflection of the worst and most paranoid parts of the man who'd married us and baptized our children. Both of us had grown up with family members who viewed race through a lens of cranky mistrust. I'd experienced Dandy's simmering resentment over the decades he'd spent being passed over for jobs because of his skin color, as well as Southside's worries that his grandkids weren't safe in white neighborhoods. Barack, meanwhile, had listened to Toot, his white grandmother, casually use ethnic stereotypes and even confess to her Black grandson that she sometimes felt afraid when running into a Black man on the street. We had lived for years with the narrow-mindedness of some of our older relatives, having accepted that no one is perfect, particularly those who'd come of age in a time of segregation.

Perhaps this had caused us to overlook the more absurd parts of Reverend Wright's preaching, even if we hadn't been present for any of the sermons in the ABC News video. Seeing the highlight reel on the news, though, we were shocked. It reminded us that when it came to race in America, the suspicion and stereotyping ran both ways.

Someone, meanwhile, had dug up my senior thesis from Princeton, written more than twenty years earlier—a survey that looked at how African American alumni felt about race and identity after being at

Princeton. For reasons I'll never understand, the conservative media was treating my paper as if it were some secret Black-power manifesto, a threat that had been unburied. It was as if instead of trying to get an A in sociology and a spot at Harvard Law School, I'd been planning a rebellion to overthrow the white majority and was now finally, through my husband's political career, getting a chance to put it in motion. "Is Michelle Obama Responsible for the Jeremiah Wright Fiasco?" was the subtitle of an online column that tore into the college-age me, suggesting that I'd been influenced by Black radical thinkers and was also a crappy writer. "To describe it as hard to read would be a mistake," the author wrote. "The thesis cannot be 'read' at all, in the strict sense of the verb. This is because it wasn't written in any known language."

I was being painted not simply as an outsider but as fully "other," so foreign that even my language couldn't be recognized. It was a small-minded and ludicrous insult, sure, but his mocking of my intellect, his marginalizing of my young self, carried with it a larger dismissiveness. Barack and I were now too well-known to be made invisible, but if people saw us as alien and trespassing, then maybe our power could be drained. The message was never said directly: *These people don't belong.* A photo of Barack wearing a turban and traditional Somali clothing that had been bestowed on him during an official visit he'd made to Kenya as a senator had shown up on a conservative website, reviving old theories that he was secretly Muslim. A few months later, the internet would burp up another anonymous and unfounded rumor, this one questioning Barack's citizenship, floating the idea that he'd been born not in Hawaii but in Kenya, which would make him ineligible to become president.

As we traveled in Ohio and Texas, in Vermont and Mississippi, I had continued to speak about optimism and unity, feeling the growing positivity of people at campaign events. All along, though, the unflattering picture of me seemed only to spread. On Fox News, there'd be discussions of my "militant anger." On the internet, there were rumors that a videotape existed of me referring to white people as "whitey," which was outlandish and just plainly untrue. In June, when Barack finally clinched the Democratic nomination, I'd greet him with a playful fist bump onstage. One Fox commentator said that this was a "terrorist fist jab," again suggesting that we were dangerous. The same network had referred to me as "Obama's Baby Mama," playing into clichés about Black-ghetto America and implying that Barack and I were not even married.

I was getting worn out, not physically, but emotionally. The punches hurt, even if I understood that they had little to do with who I really was as a person. It was as if there were some cartoon version of me out there, a woman I kept hearing about but didn't know—a too-tall, too-forceful, ready-to-destroy Godzilla of a political wife named Michelle Obama. Painfully, too, my friends would sometimes call and unload their worries on me, wanting me to reassure them that a rumor or lie they'd heard about me was not true. I'd hang up the phone feeling demoralized and hurt that I had to defend myself even to people who knew me well.

I felt as if I couldn't win, that no amount of faith or hard work would push me past my haters and their attempts to deny me my voice. I was female, Black, and strong, which to certain people translated only to "angry." It was another damaging cliché, one that's been forever used to dismiss minority women and what we've got to say.

I was now starting to actually feel a bit angry, which then made me feel worse, as if I were giving in to the haters. It's remarkable how a stereotype functions as an actual trap. How many "angry Black women" have been caught in the trap those words represent? When you aren't being listened to, why wouldn't you get louder? If you're written off as angry or emotional, doesn't that just cause an angry, emotional response?

I was exhausted by the meanness, thrown off by how personal it had become, and feeling, too, as if there were no way I could quit.

Sometime in May, the Tennessee Republican Party released an online video, replaying my remarks in Wisconsin against clips of voters saying things like "Boy, I've been proud to be an American since I was a kid." NPR's website carried a story with the headline "Is Michelle Obama an Asset or Liability?" implying that just by being me, I might be hurting Barack's campaign. Below it, in boldface, came what were apparently points of debate about me: "Refreshingly Honest or Too Direct?" and "Her Looks: Regal or Intimidating?"

I am telling you, this stuff hurt.

I sometimes blamed Barack's campaign for the position I was in. I understood that I was more active than many candidates' spouses, which made me more of a target for attacks. My instinct was to hit back, to speak up against the lies and unfair generalizations or to have Barack make some comment, but his campaign team kept telling me it was better not to respond, to march forward and simply take the hits. "This is just politics" was always the response, as if we could do nothing about it, as if we'd all moved to a new city on a new planet called Politics, where none of the normal rules applied.

Anytime my spirits started to dip, I'd punish myself further with negative thoughts: I hadn't chosen this. I'd never liked politics. I'd left my job and given my identity over to this campaign and now I was a liability? Where had my power gone?

Sitting in our kitchen in Chicago on a Sunday evening when Barack was home for a one-night stopover, I'd let all my frustrations pour out.

"I don't need to do this," I told him. "If I'm hurting the campaign, why on earth am I out there?"

I explained that Melissa, Katie, and I were feeling overmatched by the volume of media requests and the work it took to travel on the tight budget we were on. I didn't want to foul anything up and I wanted to be supportive, but we lacked the time and resources to do any more than react to the moment at hand. And when it came to the growing criticism of me, I was tired of being defenseless, tired of being seen as someone altogether different from the person I was. "I can just stay home and be with the kids if that's better," I told Barack. "I'll just be a regular wife who shows up only at the big events and smiles. Maybe that'd be a lot easier on everybody."

Barack listened sympathetically as I explained my frustrations. I could tell he was tired, eager to head upstairs and get some needed sleep. I hated sometimes how the lines had blurred between family life and political life for us. I didn't want to be another issue he needed to deal with, but then again, my existence had been fully folded into his.

"You're so much more of an asset than a liability, Michelle, you have to know that," he said, looking upset. "But if you want to stop or slow down, I completely understand. You can do whatever you want here."

He told me I should never feel like I owed anything to him or to the campaign. And if I wanted to keep going but needed more support and resources to do it, he'd figure out how to get them.

I was comforted by this, though only a little. I still felt like the first grader in the lunch line who'd just been walloped.

NOT LONG AFTER THAT, I went to see Barack's communications director, David Axelrod, at his office in Chicago and sat down with him and Valerie Jarrett to watch video of some of my public appearances. The two of them praised me for how hard I'd been working and how effectively I was able to rally Barack's supporters. But then Axe muted the volume as he replayed my speech, removing my voice so that we could look more closely at my body language, specifically my facial expressions.

What did I see? I saw myself speaking with intensity and conviction and never letting up. I always talked about the tough times many Americans were facing, as well as the inequality within our schools and our health-care system. My face reflected the seriousness of what I believed in. But it was too serious, too severe—given what most people were taught to expect from a woman. I saw my expression as a stranger might see it. I could see how the opposition had managed to use these images to portray me as a scold and make it easy to disregard my voice. It was another stereotype, another trap.

No one seemed to criticize Barack for appearing too serious or not smiling enough. I was a wife and not a candidate, so the expectation was for me to provide more lightness, more fluff. And yet, there was no question that other women were also not treated well in the world of politics. I knew that many used Hillary Clinton's gender against her, calling her domineering and a nag. Her voice was interpreted as screechy; her laugh was a cackle. Hillary was Barack's opponent, but I couldn't help but admire her ability to stand up and keep fighting amid the men who were so against women.

Reviewing videotape that day, I felt tears pricking at my eyes. I was upset. I could see now that there was a performance side to politics that I hadn't yet mastered. And I'd been out there giving speeches already for more than a year. It was harder to convey warmth in larger auditoriums. Bigger crowds required clearer facial cues, which was something I needed to work on. I was worried now that it was almost too late.

Valerie, my dear friend of more than fifteen years, reached out to squeeze my hand.

"Why didn't you guys talk to me about this sooner?" I asked. "Why didn't anyone try to help?"

The answer was that no one had been paying all that much attention. Barack's campaign staff had thought I was doing fine until I wasn't. Only now, when I was a problem, was I summoned.

For me, this was a turnaround point. The campaign team existed only to help Barack, not me or the girls. And as much as Barack's staffers respected me and valued my contribution, they'd never given me much in the way of guidance. Until that point, no one from the campaign had bothered to travel with me or show up for my events. I'd never received media training or speech prep. No one, I realized, was going to look out for me unless I pushed for it.

Knowing that the gaze was only going to intensify as we moved into the last six or so months of the campaign, Barack's team agreed, finally, that I needed real help. If I was going to continue to campaign like a candidate, I needed to be supported like one. I'd protect myself by being better organized, by insisting on having the resources I needed to do the job well. In the final weeks of the primaries, Barack's campaign began expanding my team to include a scheduler and a personal aide—Kristen Jarvis, a warmhearted former staffer from Barack's U.S. Senate office who kept me grounded in high-stress moments—plus a no-nonsense, politically experienced communications specialist named Stephanie Cutter. Working with Katie and Melissa, Stephanie helped me sharpen my message and my presentation, building toward a major speech I'd deliver late that summer at the Democratic National Convention. We were also finally granted access to a campaign plane, which allowed me to move more efficiently. I could now give media interviews during flights, get my hair and makeup done on the way to an event, or bring Sasha and Malia along with me at no extra cost.

All of it was a relief. And I do think that it allowed me to smile more, to feel less on guard.

As we planned my public appearances, Stephanie advised me to play to my strengths and to remember the things I most enjoyed talking about, which were my love for my husband and kids, my connection with working moms, and my proud Chicago roots. She recognized that I liked to joke around and told me not to hold back with my humor. It was okay, in other words, to be myself. Shortly after the primaries wrapped up, I signed on to appear on a daytime talk show, spending a happy and spirited hour with the hosts in front of a live audience, talking about the attacks against me, but also laughing about the girls and the fist bumps and the silly things people don't know about campaigning. I felt a new ease, a new ownership of my voice. The show aired to generally positive commentary. I'd worn an affordable black-and-white dress that women were suddenly scrambling to buy.

I was having an impact and beginning to enjoy myself at the same time, feeling more and more open and optimistic. I also was trying to learn from the Americans I was meeting around the country, holding discussions about work-family balance, an issue in which I had a keen interest. For me, the most humbling lessons came when I visited military communities and met with soldiers' husbands and wives.

"Tell me about your lives," I'd say. And then I'd listen as women with babies on their laps, some of them still teenagers themselves, told me stories. Some described needing to start over in settling their children into things like music lessons or enrichment programs every time they moved to a new military base. They explained how difficult it could be to maintain a career over the course of those many moves. Many young parents had trouble finding affordable child care. All of it, of course, was made more difficult by the logistical and emotional burdens of having a loved one deployed for twelve months or more at a time to a place like Afghanistan or Iraq or on an aircraft carrier in the South China Sea. Meeting these dedicated people instantly put whatever hurt I was feeling into perspective. Their sacrifices were far greater than mine. I sat in these meetings, taken aback by the fact that I knew so little about military life. I vowed to myself that if Barack was fortunate enough to be elected, I'd find some way to better support these families.

All this left me more energized to help make the final push for Barack and Joe Biden, the senator from Delaware who'd soon be announced as his vice presidential running mate. I felt emboldened to follow my instincts again, surrounded by people who had my back. At public events, I focused on making personal connections with the people I met, in small groups and in crowds of thousands. When voters got to see me as a person, they understood that the distorted pictures of me were untrue. I've learned that it's harder to hate up close.

I would go on to spend the summer of 2008 moving faster and working harder, convinced that I could make a positive difference for Barack. With the Democratic Convention in Denver drawing close, I worked with a speechwriter for the first time, a gifted young woman named Sarah Hurwitz who helped shape my ideas into a tight seventeen-minute speech. After weeks of careful preparation, I walked onstage. I stood before an audience of some twenty thousand people and a TV audience of millions more, ready to tell the world who I really was.

That night, my brother, Craig, introduced me. My mom sat in the front row of a skybox, looking a little stunned by how giant the stage for our lives had become. I spoke of my dad—his humility, his resilience, and how all that had shaped me and Craig. I tried to give Americans the most intimate view possible of Barack and his noble heart. When I finished, people applauded and applauded, and I felt a powerful blast of relief, knowing that maybe I'd done something, finally, to change people's perception of me.

It was a big moment, for sure—grand and public. But the truth is, stages, audiences, lights, and applause were becoming more normal than I'd ever thought they could be. What I lived for now were the unrehearsed, unphotographed, in-between moments where nobody was performing and no one was judging and real surprise was still possible.

For this, we need to go back to Butte, Montana, on the Fourth of July. It was the end of our day there, the summer sun finally dropping behind the western mountains, the sound of firecrackers beginning to pop in the distance. Barack was leaving for Missouri the next day, and the girls and I were headed home to Chicago. We were tired, all of us.

We'd done the parade and the picnic. We'd spent time with what felt like every last resident in the town of Butte. And now, finally, we were going to have a little gathering just for Malia.

If you asked me at the time, I'd have said that we came up short for her in the end—that her birthday felt like an afterthought in the powerful storm of the campaign. We got together in a gloomy conference room in the basement of our hotel, with Konrad, Maya, and Suhaila, plus a handful of staffers who were close with Malia, and of course the Secret Service agents, who were always close no matter what. We had some balloons, a grocery-store cake, ten candles, and a tub of ice cream. There were a few gifts bought and wrapped on the fly by someone who was not me. The mood was not exactly festive. It had simply been too long of a day. Barack and I shared a look, knowing we'd failed.

But like so many things, it was a matter of perception—how we decided to look at what was in front of us. Barack and I were focused on only our faults and insufficiencies, seeing them reflected in that drab room and thrown-together party. But Malia was looking for something different. And she saw it. She saw kind faces, people who loved her, a thickly frosted cake, a little sister and cousin by her side, a new year ahead. She'd spent the day outdoors. She'd seen a parade. Tomorrow there would be an airplane ride.

She marched over to where Barack sat and threw herself into his lap. "This," she declared, "is the best birthday *ever*!"

She didn't notice that both her mom and her dad got teary or that half the people in the room were now choked up as well. Because she was right. And suddenly we all saw it. She was ten years old that day, and everything was the best.

18

FOUR MONTHS LATER, ON NOVEMBER 4, 2008, I CAST MY
vote for Barack. The two of us went early that morning to our polling
place, which was in the gym at Beulah Shoesmith Elementary School,
just a few blocks away from our house in Chicago. We brought Sasha
and Malia along, both of them dressed and ready for school. Even on
Election Day—maybe especially on Election Day—I thought school
would be a good idea. School was routine. School was comfort. As we
walked past photographers and TV cameras to get into the gym, as
people around us talked about the historic nature of this presidential
election, I was happy to have the lunch boxes packed.

What kind of day would this be? It would be a long day. Beyond
that, none of us knew.

Barack, as he always is on high-pressure days, was more easygoing
than ever. He greeted the poll workers, picked up his ballot, and shook
hands with anyone he encountered, appearing relaxed. It made sense,
I guess. This whole thing was about to be out of his hands.

We stood shoulder to shoulder at our voting stations while the girls
leaned in closely to watch what each of us was doing.

I'd voted for Barack many times before, in state-level and national races, and this trip to the polls felt no different. Voting, for me, was a habit, a healthy ritual to be done thoughtfully and at every opportunity. My parents had taken me to the polls as a kid. I'd made a practice of bringing Sasha and Malia with me anytime I could, hoping to show them the ease and the importance of the act.

My husband's career had allowed me to witness how just a handful of votes could mean the difference not just between one candidate and another but between one value system and the next. If a few people stayed home in each neighborhood, it could determine what our kids learned in schools, which health-care options we had available, or whether or not we sent our troops to war. Voting was both simple and incredibly effective.

That day, I stared for a few extra seconds at the little bubble next to my husband's name on the voting ballot for president of the United States. After almost twenty-one months of campaigning, attacks, and exhaustion, this was it—the last thing I needed to do.

Barack glanced my way and laughed. "You still trying to make up your mind?" he said. "Need a little more time?"

If it weren't for the anxiety, an Election Day might almost be relaxing compared to the busyness of campaigning—a kind of mini-vacation between everything that's happened and whatever lies ahead. After months of everything going too fast, time slows to a crawl. Back at home, I played hostess to family and friends who stopped by our house to make small talk and help pass the hours.

At some point that morning, Barack went off to play basketball with Craig and some friends at a nearby gym, which had become a kind of Election Day custom. Barack loved nothing more than a competitive game of basketball to settle his nerves.

"Just don't let anyone break his nose," I said to Craig as the two of them walked out the door. "He's gotta be on TV later, you know."

"Way to make me responsible for everything," Craig said back, as only a brother can. And then they were gone.

If you believed the polls, it appeared that Barack should win, but I also knew he'd been working on two possible speeches for the night ahead—one for a victory, another for a defeat. We knew about a pattern that had been repeated for years in different high-profile political races involving Black candidates around the country. Black candidates would be leading in the polls, only to lose on election day. The explanation seemed to be that when it came to minority candidates, voters often hid their prejudice from pollsters, expressing it only from the privacy of the voting booth.

Throughout the campaign, I'd asked myself over and over whether America was really ready to elect a Black president, whether the country was in a strong enough place to see beyond race and move past prejudice. Finally, we were about to find out.

In mid-September, the news had turned disastrous. The U.S. economy began to spiral out of control as financial institutions and banks suddenly went bankrupt. Stocks plummeted. Companies were unable to borrow money. People's retirement savings vanished.

Barack was the right person for this moment in history. The job of being president was never going to be easy, but thanks to the financial crisis, it would be even more difficult. But Barack was calm, prepared, and smart, and I knew he could handle it. Personally I still would've been content to lose the election and go back to some version of our old lives, but I also was feeling that as a country we truly needed his help. Still, he would inherit a mess.

As evening drew closer, I felt my fingers getting numb, a nervous tingle running through my body. I couldn't really eat. I lost interest in making small talk with my mom or the friends who'd stopped in. At some point, I went upstairs just to catch a moment to myself.

Barack, it turned out, had retreated up there as well, clearly needing a moment of his own.

I found him sitting at his desk, looking over the text of his victory speech in the little book-strewn office adjacent to our bedroom—his Hole.

"You doing okay?" I said.

"Yep."

"Tired?"

"Nope." He smiled up at me, as if trying to prove it was true. Only a day earlier, we'd received news that Toot, Barack's eighty-six-year-old grandmother, had passed away in Hawaii after being sick for months with cancer. Knowing he'd missed saying good-bye to his mom, Barack had made a point of seeing Toot. We'd taken the kids to visit her late that summer, and he'd gone again on his own ten days earlier, stepping off the campaign trail for a day to sit and hold her hand. It occurred to me what a sad thing this was. Barack had lost his mom at the very beginning of his political career, two months after announcing his run for state senate. Now, as he reached its peak, his grandmother wouldn't be around to witness it. The people who'd raised him were gone.

"I'm proud of you, no matter what happens," I said. "You've done so much good."

"So have you," he said, pulling me close. "We've both done all right."

AFTER A FAMILY dinner at home, we got dressed up and rode downtown to watch election returns with a small group of friends and family in a suite the campaign had rented for us at a hotel. Our vice presidential candidate, Joe Biden, and his wife, Jill, had their own suite for friends and family across the hall.

The first results came in around 6:00 p.m., with Kentucky for the Republican candidate McCain, Vermont for Barack. Then West Virginia went for McCain, and after that so did South Carolina. My confidence lurched a little, though none of this was a surprise. Barack's advisers were buzzing in and out of the room, sharing updates as the results came in. We could see on TV that thousands of people were already gathering at Grant Park, a mile or so away on the lakefront, where election coverage was being broadcast on Jumbotron screens and where Barack would later show up to deliver one of his two speeches. There were police officers stationed on practically every corner, Coast Guard boats patrolling the lake, helicopters overhead. All of Chicago, it seemed, was holding its breath, waiting for news.

Connecticut went for Barack. Then New Hampshire. So did Massachusetts, Maine, Delaware, and Washington, D.C. When Illinois was called for Barack, we could hear cars honking and shouts of excitement from the streets below. The room had gone mostly quiet now, everyone waiting for the final results. To my right, the girls sat in their red and black dresses on a couch, and to my left, Barack, his suit coat draped elsewhere in the room, had taken a seat on another couch next to my mom, who was dressed that evening in an elegant black suit and silver earrings.

"Are you ready for this, Grandma?" I heard Barack say to her.

My mom just gave him a sideways look and shrugged, causing them both to smile. Later, though, she'd describe to me how moved she'd felt right then, struck just as I'd been by his vulnerability. America had come to see Barack as self-assured and powerful, but my mom also recognized the seriousness of his journey and the loneliness of the job ahead. Here was this man who no longer had a dad or a mom, about to be elected the leader of the free world.

The next time I looked over, I saw that she and Barack were holding hands.

IT WAS EXACTLY ten o'clock when the networks began to flash pictures of my smiling husband, declaring that Barack Hussein Obama would become the forty-fourth president of the United States. We all leaped to our feet and started yelling. Our campaign staff streamed into the room, as did the Bidens, everyone hugging.

He had done it. We'd all done it. It hardly seemed possible, but the victory was sound.

Here is where I felt like our family got launched out of a cannon and into some strange underwater universe. Things felt slow and slightly distorted, even if we were moving quickly, waved by Secret Service agents into a freight elevator, hustled out a back exit at the hotel and into a waiting SUV. Did I breathe the air as we stepped outside? Did I thank the person who held open the door as we passed by? Was I smiling? I don't know. Everything felt unreal. It had been a very long day. I could see the tiredness in the girls' faces. I'd prepared them for this next part of the night, explaining that whether Dad won or lost, we were going to have a big noisy celebration in a park.

We were gliding now in a police-escorted motorcade along Lake Shore Drive, speeding south toward Grant Park. I'd traveled this same road hundreds of times in my life ever since my bus rides home from Whitney Young. This was my city, as familiar to me as a place could be, and yet that night it felt different, transformed into something strangely quiet. It was a little like a dream.

Malia had been peering out the window of the SUV, taking it all in.

"Daddy," she said, sounding almost apologetic. "There's no one on the road. I don't think anyone's coming to your celebration."

Barack and I looked at each other and started to laugh. It was then that we realized that ours were the only cars on the street. Barack was now the next president of the United States. The Secret Service had cleared everything out, shutting down an entire section of Lake Shore Drive, blocking every intersection along the route—a standard precaution for a president, we'd soon learn. But for us, it was new.

Everything was new.

I put an arm around Malia. "The people are already there, sweetie," I said. "Don't worry, they're waiting for us."

And they were. More than 200,000 people had crammed into the park to see us. We could hear an expectant hum as we exited the vehicle and were ushered into a set of white tents that had been put up at the front of the park, forming a tunnel that led to the stage. A group of friends and family had gathered there to greet us, only now, due to Secret Service rules, they were cordoned off behind a rope. Barack put his arm around me, almost as if to make sure I was still there.

As the four of us walked onto the stage, me holding Malia's hand and Barack holding Sasha's, I saw a lot of things at once. I saw that a wall of thick, bulletproof glass had been set up around the stage. I saw an ocean of people, many of them waving little American flags. My brain could process none of it. It all felt too big.

I remember little of Barack's speech that night. Sasha, Malia, and I watched him from the wings surrounded by those glass shields and by our city and by the comfort of more than sixty-nine million votes. What stays with me is that sense of comfort, the unusual calmness of that unusually warm November night by the lake in Chicago. After so many months of going to high-energy campaign rallies with crowds whipped up into a shouting, chanting frenzy, the atmosphere in Grant Park was different. We were standing before a giant, joyful mass of Americans who were also feeling thoughtful. It was quiet. It seemed almost as if I could make out every face in the crowd. There were tears in many eyes.

Maybe the calmness was something I imagined, or maybe for all of us, it was just a product of the late hour. It was almost midnight, after all. And everyone had been waiting. We'd been waiting a long, long time.

Becoming More

19

THERE IS NO HANDBOOK FOR INCOMING FIRST LADIES
of the United States. It's not technically a job, nor is it an official government title. It comes with no salary and no spelled-out set of duties. More
than forty-three different women had served as First Lady by the time
I came to it, each of whom had done it in her own way.

I knew only a little about previous First Ladies and how they'd approached the position. I knew that Jackie Kennedy had redecorated the
White House, Rosalynn Carter had sat in on official meetings, Nancy
Reagan had gotten into some trouble accepting free designer dresses,
and Hillary Clinton had been ridiculed for working on health-care
policy with her husband's administration. Once, a couple of years earlier at a luncheon for U.S. Senate spouses, I'd watched—half in shock,
half in awe—as Laura Bush posed, serene and smiling, for ceremonial
photos with about a hundred different people, never once losing her
composure or needing a break. First Ladies showed up in the news,
having tea with important people. They sent out official greetings on
holidays and wore pretty gowns. I knew that they normally picked a
cause or two to champion as well.

I understood that I'd be measured by a different yardstick. I would be the first African American First Lady to set foot in the White House. That meant things would be different for me, and harder. People would see me as different or "other." If my white predecessors had automatically been viewed with goodwill, I knew it wasn't likely to be the same for me. I'd learned from the campaign that I had to be better, faster, smarter, and stronger than ever. My grace would need to be earned. I worried that many Americans wouldn't see themselves reflected in me, or that they wouldn't relate to my journey. I wouldn't have the luxury of settling into my new role slowly before being judged. And when it came to judgment, I was as vulnerable as ever to the unfounded fears and racial stereotypes that lay just beneath the surface of the public awareness, ready to be stirred up by rumors.

I was humbled and excited to be First Lady, but not for one second did I think I'd be sliding into some glamorous, easy role. Nobody who has the words "first" and "Black" attached to them ever would. I felt like I was standing at the foot of a mountain, knowing I'd need to climb my way up into favor.

This feeling took me all the way back to high school, when I'd shown up at Whitney Young and found myself suddenly gripped by doubt. Confidence, I'd learned then, sometimes needs to be called from within. I've repeated the same words to myself many times now, through many climbs.

Am I good enough? Yes I am.

There were seventy-six days between election day and inauguration day. It felt important for me to start setting the tone for the kind of First Lady I wanted to be. I knew I'd be happiest if I could actively work toward achieving measurable results. I intended to make good on the promises I'd made to support military families I'd met while campaigning. And then there were my ideas for planting a garden and working to improve children's health and nutrition.

I intended to arrive at the White House with a carefully thought-out strategy and a strong team backing me. I'd learned from the ugliness of the campaign, from the many ways people had sought to write me off as angry or unbecoming, that if you don't get out there and define yourself, you'll be quickly and inaccurately defined by others. I wasn't interested in waiting passively for Barack's team to give me direction. After coming through the trials of the last year, I knew that I would never allow myself to get that banged up again.

MY MIND RACED with all that needed to get done. There had been no way to plan for this transition. For a planner like me, it had been hard to sit back. But now we went into overdrive. My top priority was looking out for Sasha and Malia. I wanted to get them settled as quickly and comfortably as possible.

Thankfully, I was able to keep my key campaign staffers—Melissa, Katie, and Kristen—working with me during the transition. We immediately began to plan our family's move to Washington while also beginning to interview and hire staff for my future East Wing offices, as well as jobs in the family residence.

Barack, meanwhile, was working on filling positions for his cabinet and huddling with various experts on ways to rescue the economy. I could tell by my husband's serious expression following these sessions that the situation was worse than most Americans even understood. He was also receiving secret information about national security, and all of this was weighing on him.

Now that the Secret Service would be protecting us for years to come, the agency selected official code names for us. Barack was "Renegade," and I was "Renaissance." The girls were allowed to choose their own names from a list of options. Malia became "Radiance," and Sasha picked "Rosebud." (My mom would later get her own informal code name, "Raindance.")

When speaking to me directly, the Secret Service agents almost always called me "ma'am." As in, "This way, ma'am. Please step back, ma'am." And, "Ma'am, your car will be here shortly."

Who's "Ma'am"? I'd wanted to ask at first. Ma'am sounded to me like an older woman with a proper purse, good posture, and sensible shoes.

But I was Ma'am. Ma'am was me. It was part of this crazy transition we were in.

All this was on my mind the day I traveled to Washington to visit potential schools for Malia and Sasha. After one of my meetings, I went back to Reagan National Airport to meet Barack, who was flying in from Chicago. As was traditional for the president-elect, we'd been invited by President and Mrs. Bush to drop by for a visit to the White House and had scheduled it to coincide with my trip to look at schools. I stood waiting as Barack's plane touched down. Next to me was Cornelius Southall, one of the agents heading my security detail.

Cornelius was a square-shouldered former college football player who'd previously worked on President Bush's security team. Like all of my detail leaders, he was smart, trained to be hyperaware at every moment, a human sensor. Even then, as the two of us watched Barack's plane come to a stop maybe twenty yards away on the tarmac, he was picking up on something before I did.

"Ma'am," he said as some new piece of information arrived via his earpiece, "your life is about to change forever."

When I looked at him quizzically, he added, "Just wait."

He then pointed to the right, and I turned to look. Something massive came around the corner: it was an army of vehicles that included police cars and motorcycles, a number of black SUVs, two armored limousines with American flags mounted on their hoods, a hazmat mitigation truck, a counterassault team riding with machine guns visible, an ambulance, a signals truck equipped to detect incoming projectiles, several passenger vans, and another group of police escorts. This was the presidential motorcade. It was at least twenty vehicles long, moving in close formation, car after car after car, before finally the whole fleet rolled to a quiet halt, and the limos stopped directly in front of Barack's parked plane.

I turned to Cornelius. "Is there a clown car?" I said. "Seriously, this is what he's going to travel with now?"

He smiled. "Every day for his entire presidency, yes," he said. "It's going to look like this all the time."

I took in the spectacle, not yet knowing that Barack's protection was still only half-visible. I didn't know that he'd also, at all times, have a nearby helicopter ready to evacuate him, that sharpshooters would position themselves on rooftops along the routes he traveled, that a personal physician would always be with him in case of a medical problem, or that the vehicle he rode in contained a supply of his blood type in case he ever needed it. In a matter of weeks, just ahead of Barack's inauguration, the presidential limo would be upgraded to a newer model—aptly named the Beast—a seven-ton tank disguised as a luxury vehicle, tricked out with hidden tear-gas cannons, rupture-proof tires, and a sealed ventilation system meant to get him through a biological or chemical attack.

I was now married to one of the most heavily guarded human beings on earth. It was both relieving and distressing.

I looked to Cornelius, who waved me forward in the direction of the limo.

"You can head over now, ma'am," he said.

I'D BEEN INSIDE the White House just once before, a couple of years earlier. I'd signed myself and Malia and Sasha up for a special tour being offered during one of our visits to Washington, figuring it'd be a fun thing to do. A White House curator walked us through its grand hallways and many public rooms.

We stared at the chandeliers that dangled from the high ceiling of the East Room, where fancy balls and receptions were historically held. We inspected George Washington's red cheeks and sober expression in the massive portrait that hung on one wall. We learned, courtesy of our guide, that in the late eighteenth century First Lady Abigail Adams had used the giant space to hang her laundry and that decades later, during the Civil War, Union troops had temporarily been quartered there. A number of First Daughters' weddings had taken place in the East Room. Abraham Lincoln's and John F. Kennedy's caskets had also lain there for viewing.

Malia, who was about eight at the time, seemed mostly awestruck by the size of the place, while Sasha, at five, was doing her best not to touch the many things that weren't supposed to be touched. She held it together as we moved from the East Room to the Green Room, which had delicate emerald-silk walls and came with a story about James Madison and the War of 1812, and the Blue Room, which had French furniture and came with a story about Grover Cleveland's wedding. But when our guide asked if we'd now please follow him to the Red Room, Sasha looked up at me and, in the loud voice of a bored kindergartner, blurted out, "Oh nooo, not another *ROOM!*" I quickly shushed her and gave her the mom-look that said, "Do not embarrass me."

But who could blame her? It's a huge place, the White House, with 132 rooms, 35 bathrooms, and 28 fireplaces spread out over six floors, all of it stuffed with more history than any single tour could begin to cover. It was hard to imagine real life happening there. President Bush and First Lady Laura Bush lived with their Scottish terriers upstairs in the family residence. But we were standing then in a different area of the house, the frozen-in-time, museum-like part of the place, where the country's history was on display.

Two years later, I was arriving all over again, this time through a different door and with Barack. We were now going to see the place as our soon-to-be home.

President and Mrs. Bush greeted us at the Diplomatic Reception

Room, just off the South Lawn. The First Lady clasped my hand warmly. "Please call me Laura," she said. Her husband was just as welcoming, his bighearted Texas spirit overriding any political hard feelings. Bush, as a Republican, had naturally supported John McCain's candidacy. But he'd also vowed to make this the smoothest presidential transition in history. First Lady Laura Bush had instructed her staff to put together contact lists, calendars, and sample correspondence to help me find my footing when it came to the social obligations that came with the title. There was kindness running beneath all of it, a genuine love of country that I will always appreciate and admire.

Though President Bush mentioned nothing directly, I swore I could see the first traces of relief on his face, knowing that his time in office was almost finished, and that he could soon head home to Texas. It was time to let the next president through the door.

While our husbands walked off to the Oval Office to have a talk, Laura led me to the private wood-paneled elevator reserved for the First Family, which was operated by a gentlemanly African American in a tuxedo.

As we rode two floors up to the family residence, Laura asked how Sasha and Malia were doing. She had parented two older daughters while in the White House. A former schoolteacher and librarian, she'd used her platform as First Lady to promote education and advocate for teachers. She inspected me with warm blue eyes.

"How are you feeling?" she asked.

"A little overwhelmed," I admitted.

She smiled with what felt like real compassion. "I know. Trust me, I do."

In the moment, I wasn't able to fully understand the weight of what she was saying, but later I would think of it often. Barack and I were joining a strange and very small group made up of the Clintons, the Carters, two sets of Bushes, Nancy Reagan, and Betty Ford—the only other living families who'd experienced firsthand the unique delights and hardships of life in the White House. As different as we all were, we'd always share this bond.

Laura walked me through the residence, showing me room upon room upon room. The private area of the White House occupies the top two stories of the main historical structure—the one you'd recognize from photos with its iconic white pillars. I saw the dining room where First Families ate their meals and popped my head into the tidy kitchen, where a culinary staff was already at work on dinner. I saw the guest quarters on the top floor, scouting them out as a possible place my mom could live, if we could manage to talk her into moving in with us. I was most interested in checking out the two bedrooms that I thought would work best for Sasha and Malia, just down the hall from the master bedroom.

For me, the girls' sense of comfort and home was key. If we pared back all the fairy-tale unreality of moving into a big house that came with chefs, a bowling alley, and a swimming pool, what Barack and I were doing was something no parent really wants to do: yanking our kids midyear out of a school they loved, taking them away from their friends, and plopping them into a new home and new school without much notice. I was preoccupied by this thought, though I was also comforted by the knowledge that other moms and children had successfully done this before.

Laura took me into a pretty, light-filled room off the master bedroom that was traditionally used as the First Lady's dressing room. She pointed out the view of the Rose Garden and the Oval Office through the window, adding that it gave her comfort to be able to look out and sometimes get a sense of what her husband was doing. Hillary Clinton, she said, had shown her this same view when she'd first come to visit the White House eight years earlier. And eight years before that, her mother-in-law, Barbara Bush, had pointed out the view to Hillary.

In the coming months, I'd feel the power of connection to these other women. Hillary graciously shared wisdom over the phone, walking me through her experience picking out a school for Chelsea. I spoke with Rosalynn Carter and Nancy Reagan, both women warm and offering support. And Laura kindly invited me to return with Sasha and Malia a couple of weeks after that first visit, on a day when her own girls, Jenna and Barbara, could be there to introduce my kids to the "fun parts" of the White House, showing them everything from the plush seats of the in-house movie theater to how to slide down a sloping hallway on the top floor.

This was all heartening. I already looked forward to the day I could pass whatever wisdom I picked up to the next First Lady in line.

WE MOVED TO Washington right after our traditional Christmas holiday in Hawaii so that Sasha and Malia could start school just as their new classmates were coming back from winter break. The inauguration wasn't for another three weeks, so we stayed on the top floor of a hotel in the center of the city. Our rooms overlooked Lafayette Square and the North Lawn of the White House, where we could see the grandstand and metal bleachers being set up in preparation for the inaugural parade. On a building across from the hotel, someone had hung a massive banner that read, "Welcome Malia and Sasha." I choked up a little at the sight.

We decided to enroll Malia and Sasha at Sidwell Friends, a Quaker school with an excellent reputation. Sasha would be a second grader in the lower school, in suburban Bethesda, Maryland, and Malia would attend fifth grade on the main campus just a few miles north of the White House. Both kids would need to go to school by motorcade, escorted by Secret Service agents. Agents would also remain posted outside their classroom doors and follow them to every recess, play-date, and sports practice.

We lived in a kind of bubble now. I couldn't remember the last time

I'd run an errand by myself or walked in a park just for fun. All movements first required a discussion about both security and schedule. It was odd, being in the bubble, and not a feeling I particularly enjoyed, but I also understood it was for our safety. With a regular police escort, our vehicles no longer stopped at traffic lights. We rarely walked in or out of a building's front door when we could be rushed through a side entrance. From the Secret Service's point of view, the less visible we could be, the better.

I held on to a hope that Sasha and Malia's bubble might be different, that they could remain safe but still able to act like regular kids. I wanted them to make friends, real friends—to find kids who liked them for reasons other than that they were Barack Obama's daughters. I wanted them to learn, to have adventures, to make mistakes and bounce back. I hoped that school for them would be a place to be themselves. Sidwell Friends appealed to us for a lot of reasons. The staff knew how to safeguard the privacy of high-profile students and had already made the sorts of security accommodations that would now be needed for Malia and Sasha. Above all, I liked the feel of the place. The Quaker philosophy was all about community, built around the idea that no one individual should be prized over another, which seemed to me like a healthy counterbalance to the big fuss that now surrounded their dad.

On the first day of school, Barack and I ate an early breakfast with Malia and Sasha before helping them into their winter coats. Barack couldn't help but to offer bits of advice about surviving a first day at a new school (keep smiling, be kind, listen to your teachers), adding finally, as the two girls donned their purple backpacks, "And definitely don't pick your noses!"

My mom joined us in the hallway, and we took an elevator downstairs.

Outside the hotel, the Secret Service had put up a security tent, meant to keep us out of sight of the photographers and television crews who'd posted themselves by the entrance, eager for images of our family in transition. Barack was hoping to ride all the way to school with the girls, but he knew it would create too much of a scene. His motorcade was too big. I could read the pain of this in his face as Sasha and Malia hugged him good-bye.

My mom and I then accompanied the girls in what would become their new form of school bus—a black SUV with smoked windows made of bulletproof glass. I tried that morning to show confidence, smiling and joking with the kids. Inside, however, I felt nervous. We arrived first at the upper school campus, where Malia and I hustled past news cameras and into the building, the two of us flanked by Secret Service agents. After I delivered Malia to her new teacher, the motorcade took us to Bethesda, where I repeated the routine with little Sasha, releasing her into a sweet classroom with low tables and wide windows—what I prayed would be a safe and happy place.

I had a busy day ahead, every minute of it scheduled with meetings, but my mind would stay locked on our daughters. What kind of day were they having? What were they eating? Were they being stared at or made to feel at home? I'd later see a media photo of Sasha taken during the morning trip to school, one that brought me to tears. I believe it was snapped as I was dropping off Malia, while Sasha waited in the car with my mom. She had her round little face pressed up against the window of the SUV and was staring outward, wide-eyed, taking in the sight of photographers and onlookers, her thoughts unreadable but her expression serious.

We were asking so much of them. I sat with that thought not just for that entire day but for months and years to come.

ALL INCOMING PRESIDENTS are given federal funds for moving into the White House and redecorating, but Barack insisted we pay for everything ourselves, holding himself to a higher standard as always.

There's an age-old maxim in the Black community: *You've got to be twice as good to get half as far.* As the first African American family in the White House, we were being viewed as representatives of our race. Any error or lapse in judgment, we knew, would be magnified, read as something more than what it was.

The pace of the transition never slowed. I was bombarded with hundreds of decisions, having to pick out everything from bath towels and toothpaste to dish soap for the White House residence, choose my outfits for the inauguration ceremony and fancy balls that would follow, and coordinate the visits of the 150 or so of our close friends and relatives who'd be coming from out of town as our guests. I was less interested in the redecorating and inauguration planning than I was in figuring out what I could do with my new role. The fact that being First Lady comes with no job description gave me the freedom to choose my agenda. I wanted to ensure any effort I made helped advance the new administration's larger goals.

To my great relief, both our kids came home happy after the first day of school, and the second, and the third. Sasha brought back homework, which she'd never had before. Malia was already signed up to sing in a middle school choral concert. They reported that kids in other grades sometimes did a double take when they saw them, but everyone was nice. Each day afterward, the motorcade ride to Sidwell Friends felt a little more routine. After about a week, the girls felt comfortable enough to start traveling to school without me. My mom became their regular escort. This automatically made drop-offs and pickups a bit less of a production, involving fewer agents, vehicles, and guns.

My mom hadn't wanted to come with us to Washington, but I'd forced the issue. The girls needed her. I needed her. I liked to believe that she needed us, too. For the last few years, she'd been a nearly every-day presence in our lives, her practicality soothing everyone's worries. At seventy-one, though, she'd never lived anywhere but Chicago. She was reluctant to leave the South Side and her home on Euclid Avenue. ("I love those people, but I love my own house," she told a reporter after the election. "The White House reminds me of a museum and it's like, how do you sleep in a museum?")

I tried to explain that if she moved to Washington, she'd meet all sorts of interesting people, wouldn't have to cook or clean for herself anymore, and would have more room on the top floor of the White House than she'd ever had at home. None of this was meaningful to her. My mom didn't care about all the glamour and hype.

I'd finally called Craig. "You've got to talk to Mom for me," I said. "Please get her on board with this."

Somehow that worked. Craig was good at convincing when he needed to be.

My mom would end up staying with us in Washington for the next eight years, but she refused to get put into any bubble. She declined Secret Service protection and avoided the media in order to keep her profile low and her footprint light. She'd charm the White House housekeeping staff by insisting on doing her own laundry, and for years to come, she'd slip in and out of the residence as she pleased, walking out the gates and over to the nearest pharmacy or discount department store when she needed something, making new friends and meeting them out regularly for lunch. Anytime a stranger commented that she looked exactly like Michelle Obama's mom, she'd just give a polite shrug and say, "Yeah, I get that a lot," before carrying on with her business. As she always had, my mom did things her own way.

MY WHOLE FAMILY came for the inauguration. My aunts, uncles, and cousins came. Our friends from Hyde Park came, along with my girlfriends and their spouses. Everyone brought their kids. We'd planned festivities for the big and small people over inauguration week, including a kids' concert, a separate lunch for kids to take place during the traditional luncheon at the Capitol right after the swearing in, and a scavenger hunt and children's party at the White House that would go on while the adults went to inaugural balls.

One of the surprise blessings of the final few months of campaigning had been the natural friendship of our family with the family of Barack's vice president, Joe Biden.

I liked Jill, Joe's wife, right away, admiring her gentle fortitude and her work ethic. She'd married Joe and become stepmother to his two sons five years after his first wife and baby daughter were tragically killed in a car accident. Later, they'd had a daughter of their own. Jill had earned her degree in education and taught English at a community college throughout Joe's years as a senator but also through his two presidential campaigns. Like me, she was interested in finding new ways to support military families. She had a direct emotional connection to the issue: Beau Biden, Joe's older son, was serving in Iraq with the National Guard. He'd been granted a short leave to travel to Washington and see his dad get sworn in as vice president.

And then there were the Biden grandkids, five altogether. They'd shown up at the Democratic National Convention in Denver and immediately made friends with Sasha and Malia, hosting our girls for a sleepover in Joe's hotel suite. We were always grateful to have the Biden kids around.

Inauguration Day was bitingly cold, with temperatures never going above freezing and the wind making it feel more like fifteen degrees. That morning, Barack and I went to church with the girls, my mom, Craig and Kelly, Maya and Konrad, and Mama Kaye. All the while, we were hearing that people had begun forming lines at the National Mall before dawn, bundled up as they waited for the inaugural activities to begin. Nearly two million people flooded the Mall, arriving from all parts of the country, a sea of diversity, energy, and hope stretching for more than a mile from the U.S. Capitol past the Washington Monument.

After church, Barack and I headed to the White House to join up with Joe and Jill, along with President Bush, Vice President Dick Cheney, and their wives, all of us gathering for coffee and tea before motorcading together to the Capitol for the swearing in. At some point earlier, Barack had received the authorization codes that would allow him to access the country's nuclear arsenal and a briefing on the protocols for using them. From now on, wherever he went, he'd be closely trailed by a military aide carrying a forty-five-pound briefcase containing launch authentication codes and sophisticated communications devices, often referred to as the nuclear football. That, too, was heavy.

For me, the ceremony itself would become another one of those strange, slowed-down experiences so enormous I couldn't fully process what was going on. We were ushered to a private room in the Capitol ahead of the ceremony so that the girls could have a snack and Barack could take a few minutes with me to practice putting his hand on the small red Bible that had belonged 150 years earlier to Abraham Lincoln. At that same moment, many of our friends, relatives, and colleagues were finding their seats on the platform outside. It occurred to me later that this was probably the first time in history that so many people of color had sat before the public and a global television audience, acknowledged as VIPs at an American inauguration.

Barack and I both knew what this day represented to many Americans, especially those who'd been a part of the civil rights movement. He'd made a point of including the Tuskegee Airmen, the history-making African American pilots and ground crews who fought in World War II, among his guests. He'd also invited the group known as the Little Rock Nine, the nine Black students who in 1957 had been among the first to test the Supreme Court's *Brown v. Board of Education* decision by enrolling at an all-white high school in Arkansas, enduring many months of cruelty and abuse in the name of a higher principle. All of them were senior citizens now, their hair graying and shoulders curving, a sign of the decades they'd lived and maybe also the weight they'd carried for future generations. Barack had often said that he aspired to climb the steps of the White House because the Little Rock Nine had dared to climb the steps of Central High School. Of every legacy we belonged to, this was perhaps the most important.

Almost exactly at noon, we stood before the country with our two girls. I remember really only the smallest things—how brightly the sun fell across Barack's forehead just then, how a respectful hush came over the crowd as the Supreme Court chief justice, John Roberts, began the proceedings. I remember how Sasha, too small for her presence to register amid a sea of adults, stood proudly on a footstool in order to stay visible. I remember the crispness of the air. I lifted Lincoln's Bible, and Barack placed his left hand on it, vowing to protect the U.S. Constitution and solemnly agreeing to take on the country's every concern. It was weighty and at the same time it was joyful, a feeling mirrored in the inaugural speech Barack would then deliver.

"On this day," he said, "we gather because we have chosen hope over fear, unity of purpose over conflict and discord."

I saw that truth mirrored again and again in the faces of the people who stood shivering in the cold to witness it. There were people in every direction, as far back as I could see. They filled every inch of the National Mall and the parade route. I felt their support for our family. We were making a pact, all of us. You've got us; we've got you.

I WAS PROUD that Malia and Sasha were quickly learning what it meant to be watched publicly.

We climbed into the presidential limo and began our slow crawl to the White House, leading the inaugural parade. I marveled at how our daughters had managed themselves perfectly throughout the inauguration, never fidgeting, slouching, or forgetting to smile. We still had many thousands of people watching from the sides of the road and on television as the motorcade made its way up Pennsylvania Avenue, though the darkened windows made it difficult for anyone to see inside. When Barack and I stepped out to walk a short stretch of the parade route and wave to the public, Malia and Sasha stayed behind inside the warm cocoon of the moving limo. It seemed to hit them then that they were finally relatively alone and out of sight.

By the time Barack and I climbed back in, the two girls were breathless and laughing, having released themselves from all ceremonial dignity. They'd shucked off their hats and messed up each other's hair and were engaged in a sisterly tickle fight. Tired out, finally, they sprawled across the seats and rode the rest of the way with their feet kicked up, blasting Beyoncé on the car stereo as if it were just any old day.

Barack and I both felt a kind of sweet relief just then. We were the First Family now, but we were also still ourselves.

As the sun began to set on Inauguration Day, the air temperature dropped further. Barack and I spent the next two hours in an outdoor reviewing stand in front of the White House, watching bands and floats from all fifty states pass by us on Pennsylvania Avenue. It was so cold that at some point, I stopped feeling my toes, even after someone passed me a blanket to wrap around my legs and feet. It was nearly 7:00 p.m. when the last marching band finished and Barack and I walked into the White House, arriving for the first time as residents. Over the course of the afternoon, the staff whisked the Bushes' belongings out and our belongings in. The carpets had been steamed to help keep Malia's allergies from being activated by traces of the former president's dogs. Furniture was brought in and arranged, floral decorations set out. By the time we rode the elevator upstairs, our clothes were organized neatly in the closets; the kitchen pantry had been stocked with our favorite foods. The White House butlers who staffed the residence, mostly African American men who were our age or older, stood poised to help us with anything we needed.

We were due at the first of ten inaugural balls in less than an hour. I remember seeing very few people upstairs beyond the butlers, who were strangers to me. I remember, in fact, feeling a little lonely as I moved down a long hallway, past a bunch of closed doors. For the last two years, I'd been constantly surrounded by people, with Melissa, Katie, and Kristen always right by my side. Now, suddenly, I felt very much on my own. The kids had already headed to another part of the house for their evening of fun. My mom, Craig, and Maya were staying with us but had been packed into cars and shuttled off already to the night's festivities. A hairdresser waited to style me; my gown hung on a rack. Barack had disappeared to take a shower and put on his tux.

It had been an incredible, symbolic day for our family and I hoped for the country, but it was also a kind of ultramarathon. I had only about five minutes alone to soak in a warm bath and get ready for what came next. I'd have my hair touched up and makeup redone, and then I'd slip into the ivory silk chiffon gown I'd picked for the night ahead, specially made for me by a young designer named Jason Wu. The dress had a single shoulder strap and delicate organza flowers sewn across it, each one with a tiny crystal at its center, and a full skirt that cascaded richly to the floor.

In my life so far, I'd worn very few gowns, but Jason Wu's creation performed a little miracle, making me feel soft and beautiful, transforming me if not into a full-blown ballroom princess, then at least into a woman capable of climbing onto another stage. I was now FLOTUS—First Lady of the United States—to Barack's POTUS. It was time to celebrate.

That night, Barack and I went to the Neighborhood Ball, the first inaugural ball ever to be broadly accessible and affordable to the general public and where Beyoncé—real-life Beyoncé—sang a stunning, full-throated rendition of the R&B classic "At Last," which we'd chosen as our "first dance" song. From there, we moved on to a Home States Ball and after that to the Commander in Chief Ball, then onward to the Youth Ball, and six more beyond that. Our stay at each one was relatively brief and pretty much exactly the same: A band played "Hail to the Chief," Barack made a few remarks, we tried to beam our appreciation to those who'd come, and as everyone stood and watched, we slow danced yet another time to "At Last."

I held on to my husband each time, my eyes finding the calm in his. We were still the same duo we'd been for twenty years now and still connected by a grounding love, our different personalities balancing each other. This was one thing I was always content to show.

As the hour got late, however, I could feel myself starting to sag.

The best part of the evening was supposed to be what came last— a private party being held for a couple hundred of our friends back at the White House. It was there that we'd finally be able to let down and stop worrying about how we appeared. For sure, I'd be taking off my shoes.

It was close to 2:00 a.m. by the time we got ourselves there. Barack and I walked across the marble floors leading to the East Room to find the party in full swing, drinks flowing and elegantly dressed people swirling beneath the sparkling chandeliers. Wynton Marsalis and his band were playing jazz on a small stage at the back of the room. I saw friends from nearly every phase of my life—Princeton friends, Harvard friends, Chicago friends, family members galore. These were the people I wanted to laugh with, to say, *How did we all get here?*

But I was done. I'd hit a final fence line. I was also thinking ahead, knowing that the next morning—really just a matter of hours from now—we'd be going to the National Prayer Service and after that we'd stand and greet two hundred members of the public who were coming to visit the White House. Barack looked at me, reading my thoughts. "You don't need to do this," he said. "It's okay."

Partygoers were moving toward me now, eager to interact. Here came a donor. Here was the mayor of a big city. "Michelle! Michelle!" people were calling. I was so exhausted I thought I might cry.

As Barack stepped into the room, I froze for a split second, then turned and fled. I had no energy left to make excuses or even wave to my friends. I walked quickly away over the thick red carpet, ignoring the agents who trailed behind me, ignoring everything as I found the elevator to the residence and took myself there—down an unfamiliar hallway and into an unfamiliar room, out of my shoes and out of my gown and into our strange new bed.

20

PEOPLE ASK WHAT IT'S LIKE TO LIVE IN THE WHITE House. I sometimes say that it's a bit like what I imagine living in a fancy hotel might be like, only the fancy hotel has no other guests in it—just you and your family. There are fresh flowers everywhere, with new ones brought in almost every day. The building feels old and a little intimidating. The walls are so thick and the floors so solid that sound gets absorbed quickly. The windows are grand and tall and also fitted with bomb-resistant glass, kept shut at all times for security reasons, which further adds to the stillness. The place is kept perfectly clean. There's a staff made up of ushers, chefs, housekeepers, florists, and also electricians, painters, and plumbers, everyone coming and going politely and quietly, doing their best to keep a low profile, waiting until you've moved out of a room before slipping in to change the towels or put a fresh flower in the little vase at the side of your bed.

The rooms are big, all of them. Even the bathrooms and closets are bigger than anything I'd ever experienced. Our bedroom had not just a beautiful four-poster bed with a canopy overhead, but also a fireplace and a sitting area, with a couch, a coffee table, and a couple of upholstered chairs. There were five bathrooms for the five of us living in the residence, plus another ten spare bathrooms to go with them. I had a closet connected to a spacious dressing room—the same room from which Laura Bush had shown me the Rose Garden view. This became my private office, the place where I could sit quietly and read, work, or watch TV, dressed in a T-shirt and a pair of sweatpants, blessedly out of sight of everyone.

I understood how lucky we were to be living this way. The master suite in the residence was bigger than the entire upstairs apartment my family had shared when I was growing up on Euclid Avenue. There was a painting by a famous French artist hanging outside my bedroom door and a bronze sculpture in our dining room. I was a child of the South Side, now raising daughters who slept in rooms designed by a decorator and who could custom order their breakfast from a chef.

I had these thoughts sometimes, and they made me dizzy.

I tried, in my way, to loosen the formalities of the place. I made it clear to the housekeeping staff that our girls would make their own beds every morning. I told Malia and Sasha to act as they'd always acted—to be polite and gracious and to not ask for anything more than what they absolutely needed or couldn't get for themselves. But it was important to me that our daughters continue to feel free to act like kids despite the formality of the place. *Yes, you can throw balls in the hallway,* I told them. *Yes, you can rummage through the pantry looking for snacks.* I made sure they knew they didn't have to ask permission to go outside and play. I was heartened one afternoon during a snowstorm when I caught sight of the two of them through the window, sledding on the slope of the South Lawn, using plastic trays lent to them by the kitchen staff.

The truth was that the girls and I were supporting players; we benefitted because our happiness was tied to Barack's. We were protected for one reason, which was that if we were not safe, he would be distracted and unable to lead the nation. Everything about how the

White House works, one learns, is designed to increase the well-being, efficiency, and overall power of one person—and that's the president. Barack was now surrounded by people whose job was to treat him like a precious gem. It sometimes felt like a throwback to older times, when a household revolved solely around the man's needs. This was the opposite of what I wanted our daughters to think was normal. Barack, too, was uncomfortable with the attention, though he had little control over all the fuss.

He now had about fifty staffers reading and answering his mail. He had Marine helicopter pilots to fly him anywhere he needed to go, and a team that organized thick briefing books so he could stay current on the issues and make educated decisions. He had a crew of chefs looking after his nutrition, and grocery shoppers who made sure our food was safe by making anonymous runs to stores, picking up supplies without ever revealing whom they worked for.

As long as I've known him, Barack has never enjoyed shopping, cooking, or home maintenance of any kind. He's not someone who keeps power tools in the basement or shakes off work stress by making a fancy meal or trimming hedges. Not having to worry about any domestic chores made him happy, if only because it allowed his brain to focus on bigger, more important things.

Most amusing to me was the fact that he now had three personal military valets whose duties included standing watch over his closet, making sure his shoes were shined, his shirts pressed, his gym clothes always fresh and folded. Life in the White House was very different from life in the Hole.

"You see how neat I am now?" Barack said to me one day as we sat at breakfast, his eyes showing amusement. "Have you looked in my closet?"

"I have," I said, smiling back. "And you get no credit for any of it."

.   .   .

IN HIS FIRST month in office, Barack signed the Lilly Ledbetter Fair Pay Act, which helped protect workers from wage discrimination based on gender, race, or age. He ordered the end of the use of torture in interrogations and pushed a major bill through Congress that would help the economy. To me, he seemed to be on a roll. The changes he'd promised were becoming real.

As an added bonus, he was showing up for dinner on time.

For me and the girls, this was the happy shift that came from living in the White House with the president of the United States instead of in Chicago with a dad who served in some faraway senate and was often out campaigning for higher office. We had access, at long last, to Dad. His life was more orderly now. He worked a ridiculous number of hours, as he always had, but at 6:30 p.m. sharp he'd get on the elevator and ride upstairs to have a family meal, even if he often had to go right back down to the Oval Office afterward. My mom sometimes joined us for dinner, too, though she'd fallen into her own routine. She'd come down to say hello before accompanying Malia and Sasha to school but mostly chose to leave us alone in the evenings. Instead, she'd eat dinner upstairs in the solarium next to her bedroom while *Jeopardy!* was on. Even when we asked her to stay, she'd usually wave us off. "You all need your time," she'd say.

For the first few months in the White House, I felt the need to be watchful over everything. One of my earliest lessons was that it could be costly to live there. While we stayed rent-free and had our utilities and staffing paid for, we had to cover all other living expenses, which seemed to add up quickly, especially given the fancy-hotel quality of everything. We got an itemized bill each month for every food item and roll of toilet paper. We paid for every guest who came for an overnight stay or joined us for a meal. I had to keep a close eye on the food we ate, because if Barack ever casually said that he liked the taste of some exotic fruit at breakfast or the sushi on his dinner plate, the kitchen staff took note and put those foods on the menu regularly.

Only later, inspecting the bill, would we realize that some of these items were being flown in at great expense from overseas.

Most of my watchfulness in those early months, though, was focused on Malia and Sasha. I paid attention to their moods, quizzing them on their feelings and how they were getting along with other children. I tried not to overreact anytime they reported making a new friend, though inwardly I was thrilled. I understood by now that there was no straightforward way to arrange playdates at the White House or outings for the kids, but slowly we were figuring out a system.

I was allowed to use a personal phone but had been advised to limit my contacts to only about ten of my closest friends—the people who loved and supported me unconditionally. Most of my communications were managed by Melissa, who was now my deputy chief of staff and knew my life better than anyone. She kept track of all my cousins, all my college friends. We gave out her phone number and email address instead of mine, directing all requests to her. Old acquaintances and distant relatives were surfacing from nowhere with a flood of questions. Could Barack speak at somebody's graduation? Could I please give a speech for somebody's nonprofit? Would we come to this party or that fund-raiser? Most of it was good-hearted, but it was too much for me to absorb all at once.

When it came to the day-to-day lives of our girls, I often had to rely on young staffers to help. My team met early on with teachers and administrators at Sidwell, recording important dates for school events and answering questions from teachers. As the girls began making social plans outside school, my personal assistant collected the phone numbers of other parents, organizing pickups and drop-offs for playdates. Just as I always had in Chicago, I made a point of trying to get to know the parents of the girls' new friends, inviting a few moms over for lunch and introducing myself to others during school events. These interactions could be awkward. I knew it sometimes took a minute for new acquaintances to move past whatever they thought they knew about me and Barack from TV or the news, and to see me simply, if possible, as Malia's or Sasha's mom.

It was awkward to explain to people that before Sasha could come to little Julia's birthday party, the Secret Service would need to stop by and do a security sweep. It was awkward to require Social Security numbers from any parent or caregiver who was going to drive a kid over to our house to play. It was all awkward, but it was all necessary. I didn't like that there was this strange little divide to be crossed anytime I met someone new, but I was relieved to see that it was far different for Sasha and Malia, who went dashing outside to greet their school friends as they got dropped off at the White House, grabbing them by the hand and running giggling inside. Kids care about fame, it turns out, for only a few minutes. After that, they just want to have fun.

PART OF BEING First Lady involved hosting traditional parties and dinners, beginning with the Governors' Ball in February. The same went for the annual Easter Egg Roll, an outdoor family celebration that had been started in 1878 and involved thousands of people. There were also springtime luncheons I would attend in honor of congressional and Senate spouses—similar to the one where I'd seen Laura Bush smiling so unflappably while having an official photo taken with every single guest.

For me, these events could feel like distractions from what I hoped would be more impactful work, but I also started thinking about ways I could update them. I was thinking that life in the White House could be modernized without losing any of its established history and tradition. Over time, Barack and I would take steps in this direction, hanging more abstract art and works by African American artists on the walls and mixing contemporary furniture in with the antiques. In the Oval Office, Barack swapped out a bust of Winston Churchill and replaced it with a bust of Martin Luther King Jr. And we gave the tuxedoed White House butlers the option of dressing more casually on days when there were no public events, introducing a khaki and golf shirt option.

Barack and I knew we wanted to make the White House more open. When we hosted an event, I wanted everyday people to show up, not just those used to fancy attire. And I wanted more kids around, because kids made everything better. I hoped to make the Easter Egg Roll open to more people—adding more slots for city schoolchildren and military families to go with the tickets guaranteed to the children and grandchildren of members of Congress and other VIPs. Lastly, if I was going to sit and lunch with the spouses of the House and the Senate, couldn't I also invite them to join me out in the city for a community service project?

I knew what mattered to me. I didn't want to be some sort of well-dressed ornament who showed up at parties and ribbon cuttings. I wanted to do things that were purposeful and lasting. My first real effort, I decided, would be the garden.

I was not a gardener and never had been in my life, but thanks to Sam Kass and our family's efforts to eat better at home, I knew that strawberries were at their most juicy in June, that darker-leaf lettuces had the most nutrients, and that it wasn't so hard to make kale chips in the oven. I saw my daughters eating things like spring pea salad and cauliflower mac and cheese and understood that until recently most of what we knew about food had come through food-industry advertising of everything boxed, frozen, or otherwise processed for convenience. Nobody, really, was out there advertising the fresh, healthy stuff—the satisfying crunch of a fresh carrot or the sweetness of a tomato plucked right off the vine.

Planting a garden at the White House was my response to this problem, and I hoped it would signal the start of something bigger. Barack's administration was focused on helping people get affordable health care, and for me the garden was a way to offer a similar message about healthy living. I saw it as an early test of what I might be able to accomplish as First Lady. I thought of the garden as a kind of outdoor classroom, a place kids could visit to learn about growing food.

But there was more to it than that. I planned to use the work we did in the garden to spark a conversation about nutrition, about how food was produced, labeled, and marketed and the ways that was affecting people's health. I especially wanted these topics to be discussed at schools and among parents, and I knew that speaking on these topics from the White House would challenge big food and beverage companies to change the way they'd been doing business for decades.

The truth was, I really didn't know how any of it would go over. But as I directed Sam, who'd joined the White House staff, to begin taking steps to create the garden, I knew I was ready to find out.

My optimism in those first months was dampened by one thing, and that was politics. We lived in Washington now, right up close to the ugly Republican-versus-Democrat dynamic I'd tried for years to avoid, even as Barack had chosen to work inside it. Now that he was president, these forces all but ruled his every day. Weeks earlier, before the inauguration, the conservative radio host Rush Limbaugh announced, "I hope Obama fails." I'd watched with dismay as Republicans in Congress fought Barack's every effort to fix the economic crisis, refusing to support policies that would cut taxes and save or create millions of jobs. On the day he took office, the American economy was collapsing as fast as or faster than it had at the onset of the Great Depression. Nearly 750,000 jobs had been lost that January alone. And while Barack had campaigned on the idea that it was possible to build agreement between parties, that Americans were at heart more united than divided, the Republican Party was making a deliberate effort, in a time of dire national emergency no less, to prove him wrong.

This was on my mind during the evening of February 24, when Barack addressed a joint session of Congress. The event is meant to give any newly inaugurated president a chance to explain their goals for the coming year in a speech televised live and delivered in the hall of the House of Representatives with Supreme Court justices, cabinet members, military generals, and members of Congress present. By tradition, lawmakers dramatically express their approval or disapproval of the president's ideas by either leaping to their feet in repeat standing ovations or remaining seated and sullen.

I took my seat that evening in the balcony between a fourteen-year-old who'd written a heartfelt letter to her president and a gracious veteran of the Iraq war, all of us waiting for my husband to arrive. From where I sat, I could see most of the room below. It was an unusual, bird's-eye view of our country's leaders, an ocean of whiteness and maleness dressed in dark suits. The absence of diversity was glaring—honestly, it was embarrassing—for a modern, multicultural country. It was most dramatic among the Republicans. At the time, there were just seven nonwhite Republicans in Congress—none of them African American and only one a woman. Overall, four out of five members of Congress were male.

A few minutes later, the spectacle began with a thunderclap—the beating of a gavel and the call of the sergeant at arms. The crowd stood, applauding for more than five minutes straight as elected leaders jostled for position. At the center of the storm, surrounded by a knot of security agents and a backward-walking videographer, was Barack, shaking hands and beaming as he slowly made his way through the room and toward the podium.

Something about seeing my husband down there amid the crush of lawmakers and security made the size and difficulty of the job suddenly very real, especially because he'd need to win over more than half of Congress to get anything done.

Barack's speech that night was detailed and sober-minded, acknowledging all the challenges the nation faced, including the bad economy, wars, and possible terrorist attacks. He was careful to be realistic but also to sound notes of hope, reminding his listeners of our resilience as a nation, our ability to rebound after tough times.

I watched from the balcony as Republican members of Congress stayed seated through most of it, appearing stubborn and angry, their arms folded and their frowns deliberate, looking like children who hadn't gotten their way. They would fight everything Barack did, I realized, whether it was good for the country or not. More than anything, it seemed they just wanted Barack to fail. I confess that in that moment, I did wonder whether there was any path forward.

WHEN I WAS A GIRL, I had vague ideas about how my life could be better. I'd go over to play at the Gore sisters' house and envy the fact that their family had a whole house to themselves. I wished my family could afford a nicer car. I couldn't help but notice who among my friends had more bracelets or Barbies than I did, or who got to buy their clothes at the mall instead of having a mom who sewed everything on the cheap at home. As a kid, you learn to measure and make comparisons long before you understand the size or value of anything. Eventually, if you're lucky, you learn that you've been measuring all wrong.

We lived in the White House now. Very slowly, it was starting to feel familiar. Not because I'd ever grow used to how big and luxurious everything was, but because this was where my family slept, ate, laughed, and lived. In the girls' rooms we'd put on display the growing collections of trinkets that Barack would bring home from his various travels—snow globes for Sasha, key chains for Malia. We began to make small changes to the residence, adding modern lighting and scented candles that made the place feel more like home. I would never take our good fortune or comfort for granted, though what I began to appreciate more was the humanity of the place.

Even my mom, who'd fretted about the museum-like formality of the White House, soon learned that there was more there than it first appeared. The place was full of people not all that different from us. A number of the butlers had worked for many years in the White House, tending to every family that came through. Their quiet dignity reminded me of my great-uncle Terry, who'd lived downstairs when I was growing up on Euclid Avenue, mowing our lawn in dress shoes and suspenders. I tried to make sure that our interactions with staff were respectful and positive. I wanted to make sure they never felt invisible. They were careful to respect our privacy, but also were always open and welcoming, and gradually we became close. They instinctively sensed when to give me some space or when I could stand some gentle ribbing. Often they were talking trash about their favorite sports teams in the kitchen, where they liked to fill me in on the latest staff gossip or the exploits of their grandchildren as I looked over the morning headlines. If there was a college basketball game playing on the TV in the evening, Barack came in sometimes to join them for a little while to watch. Sasha and Malia came to love the welcoming spirit of the kitchen, slipping in to make smoothies or pop popcorn after school. Many of the staff took a special shine to my mom, stopping in to catch up with her upstairs.

It took some time for me to be able to recognize the voices of the different White House phone operators who gave me wake-up calls in the morning or connected me with the East Wing offices downstairs, but soon they, too, became familiar and friendly. We'd chat about the weather, or I'd joke about how I often had to be roused hours earlier than Barack to have my hair done ahead of official events. These interactions were quick, but in some small way they made life feel a little more normal.

One of the more experienced butlers, a white-haired African American man named James Ramsey, had served since the Carter administration forty years ago. Every so often, he'd hand me the latest copy of *Jet* magazine, smiling proudly and saying, "I got you covered, Mrs. Obama." Life was better, always, when we could measure the warmth.

I'D BEEN WALKING around thinking that our new house was big and grand to the point of being over the top, but then in April I went to England and met Her Majesty the Queen.

This was the first international trip Barack and I made together since the election, flying to London on Air Force One so that he could attend a meeting of world leaders. It was Barack's first big international meeting since he became president, and his main job was to clean up a mess, in this case absorbing the frustration of other world leaders who felt the United States had missed important opportunities to prevent the economic disaster all of them were now dealing with.

Beginning to feel more confident that Sasha and Malia were comfortable in their routines at school, I'd left my mom in charge for the few days I'd be abroad, knowing that she'd immediately relax all my regular rules about getting to bed early and eating every vegetable served at dinner. My mom loved being a grandmother, especially the part where she got to throw over all my rules in favor of her own looser and lighter style. Her way of caring for kids was much more relaxed than when Craig and I were little, and the girls were always thrilled to have Grandma in charge.

Britain's prime minister was hosting the meetings that Barack was attending, but the Queen would also have everyone over to Buckingham Palace for a ceremonial hello. Because of America and Great Britain's close relationship and also, I suppose, because we were new, Barack and I were invited to arrive at the palace early for a private audience with the Queen.

I had no experience meeting royalty. I knew that I could either curtsy or shake the Queen's hand. I knew that we were to refer to her as "Your Majesty," while her husband, Prince Philip, the Duke of Edinburgh, went by "Your Royal Highness." Other than that, I wasn't sure what to expect as our motorcade rolled through the tall iron gates at the entrance to the palace, past onlookers pressed at the fences, past a collection of guards and a royal horn player, through an interior arch and up to the courtyard, where the official master of the household waited outside to greet us.

It turns out that Buckingham Palace is big—so big that it almost defies description. It has 775 rooms and is fifteen times the size of the White House. In the years to come, Barack and I would be lucky enough to return there a few times as invited guests. On our later trips, we'd sleep in a luxurious bedroom suite on the ground floor of the palace, looked after by liveried footmen and ladies-in-waiting. We'd attend a formal banquet in the ballroom, eating with forks and knives coated in gold. At one point, as we were given a tour, we were told things like "This is our Blue Room," our guide gesturing into a vast hall that was five times the size of our Blue Room back home. The Queen's head usher one day would take me, my mom, and the girls through the palace Rose Garden, which contained thousands of flaw-lessly blooming flowers and occupied nearly an acre of land, making the few rosebushes we so proudly kept outside the Oval Office suddenly seem a tad less impressive. I found Buckingham Palace breathtaking and incomprehensible at the same time.

On that first visit, we were escorted to the Queen's private apart-ment and shown into a sitting room where she and Prince Philip stood waiting to receive us. Queen Elizabeth II was eighty-two years old then, extremely small and graceful with a delicate smile and her white hair curled regally away from her forehead. She wore a pale pink dress and a set of pearls and kept a black purse draped properly over one arm. We shook hands and posed for a photo. The Queen politely inquired about our jet lag and invited us to sit down.

Sitting with the Queen, I had to will myself to stop focusing on the splendor of the setting and the awe I felt coming face-to-face with an honest-to-goodness icon. I'd seen Her Majesty's face dozens of times before, in history books, on television, and on currency, but here she was in the flesh, giving me her full attention and asking questions. She was warm and personable, and I tried to be the same. The Queen was as human as the rest of us. I liked her immediately.

Later that afternoon, Barack and I floated around at the palace reception, eating canapés with the other world leaders and their spouses. I chatted with the chancellor of Germany and the president of France. I met the king of Saudi Arabia, the president of Argentina, the prime ministers of Japan and Ethiopia. I did my best to remember who came from which nation and which spouse went with whom, careful not to say too much for fear of getting anything wrong. Overall, it was a dignified, friendly affair and a reminder that even heads of state are capable of talking about their children and joking about the British weather.

At some point toward the end of the party, I turned my head to find that Queen Elizabeth had appeared at my elbow, the two of us suddenly alone together in the otherwise crowded room. She was wearing a pair of pristine white gloves and appeared just as fresh as she'd been hours earlier when we first met. She smiled up at me.

"You're so tall," she remarked, cocking her head.

"Well," I said, chuckling, "the shoes give me a couple of inches. But yes, I'm tall."

The Queen then glanced down at the pair of black high heels I was wearing. She shook her head.

"These shoes are unpleasant, are they not?" she said. She gestured with some frustration at her own black dress shoes.

I confessed then to the Queen that my feet were hurting. She confessed that hers hurt, too. We looked at each other then with identical expressions, like, *When is all this standing around with world leaders going to finally wrap up?* And with this, she busted out with a fully charming laugh.

Forget that she sometimes wore a diamond crown and that I'd flown to London on the presidential jet; we were just two tired ladies whose feet hurt. I then did what's instinctive to me anytime I feel connected to a new person, which is to express my feelings outwardly. I laid a hand affectionately across her shoulder.

I couldn't have known it in the moment, but this would become a big deal. I'd touched the Queen of England, which I'd soon learn was *not done*. Our interaction was caught on camera, and in the coming days it would be shown again and again in media reports all over the world: "A Breach in Protocol!" "Michelle Obama Dares to Hug the Queen!" It revived some of the campaign-era speculation that I was improper and lacking the standard elegance of a First Lady, and I worried that I'd possibly distracted from Barack's efforts abroad. But I tried not to let the criticism upset me. If I hadn't done the proper thing at Buckingham Palace, I had at least done the human thing. I reckon that the Queen was okay with it, too, because when I touched her, she only pulled closer, resting a gloved hand lightly on the small of my back.

The following day, while Barack attended meetings, I went to visit a school for girls. It was a government-funded, inner-city school, not far from a set of council estates, which is what public-housing projects are called in England. More than 90 percent of the school's nine hundred students were Black or from an ethnic minority; a fifth of them were the children of immigrants or asylum seekers. I was drawn to it because it was a diverse school with not much money and yet had been recognized as academically outstanding. I also wanted to make sure that when I visited a new country as First Lady, I really visited it— meaning that I'd have a chance to meet the people who actually lived there, not just those who governed them. Doing that would allow me to find new ways to bring a little extra warmth to those otherwise staid visits. I aimed to do it with every foreign trip, beginning in England.

I wasn't fully prepared, though, to feel what I did when I set foot inside the Elizabeth Garrett Anderson School and was led to an auditorium where about two hundred students had gathered to watch some of their classmates perform and then hear me speak. The school was named after a pioneering doctor who also became the first female mayor elected in England. The building itself was nothing special—a boxy brick building on a normal-looking street. But as I settled into a folding chair onstage and started watching the performance—which included a Shakespeare scene, a modern dance, and a chorus singing a beautiful rendition of a Whitney Houston song—something inside me began to quake. I almost felt myself falling backward into my own past.

You had only to look around at the faces in the room to know that despite their strengths these girls would need to work hard to be seen. There were girls in *hijab,* girls for whom English was a second language, girls whose skin made up every shade of brown. I knew they'd have to push back against the stereotypes that would get put on them, all the ways they'd be defined before they'd had a chance to define themselves. They'd need to fight the invisibility that comes with being poor, female, and of color. They'd have to work to find their voices and not be diminished, to keep themselves from getting beaten down. They would have to work just to learn.

But their faces were hopeful, and now so was I. For me it was a strange, quiet revelation: They were me, as I'd once been. And I was them, as they could be. The school was filled with the energy and power of nine hundred girls striving.

When the performance was done and I went to the microphone to speak, I could barely contain my emotion. I had prepared a speech, but suddenly it didn't seem right. Looking up at the girls, I just began to talk, explaining that though I had come from far away, carrying this

Our daughters grew up during our time in the White House. This was Sasha's eleventh birthday, one of the eight birthdays she celebrated during Barack's presidency.
→

Hugs are my favorite way to simply connect, like here with the girls from London's Elizabeth Garrett Anderson School.
←

I loved the White House garden because it helped promote nutrition and healthy living, but also because it's where I could get my hands dirty with kids as we rooted around in the soil.
→

I am so inspired by the
optimism and sacrifice of
military service members
and their families.

A hug is not always enough. Life can be unfair, like for Cleopatra Cowley-Pendleton, who lost her daughter, Hadiya, to gun violence in Chicago.

←

I greeted the girls when they came back from school nearly every day.

→

We usually stayed out of Barack's way at work, but we surprised him in the Oval Office on his birthday.

←

Our dogs, Bo (pictured here) and Sunny, always brightened our days.
←

We're deeply grateful to all of the White House staff who supported us for eight years. We celebrated a lot of milestones together, like the birthday of assistant usher Reggie Dixon.
→

We tried to maintain a sense of normalcy in our lives and always showed up for our girls, like when Malia, Barack, and I cheered on Sasha's basketball team, the Vipers.
←

The girls relax on Bright Star, the call sign for the First Lady's plane.

→

↑

We made sure our girls had the opportunity to do standard teenage things, like learning to drive a car, even if it meant having driving lessons with the Secret Service.

↑

The Fourth of July always gives us a lot to celebrate, since it's also Malia's birthday.

We joined the late congressman John Lewis and other civil rights leaders for the fiftieth anniversary of the March across the Edmund Pettus Bridge in Selma, Alabama. Being at the site of the infamous civil rights conflict reminded me how far our country has come, and how far we still have to go, to achieve equality.

↓

↑

Being the First
Family came with
unique privileges
and challenges,
but through it all,
we stayed true to
ourselves.

strange title of First Lady of the United States, I was more like them than they knew. That I, too, was from a working-class neighborhood, raised by a family of modest means and loving spirit, that I'd realized early on that school was where I could start defining myself—that an education was a thing worth working for, that it would help spring them forward in the world.

At this point, I'd been First Lady for just over two months. At times, I'd felt overwhelmed by the pace, unworthy of the glamour, anxious about our children, and uncertain of my purpose. There are pieces of public life, of giving up one's privacy to become a walking, talking symbol of a nation, that can feel like they're stripping away part of your identity. But here, finally, speaking to those girls, I felt something completely different and pure—a fitting together of my old self with this new role. *Are you good enough? Yes, you are, all of you.* I told the students of Elizabeth Garrett Anderson that they'd touched my heart. I told them that they were precious, because they truly were. And when my talk was over, I did what was instinctive. I hugged absolutely every single girl I could reach.

BACK IN WASHINGTON, spring had arrived. The sun came up earlier and stayed out a little longer each day. I watched as the slope of the South Lawn gradually turned a lush green. My staff and I had spent the past two months working to turn my idea for a garden into reality, which hadn't been easy. For one thing, we'd had to persuade the National Park Service and the White House grounds team to tear up a patch of one of the most famous lawns in the world. The very suggestion had been met with resistance, but eventually we got our way.

Several days after I returned from Europe, I hosted a group of students from Bancroft Elementary School, a local bilingual school. Weeks earlier, we'd used shovels and hoes to prepare the soil. The same kids were back to help me do the planting. Our patch of dirt sat not far from the southern fence where tourists often gathered to gaze up at the White House. I was glad that this would now be a part of their view.

Or at least I hoped to be glad at some point. Because with a garden you never know for sure what will or won't happen—whether anything, in fact, will grow. "Honestly," I'd said to Sam before anyone arrived that morning to watch the planting, "this better work."

That day, I knelt with a bunch of fifth graders as we carefully put seedlings into the ground, patting the dirt into place around the fragile stalks. The kids asked me questions, some about vegetables and the tasks at hand, but also things like "Where's the president?" and "How come he's not helping?" It took only a little while before most of them seemed to lose track of me, their focus centered instead on the fit of their garden gloves and the worms in the soil. I loved being with children. It was, and would be throughout the entirety of my time in the White House, a way to escape my First Lady worries. Kids made me feel like myself again. To them, I was just a nice, kinda-tall lady.

As the morning went on, we planted lettuce and spinach, fennel and broccoli. We put in carrots and collard greens and onions and shell peas. We planted berry bushes and a lot of herbs. What would come from it? I didn't know, the same way I didn't know what lay ahead for us in the White House, nor what lay ahead for the country or for any of these sweet children surrounding me. All we could do then was put our faith into the effort, trusting that with sun and rain and time, something half-decent would push up through the dirt.

21

ONE SATURDAY EVENING AT THE END OF MAY, BARACK took me out on a date. In the four months since becoming president, he'd been spending his days working on ways to fulfill the promises he made to voters during the campaign. Now he was making good on a promise to me. We were going to New York, to have dinner and see a show.

For years in Chicago, our date nights had been an important part of every week, an activity we protected no matter what. I love talking to my husband across a small table in a low-lit room. I always have, and I expect I always will. Barack is a good listener, patient and thoughtful. I love how he tips his head back when he laughs. I love the lightness in his eyes, the kindness at his core. Having an unrushed meal together has always been a way for us to be reminded of the excitement we felt during that first hot summer when we met.

I dressed up for our New York date, putting on a black cocktail dress and lipstick, styling my hair in an elegant updo. I felt a fluttering excitement at the prospect of a getaway, of time alone with my husband. In the last few months, we'd hosted dinners and gone to performances together, but it was almost always in an official capacity and with lots of other people. This was to be a true night off.

Barack had dressed in a dark suit with no tie. We kissed the girls and my mom good-bye and walked hand in hand across the South Lawn and climbed onto Marine One, the presidential helicopter, which took us to Andrews Air Force Base. We next boarded a small Air Force plane, flew to JFK Airport, and were then helicoptered into Manhattan. Our movements had been planned meticulously in advance by our scheduling teams and the Secret Service to maximize efficiency and security.

Barack had chosen a small, tucked-away restaurant near Washington Square Park that he knew I'd love for its emphasis on locally grown foods. As we motorcaded the last stretch of the journey from the helipad to Greenwich Village, I noted the lights of the cop cars being used to barricade the cross streets, feeling a twinge of guilt at the traffic problems we were causing.

At the restaurant, we were shown to a table in a quiet corner of the room as around us people tried not to stare at us. But there was no hiding our arrival. Anyone who came in after we did would have to get swept with a security wand by a Secret Service team, a process that was usually quick but still an inconvenience. For this, I felt another twinge.

Our conversation stayed light. Four months into our lives as president and First Lady, we were still figuring out how our new identities would change our life together. These days, there was almost no part of Barack's complicated life that didn't in some way impact mine—his team's decision to schedule a foreign trip during the girls' summer vacation, for example, or whether my chief of staff was being listened to at morning staff meetings in the West Wing, the part of the White House where the president's office is. But I tried in general to avoid discussing these things at dinner, doing what I could to keep White

House business out of our personal time, not just this night, but every night.

Sometimes Barack wanted to talk about work, though more often than not he avoided it. So much of his job was just plain grueling, the challenges huge and often seemingly impossible to resolve. Anytime old friends came to visit us at the White House, they were amused by the intensity with which both Barack and I quizzed them about their jobs, their kids, their hobbies, anything. The two of us were always less interested in talking about the complexities of our new existence and more interested in sponging up bits of gossip and everyday news from home. Both of us craved glimpses of regular life.

That evening in New York, we ate and talked in the candlelight, enjoying the feeling that we'd stolen away. The White House is a remarkably beautiful and comfortable place, a fortress disguised as a home, and from the point of view of the Secret Service agents tasked with protecting us, it would probably be ideal if we never left its grounds. We respected the watchfulness, but it could feel like a form of confinement. I struggled sometimes, trying to balance my needs with what was convenient for others. If anyone in our family wanted to step outside onto the Truman Balcony—the lovely terrace that overlooked the South Lawn, and the only semiprivate outdoor space we had at the White House—we needed to first alert the Secret Service so that they could shut down the street that was in view of the balcony, clearing out the flocks of tourists who gathered there at all hours of the day and night to look at the White House. There were many times when I thought I'd go out to sit on the balcony, but then reconsidered, realizing the hassle I would cause, the vacations I'd be interrupting, all because I thought it would be nice to have a cup of tea outdoors.

Setting aside the business of the country, Barack and I never lacked for things to discuss. We talked that night over dinner about Malia's flute lessons and Sasha's ongoing devotion to her Blankie, which she kept draped over her head as she slept at night. When I told a funny story about how a makeup artist recently tried and failed to put false eyelashes on my mom before a photo shoot, Barack tipped his head and laughed, exactly the way I knew he would. And we had a new and entertaining family member to discuss, an energetic, seven-month-old Portuguese water dog we'd named Bo. He was a fulfillment of the promise we'd made to the girls during the campaign and was hypoallergenic so he wouldn't trigger Malia's allergies. The girls had taken to playing hide-and-seek with him on the South Lawn, crouching behind trees and shouting his name as he scampered across the open grass, following their voices. All of us loved Bo.

When we finished our meal and stood up to leave, the diners around us rose to their feet and applauded, which struck me as both kind and unnecessary. It's possible that some of them were glad to see us go.

As our motorcade zipped up Sixth Avenue to take us to see a play, I felt acutely how our mere presence was disrupting people's normal lives. When we got to the theater, our fellow theatergoers were now waiting in line to pass through metal detectors that normally weren't there and the performers would need to wait an extra forty-five minutes to start the show due to the security checks. The play, when it finally began, was marvelous—a drama by August Wilson set during the Great Migration, when millions of African Americans left the South and flooded into the Midwest, just as my relatives on both sides had done. Sitting in the dark next to Barack, I was spellbound, a little emotional, and for a short while able to get lost in the performance and the sense of quiet contentment that came with just being off duty and out in the world.

As we flew back to Washington late that night, I already knew it would be a long time before we did anything like this again. Barack's political opponents would criticize him for taking me to New York to see a show, saying that our date had been extravagant and costly. I was reminded that the critics would always be there. The Republicans would never let up. Optics would always rule our lives.

With our date Barack and I had proven that we *could* step away for a romantic evening the way we used to, years earlier, before his political life took over. We could, as First Couple, feel close and connected, enjoying a meal and a show in a city we both loved. The harder part was feeling that we had been a little selfish in making that choice, knowing that our date night had required hours of advance meetings between security teams and local police. It had involved extra work for our staffers, for the theater, for the waiters at the restaurant, for the people who had been stuck in traffic due to our motorcade. It was part of the new heaviness we lived with. There were just too many people involved, too many affected, for anything to feel light.

FROM THE TRUMAN BALCONY, I could see the fullness of the garden taking shape. For me, it was a rewarding sight—half-grown shoots, carrot and onion stalks just beginning to rise, the patches of spinach dense and green, with bright red and yellow flowers blooming around the edges. We were growing food.

In late June, our original garden-helper crew from Bancroft Elementary joined me for our first harvest, kneeling together in the dirt to tear off lettuce leaves and strip pea pods from their stems. This time they were also entertained by Bo, our puppy, bounding in circles around the trees before sprawling belly-up in the sun between the raised beds.

After our harvest, Sam and the schoolkids made salads with their fresh-picked lettuce and peas in the kitchen, which we then ate with baked chicken, followed by cupcakes topped with garden berries. In ten weeks, the garden had generated over ninety pounds of produce—from only about $200 worth of seeds and mulch.

The garden was popular and the garden was wholesome, but I also knew that for some people it wouldn't feel like enough. I understood that I was being watched with anticipation, especially by women, maybe especially by professional working women, who wondered whether I'd set aside my education and management experience to fit the mold of a traditional First Lady who just hosted tea parties and chose fancy linens. People seemed worried that I wasn't going to show my full self.

Regardless of what I chose to do, I knew I was bound to disappoint someone. The campaign had taught me that my every move and facial expression would be read a dozen different ways. Some people would continue to see me as hard-driving and angry. Feminists would see my garden and messages about healthy eating as evidence that I was not using my power and my voice fully or loudly enough. Several months before Barack was elected, I'd told a magazine interviewer that my primary focus in the White House would be to continue my role as "mom in chief" in our family. I'd said it casually, but the phrase caught hold and was spread widely by the media. Some Americans embraced it, understanding the amount of organization and drive it takes to raise children. Others, meanwhile, seemed horrified, thinking that as First Lady I'd do nothing but pipe-cleaner craft projects with my kids.

The truth was, I intended to do everything—to work with purpose and parent with care—same as I always had. The only difference now was that a lot of people were watching.

My preferred way to work, at least at first, was quietly. I wanted to be methodical in putting together a larger plan, waiting until I had full confidence in what I was presenting before going public with any of it. The interest and enthusiasm we'd generated with the garden—the positive news coverage, the letters pouring in from around the country— only confirmed for me that I could generate buzz around a good idea. Now I wanted to highlight a larger issue and push for larger solutions.

At the time Barack took office, nearly a third of American children were overweight or obese. Over the previous three decades, rates of childhood obesity had tripled. More kids were being diagnosed with high blood pressure and type 2 diabetes. Military leaders were reporting that obesity was one of the most common disqualifiers for service.

The problem was woven into every aspect of family life, from the high price of fresh fruits to cuts in funding for sports and recreation programs in public schools. TV, computers, and video games competed for kids' time, and in some neighborhoods staying indoors felt like a safer choice than going outside to play, as Craig and I had done when we were kids. Many families didn't have grocery stores in their neighborhoods, or had trouble finding and affording fresh fruits and vegetables. Meanwhile, portion sizes at restaurants were increasing. Advertising slogans for sugary cereal, microwavable convenience foods, and supersized everything were downloaded directly into the minds of children watching cartoons.

I knew that if I were to try to declare war on sugary drinks marketed to kids, it would likely be opposed not just by the big beverage companies but also by farmers who supplied the corn used in many sweeteners. If I were to advocate for healthier school lunches, I'd put myself on a collision course with the big corporations that often dictated what food ended up on a fourth grader's tray at the cafeteria.

Still, it felt to me like the right time to push for change. I was neither the first nor the only person to be drawn to these issues. Across America, a growing healthy food movement was gaining strength. Urban farmers were experimenting in cities across the country. Republicans and Democrats alike had tackled the problem in states and towns, investing in healthy living, building more sidewalks and community gardens—proof that there was common ground to be explored.

My small team and I began meeting with experts to formulate a plan. We decided to keep our work focused on children because it's tough to get grown-ups to change their habits. We felt certain we'd stand a better chance if we tried to help kids think differently about food and exercise from an early age. And who could take issue with us if we were genuinely looking out for kids?

My own kids were out of school for the summer. I'd committed myself to spending three days a week working as First Lady while reserving the rest of my time for family. Rather than put the girls in day camps, I decided to run what I called Camp Obama, where we'd invite a few friends and make local excursions, getting to know the area in which we now lived. We went to Monticello and Mount Vernon and explored caves in the Shenandoah Valley. We visited the Bureau of Engraving and Printing to see how dollars got made and toured Frederick Douglass's house in the southeast part of Washington, learning how an enslaved person could become a scholar and a hero. For a while, I required the girls to write up a little report after each visit, summarizing what they had learned, though eventually they started protesting and I let the idea go.

As often as we could, we scheduled these outings for first thing in the morning or late in the day so that the Secret Service could secure an area without causing too much of a hassle. We were still a nuisance, I knew, but when it came to the girls, I tried to let go of any guilt. I wanted our kids to be able to move with the same kind of freedom that other kids had. One day, earlier in the year, I'd had a dustup with the Secret Service when Malia had been invited to join a group of school friends who were making a spur-of-the-moment trip to get some ice cream. Because for security reasons she wasn't allowed to ride in another family's car, Malia was told she'd have to wait an hour while the leader of her security detail was summoned, which of course then delayed everyone involved.

This was exactly the kind of heaviness I didn't want for my daughters. I couldn't contain my irritation. To me, it made no sense.

"This isn't how families work or how ice cream runs work," I said. "If you're going to protect a kid, you've got to be able to move like a kid." I insisted that the agents revise their procedures so that in the future Malia and Sasha could leave the White House safely and without some massive advance planning effort. Barack and I had by now let go of the idea that we could be spontaneous. We'd surrendered to the idea that there was no longer room for impulsiveness and playfulness in our own lives. But for our girls, we'd fight to keep that possibility alive.

SOMETIME DURING BARACK'S campaign, people had begun paying attention to my clothes. Or at least the media paid attention, which led fashion bloggers to pay attention, which seemed then to provoke all manner of commentary across the internet. I don't know why this was, exactly—possibly because I'm tall and unafraid of bold patterns—but so it seemed to be.

Everything I wore got reported in the news. When I wore flats instead of heels, it got reported in the news. My pearls, my belts, my cardigans, my dresses, my choice of white for an inaugural gown— all seemed to trigger an avalanche of opinions and instant feedback. I wore a sleeveless dress to Barack's address to the joint session of Congress and for my official White House photo, and suddenly my arms were making headlines. When we went on a family trip in the Grand Canyon, I was criticized when I was photographed getting off Air Force One (in 106-degree heat, I might add) dressed in a pair of shorts. It sometimes seemed that my clothes mattered more to people than anything I had to say. In London, I'd been moved to tears while speaking to the girls at the Elizabeth Garrett Anderson School, only to learn that the first question asked by a reporter covering the event had been "Who made her dress?"

This stuff got me down, but I tried to see it as an opportunity to learn and find power inside a situation I'd never have chosen for myself. If people flipped through a magazine primarily to see the clothes I was wearing, I hoped they'd also see the military spouse standing next to me or read what I had to say about children's health. I even agreed to appear on the cover of *Vogue,* because it mattered every time a woman of color showed up on the cover of a magazine. Also, I insisted on choosing my own outfits, wearing dresses by young and diverse designers like Jason Wu and Narciso Rodriguez, a gifted Latino designer, for photo shoots.

I knew a little about fashion, but not a lot. As a working mom, I'd really been too busy to put much thought into what I wore. During the campaign, I'd done most of my shopping at a boutique in Chicago where I'd had the good fortune of meeting a young sales associate named Meredith Koop. Meredith was sharp and knowledgeable about different designers and had a playful sense of color and texture. After Barack's election, I was able to persuade her to move to Washington and work with me as a personal aide and wardrobe stylist. Very quickly, she also became a trusted friend.

A couple of times a month, Meredith would roll several big racks of clothing into my dressing room in the residence, and we'd spend an hour or two trying things on, pairing outfits with whatever was on my schedule in the coming weeks. I paid for all my own clothes and accessories—with the exception of some items like the fancy gowns I wore to formal events, which were lent to me by the designers and would later be donated to the National Archives. When it came to my choices, I tried to be somewhat unpredictable, to prevent anyone from reading any sort of message into what I wore. It was a thin line to walk. I was supposed to stand out without overshadowing others, to blend in but not fade away. As a Black woman, too, I knew I'd be criticized if I was perceived as being showy and high end, and I'd be criticized also if I was too casual. So I mixed it up. I'd match a high-end Michael Kors skirt with a T-shirt from Gap. I wore something from Target one day and Diane von Furstenberg the next. I wanted to draw attention to and celebrate American designers, most especially those who were less well known. For me, my choices were simply a way to use all the attention I received to boost a diverse set of up-and-comers.

It required time, thought, and money—more money than I'd spent on clothing ever before—to make sure my outfits were always appropriate. It also required careful research by Meredith, particularly on foreign trips. She'd spend hours making sure the designers, colors, and styles we chose paid proper respect to the people and countries we visited. Meredith also shopped for Sasha and Malia ahead of public events, which added to the overall expense, but they, too, had the public gaze upon them. I sighed sometimes, watching Barack pull the same dark suit out of his closet and head off to work without even needing a comb. His biggest fashion consideration for a public moment was whether to have his suit jacket on or off. Tie or no tie?

We were careful, Meredith and I, to always be prepared. In my dressing room, I'd put on a new dress and then squat, lunge, and pinwheel my arms, just to be sure I could move. When I traveled, I brought backup outfits, anticipating shifts in weather and schedule, not to mention nightmare scenarios involving spills or broken zippers. I learned, too, that it was important to always pack a dress suitable for a funeral, because Barack sometimes got called with little notice to be there as soldiers, senators, and world leaders were laid to rest.

I came to depend heavily on Meredith but also equally on Johnny Wright, my fast-talking, hard-laughing hurricane of a hairdresser, and Carl Ray, my soft-spoken and meticulous makeup artist. Together, the three of them gave me the confidence I needed to step out in public each day, all of us knowing that a slipup would lead to a flurry of ridicule and nasty comments. I never expected to be someone who hired others to maintain my image, and at first the idea made me uncomfortable. But I quickly found out a truth that no one talks about: Today, virtually every woman in public life—politicians, celebrities, you name it—has some version of Meredith, Johnny, and Carl. It's all but a requirement, a built-in fee for the way women are judged by their appearance more than men.

DURING THAT FIRST year in the White House, I found myself picking up books either by or about previous First Ladies, but each time I'd lay them down again. I almost didn't want to know what was the same and what was different about any of us.

I did, in September, have a pleasant overdue lunch with Hillary Clinton in the residence dining room. We discussed what she had experienced when she was First Lady. She was honest with me about how she'd misjudged the country's readiness to have a proactive professional woman in the role of First Lady. As First Lady of Arkansas, Hillary had kept her job as a lawyer while also helping with her husband's efforts to improve health care and education. When her husband was elected president, she came to Washington with the same desire and energy to contribute, but she had been criticized for taking on an active role in the White House's work on health-care reform. The message had been delivered loud and clear: Voters had elected her husband and not her. First Ladies had no place in the West Wing. She'd tried to do too much too quickly, it seemed, and had run straight into a wall.

I myself tried to be mindful of that wall, taking care not to get directly involved with West Wing business. I relied instead on my staff to communicate daily with Barack's, exchanging advice and reviewing our schedules and plans. His advisers in my opinion could be overly fretful about appearances. At one point, when I decided to get bangs cut into my hair, my staff would feel the need to first run the idea past Barack's staff, just to make sure there wouldn't be a problem.

Almost a year into Barack's presidency, the economy was still struggling. I knew from experience that even during hard times, maybe especially during hard times, it was still okay to laugh. You had to find ways to have fun. On this front, my team had been clashing with Barack's communications staff over an idea I'd had to host a Halloween party for kids at the White House. Barack's staff thought it would be seen as too showy and expensive. "The optics are just bad" was how they put it. This meant it wouldn't look good to the public when so many families were facing hard times. I disagreed, arguing that a Halloween party for local kids and military families who'd never seen the White House before was a perfectly appropriate use for a tiny slice of our entertaining budget.

At some point his team stopped fighting our idea. At the end of October, to my great delight, a thousand-pound pumpkin sat on the White House lawn. A brass band of skeletons played jazz music, while a giant black spider descended from the North Portico. I stood in front of the White House, dressed as a leopard—in black pants, a spotted top, and a pair of cat ears on a headband—as Barack, who was never much of a costume guy even before optics mattered, stood next to me in a humdrum sweater. That night, we handed out bags of cookies, dried fruits, and M&M's in a box emblazoned with the presidential seal as more than two thousand little princesses, grim reapers, pirates, superheroes, ghosts, and football players traipsed up the lawn to meet us. As far as I was concerned, the optics were just right.

THE GARDEN CHURNED through the seasons, teaching us all sorts of things. We grew cantaloupes that turned out pale and tasteless. Rainstorms washed away our topsoil. Birds snacked on our blueberries. Beetles went after the cucumbers. If something went wrong, we made small adjustments and carried on. Our dinners in the residence now often included broccoli, carrots, and kale grown on the South Lawn. We started donating a portion of every harvest to Miriam's Kitchen, a local nonprofit that served the homeless. We began to pickle vegetables and present them as gifts to visiting dignitaries, along with jars of honey from our new beehives. Among the staff, the garden became

315

a source of pride. Its early doubters had quickly become fans. For me, the garden was simple, abundant, and healthy—a symbol of diligence and faith. It was beautiful while also being powerful. And it made people happy.

Over the previous few months, my staff and I had spoken with children's health experts to help us develop our efforts into something bigger. We'd give parents better information to help them make healthy choices for their families. We'd work to create healthier schools. We'd try to improve access to nutritious food. And we'd find more ways for young people to be physically active. Knowing that the way we introduced our initiatives would matter, my communications team worked to make the campaign look fun. All the while, Barack's staff was apparently fretting about my plans, worried I'd come off as a know-it-all at a time when Americans were suspicious of anything that looked like the government was telling them what to do.

My goal was to make this about more than government. When it came to the way families actually lived, I wanted to speak directly to moms, dads, and especially kids.

I did interviews with health magazines geared toward parents and kids. I hula-hooped on the South Lawn to show that exercise could be fun and made a guest appearance on *Sesame Street*, talking about vegetables with Elmo and Big Bird. Anytime I spoke to reporters from the White House garden, I mentioned that many Americans had trouble finding fresh produce in their communities and spoke about the health-care costs connected to rising obesity levels. To make sure we had buy-in from everyone we'd need to make the initiative a success, we spent weeks and weeks quietly holding meetings with different groups to perfect our plan and message.

In February 2010, I was finally ready to share my vision. On a cold Tuesday afternoon, I stood in the State Dining Room at the White House, surrounded by kids and government officials, sports figures and mayors, along with leaders in medicine, education, and food production, plus the media, to proudly announce our new initiative. We'd decided to name it Let's Move! It centered on one goal—ending the childhood obesity epidemic within a generation.

What was important to me was that we weren't just announcing some pie-in-the-sky set of wishes. The effort was real, and the work was well under way. Barack had signed a memo earlier that day to create a new task force on childhood obesity. The three major corporate suppliers of school lunches had announced that they would cut the amount of salt, sugar, and fat in the meals they served. The American Beverage Association had promised to label its ingredients more clearly. We'd encouraged pediatricians to regularly measure body mass index, which determined whether a person's weight fell within a healthy range for their height and age. We'd persuaded Disney, NBC, and Warner Bros. to air public service announcements and invest in special programming that encouraged kids to make healthy lifestyle choices. Leaders from professional sports leagues had agreed to promote a 60 Minutes of Play a Day campaign to help get kids moving more.

And that was just the start. We had plans to help bring green-grocers into urban neighborhoods and rural areas known as "food deserts" due to the lack of stores selling healthy food. We'd also push for more accurate nutritional information on food packaging. Along the way, we'd work to hold businesses responsible for their decisions that impacted children's health.

It would take commitment and organization to make all this happen, I knew, but that was exactly the kind of work I liked. We were taking on a huge issue, but now as First Lady I was operating from a huge platform. I was beginning to realize that all the things that felt odd to me about my new existence—the strangeness of fame, the hawkeyed attention paid to my image, the vagueness of my job description— could be used in service of real goals. I was energized. Here, finally, was a way to show my full self.

22

ONE SPRING MORNING, BARACK AND THE GIRLS AND I were summoned downstairs from the residence to the South Lawn. A man I'd never seen before stood waiting for us in the driveway. He had a friendly face and a salt-and-pepper mustache that gave him an air of dignity. He introduced himself as Lloyd.

"Mr. President, Mrs. Obama," he said. "We thought you and the girls might like a little change of pace, and so we've arranged a petting zoo for you." He smiled broadly at us. "Never before has a First Family participated in something like this."

The man gestured to his left and we looked. About thirty yards away, lounging in the shade of the cedar trees, were four big, beautiful cats. There was a lion, a tiger, a sleek black panther, and a slender, spotted cheetah. From where I stood, I could see no fences or chains. There seemed to be nothing penning them in. It all felt odd to me. Most certainly a change of pace.

"Thank you. This is so thoughtful," I said, hoping I sounded gracious. "Am I right—Lloyd, is it?—that there's no fence or anything? Isn't that a little dangerous for kids?"

"Well, yes, of course, we thought about that," Lloyd said. "We figured your family would enjoy the animals more if they were roaming free, like they would in the wild. So we've sedated them for your safety. They're no harm to you." He gave a reassuring wave. "Go ahead, get closer. Enjoy!"

Barack and I took Malia's and Sasha's hands and made our way across the still-dewy grass. The animals were larger than I expected, their tails flicking as they watched us approach. I'd never seen anything like it, four cats in a companionable line. The lion stirred slightly as we drew closer. I saw the panther's eyes tracking us, the tiger's ears flattening just a little. Then, without warning, the cheetah shot out from the shade with blinding speed, rocketing right at us.

I panicked, grabbing Sasha by the arm, sprinting with her back up the lawn toward the house, trusting that Barack and Malia were doing the same. I heard the animals leap to their feet and come after us.

Lloyd stood in the doorway, looking unfazed.

"I thought you said they were sedated!" I yelled.

"Don't worry, ma'am," he called back. "We've got a plan for exactly this scenario!" Secret Service agents swarmed past him, carrying what looked to be guns loaded with tranquilizer darts. Just then, I felt Sasha slip out of my grasp.

I turned back toward the lawn, horrified to see my family being chased by wild animals and the wild animals being chased by agents, who were firing their guns.

"This is your plan?" I screamed. *"Are you kidding me?"*

Just then, the cheetah let out a snarl and launched itself at Sasha, its claws out, its body seeming to fly. An agent took a shot, missing the animal but scaring it enough to make it retreat. I was relieved for a split second, but then I saw it—a white-and-orange tranquilizer dart lodged in Sasha's right arm.

I lurched upward in bed, heart hammering, my body soaked in

sweat, only to find my husband curled in comfortable sleep beside me. I'd had a very bad dream.

I CONTINUED TO feel as if we were falling backward, our whole family in a giant trust fall. I had confidence in all the support we had in the White House, but still I could feel vulnerable, knowing that everything from the safety of our daughters to the planning of my movements lay almost entirely in the hands of other people. Growing up on Euclid Avenue, I'd been taught that self-sufficiency was everything. I'd been raised to handle my own business, but now that seemed almost impossible. Things got handled for me. Before I traveled, staffers drove the routes I'd take, timing my travel down to the minute, scheduling my bathroom breaks in advance. Agents took my girls to playdates. Housekeepers collected our laundry. I no longer drove a car or carried cash or house keys. Aides took phone calls, attended meetings, and drafted statements on my behalf.

All of this was marvelous and helpful, freeing me up to focus on the things I felt were most important. But occasionally it left me—a detail person—feeling as if I'd lost control of the details. Which is when the lions and cheetahs started to lurk.

There was also much that couldn't be planned for. When you're married to the president, you come to understand quickly that the world is full of chaos, that disasters happen without notice, disrupting whatever calm you might feel. The news could never be ignored: An earthquake devastates Haiti. A mechanical problem on an underwater oil rig off the coast of Louisiana sends millions of barrels of crude oil gushing into the Gulf of Mexico. Revolution stirs in Egypt. A gunman opens fire in the parking lot of an Arizona supermarket, killing six people and seriously injuring a U.S. congresswoman.

I read a set of news clips sent by my staff each morning and knew that Barack would have to respond to every new development. He'd be blamed for things he couldn't control, pushed to solve frightening problems in faraway nations. His job was to take the chaos and somehow turn it into calm leadership. Every day of the week, every week of the year.

I tried as best I could not to let the uncertainties of the world impact my day-to-day work as First Lady, but sometimes there was no getting around it. How Barack and I behaved in the face of instability mattered. We understood that we represented the nation and it was up to us to model reason, compassion, and consistency and be present when there was tragedy, or hardship, or confusion. After the Louisiana oil spill—the worst in U.S. history—had finally been contained, we made a family trip to Florida, during which Barack took Sasha for a swim to show everyone that it was safe to return to the Gulf of Mexico for vacations. It was a small gesture, but the message was bigger: *If he trusts the water, then so can you.* When we traveled somewhere after a tragedy, it was often to remind Americans not to look too quickly past the pain of others. I tried to highlight the efforts of relief workers, educators, or community volunteers—anyone who gave more when things got rough. When an earthquake struck Haiti, Jill Biden and I visited a group of local artists who were doing art therapy with displaced children. Despite the heart-wrenching devastation around them and their losses, and thanks to the adults around them, the children still bubbled with hope.

Grief and resilience live together. I learned this not just once as First Lady but many times over.

As often as I could, I visited military hospitals where American troops were recovering from the wounds of war. The first time I went to Walter Reed National Military Medical Center, I was scheduled to be there for ninety minutes, but instead I ended up staying about four hours.

Walter Reed tended to injured service members who were evacuated out of Iraq and Afghanistan. Some troops stayed only a few days, while others were there for months. The hospital employed top-notch military surgeons and offered excellent rehabilitation services, geared to handle the most devastating of battlefield injuries.

As much as I tried to prepare for everything in life, there was no preparing for the interactions I had with wounded veterans and their families. As I've said before, I grew up knowing little about the military. My dad had spent two years in the Army, but that was well before I was born. Until Barack started campaigning, I'd had no exposure to the orderly bustle of an Army base or the modest homes that housed service members with families. War, for me, had always been terrifying but also distant. War had involved places I couldn't imagine and people I didn't know. To view it this way, I see now, had been a luxury.

When I arrived at a hospital, I was usually met by a nurse, handed a set of scrubs to wear, and told to sanitize my hands each time I entered a room. Before opening a new door, I'd get a quick briefing on the service member and his or her situation. A few patients would decline to meet me, possibly because they weren't feeling well enough or maybe for political reasons. Either way, I understood. The last thing I wanted to be was a burden.

My visits to each room were as short or long as the service member wanted them to be. Every conversation was private, with no media or staff observing. The mood was sometimes somber, sometimes light. We'd talk about sports, or our home states, or our children. Or Afghanistan and what had happened to them there. We sometimes discussed what they needed and also what they didn't need, which—as they'd often tell me—was anyone's pity.

At one point, I encountered a piece of red poster board taped to a doorway, with a message written in black marker that seemed to say it all:

ATTENTION TO ALL THOSE WHO ENTER HERE:
If you are coming into this room with sorrow or to feel sorry for my wounds, go elsewhere. The wounds I received, I got in a job I love, doing it for people I love, supporting the freedom of a country I deeply love. I am incredibly tough and will make a full recovery.

This was resilience. It was reflective of a larger spirit of self-sufficiency and pride I'd seen in all parts of the military. I sat one day with a man who'd gone off young and healthy to an overseas mission, leaving behind a pregnant wife, and had come back quadriplegic, unable to move his arms or legs. As we talked, their baby—a tiny newborn with a pink face—lay swaddled in a blanket on his chest. I met another service member who'd had a leg amputated and asked me a lot of questions about the Secret Service. He explained cheerily that he'd once hoped to become an agent after leaving the military, but that given the injury he was now figuring out a new plan.

Then there were the families. I introduced myself to the wives and husbands, moms and dads, cousins and friends I found by the bedside, people who had often put the rest of their lives on hold in order to stay close to their loved one. Sometimes they were the only ones I could talk to, as their loved one lay nearby, heavily sedated or asleep. These family members carried their own weight. Some came from generations of military service, while others were teenage girlfriends who'd become brides just ahead of a deployment—their futures now having taken a sudden, complicated turn. I can no longer count the number of moms with whom I've cried, their sadness so deep that all we could do was lace our hands together and pray silently through tears.

What I saw of military life left me humbled. As long as I'd been alive, I'd never encountered the kind of strength and loyalty that I found in those rooms.

One day at a military hospital in San Antonio, Texas, I noticed a commotion in the hallway. Nurses shuffled urgently in and out of the room I was about to enter. "He won't stay in bed," I heard someone whisper. Inside, I found a broad-shouldered young man from rural Texas who had multiple injuries and whose body had been severely burned. He was in agony, tearing off the bedsheets and trying to slide his feet to the floor.

It took us all a minute to understand what he was doing. Despite his pain, he was trying to stand up and salute the wife of his commander in chief.

SOMETIME EARLY IN 2011, Barack mentioned the name "Osama bin Laden." We'd just finished dinner and Sasha and Malia had run off to do their homework, leaving the two of us alone in the residence dining room.

"We think we know where he is," Barack said. "We may go in and try to take him out, but nothing's sure."

Bin Laden was the brain behind the 9/11 terrorist attacks on America and the world's most wanted man. Capturing or killing him had been one of Barack's top priorities when he took office. I knew it would mean something to the nation, especially to the military service members who'd spent years trying to protect us from al-Qaeda and to all those who'd lost loved ones on September 11.

I could tell from Barack's grim tone that the decision about what to do weighed heavily on him, though I knew better than to ask too many questions. I knew that he now spent his days surrounded by expert advisers and had access to all kinds of top-secret information, and as far as I was concerned, he needed no input from me. In general, I hoped that time with me and the girls would always be a break from the stress, even though work was forever close by.

Barack has always been good at setting aside his work to be present and undistracted when he was with us. It was something we'd learned together over time as our work lives had grown increasingly busy and intense. Fences needed to go up; boundaries required protecting. Bin Laden was not invited to dinner, nor was the humanitarian crisis in Libya, nor were the Tea Party Republicans. We had kids, and kids need room to speak and grow. Our family time was when we put aside our big worries so that the small could rightly take over. Barack and I would sit at dinner, hearing tales from the school playground or listening to the details of Malia's research project on endangered animals, feeling as if these were the most important things in the world. Because they were. They deserved to be.

Even as we ate, the work piled up. Part of the White House ritual was that two binders got delivered every evening, one for me and a much thicker, leather-bound one for Barack. Each contained papers from our offices, which we were expected to read overnight.

After we tucked the kids into bed, Barack would normally disappear into the Treaty Room with his binder, while I took mine to the sitting area in my dressing room, where I'd spend an hour or two each night or early in the morning going through what was inside.

A year after launching Let's Move!, we were seeing results. We'd helped install six thousand salad bars in school cafeterias and were recruiting local chefs to help schools serve meals that were not just healthy but tasty. Walmart had joined our effort by pledging to cut the amount of sugar, salt, and fat in its food products and to reduce prices on produce. And we'd enlisted mayors from five hundred cities and towns across the country to commit to tackling childhood obesity.

Most important, over the course of 2010, I'd worked hard to help push a new child nutrition bill through Congress. The bill would expand children's access to healthy, high-quality food in public schools. As much as I was generally happy to stay out of politics and policy making, this had been my big fight—the issue for which I was willing to hurl myself into the ring. I'd spent hours making calls to senators and representatives, trying to convince them that our children deserved better than what they were getting. I'd talked about it endlessly with Barack, his advisers, anyone who would listen. The new law added more fresh fruits and vegetables, whole grains, and low-fat dairy to roughly forty-three million meals served daily. It limited the junk food that got sold to children in vending machines on school property and gave money to schools to establish gardens and use locally grown produce. Barack and his advisers pushed hard for the bill, too. After Republicans won control of the House of Representatives in the midterm elections, he made the effort a priority in his dealings with lawmakers. In early December the bill was officially passed. I stood proudly next to Barack eleven days later as he signed it into law, surrounded by children at a local elementary school.

As with the garden, I was trying to grow something—a chorus of voices speaking up for children and their health. I saw my work as complementing Barack's success in establishing the 2010 Affordable Care Act, which greatly increased access to health insurance for all Americans. And I was now also focused on getting a new effort called Joining Forces off the ground—this one in collaboration with Jill Biden, whose son Beau had recently returned safely from military service in Iraq. This work, too, would serve to support Barack's duties as commander in chief.

Knowing that we owed more to our service members and their families than just thank-yous, Jill and I had been collaborating to come up with specific ways to support the military community. Barack had kicked things off earlier in the year by asking each government agency to find new ways to support military families. I reached out to the country's most powerful CEOs, getting them to agree to hire a significant number of veterans and military spouses. Jill would get pledges from colleges and universities to train teachers and professors to better understand the needs of military children. We also wanted to fight the shame surrounding the mental health issues that followed some of our troops home, and planned to encourage writers and producers in Hollywood to include military stories in their movies and TV shows.

The issues I was working on weren't simple, but still they were manageable in ways that much of what kept my husband at his desk at night was not. As had been the case since I first met him, nighttime was when Barack could think without distraction. If he got hungry, a valet would bring him a small dish of figs or nuts. He was no longer smoking, thankfully, though he'd often chew a piece of nicotine gum. Most nights of the week, he stayed at his desk until 1:00 or 2:00 in the morning, reading memos, rewriting speeches, and responding to email while ESPN played low on the TV. He always took a break to come kiss me and the girls good night.

I was used to it by now—his devotion to the never-finished task of governing. For years, the girls and I had shared Barack with his constituents, and now there were more than 300 million of them. Leaving him alone in the Treaty Room at night, I wondered sometimes if they had any sense of how lucky they were.

The last bit of work he did, usually at some hour past midnight, was to read letters from American citizens. Since the start of his presidency, Barack had asked his staff to include ten letters or messages from constituents inside his briefing book, selected from the roughly fifteen thousand letters and emails that poured in daily. He read each one carefully, jotting responses in the margins so that a staffer could prepare a reply or forward a concern on to a cabinet secretary. He read letters from soldiers. From prison inmates. From cancer patients struggling to pay health-care premiums and from people who'd lost their homes to foreclosure. From gay people who hoped to be able to legally marry and from Republicans who felt he was ruining the country. From moms, grandfathers, and young children. He read letters from people who appreciated what he did and from others who wanted to let him know he was an idiot.

He read all of it, seeing it as part of the responsibility that came with the oath. He had a hard and lonely job—the hardest and loneliest in the world, it often seemed to me—but he knew that he had an obligation to listen to the concerns of all the American people.

ON MONDAY and Wednesday evenings, Sasha, who was now ten, had swim-team practice. I went sometimes to watch her do her workouts, trying to slip unnoticed into the small room next to the pool where parents could sit and observe practice through a window.

Navigating a busy athletic facility during peak workout hours posed a challenge for the agents on my security detail, but they managed it well. For my part, I'd become an expert at walking quickly and lowering my gaze when passing through public spaces, which helped keep things efficient. I zipped past university students busy with their weight workouts and Zumba classes in full swing. Sometimes nobody seemed to notice. Other times, I'd feel the disturbance without even needing to look up, aware of the ripple I caused as people murmured or occasionally just shouted, "Hey, that's Michelle Obama!" But it was never more than a ripple and it happened quickly. I was like an apparition, there and gone before the sight had really registered.

On practice nights, the seats by the pool were generally empty, aside from a handful of other parents chatting as they waited for their kids to be done. I'd find a quiet spot, sit down, and focus on the swimming.

I loved any time I could glimpse my daughters in their own worlds—free from the White House, free from their parents, in the spaces and relationships they'd forged for themselves. Sasha was a strong swimmer, enthusiastic about breaststroke and intent on mastering the butterfly. She wore a navy-blue swim cap and a one-piece bathing suit and motored through her laps, stopping once in a while to take advice from the coaches, chatting merrily with her teammates during the prescribed breaks.

For me, there was nothing more enjoyable than sitting barely noticed by the people around me and witnessing the miracle of a girl—our girl—growing independent and whole. We had thrust our daughters into all the strangeness and intensity of White House life, not knowing how it would impact them or what they'd take from the experience. I tried to make our daughters' exposure to the wider world as positive as possible, realizing that Barack and I had a unique opportunity to show them history up close. When Barack had foreign trips that coincided with school vacations, we traveled as a family. We'd brought them on trips that included visits to the Kremlin in Moscow and the Vatican in Rome. They'd met the Russian president, toured the Pantheon and the Roman Colosseum, and passed through the "Door of No Return" in Ghana, the departure point for untold numbers of Africans who'd been sold into slavery.

I was learning that each child took in what she could and from her own perspective. Sasha had returned home from our summer travels to start third grade. Walking around her classroom at parents' night that fall, I'd come across a short "What I Did on My Summer Vacation" essay she'd written, hanging alongside those of her classmates on one of the walls. "I went to Rome and I met the Pope," Sasha had written. "He was missing part of his thumb."

I could not tell you what Pope Benedict XVI's thumb looks like, whether some part of it isn't there. But we'd taken an observant, matter-of-fact eight-year-old to Rome, Moscow, and Accra, and this is what she'd brought back. Her view of history was, at that point, waist-high.

As much as we tried to create a buffer between the girls and the more complicated aspects of Barack's job, I knew that Sasha and Malia still had a lot to take in. They were living with world events in a way that few children did, living with news occasionally happening right under our roof. They were living with the fact that their dad got called away sometimes for national emergencies, and that always and no matter what there'd be some people who criticized and opposed him. This feeling of threat reminded me of my dream in which the lions and cheetahs were very close by.

Over the course of the winter of 2011, the reality-show host and New York real-estate developer Donald Trump was beginning to make noise about possibly running for the Republican presidential nomination in 2012. Mostly, it seemed Trump was just making noise in general, yammering uninformed criticisms of Barack and openly questioning whether he was even an American citizen. During the previous presidential campaign, some people had started a false rumor that Barack's Hawaiian birth certificate was a hoax and that he'd in fact been born in Kenya. These people became known as "birthers." and Trump was now making increasingly outlandish claims on television, insisting that the 1961 Honolulu newspaper announcements of Barack's birth were fake and that none of his kindergarten classmates remembered him. All the while, news outlets—particularly the more conservative ones—were gleefully repeating his groundless claims.

The whole thing was crazy and mean-spirited, of course. The birthers hardly concealed their racism and xenophobia, a fear of foreigners. But it was also dangerous, deliberately meant to stir up the wingnuts and kooks. I feared the reaction of people who believed these lies. The Secret Service occasionally told me about the more serious threats that came in and I tried not to worry, but sometimes I couldn't help it. What if someone with an unstable mind loaded a gun and drove to Washington? What if that person went looking for our girls? Donald Trump, with his loud and reckless claims, was putting my family's safety at risk. And for this, I'd never forgive him.

We had little choice, though, but to push the fears away and to simply live. The people who tried to define us as different or as "other" had been doing so for years already. We did everything we could to rise above their lies, trusting that the way Barack and I lived our lives would show people the truth about who we really were. I'd lived with well-intentioned concerns for our safety since almost the day Barack first decided to run for president. "We're praying nobody hurts you," people used to say, clasping my hand at campaign events. I'd heard it from people of all races, all backgrounds, all ages—a reminder of the goodness and generosity that existed in our country. "We pray for you and your family every day."

I kept their words with me. I felt the protection of those millions of decent people who prayed for our safety. Barack and I both relied on our personal faith as well. We went to church only rarely now, mostly because it had become such a spectacle, with reporters shouting questions as we walked in to worship. Ever since the scrutiny of our former pastor the Reverend Jeremiah Wright had become an issue in Barack's first presidential campaign, ever since opponents had tried to use faith as a weapon—suggesting that Barack was a "secret Muslim"— we'd made the choice to exercise our faith privately and at home. We prayed each night before dinner and organized a few sessions of Sunday school at the White House for our daughters. We didn't join a church in Washington, because we didn't want to subject another congregation to the kind of attacks that had rained down on our church in Chicago. It was a sacrifice, though. I missed the warmth of a spiritual community. Every night, I'd look over and see Barack lying with his eyes closed on the other side of the bed, quietly saying his prayers.

Months after the birther rumors picked up steam, on a Friday night in November, a man parked his car on Constitution Avenue and started firing a semiautomatic rifle out the window, aimed at the top floors of the White House. A bullet hit one of the windows in the Yellow Oval Room, where I sometimes liked to sit and have tea. Another lodged itself in a window frame, and more bounced off the roof. Barack and I were out that night, as was Malia, but Sasha and my mom were both at home, though unaware and unharmed. Before the glass was replaced, I often found myself staring at the thick round crater that had been left by the bullet, reminded of how vulnerable we were.

In general, I understood that it was better for all of us not to acknowledge the hate or dwell on the risk, even when others brought it up. Malia would eventually join the high school tennis team at Sidwell, which practiced on the school courts visible from the street. She was there one day when a woman, the mom of another student, approached her, gesturing at the busy road running past the courts. "Aren't you afraid out here?" she asked.

My daughter, as she grew, was learning to use her voice, discovering her own ways to set the boundaries she needed. "If you're asking me whether I ponder my death every day," she said to the woman, as politely as she could, "the answer is no."

A couple of years later, that same mom would come up to me at a parent event at school and pass me a heartfelt note of apology, saying that she'd understood her mistake right away—having put worries on a child who could do nothing about them. It meant a lot to me that she'd thought so much about it. She'd heard, in Malia's answer, both the resilience and the vulnerability, an echo of all that we lived with and all we tried to keep at bay. She'd also understood that the only thing our girl could do, that day and every day after it, was get back on the court and hit another ball.

EVERY CHALLENGE, of course, is relative. I knew my kids were growing up with more advantages than most families could imagine. Our girls had a beautiful home, food on the table, devoted adults around them, and encouragement and resources when it came to getting an education. I put everything I had into Malia and Sasha and their development, but as First Lady I was mindful, too, of a bigger duty. I felt that I owed more to children in general, and in particular to girls. I understood that people were surprised by my life story—an urban Black girl vaulting through Ivy League schools and executive jobs and landing in the White House. I understood that my journey was unusual, but there was no good reason why it had to be. There had been so many times in my life when I'd found myself the only woman of color—or even the only woman, period—sitting at a conference table or attending a VIP gathering. If I was the first at some of these things, I wanted to make sure that others were coming up behind me. As my mom still says anytime someone starts gushing about me and Craig and our various accomplishments, "They're not special at all. The South Side is filled with kids like that." We just needed to help get them into those rooms.

The important parts of my story, I was realizing, lay less in my actual accomplishments and more in what held them up—the many small ways I'd been supported over the years, and the people who'd helped build my confidence over time. I remembered every person who'd ever waved me forward. Each of them did his or her best to prepare me to overcome all the slights and indignities I was certain to encounter in the places I was headed—all those environments built primarily for and by people who were neither Black nor female.

I thought of my great-aunt Robbie and her high piano standards, how she'd taught me to lift my chin and play my heart out on a baby grand even if all I'd ever known was an upright with broken keys. I thought of my dad, who showed me how to box and throw a football, same as Craig. There were Mr. Martinez and Mr. Bennett, my teachers who never dismissed my opinions. There was my mom, my most dedicated supporter, who had saved me from wasting away in a dreary second-grade classroom. At Princeton, I'd had Czerny Brasuell, who encouraged me to take new risks. And as a young professional, I'd had, among others, Susan Sher and Valerie Jarrett, who showed me what it looked like to be a working mom and opened doors for me, certain I had something to offer.

These were people who mostly didn't know one another and would never have occasion to meet, many of whom I'd fallen out of touch with myself. But for me, they formed a meaningful constellation.

These were my boosters, my believers, my own personal gospel choir, singing, *Yes, kid, you got this!* all the way through.

I'd never forgotten it. I'd tried, even as a junior lawyer, to pay it forward, encouraging curiosity when I saw it, drawing younger people into important conversations. If a legal assistant asked me a question about her future, I'd open my office door and share my journey or offer some advice. If someone wanted guidance or help making a connection, I did what I could to give it. Later, during my time at Public Allies, I saw the benefits of more formal mentoring firsthand. I knew from my own life experience that when someone shows real interest in your learning and development, even if only for ten minutes in a busy day, it matters. It matters especially for women, for minorities, for anyone society is quick to overlook.

With this in mind, I'd started a leadership and mentoring program at the White House, inviting twenty sophomore and junior girls from high schools around Greater D.C. to join us for monthly get-togethers. We'd have informal chats, field trips, and workshops on everything from choosing a career to understanding how money works.

We paired each teen with a female mentor who would give her guidance and advice. Students were nominated by their principals or guidance counselors and would stay with us until they graduated. We had girls from military families, girls from immigrant families, a teen mom, a girl who'd lived in a homeless shelter. They were smart, curious young women, all of them. No different from me. No different from my daughters. I watched over time as the girls formed friendships and close relationships with one another and with the adults around them. I spent hours talking with them in a big circle, munching popcorn and trading our thoughts about college applications, body image, and boys. No topic was off-limits. We ended up laughing a lot. More than anything, I hoped this was what they'd carry forward into the future—the ease, the sense of community, the encouragement to speak and be heard.

My wish for them was the same one I had for Sasha and Malia—that in learning to feel comfortable at the White House, they'd go on to feel comfortable and confident in any room, sitting at any table, raising their voices inside any group.

WE'D LIVED INSIDE the bubble of the presidency for more than two years now. I looked for ways to widen that bubble as much as I could. Barack and I continued to open the White House up to more people, most especially children, hoping to make its grandeur feel inclusive. We invited local schoolkids to come over to take in the official welcome ceremonies for foreign dignitaries and taste the food that would be served at the state dinner. When musicians were coming for an evening performance, we asked them to show up early to help with a youth workshop. We wanted to highlight the importance of exposing children to the arts. I loved the sight of high schoolers mingling with John Legend, Justin Timberlake, and Alison Krauss as well as legends like Smokey Robinson and Patti LaBelle. For me, it was a throwback to the way I'd been raised—the jazz at Southside's house, the piano recitals put on by my great-aunt Robbie, my family's trips to museums. I knew how arts and culture contributed to the development of a child. And it made me feel at home. Barack and I swayed to the beat together in the front row of every performance. Even my mom, who generally steered clear of public appearances, always made her way down to the state floor anytime music was playing.

We added celebrations of dance and other arts to the mix, bringing in upcoming artists to showcase new work. In 2009, we'd put on the first-ever White House poetry and spoken-word event, listening as a young composer named Lin-Manuel Miranda stood up and astonished everyone with a piece from a project he was just beginning to put together, describing it as a "concept album about the life of someone I think embodies hip-hop . . . Treasury secretary Alexander Hamilton."

I remember shaking his hand and saying, "Hey, good luck with the Hamilton thing."

In any given day, we were exposed to so much. Glamour, excellence, devastation, hope. Everything lived side by side, and all the while we had two kids trying to lead their own lives apart from what was going on at home. I did what I could to make sure that the girls and I remained connected to the everyday world and to find moments of normal, regular life. During soccer and lacrosse seasons, I went to many of Sasha's and Malia's home games, taking my place on the sidelines alongside other parents, politely turning down anyone who asked to take a photo, though I was always happy to talk. After Malia started tennis, I watched her matches through the window of a Secret Service vehicle parked near the courts, not wanting to create a distraction. Only when it was over would I get out to give her a hug.

It was harder for Barack to experience these normal moments. He attended school functions and the girls' sporting events as he could, but his security team was always easy to spot. The point was to send a clear message to the world that nobody could harm the president of the United States. I was glad for this, but it could be a little much.

This same thought would occur to Malia one day as Barack and I were heading with her to one of Sasha's events at Sidwell's lower school. The three of us were crossing an open outdoor courtyard, passing a group of kindergartners in the middle of their recess, swinging from a set of monkey bars and running around the wood-chipped play area. I'm not sure if the little kids had spotted the squad of Secret Service snipers dressed all in black and spread out across the rooftops of the school buildings with their assault rifles visible, but Malia had.

She looked from the snipers to the kindergartners, then back to her dad, giving him a teasing look. "Really, Dad?" she said. "Seriously?"

All Barack could do was smile and shrug. There was no ducking the seriousness of his job.

To be sure, none of us ever stepped outside the bubble. Following our early negotiations with the Secret Service, Sasha and Malia were doing things like going to friends' bat mitzvahs, washing cars for the school fund-raiser, and even hanging out at the mall, always with agents and often with my mom tagging along, but they were now at least able to get around as much as their peers. Sasha's agents, including Beth Celestini and Lawrence Tucker—whom everyone called L.T.—had become beloved fixtures at Sidwell. Families often sent in extra cupcakes for the agents when there were classroom birthday celebrations.

All of us grew close to our agents over time. When we were out in public, they were silent and hyperalert, but anytime we were backstage or on plane rides, they'd loosen up, sharing stories and joking around. "Stone-faced softies," I used to call them, teasingly. Over all the hours we spent together and many miles traveled, we became real friends. I grieved their losses with them and celebrated when their kids hit significant milestones. I was always aware of the seriousness of their duties, what they were willing to sacrifice in order to keep me safe, and I never took it for granted.

Like my daughters, I was creating a private life to go along with my official one. I'd found there were ways to keep a low profile when I needed to, helped by the Secret Service's willingness to be flexible. I was sometimes allowed to travel in an unmarked van and with a lighter security escort. I managed to make lightning-strike shopping trips from time to time, coming and going from a place before anyone really registered I was there. After Bo expertly disemboweled or shredded every last dog toy bought for him by the staff who did our regular shopping, I personally escorted him over to PetSmart one morning. And for a short while, I enjoyed glorious anonymity while browsing for better chew toys as Bo—who was as delighted by the novelty of the outing as I was—loafed next to me on a leash.

Anytime I went somewhere without a fuss, it felt like a small victory. Maybe six months after the PetSmart trip, I made a giddy run to the local Target, disguised in a baseball cap and sunglasses. My security detail wore shorts and sneakers and ditched their earpieces, doing their best not to stand out as they trailed me and my assistant Kristin Jones through the store. We wandered every single aisle. I found a couple of games for Sasha and Malia, and for the first time in several years I was able to pick out a card to give to Barack on our anniversary.

I went home overjoyed. Sometimes the smallest things felt huge.

As time went by, I added new adventures to my routine. I started to meet friends occasionally out for dinner in restaurants or at their homes. Sometimes I'd go to a park and take long walks along the Potomac River. I'd have agents walking ahead of and behind me on these excursions, but at a distance. I'd begin leaving the White House to hit workout classes around the city, slipping into the room at the last minute and leaving as soon as class was done to avoid causing a disturbance. The most liberating activity of all turned out to be downhill skiing. I didn't have much experience skiing, but it quickly became a passion. Taking advantage of the unusually heavy winters we'd had during our first two years in Washington, I made a few day trips with the girls and some friends to a tiny ski area called Liberty Mountain, near Gettysburg, where we found we could don helmets, scarves, and goggles and blend into any crowd. Gliding down a ski slope, I was outdoors, in motion, and unrecognized—all at once. For me, it was like flying.

I loved blending in—it was a way to feel like myself, to remain Michelle Robinson from the South Side inside this larger sweep of history. I knit my old life into my new one, my private concerns into my public work. In D.C., I'd made a handful of new friends—a couple of Sasha's and Malia's classmates' moms and a few people I'd met in the course of White House duties. These were women who cared less about my last name or home address and more about who I was as a person. It's funny how quickly you can tell who's there for you and who's just faking friendship. Barack and I sometimes talked about it with Sasha and Malia over dinner, the fact that there were people, children and adults, who hovered at the edges of our friend groups seeming a little too eager—"thirsty," as we called it.

I'd learned many years earlier to hold my true friends close. I was still deeply connected to the group of women who had started gathering for Saturday playdates with our kids years earlier, back in Chicago. These were the friends who'd held me together, dropping off groceries when I was too busy to shop, picking up the girls for ballet when I was behind on work or just needing a break. A number of them had hopped planes to join me for stops on the campaign trail, giving me emotional support when I needed it most. Friendships between women are built of a thousand small kindnesses like these, swapped back and forth and over again.

I started to make a deliberate effort to bring together old friends and new. Every few months, I invited twelve or so of my closest friends to join me for a weekend at Camp David, the woodsy, summer-camp-like presidential retreat in the mountains of northern Maryland. I started referring to these gatherings as "Boot Camp," in part because I forced everyone to work out with me several times a day.

Many of my friends had busy family lives and heavy-duty jobs. I understood it wasn't always easy for them to get away. But this was part of the point. We were all so used to sacrificing for our kids, our spouses, and our work. I had learned through my years of trying to find balance in my life that it was okay to flip those priorities and care only for ourselves once in a while, to say *Sorry, folks, I'm doing this for me.*

Boot Camp weekends became a way for us to connect and recharge. We stayed in cozy, wood-paneled cabins surrounded by forest, buzzed around in golf carts, and rode bikes. We played dodgeball and did burpees and downward dogs. I sometimes invited a few young staffers along, and it was mind-blowing to see Susan Sher, in her late sixties, spider crawling across the floor next to MacKenzie Smith, my young scheduler who'd been a soccer player in college. We ate healthy meals, got a lot of exercise, and talked and talked and talked, sharing our thoughts and experiences and offering advice or funny stories. We steadied one another just by listening. And saying good-bye at the end of each weekend, we vowed we'd do it all again soon.

My friends made me whole, as they always have and always will. They gave me a lift anytime I felt down or frustrated or had less access to Barack. They grounded me when I felt the pressures of being judged, having everything from my choice of nail-polish color to the size of my hips examined and discussed publicly. And they helped me ride out the big, unsettling waves that sometimes hit without notice.

On the first Sunday in May 2011, I went to dinner with two friends at a restaurant downtown, leaving Barack and my mom in charge of the girls at home. The weekend had seemed especially busy. Barack had been pulled into a flurry of briefings that afternoon, and we'd spent Saturday evening at the White House Correspondents' Dinner, where in his speech Barack made a few pointed jokes about Donald Trump's *Celebrity Apprentice* career and his birther theories. I couldn't see him from my seat, but Trump had been in attendance. During Barack's monologue, news cameras zeroed in on him, stone-faced and stewing.

For us, Sunday nights tended to be quiet and free. The girls were usually tired after a weekend of sports and socializing. That night, after catching up with my friends over dinner, I arrived home around 10:00, greeted at the door by an usher, as I always was. Already, I could tell something was going on, sensing a different-from-normal level of activity on the ground floor of the White House. I asked the usher if he knew where the president was.

"I believe he's upstairs, ma'am," he said, "getting ready to address the nation."

This is how I realized that it had finally happened. I'd spent the last two days trying to act completely normal, pretending I didn't know that something dangerous and important was about to take place.

After months of careful preparation and a tense final decision, seven thousand miles from the White House and under cover of darkness, an elite team of U.S. Navy SEALs had stormed a mysterious compound in Abbottabad, Pakistan, looking for the terrorist Osama bin Laden.

Barack was coming out of our bedroom as I walked down the hall. He was dressed in a suit and red tie and seemed thoroughly jacked up on adrenaline. He'd been carrying the pressure of this decision for months.

"We got him," he said. "And no one got hurt."

We hugged. Osama bin Laden had been killed. No American lives had been lost. Barack had taken an enormous risk—one that could have cost him his presidency—and it had all gone okay.

The news was already traveling across the world. People were clogging the streets around the White House, spilling out of restaurants, hotels, and apartment buildings, filling the night air with celebratory shouts. The sound of it grew so loud it roused Malia from sleep in her bedroom, even through the bulletproof windows that were meant to shut everything out.

That night, there was no inside or outside, anyway. In cities across the country, people had taken to the streets, drawn by an impulse to be close to others, linked not just by patriotism but by the communal grief that had been born on 9/11 and the years of worries that we'd be attacked again. I thought about every military base I'd ever visited, all those soldiers working to recover from their wounds, the many people who'd sent family members to a faraway place in the name of protecting our country, the thousands of children who'd lost a parent on that horrible, sad day. There was no restoring any one of those losses, I knew. Nobody's death would ever replace a life. I'm not sure anyone's death is reason to celebrate, ever. But what America got that night was a moment of release, a chance to feel its own resilience.

23

TIME SEEMED TO LOOP AND LEAP, MAKING IT FEEL impossible to measure or track. Each day was packed. Each week and month and year we spent in the White House was packed. I'd get to Friday and need to work to remember how Monday and Tuesday had gone. I'd sit down to dinner sometimes and wonder where and how lunch had happened. Even now, I still find it hard to process. The velocity was too great, the time for reflection too limited. A single afternoon could hold a couple of official events, several meetings, and a photo shoot. I might visit several states in a day, or speak to twelve thousand people, or have four hundred kids over to do jumping jacks with me on the South Lawn. All this before putting on a fancy dress for a party at night. I used my days off to tend to Sasha and Malia and their lives, before going back "up" again—back into hair, makeup, and wardrobe. Back into the vortex of the public eye.

As we moved toward Barack's reelection year in 2012, I felt that I couldn't and shouldn't rest. I was still earning my grace. I thought often of what I owed and to whom. I carried a history with me, and it wasn't that of presidents or First Ladies. I'd never related to the story of John Quincy Adams the way I did to that of Sojourner Truth, or been moved by Woodrow Wilson the way I was by Harriet Tubman. The struggles of Rosa Parks and Coretta Scott King were more familiar to me than those of Eleanor Roosevelt or Mamie Eisenhower. I carried their histories, along with those of my mom and grandmothers. None of these women could ever have imagined a life like the one I now had. Yet they'd persisted, paving the way for someone like me. I wanted to show up in the world in a way that honored who they were.

I felt pressure not to mess anything up. Though I was thought of as a popular First Lady, I couldn't help but feel haunted by the ways I'd been criticized, by the people who'd made assumptions about me based on the color of my skin. So I rehearsed my speeches again and again, and made sure every one of our events ran smoothly and on time. I pushed even harder to continue growing the reach of my Let's Move! and Joining Forces initiatives with my team. I was focused on not wasting any of the opportunities I now had, but sometimes I had to remind myself just to breathe.

With another presidential election coming up, Barack and I both knew that the months of campaigning ahead would involve extra travel, extra strategizing, and extra worry. And the responsibility was huge. Everyone working in the White House lived in the limbo of not knowing whether we'd get a second term to continue the progress we'd made so far. I tried not to even consider the possibility that Barack might lose the election, but it was there—a kernel of fear deep down.

The country was still recovering from the economic crisis. Many people blamed Barack. In the relief following the death of Osama bin Laden, his approval ratings had spiked, hitting a two-year high, but then, just a few months later, following political brawls and worries about a new recession, they'd plunged to the lowest they'd been.

As this commotion was beginning, I flew to South Africa for a goodwill visit. Sasha and Malia's school year had just ended, so they were able to join me, along with my mom and Craig's kids Leslie and Avery, who were now teenagers. I was headed there to give a speech at a forum for young African women leaders from around the continent. We'd also filled my schedule with community events connected to wellness and education, as well as visits with local leaders and U.S. consulate workers.

It had taken no time at all for us to get swept up in South Africa's energy. In Johannesburg, we toured the Apartheid Museum, which explored the country's history of racial segregation. We danced and read books with young children at a community center in one of the Black townships north of the city. At a soccer stadium in Cape Town, we met community organizers and health workers who were using youth sports programs to help educate children about HIV/AIDS, and were introduced to Archbishop Desmond Tutu, the legendary theologian and activist who'd helped end apartheid in South Africa. Tutu was seventy-nine years old, a barrel-chested man with bright eyes and an irrepressible laugh. Hearing that I was at the stadium to promote fitness, he insisted on doing push-ups with me in front of a cheering pack of kids.

During those few days in South Africa, I felt myself floating. This visit was a long way from my first trip to Kenya, when I'd ridden around with Barack in *matatus* and pushed Auma's broken-down VW along the side of a dusty road. What I felt was one part jet lag, maybe, but two parts something more meaningful and energizing. It was as if we'd stepped into the larger crosscurrents of culture and history, reminded suddenly of how small we really were in the wider arc of time. Seeing the faces of the seventy-six young women who'd been chosen to attend the leadership forum because they were doing meaningful work in their communities, I fought back tears. They gave me hope. They made me feel old in the best possible way. A full 60 percent of Africa's population at the time was under the age of twenty-five. Here were women, all of them under thirty and some as young as sixteen, who were building nonprofits, training other women to be entrepreneurs, and risking imprisonment to report on government corruption. And now they were being connected, trained, and encouraged. I hoped this would only increase their power.

The most surreal moment of all, though, had come early, on just the second day of our trip. My family and I had been at the Nelson Mandela Foundation headquarters in Johannesburg, visiting with Graça Machel, a well-known humanitarian and Mandela's wife, when we received word that Mandela himself would be happy to greet us at his home nearby.

We went immediately, of course. Nelson Mandela was ninety-two at the time. He'd been hospitalized with lung issues earlier in the year. I was told he rarely received guests. Barack had met him six years earlier, as a senator, when Mandela had visited Washington. He'd kept a framed photo of their meeting on the wall of his office ever since. Even my kids—Sasha, ten, and Malia, about to turn thirteen—understood what a big deal this was. Even my usually unfazed mom looked a little stunned.

There was no one alive who'd had a more meaningful impact on the world than Nelson Mandela had, at least by my measure. He'd been a young man in the 1940s when he first joined the African National Congress and began boldly challenging the all-white South African government and its deep-seated racist policies. He'd been forty-four years old when he was sent to prison for his activism, and seventy-one when he was finally released in 1990. Surviving twenty-seven years of deprivation and isolation as a prisoner, having had many of his friends tortured and killed under the apartheid rule, Mandela managed to negotiate—rather than fight—with government leaders, bringing about a miraculously peaceful transition to a true democracy in South Africa and ultimately becoming its first president.

Mandela lived on a leafy suburban street in a home set behind butter-colored concrete walls. Graça Machel ushered us through a courtyard shaded by trees and into the house, where in a wide, sunlit room her husband sat in an armchair. He had sparse, snowy hair and wore a brown batik shirt. Someone had laid a white blanket across his lap. He was surrounded by several generations of relatives, all of whom welcomed us enthusiastically. Something in the brightness of the room, the liveliness of the family, and the squinty smile of the patriarch Mandela reminded me of going to my grandfather Southside's house when I was a kid. I'd been nervous to come, but now I relaxed.

The truth is I'm not sure that Mandela himself completely grasped who we were. He was an old man at this point, his attention seeming to drift, his hearing a little weak. "This is *Michelle Obama*!" Graça Machel said, leaning close to his ear. "The wife of the U.S. president!"

"Oh, lovely," murmured Nelson Mandela. "Lovely."

He looked at me with genuine interest, though in truth I could have been anyone. It seemed clear that he brought this same degree of warmth to every person who crossed his path. My interaction with Mandela was both quiet and profound—maybe more profound, even, for its quietness. His life's words had mostly been spoken now, his speeches and letters, his books and protest chants, already etched not just into his story but into humanity's as a whole. I could feel all of it in the brief moment I had with him—the dignity and spirit that had coaxed equality from a place where none had existed.

I was still thinking about Mandela five days later as we flew back to the United States. Sasha and Malia lay sprawled beneath blankets next to their cousins; my mom dozed in a seat nearby. Farther back in the plane, staff and Secret Service members were watching movies and catching up on sleep. The engines hummed. I felt alone and not alone. I thought about the young African women I'd met at the leadership forum, all of them now headed back to their own communities to pick up their work again, persevering through whatever uncertainties they faced.

Mandela had gone to jail for his principles. He'd missed seeing his kids grow up, and then he'd missed seeing many of his grandkids grow up, too. All this without bitterness. All this still believing that the better nature of his country would at some point prevail. He'd worked and waited, tolerant and undiscouraged, to see it happen.

I flew home propelled by that spirit. Life was teaching me that progress and change happen slowly. Not in two years, four years, or even a lifetime. We were planting seeds of change, the fruit of which we might never see. We had to be patient.

THREE TIMES OVER the course of the fall of 2011, Barack proposed bills that would create thousands of jobs for Americans, including more opportunities for teachers and first responders. Three times the Republicans blocked them, never even allowing a vote.

"The single most important thing we want to achieve," Senator Mitch McConnell had declared a year earlier, laying out his party's goals, "is for President Obama to be a one-term president." It was that simple. The Republican Congress was devoted to seeing Barack fail above all else. It seemed they weren't prioritizing the running of the country or the fact that people needed jobs. Their own power came first.

I found it disappointing, infuriating, sometimes crushing. This was politics, yes, but in its most pessimistic and negative form, seemingly disconnected from any larger sense of purpose. I felt emotions that perhaps Barack couldn't afford to feel. He stayed locked in his work, riding out the bumps and compromising where he could, clinging to the sensible optimism that had always guided him. I thought of him as being like an old copper pot—seasoned by fire, dinged up but still shiny.

Returning to the campaign trail that fall took us out of Washington and back to communities all around the country again. There we could hug and shake hands with supporters, listening to their ideas and concerns. It was a chance to be reminded that American citizens are mostly more positive and hopeful than their elected leaders. We just needed them to get out and vote. I'd been disappointed that millions of people had sat out during the 2010 midterm elections, effectively handing Barack a divided Congress that could barely manage to make a law.

Despite the challenges, there was plenty to feel hopeful about, too. By the end of 2011, the last American soldiers had left Iraq. A gradual drawdown of troops was under way in Afghanistan. Major parts of the Affordable Care Act had also gone into effect, giving more people access to health care. All this was forward motion, I reminded myself, steps taken along the broader path.

Even with an entire political party plotting to see Barack fail, we had no choice but to stay positive and carry on. It was similar to when the Sidwell mom had asked Malia if she feared for her life at tennis practice. What can you do, really, but go out and hit another ball? So we worked. Both of us worked. I threw myself into my initiatives. Under the banner of Let's Move! we continued to rack up results. My team and I persuaded a big restaurant company that served 400 million meals to Americans each year to make healthy changes to the kind of food it served. With a company that big, even a small shift— like removing tempting photos of cool, icy glasses of soda from the kids' menus—could have a real impact.

A First Lady's power is a curious thing—as soft and undefined as the role itself. And yet I was learning to harness it. Tradition called for me not to challenge the nation, but instead simply to be devoted to the president. I was beginning to see, though, that I had more power than that. I had influence in the form of being something of a curiosity— a Black First Lady, a professional woman, a mom of young kids. People seemed to want to know about my clothes, my shoes, and my hairstyles, but they also had to see why I made the choices I did. I was learning how to connect my message to my image and to influence how people saw me. I could put on an interesting outfit, crack a joke, and talk about kids' nutrition without being totally boring. I could give a shout-out to a company that was hiring members of the military community, or drop to the floor for an on-air push-up contest with Ellen DeGeneres (and win it, earning bragging rights forever) in the name of Let's Move!

I've always had mainstream tastes and enjoyed popular culture. Though I'd moved through exclusive places like Princeton and my Chicago law firm, and though I now occasionally found myself wearing diamonds and a ball gown, I'd never stopped reading *People* magazine or let go of my love of a good sitcom. I watched Oprah and Ellen far more often than I'd ever tuned in to political news shows, and to this day nothing pleases me more than the tidy triumph delivered by a home-makeover show.

Because of this, I saw ways to connect with Americans that Barack and his West Wing advisers didn't fully recognize at first. Rather than doing interviews with big newspapers or cable news outlets, I began sitting down with influential "mommy bloggers" who reached an enormous and aware audience of women. Watching my young staffers interact with their phones, seeing Malia and Sasha start to take in news and chat with their high school friends via social media, I realized there was opportunity there as well. I crafted my first tweet in the fall of 2011 to promote Joining Forces and then watched it zing through the strange, boundless online world where people increasingly spent their time.

It was a revelation. With my soft power, I was finding I could be strong.

If reporters and television cameras wanted to follow me, then I was going to take them places that brought attention to important issues. They could come watch me and Jill Biden paint a wall, for example, at a modest house in Washington. There was nothing inherently interesting about two ladies with paint rollers, but it brought everyone to the doorstep of Sergeant Johnny Agbi.

Sergeant Agbi was a young Army medic who had been badly

injured in a helicopter attack, requiring a long rehabilitation at Walter Reed hospital. His home was now being fixed up to accommodate his wheelchair—its doorways widened, its kitchen sink lowered—by a group of volunteers who'd renovated a thousand homes for veterans in need. The cameras caught all of it—the soldier, his house, the goodwill and energy being poured in. The reporters interviewed not just me and Jill but Sergeant Agbi and the folks who'd done the real work. For me, this was how it should be. The public's attention belonged here.

ON ELECTION DAY—November 6, 2012—my fears sat with me quietly. Barack and the girls and I were back at home in Chicago, waiting for an entire nation to accept or reject us. This vote, for me, was more stressful than any other we'd gone through. It felt like a judgment not only on Barack's performance in running the country but also on his character, on our very presence in the White House. Our girls had established a strong community for themselves and regular routines that I didn't want to upend yet again. I was so invested now, having given over four years of our family's life, that it was impossible not to feel everything a bit personally.

Polls showed Barack with only a slight lead over the Republican candidate Mitt Romney. The campaign had worn us out even more than I'd anticipated, and we could read the exhaustion on the faces of our hardworking staffers. Though they aimed never to show it, they were worried about the possibility that Barack could be voted out of office.

Throughout it, Barack stayed calm, though I could see what the pressure did to him. During the final weeks, he began to look a little pale and even skinnier than usual. I'd watched with concern as he tried to do everything—soothe the worriers, finish out the campaign, and govern all at once.

As polls on the East Coast began to close that evening, I headed up to the third floor of our house, where my team had set up a kind of hair and makeup salon to prepare for the public part of the night ahead. Meredith had steamed and readied clothes for me, my mom, and the girls. Johnny and Carl were doing my hair and makeup. In keeping with tradition, Barack had gone out to play basketball earlier in the day and had since settled into his office to put finishing touches on his speeches.

I deliberately kept the TV off. If there was news, good or bad, I wanted to hear it directly from Barack or Melissa, or someone else close to me. The babble of news anchors always jangled my nerves. I didn't want the details: I just wanted to know how to feel.

It was after 8:00 p.m. now, which meant there had to be some early results coming in. I emailed Valerie, Melissa, and Tina Tchen, who in 2011 had become my new chief of staff, asking them what they knew.

I waited fifteen minutes, then thirty. Nobody responded. The room around me began to feel strangely silent. My mom sat in the kitchen downstairs, reading a magazine. Meredith was getting the girls ready for the evening. Johnny ran a flat iron over my hair. Was I being paranoid, or were people not looking me in the eye? Did they somehow know something I didn't?

As more time passed, my head started to throb. I didn't dare turn on the news, assuming suddenly that it was bad. For every minute my phone lay silent in my lap, my doubts grew stronger and louder. Maybe we hadn't worked hard enough. Maybe we didn't deserve another term. My hands had started to shake.

I was just about ready to pass out from the anxiety when Barack came trotting up the stairs, wearing his big old confident grin. His worries were well behind him already. "We're kicking butt," he said, looking surprised that I didn't know it already. "It's basically done."

It turned out that downstairs, the mood had been jubilant all along, the basement TV pumping out a consistent stream of good news. The problem for me was that my cell service had somehow disconnected, never sending out or receiving messages. I'd allowed myself to get trapped in my own head. Nobody had known I was worrying, not even the people in the room with me.

Barack would win all but one of the battleground states that night. He'd win among young people, minorities, and women, just as he had in 2008. Despite everything the Republicans had done to try to block his success, his vision had prevailed. We'd asked Americans for permission to keep working—to finish strong—and now we'd gotten it. The relief was immediate. *Are we good enough? Yes we are.*

At some late hour, Mitt Romney called to admit defeat. Once again, we found ourselves dressed up and waving from a stage, four Obamas and a lot of confetti, glad to have another four years.

The certainty that came with reelection held me steady. We had more time to further our goals. We could be more patient with our push for progress. We had a sense of the future now, which made me happy. We could keep Sasha and Malia enrolled at school; our staff could stay in their jobs; our ideas still mattered. And when these next four years were over, we'd be truly done, which made me happiest of all.

The truth is that the future would arrive with its own surprises— some joyous, some unspeakably tragic. Four more years in the White House meant four more years of being symbols of America, absorbing and responding to whatever came our country's way. And now the future was coming in our direction, maybe faster than we knew.

FIVE WEEKS LATER, a gunman walked into Sandy Hook Elementary School in Newtown, Connecticut, and started killing children.

I had just finished giving a short speech across the street from the White House and was scheduled to then go visit a children's hospital when Tina pulled me aside to tell me what had happened. While I'd been speaking, she and several others had seen the headlines on their phones. They'd sat there trying to hide their emotions as I wrapped up my remarks.

The news Tina gave me was so horrifying and sad I could barely process what she was saying.

She said Barack was in the Oval Office by himself. "He's asking for you to come," she said. "Right away."

My husband needed me. This would be the only time in eight years that he'd ask for my presence in the middle of a workday. Usually, work was work and home was home, but for us, as for many people, the tragedy in Newtown shattered every window and blew down every fence. When I walked into the Oval Office, Barack and I embraced silently. There was nothing to say. No words.

What a lot of people don't know is that the president sees almost all information related to the country's well-being. Being a fact guy, Barack always asked for more detail rather than less, so that he could offer a truly informed response. As he saw it, it was his responsibility to look rather than look away, to stay upright when the rest of us felt ready to fall down.

Which is to say that by the time I found him, he'd heard everything about the terrible scene at Sandy Hook. His shock and grief would never compare with that of the first responders who'd rushed in to secure the building and evacuate survivors from the school. It was nothing next to that of the parents who had to wait outside the building, praying that they'd see their child's face again. And it was nothing at all next to the unimaginable grief of the parents who lost their children that day.

But still, those images of what happened at Sandy Hook left Barack devastated.

Like me, he loved children in a deep and genuine way. Beyond being a doting dad, he regularly brought kids into the Oval Office to show them around. He asked to hold babies. He lit up anytime he got to visit a school science fair or a youth sporting event. The previous winter, he'd added a whole new level of delight to his existence when he started volunteering as an assistant coach for Sasha's middle school basketball team. The proximity of children made everything lighter for him. He knew as well as anyone the promise lost with those twenty young lives.

Staying upright after Newtown was probably the hardest thing he'd ever had to do. When Malia and Sasha came home from school later that day, Barack and I hugged them tight. It was hard to know what to say or not say to our girls about the shooting. Parents all around the country, we knew, were dealing with the same thing.

Later that day, Barack wiped away tears as he held a press conference, trying to put together words that might provide some comfort, but understanding that truly there was no comfort to be had. The best he could do was to offer his resolve to prevent more massacres by passing basic, sensible laws concerning how guns were sold.

I watched him step forward, knowing that I myself wasn't ready. In nearly four years as First Lady, I had consoled often. I'd prayed with people whose homes had been shredded in an instant by a tornado. I'd put my arms around men, women, and children who'd lost loved ones to war, to terrorist attacks, and to violence on street corners near their own homes. In the previous four months, I'd paid visits to people who'd survived mass shootings at a movie theater and inside a Sikh temple. It was devastating, every time. I'd tried always to bring the most calm and open part of myself to these meetings, to lend my own strength by being caring and present, sitting quietly on the riverbed of other people's pain. But two days after the shooting at Sandy Hook, when Barack traveled to Newtown to speak at a prayer vigil being held for the victims, I couldn't bring myself to join him. I was so shaken by it that I had no strength available to lend. I'd been First Lady for almost four years, and there had been too much killing already—too many senseless preventable deaths and too little action. I wasn't sure what comfort I could ever give to someone whose six-year-old had been gunned down at school.

Instead, like a lot of parents, I clung to my children. It was nearly Christmas, and Sasha was among a group of local children selected to join the Moscow Ballet for two performances of *The Nutcracker,* happening on the same day as the vigil in Newtown. Barack managed to slip into a back row and watch the dress rehearsal before leaving for Connecticut. I went to the evening show.

The ballet was beautiful, with its prince in a moonlit forest and its swirling pageantry of sweets. Sasha played a mouse, dressed in a black leotard with fuzzy ears and a tail, performing her part while a sleigh drifted through the swelling orchestral music and showers of glittering fake snow. My eyes never left her. My whole being was grateful for her. Sasha stood bright-eyed onstage, looking at first like she couldn't believe where she was, as if she found the whole scene dazzling and unreal. Which of course it was. But she was young enough still that she could give herself over to it, allowing herself to move through this heaven where nobody spoke and everyone danced, and a holiday was always just about to arrive.

BEAR WITH ME, because this doesn't get easier. It would be one thing if America were a simple place with a simple story. If I could say that everything around me was orderly and sweet. If there were no steps backward. And if every sadness turned out at least to have a happy ending.

But that's not America, and it's not me, either. I'm not going to try to bend this into any kind of perfect shape.

In many ways, Barack's second term would turn out to be easier than his first. We'd learned so much in four years, surrounding ourselves with the right people, building systems that worked. We knew enough now to avoid some of the small mistakes that had been made the first time around, beginning on Inauguration Day in January 2013, when I requested that the viewing stand for the parade be fully heated this time so our feet wouldn't freeze. We had four years still to go, and if I'd learned anything, it was to relax and try to pace myself.

Sitting next to Barack at the Inauguration Day parade after he'd renewed his vows to the country, I watched the flow of floats and the marching bands, already able to enjoy more than I had our first time around. From my viewpoint, I could barely make out the individual faces of the performers. There were thousands of them, each with his or her own story. Thousands of others had come to D.C. to perform in the events leading up to the inauguration, and tens of thousands more had come to watch.

Later, I'd wish almost frantically that I'd been able to catch sight of Hadiya Pendleton, a graceful Black girl wearing a sparkling gold head-band and a blue majorette's uniform that day. She'd come with the King College Prep marching band from the South Side of Chicago to perform at some of the side events. I wanted to believe that I somehow would have had the occasion to see her inside the great wash of people flowing through the city—a fifteen-year-old girl having a big moment, having ridden a bus all the way to Washington with her bandmates. At home in Chicago, Hadiya lived with her parents and her little brother, about two miles from our house. She was an honor student who liked to tell people she wanted to go to Harvard someday. She'd begun planning her sweet-sixteen birthday party. She loved Chinese food and cheeseburgers and going for ice cream with friends.

I learned these things about Hadiya several weeks later, at her funeral. Eight days after the inauguration, Hadiya Pendleton was shot and killed in a public park in Chicago, not far from her school. She and a group of friends had been standing under a metal shelter next to a playground, waiting for a rainstorm to pass. They'd been mistaken for gang members and shot by an eighteen-year-old belonging to a different gang. Hadiya had been hit in the back as she tried to run for cover. Two of her friends were injured. All this at 2:20 on a Tuesday afternoon.

I wish I'd seen her alive, if only to have a memory to share with her mom, now that the memories of her daughter had been cut short and were things to be collected and hung on to.

I went to Hadiya's funeral because it felt like the right thing to do. I'd stayed back when Barack went to the Newtown memorial, but now was my time to step up. My hope was that my presence would help bring attention to the many innocent kids being gunned down in city streets almost every day. I hoped that this kind of tragedy, as well as the horror of Newtown, would prompt Americans to demand reasonable gun laws. Hadiya Pendleton came from a close-knit, working-class South Side family, much like my own. Put simply, I could have known her. I could have been her once, even. And had she taken a different route home from school that day, or even moved six inches left instead of six inches right when the gunfire started, she could have been me.

"I did everything I was supposed to," her mom told me when we met just before the funeral started, her brown eyes leaking tears. Cleopatra Cowley-Pendleton was a warm woman with a soft voice and close-cropped hair who worked in customer service. On the day of her daughter's funeral, she wore a giant pink flower pinned to her lapel. She and her husband, Nathaniel, had watched over Hadiya carefully, encouraging her to apply to King, a selective public high school. They made sure she had little time to be out on the streets, signing her up for volleyball, cheerleading, and a dance group at church. As my parents had once done for me, they'd made sacrifices so that she could be exposed to things outside her neighborhood. She was planning to go to Europe with the marching band that spring, and she'd loved her visit to Washington.

"It's so clean there, Mom," she'd reported to Cleopatra after returning. "I think I'm going to go into politics."

Instead, Hadiya Pendleton became one of three people who died in separate incidents of gun violence in Chicago on that one January day. She was the thirty-sixth person in Chicago killed in gun violence that year, and the year was at that point just twenty-nine days old. Nearly all those victims were Black. For all her hopes and hard work, Hadiya became a symbol of the wrong thing.

Her funeral was filled with people, another broken community jammed into a church. Cleopatra stood up and spoke about her daughter. Hadiya's friends stood up and told stories about her, each one expressing feelings of outrage and helplessness. These were teenagers, asking not just *why* but *why so often?* There were powerful adults in the room that day, including the mayor and the governor, all of us packed into pews and left to deal privately with our grief and guilt as the choir sang with such force that it shook the floor of the church.

IT WAS IMPORTANT to me to be more than a consoler. In my life I'd heard plenty of empty words coming from important people. They'd say a lot during times of crisis without taking action afterward. I was determined to be someone who told the truth, using my voice to lift up the voiceless when I could, and to not disappear when people needed me most. I was aware that when I showed up somewhere, it looked dramatic from the outside—the motorcade, the agents, the aides, and the media, with me at the center. I didn't like what this did to my meetings with new people. Sometimes my presence caused people to stammer or go silent, unsure of how to be themselves. It's why I often tried to introduce myself with a hug, to slow down the moment and be real.

I tried to build relationships with the people I met, especially those who didn't normally have access to the exclusive world I now lived in. I wanted to share the brightness as I could. I invited Hadiya Pendleton's parents to sit next to me at Barack's State of the Union speech a few days after the funeral and then hosted the family at the White House for the Easter Egg Roll. Cleopatra, who became a vocal advocate for violence prevention, also returned a couple of times to attend different meetings on the issue at the White House. I wrote letters to the girls from the Elizabeth Garrett Anderson School in London who had so deeply moved me, encouraging them to stay hopeful and keep working, despite their lack of privilege. In 2011, I'd taken a group of thirty-seven girls from the school to visit the University of Oxford, not the high achievers but students whose teachers thought they weren't yet reaching their potential. The idea was to give them a glimpse of what was possible if they believed in themselves as I believed in them. I'd also hosted students from the school at the White House during the British prime minister's state visit. I felt it was important to connect with the kids multiple times and in multiple ways in order for them to know that it was all real.

My early successes in life were, I knew, the result of the love and high expectations that I was surrounded by as a child, both at home and at school. This understanding was what drove my White House mentoring program, as well as a new education initiative my staff and I were now preparing, called Reach Higher. I wanted to encourage kids to work hard to get to college and, once there, to stick with it. A college education would only become more important for young people finding jobs. Reach Higher would help them along the way, providing more support for school counselors and easier access to federal financial aid.

I'd been lucky to have parents, teachers, and mentors who'd fed me with a consistent, simple message: *You matter.* As an adult, I wanted to pass those words to a new generation. It was the message I gave my own daughters, who were lucky to have it reinforced by their school and their privileged circumstances, and I was determined to let every young person I met know that they mattered too. I wanted to be the opposite of the guidance counselor I'd had in high school, who'd told me I wasn't Princeton material. I have found that kids will invest more when they feel they're being invested in. And the students at Elizabeth Garrett Anderson demonstrated this—their test scores jumped significantly after I'd started connecting with them. Any credit for improvement really belonged to the girls and their teachers, but I understood that there was power in showing children my respect.

"All of us believe you belong here," I'd said to the Elizabeth Garrett Anderson girls as they sat, many of them looking awestruck, in the Gothic old-world dining hall at Oxford, surrounded by university professors and students who'd come out for the day to mentor them. I said something similar anytime we had kids visit the White House—teens we invited from the Standing Rock Sioux Reservation; children from local schools who showed up to work in the garden; high schoolers who came for our career days and workshops in fashion, music, and poetry; even kids I only got to give a quick but tight hug. The message was always the same. *You belong. You matter. I think highly of you.*

TWO MONTHS AFTER Hadiya Pendleton's funeral, I returned to Chicago. I'd directed Tina Tchen, my chief of staff, to gather support for violence prevention there.

After Hadiya's death, Tina had leveraged her local contacts in Chicago to expand community programs for at-risk youth across the city. Her efforts had helped raise millions of dollars in donations in just a few weeks. On a cool day in April, Tina and I flew out to attend a meeting of community leaders discussing youth empowerment, and also to meet a new group of kids.

When I was young, the South Side neighborhood of Englewood had been a rough place but not necessarily as deadly as it was now. In junior high, I'd traveled to Englewood for weekly biology labs at a community college there. Now, years later, as my motorcade made its way past vacant lots and empty burned-out buildings, it looked to me as if the only thriving businesses left were the liquor stores. In the previous year, twenty-nine of the school's current and recent students had been shot, eight of them fatally. These numbers were astonishing to me and my staff, but the sad fact is that urban schools around the country were contending with epidemic levels of gun violence. Amid all the talk of youth empowerment, it seemed important to actually sit down and hear from the youth.

I thought back to my own childhood and my own neighborhood, and how the word "ghetto" got thrown around like a threat. Even the suggestion of it, I understood now, caused middle-class families to flee for the suburbs. "Ghetto" marked a place as both Black and hopeless. It was a label that predicted failure and sped up its arrival. It closed corner groceries and gas stations. It undermined schools and teachers who were trying to inspire self-worth in neighborhood kids. It was a word everyone tried to run from, but it could come to define a community quick.

In the middle of West Englewood sat Harper High School, a large sand-brick building. I met the school's principal, Leonetta Sanders, a quick-moving African American woman, and two school social workers who were deeply involved in the lives of the 510 kids enrolled at Harper, most of them from low-income families. One of the social workers, Crystal Smith, could often be found in Harper's hallways between classes, giving students boosts of positivity. She'd call out, "I'm so proud of you!" and "I see you trying hard!" She'd shout, "I appreciate you in advance!" for every good choice she trusted those students would make.

In the school library that day, I joined a circle of twenty-two Harper students—all African American, mostly juniors and seniors. Most were eager to talk. They described a constant fear of gangs and violence. Some explained that their parents were absent or struggling with addiction. A couple had spent time in juvenile detention centers. A junior named Thomas had witnessed a good friend—a sixteen-year-old girl—get shot and killed the previous summer. He'd also been there when his older brother, who had been partially paralyzed due to a gunshot injury, was shot and wounded in the same incident while sitting outside in his wheelchair. Nearly every kid there that day had lost someone—a friend, relative, neighbor—to a bullet. Meanwhile, most of them had never been as far as downtown Chicago, and had never seen the lakefront beaches and attractions only a half hour from their neighborhood.

At one point, one of the social workers spoke up, saying to the group, "Eighty degrees and sunny!" Everyone in the circle began nodding, glumly. I wasn't sure why. "Tell Mrs. Obama," she said. "What goes through your mind when you wake up in the morning and hear the weather forecast is eighty and sunny?"

She clearly knew the answer, but wanted me to hear it. A day like that, the Harper students all agreed, was no good. When the weather was nice, the gangs got more active. The shooting got worse.

These kids had adapted to the upside-down rules dictated by their environment, staying indoors when the weather was good, changing the routes they took to and from school each day depending on where the gangs were hanging out. Sometimes, they told me, taking the safest path home meant walking right down the middle of the street as cars sped past them on both sides. This way they could more easily see fights or possible shooters and avoid them. And it gave them more time to run.

America is not a simple place. Its contradictions set me spinning. In my time as First Lady, I'd found myself at fund-raisers held in big fancy apartments, with wealthy people who claimed to be passionate about education and children's issues but didn't really want their taxes raised in order to fund solutions.

And now I was at Harper, listening to children talking about how to stay alive. I admired their resilience—their ability to withstand the challenges they faced—and I wished desperately that they didn't need it so much.

One of them then gave me a direct look. "It's nice that you're here and all," he said with a shrug. "But what're you actually going to do about any of this?"

To them, I represented Washington, D.C., as much as I did the South Side. And when it came to Washington, I felt I owed them the truth.

"Honestly," I began, "I know you're dealing with a lot here, but no one's going to save you anytime soon. Most people in Washington aren't even trying. A lot of them don't even know you exist." I explained to those students that progress is slow, that they couldn't afford to simply sit and wait for change to come. Many Americans didn't want their taxes raised, even if it meant having more money to support kids in school. Congress was too busy with political bickering to put enough money into education or magical turnarounds for their community. Even after the horror of Newtown, Congress appeared determined to block any measure that could help keep guns out of the wrong hands. Politics was a mess, I said. On this front, I had nothing terribly uplifting or encouraging to say.

I went on, though, to make a different pitch, one that came directly from my South Side self. *Use school,* I said.

These kids had just spent an hour telling me stories that were tragic and unsettling, but I reminded them that those same stories also showed their persistence, self-reliance, and ability to overcome. I assured them that they already had what it would take to succeed. Here they were, sitting in a school that was offering them a free education. And there were a whole lot of committed and caring adults inside that school who thought they mattered. About six weeks later, thanks to donations from local businesspeople, a group of Harper students would come to the White House, to visit with me and Barack personally, and also spend time at Howard University, learning what college was about. I hoped that they could see themselves getting there.

I will never pretend that words or hugs from a First Lady alone can turn somebody's life around or that there's any easy path for students trying to navigate what those teens at Harper were dealing with. No story is that simple. And of course, every one of us sitting in the library that day knew this. But I was there to push back against the old and damaging narrative about being a Black urban kid in America, the one that predicted failure and then sped up its arrival. If I could point out those students' strengths and give them some glimpse of a way forward, then I would always do it. It was a small difference I could make.

24

IN THE SPRING OF 2015, MALIA ANNOUNCED THAT SHE'D been invited to the prom by a boy she kind of liked. She was sixteen then, finishing her junior year at Sidwell. To us, she was still our kid, long-legged and enthusiastic as she'd always been, though every day she seemed to become a little more adult. She was now nearly as tall as I was and starting to think about applying to college. She was a good student, curious and self-possessed, a collector of details much like her dad. She'd become fascinated by films and filmmaking. The previous summer she'd approached Steven Spielberg one evening when he'd come to the White House for a dinner party, asking him so many questions that he followed up with an offer to let her intern on a TV series he was producing. Our girl was finding her way.

Normally, for security reasons, Malia and Sasha weren't allowed to ride in anyone else's car. Malia had a provisional license by then and was able to drive herself around town, though always with agents following in their own vehicle. But still, since moving to Washington at the age of ten, she'd never once ridden a bus or the Metro or been driven by someone who didn't work for the Secret Service. For prom night, though, we were making an exception.

That evening, her date arrived in his car, clearing security at the southeast gate of the White House, and then gamely—bravely—walking into the Diplomatic Reception Room, which we called the Dip Room, dressed in a black suit. "Just be cool please, okay?" Malia had said to me and Barack, her embarrassment already beginning to smolder as we headed downstairs to meet her date. I was barefoot, and Barack was in flip-flops. Malia wore a long black skirt and an elegant bare-shouldered top. She looked beautiful.

I think we did manage to play it cool, though Malia still laughs, remembering it all as a bit excruciating. Barack and I shook the young man's hand, snapped a few pictures, and gave our daughter a hug before sending them on their way. We couldn't help taking comfort in the knowledge that Malia's security detail would basically ride the boy's bumper all the way to the restaurant where they were going for dinner before the dance and remain on quiet duty throughout the night.

From a parent's point of view, it wasn't a bad way to raise teenagers—knowing that a set of watchful adults was trailing them at all times, tasked with extricating them from any sort of emergency. From a teenager's standpoint, this was understandably a complete and total drag. As with many aspects of life in the White House, we were left to sort out where and how to draw the line for our family, how to balance the security needs of the presidency against the needs of two teenagers growing on their own.

Once they got to high school, we gave the girls curfews—first 11:00 and eventually midnight—and enforced them, according to Malia and Sasha, more strictly than many of their friends' parents did. If I was concerned about their safety or whereabouts, I could always check in with the agents, but I tried not to. It was important to me that the kids trusted their security team. Instead, I did what I think a lot of parents do and relied on a network of other parents for information, all of us pooling what we knew about where the flock of them was going and whether there'd be an adult in charge. Of course, our girls carried extra responsibility because of who their dad was. Their screwups could make headlines. Barack and I both recognized how unfair this was. Both of us had pushed boundaries and done dumb things as teenagers, and we'd been fortunate to do it all without the eyes of a nation on us.

Malia had been eight when Barack sat on the edge of her bed in Chicago and asked if she thought it was okay for him to run for president. I think now of how little she'd known at the time, how little any of us could have known. It meant one thing to be a child in the White House. It meant something different to try to grow into an adult there. How could Malia have guessed that she'd have men with guns following her to prom someday? Our kids were coming of age during what felt like a unique time. Barack was the first president in a new era when smartphones were becoming common, changing forever people's ideas and standards about privacy. Selfies, data hacks, Snapchats, and Kardashians had become part of the nation's vocabulary during our time in the White House. As teens for whom social media was an important part of their lives, our daughters lived this change more deeply than Barack or me. As Malia and Sasha moved around Washington with their friends after school or on weekends, strangers pointed their phones in their direction, or even demanded to take a selfie with them. "You do know that I'm a child, right?" Malia would sometimes say when turning someone down.

Barack and I did what we could to protect our kids from the public spotlight. We turned down all media requests for them and worked to keep their everyday lives largely out of sight. Their Secret Service escorts tried to be less obvious when following the girls around in public, wearing shorts and T-shirts instead of suits and swapping their earpieces and wrist microphones for earbud headsets, in order to better blend in at teenage hangouts. We strongly disapproved of the publication of any photos of our children that weren't connected to an official event, and the White House press office made this clear to the media. Anytime an image of one of the girls surfaced on a gossip site, my team made phone calls to get it taken down.

Guarding the girls' privacy meant finding other ways to satisfy the public's curiosity about our family. Early in Barack's second term, we'd added a new puppy to the household—Sunny—a free-spirited rambler who seemed to see no point in being house-trained. The dogs added a lightness to everything. They were living proof that the White House was a home. Knowing that Malia and Sasha were basically off-limits, the White House communications teams began requesting the dogs for official appearances, including mingling with members of the media or children coming for a tour. Bo starred in a promotional video for the Easter Egg Roll. He and Sunny posed with me for photos in a campaign to urge people to sign up for health-care coverage. They made excellent Obama representatives, immune to criticism and unaware of their own fame.

LIKE ALL KIDS, Sasha and Malia outgrew things over time. Since the first year of Barack's presidency, they had joined him while he performed what had to be the most ridiculous ritual of the office—pardoning a live turkey just ahead of the Thanksgiving holiday. For the first five years, they'd smiled and giggled as their dad cracked corny jokes. But by the sixth year, at thirteen and sixteen, they were too old to even pretend it was funny. Photos of the two of them looking bored and resentful appeared all over the internet—Sasha stone-faced, Malia with her arms crossed—as they stood next to the president and the oblivious turkey. A *USA Today* headline summed it up fairly enough: "Malia and Sasha Obama Are So Done with Their Dad's Turkey Pardon."

Their attendance at the pardon, as well as at nearly every White House event, became entirely optional. These were happy, well-adjusted teens with rich lives full of activities and social interests having nothing to do with their parents. Our kids had their own agendas, which left them less impressed with even the more fun parts of ours.

"Don't you want to come downstairs tonight and hear Paul McCartney play?"

"Mom, please. No."

There was often music blasting from Malia's room. Sasha and her friends were fond of cooking shows and sometimes took over the kitchen to decorate cookies or whip up elaborate meals for themselves. Both our daughters appreciated the relative anonymity they enjoyed when going on school trips or joining friends' families for vacations (their agents always in tow). Sasha loved nothing more than to pick out her own snacks at Dulles International Airport before boarding a packed commercial flight, simply because it was so different from the fussy presidential routine that went on at Andrews Air Force Base and had become our family's norm.

Traveling with us did have its advantages. Before Barack's presidency was over, our girls would enjoy a baseball game in Havana, walk along the Great Wall of China, and visit the Christ the Redeemer statue in Brazil. But it could also be a pain in the neck. In Malia's junior year, the two of us had gone to spend a day visiting colleges in New York City, setting up tours at New York University and Columbia. It had worked fine for a while. We'd moved through NYU's campus at a brisk pace, as it was still early and many students were not yet up for the day. We'd checked out classrooms, poked our heads into a dorm room, and chatted with a dean before heading uptown to grab an early lunch and move on to the next tour.

The problem is that there's no hiding a First Lady–sized motorcade, especially on the island of Manhattan in the middle of a weekday. By the time we finished eating, about a hundred people had gathered on the sidewalk outside the restaurant. We stepped out to find dozens of cell phones hoisted in our direction as we were engulfed by a chorus of cheers. This attention was supportive—"Come to Columbia, Malia!" people were shouting—but it was not especially useful for a girl who was trying quietly to imagine her own future.

I knew immediately what I needed to do, and that was to step away—to let Malia go see the next campus without me. Kristin Jones, my personal assistant, became her escort instead. Without me there, Malia's odds of being recognized went down. She could move faster and with a lot fewer agents. Without me, she could maybe look like just another kid walking the quad.

Kristin, in her late twenties and a California native, was like a big sister to both my girls anyway. Along with another staff member, Kristen Jarvis, she was closely involved in our family's life. "The Kristins," as we called them, stood in for us often, attending meetings and interacting with teachers, coaches, and other parents when Barack and I weren't able. With the girls, they were protective, loving, and far hipper than I'd ever be in the eyes of my kids. Malia and Sasha trusted them deeply, seeking their advice on everything from what to wear and social media to the increasing proximity of boys.

While Malia toured Columbia that afternoon, I waited in the basement of an academic building on campus designated safe by the Secret Service. I sat alone and unnoticed until it was time to leave, wishing I'd at least brought a book to read. It hurt a little to be down there, I'll admit. I felt a kind of loneliness that probably had less to do with the fact that I was by myself and more to do with the idea that, like it or not, our first baby was going to grow up and leave.

WE WEREN'T AT the end of the presidency yet, but already I was beginning to feel reflective. I found myself tallying the gains and losses, what had been sacrificed and what we could count as progress—in our country, in our family. Had we done all we could? Were we going to come out of this in one piece?

I tried to think back and remember how it was that my life had swerved away from the predictable, control-freak fantasy existence I'd pictured for myself—the one with the steady salary, a house to live in forever, a routine to my days. At what point had I chosen a different path? When had I allowed the chaos inside? Had it been on the summer night when I lowered my ice cream cone and leaned in to kiss Barack for the first time? Was it the day I'd finally walked away from my career in law, convinced I'd find something more fulfilling?

My mind sometimes landed back in the church basement on the Far South Side of Chicago, where I'd gone twenty-five years earlier to see Barack as he spoke to a neighborhood group that was struggling to push back against hopelessness and lack of concern. Listening to the conversation that evening, I'd heard something familiar spoken in a new way. I knew it was possible to have one's feet planted in reality but also pointed in the direction of progress. It was what I'd done as a kid on Euclid Avenue, what my family—and marginalized people more generally—had always done. You got somewhere by building a better reality, if at first only in your own mind. Or as Barack had put it that night, you may live in the world as it is, but you can still work to create the world as it should be.

I'd known the guy for only a couple of months then, but looking back I see that this was my swerve. In that moment, without saying a word, I'd signed on for a lifetime of us, and a lifetime of this.

All these years later, I was thankful for the progress I saw. In 2015, I was still making visits to Walter Reed, but each time it seemed there were fewer wounded warriors to visit. The United States had fewer service members at risk overseas, fewer injuries needing care, fewer moms with their hearts broken. This, to me, was progress.

Progress was the Centers for Disease Control reporting that childhood obesity rates seemed to be leveling off. It was two thousand high school students in Detroit showing up to help me celebrate College Signing Day, a holiday we'd helped expand as a part of Reach Higher, to mark the day when young people committed to their colleges. Progress was more secure access to health care for every American. It was an economy with nearly five straight years of continuous job growth.

I took this all in as proof that as a country we were capable of building a better reality. But still, we lived in the world as it is.

A year and a half after the shooting at Newtown, Congress had passed not a single gun-control measure. Bin Laden was gone, but a new terrorist group called ISIS had arrived. The homicide rate in Chicago was going up rather than down. A Black teen named Michael Brown was shot by a cop in Ferguson, Missouri, his body left in the middle of the road for hours. A Black teen named Laquan McDonald was shot sixteen times by police in Chicago, including nine times in the back. A Black boy named Tamir Rice was shot dead by police in Cleveland while playing with a toy gun. A Black man named Freddie Gray died after being neglected in police custody in Baltimore. A Black man named Eric Garner was killed by police after being put in a choke hold during his arrest on Staten Island. All this was evidence of something harmful and unchanging in America. When Barack was first elected, some commentators had declared that our country was entering a "post-racial" era, in which skin color would no longer matter. Here was proof of how wrong they'd been. As Americans obsessed over the threat of terrorism, many were overlooking the racism and bigotry that were tearing our nation apart.

Late in June 2015, Barack and I flew to Charleston, South Carolina, to sit with another grieving community—this time at the funeral of a pastor named Clementa Pinckney. Pastor Pinckney had been one of nine people killed in a racially motivated shooting earlier in the month at an African Methodist Episcopal church known simply as Mother Emanuel. The victims, all African Americans, had welcomed an unemployed twenty-one-year-old white man—a stranger to them all—into their Bible study group. He'd sat with them; then, after the group bowed their heads in prayer, he stood up and began shooting.

In the middle of it, he was reported to have said that he had to do it because Black people were taking over the country.

After delivering a moving eulogy for Reverend Pinckney and acknowledging the deep tragedy of the moment, Barack surprised everyone by leading the congregation in a slow and soulful rendition of "Amazing Grace." It was a simple plea for hope, a call to persist. Everyone in the room joined in. For more than six years now, Barack and I had lived with an awareness that we ourselves were an irritation to some. As minorities across the country were gradually beginning to take on more powerful roles in politics, business, and entertainment, our family had become the most prominent example. Our presence in the White House had been celebrated by millions of Americans, but it also contributed to a sense of fear and resentment among others. The hatred was old and deep and as dangerous as ever.

We lived with it as a family, and we lived with it as a nation. And we carried on, as gracefully as we could.

THE SAME DAY as the funeral service in Charleston—June 26, 2015—the Supreme Court of the United States issued a landmark decision. Same-sex couples now officially had the right to marry in all fifty states. This battle had been fought methodically over decades, state by state, court by court. Like any civil rights struggle it had required the persistence and courage of many people. A joyful crowd chanted, "Love has won!" on the steps of the Supreme Court. Couples were flocking to city halls and county courthouses to finally wed. Rainbow flags—a symbol of pride—waved on street corners around the country.

All this had helped lift us through a sad day in South Carolina. Returning home to the White House, we'd changed out of our funeral clothes, had a quick dinner with the girls, and then Barack had disappeared into the Treaty Room to flip on ESPN and catch up on work.

I was heading to my dressing room when I caught sight of a purplish glow through one of the north-facing windows of the residence.

Our staff had illuminated the White House in the rainbow colors of the pride flag. Looking out the window, I saw that beyond the gates a big crowd of people had gathered in the summer dusk to see the White House transformed in celebration of marriage equality. The Supreme Court's decision had touched so many people. From where I stood, I could see the exuberance of everyone celebrating outside, but I could hear nothing. It was an odd part of our reality. The White House was a silent, sealed fortress, almost all sound blocked by the thickness of its windows and walls. The Marine One helicopter could land on one side of the house, its rotor blades kicking up gale-force winds and slamming tree branches, but inside the residence we'd hear nothing. I usually figured out that Barack had arrived home from a trip not by the sound of his helicopter but rather by the smell of its fuel, which somehow managed to permeate.

Oftentimes, I was happy to withdraw into the protected hush of the residence at the end of a long day. But this night felt different. After a day spent grieving in Charleston, I was looking at a giant party starting just outside my window. Hundreds of people were staring up at our house. I wanted to see it the way they did. I found myself suddenly desperate to join the celebration.

I stuck my head into the Treaty Room. "You want to go out and look at the lights?" I asked Barack. "There are tons of people out there."

He laughed. "You know I can't do tons of people."

Sasha was in her room, engrossed in her iPad. "You want to go see the rainbow lights with me?" I asked.

"Nope."

This left Malia, who surprised me a little by immediately signing on. We were going on an adventure—outside, where people were gathered—and we weren't going to ask anyone's permission.

Normally, we checked in with the Secret Service agents posted by the elevator anytime we wanted to leave the residence, whether it was to go downstairs to watch a movie or to take the dogs out for a walk. Not tonight. Malia and I just busted past the agents on duty, neither one of us making eye contact. We bypassed the elevator, moving quickly down a stairwell. I could hear dress shoes clicking down the stairs behind us, the agents trying to keep up. Malia gave me a devilish smirk. She wasn't used to my breaking the rules.

Reaching the State Floor, we made our way toward the tall set of doors leading to the North Portico, when we heard a voice.

"Hello, ma'am! Can I help you?" It was Claire Faulkner, the usher on night duty. She was a friendly, soft-spoken brunette who I assumed had been tipped off by the agents whispering into their wrist pieces behind us.

I looked over my shoulder at her without breaking my stride. "Oh, we're just going outside," I said, "to see the lights."

Claire's eyebrows lifted. We ignored her. Arriving at the door, I grabbed its thick golden handle and pulled. But the door wouldn't budge. Nine months earlier, an intruder wielding a knife had somehow managed to jump a fence and barge through this same door, running through the State Floor before being tackled by a Secret Service officer. In response, security began locking the door.

I turned to the group of agents behind us. "How do you open this thing?" I said, to no one in particular. "There's got to be a key."

"Ma'am?" Claire said. "I'm not sure that's the door you want. Every network news camera is aimed at the north side of the White House right now."

She did have a point. My hair was a mess and I was in flip-flops, shorts, and a T-shirt. Not exactly dressed for a public appearance.

"Okay," I said. "But can't we get out there without being seen?"

Malia and I weren't going to give up. We were going to get ourselves outside.

Someone then suggested trying one of the loading doors on the ground floor, where trucks came to deliver food and office supplies. Our band began moving that way. Malia hooked her arm with mine. We were giddy now.

"We're getting out!" I said.

"Yeah we are!" she said.

We made our way down a marble staircase and over red carpets, around the busts of George Washington and Benjamin Franklin and past the kitchen until suddenly we were outdoors. The humid summer air hit our faces. I could see fireflies blinking on the lawn. And there it was, the hum of the public, people whooping and celebrating outside the iron gates. It had taken us ten minutes to get out of our own home, but we'd done it. We were outside, standing on a patch of lawn off to one side, out of sight of the public but with a beautiful, close-up view of the White House, lit up in pride.

Malia and I leaned into each other, happy to have found our way there.

AS HAPPENS IN POLITICS, new winds were already beginning to gather and blow. By the fall of 2015, the next presidential campaign was in full swing. More than a dozen Republicans were running, including governors and senators. Meanwhile, Democrats were quickly moving toward choosing between Hillary Clinton and Bernie Sanders, the liberal, longtime independent senator from Vermont.

Donald Trump had announced his candidacy for president early in the summer, standing inside Trump Tower in Manhattan and railing on Mexican immigrants. He also talked about the "losers" he said were running the country. I figured he was just trying to get attention because he could. Nothing in how he conducted himself suggested that he was serious about wanting to govern.

I was following the campaign, but not as closely as in years past. Instead, I'd been busy working on my fourth initiative as First Lady, called Let Girls Learn. Barack and I had launched it together in the spring. It was an ambitious effort focused on helping adolescent girls around the world have better access to education. Over the course of nearly seven years now as First Lady, I'd been struck again and again by both the promise and the vulnerability of young women in our world, from the immigrant girls I'd met at the Elizabeth Garrett Anderson School to Malala Yousafzai, the Pakistani teenager who'd been brutally attacked by members of the Taliban, a group of militant Islamists who believed that girls shouldn't go to school. Malala came to the White House to speak with me, Barack, and Malia about her advocacy on behalf of girls' education.

I was horrified when, about six months after her visit, 276 Nigerian schoolgirls were kidnapped by the extremist group Boko Haram, intent on causing Nigerian families to fear sending their daughters to school. This disturbing event had prompted me, for the first and only time during the presidency, to sub for Barack during his weekly address to the nation, speaking emotionally about how we needed to work harder at protecting and encouraging girls worldwide.

I felt it all personally. Education had been the primary instrument of change in my own life, my lever upward in the world. I was appalled that many girls—more than 98 million worldwide, in fact—didn't have access to it. Some girls weren't able to attend school because their families needed them to work. Sometimes the nearest school was far away or too expensive, or the risk of being assaulted while getting there was too great. Often a mix of poverty and traditional expectations of girls' roles combined to keep girls uneducated. This effectively locked them out of future opportunities. There seemed to be an idea in certain parts of the world that it was simply not worth it to put a girl in school, even though studies showed that educating girls and women and allowing them to work would boost a country's income.

Barack and I were committed to changing the ideas about what made a young woman valuable to a society. He worked to secure hundreds of millions of dollars in government resources. The two of us together urged other countries' governments to support programming for girls' education.

By now, I knew how to make a little noise for a cause. I understood Americans might feel disconnected from the struggles of people in faraway countries, so I tried to bring it home, calling up celebrities to lend their star power at events and on social media. I'd enlist the help of Janelle Monáe, Zendaya, Kelly Clarkson, and other talents to release a catchy pop song written by Diane Warren called "This Is for My Girls," the proceeds of which would go toward funding girls' education globally.

And lastly, I'd do something that was a little terrifying for me, which was to sing, making an appearance on the late-night host James Corden's hilarious "Carpool Karaoke" series. The two of us circled the South Lawn in a black SUV. We belted out "Signed, Sealed, Delivered I'm Yours," "Single Ladies," and finally—the reason I'd signed on to do it in the first place—"This Is for My Girls," with a guest appearance from Missy Elliott, who slipped into the backseat and rapped along with us. I'd practiced for my karaoke session for weeks, memorizing every beat to every song. The goal was to have it look fun and light, but behind it was a larger purpose—to keep connecting people with the issue of girls' education. My segment with James had forty-five million views on YouTube within the first three months, making every bit of the effort worth it.

TOWARD THE END OF 2015, Barack, the girls, and I flew to Hawaii to spend Christmas as we always did, renting a house with wide windows that looked out on the beach. As we had for the last six years, we took time on Christmas Day to visit with service members and their families at a nearby Marine Corps base. And as it had been right through his time as president, for Barack the vacation was only a semi-vacation. He took phone calls, sat for daily briefings, and was consulting with advisers and aides who were all staying at a hotel close by. It made me wonder whether he'd remember how to fully relax when the time actually came for us to leave the presidency behind.

Though I was allowing myself to dream a little, I still couldn't picture how any of this would end.

Returning to Washington to begin our final year in the White House, we knew the clock was ticking now. I began what would become a long series of "lasts." There was the last Governors' Ball, the last Easter Egg Roll, the last White House Correspondents' Dinner. Barack and I also made a last state visit to the United Kingdom together, which included a quick trip to see our friend the Queen.

Barack had always felt a special fondness for Queen Elizabeth, who reminded him of his no-nonsense grandmother, Toot. One afternoon in April 2016, the two of us took a helicopter from London to Windsor Castle in the countryside west of the city. As was always the case, our advance team instructed us on the proper procedure ahead of time: We'd greet the royals formally before getting into their vehicle to make the short drive. I'd sit in the front next to ninety-four-year-old Prince Philip, who would drive, and Barack would sit next to the Queen in the backseat.

It would be the first time in more than eight years that the two of us had been driven by anyone other than a Secret Service agent, or ridden in a car together without agents. This seemed to matter to our security teams, the same way doing things the right way mattered to the advance teams, who fretted endlessly over our movements and interactions, making sure that every last little thing looked right and went smoothly.

After we'd touched down in a field on the palace grounds and said our hellos, however, the Queen abruptly threw a wrench into everything by gesturing for me to join her in the backseat of the Range Rover. I froze, unsure whether it was more polite to go along with it or to insist that Barack take his proper seat by her side.

The Queen immediately picked up on my hesitation. And was having none of it.

"Did they give you some rule about this?" she said, dismissing all the fuss with a wave of her hand. "That's rubbish. Sit wherever you want."

FOR ME, giving commencement speeches at graduation ceremonies was an important springtime ritual. Each year I delivered a few of them, focusing on the sorts of high schools and colleges that normally didn't land high-profile speakers. In 2015, I'd gone back to the South Side of Chicago to speak at the graduation at King College Prep, the high school from which Hadiya Pendleton would have graduated had she lived long enough. Her spirit was honored at the ceremony by an empty chair, which her classmates had decorated with sunflowers and purple fabric.

For my final round of graduation speeches as First Lady, I spoke at Jackson State University in Mississippi, a historically Black school, using the opportunity to talk about striving for excellence. I spoke at the City College of New York, emphasizing the value of diversity and immigration. And on May 26, which happened to be the day Donald Trump clinched the Republican nomination for president, I was in New Mexico, speaking to a class of Native American students who were graduating from a small residential high school, nearly all of them headed next to college. The deeper I got into the experience of being First Lady, the more emboldened I felt to speak honestly and directly about what it meant to be marginalized by race and gender. My intention was to give young people a perspective on the hate surfacing in the news and in conversations about politics and to give them a reason to hope.

I tried to communicate the one message about myself and my place in the world that I felt might really mean something. Which was that I knew invisibility. I'd lived invisibility. I came from a history of invisibility. I was the great-great-granddaughter of a slave named Jim Robinson, who was probably buried in an unmarked grave somewhere on a South Carolina plantation. And in standing in front of students who were thinking about the future, I offered testament to the idea that it was possible, at least in some ways, to overcome invisibility.

The last commencement I attended that spring was personal—Malia's graduation from high school, held on a warm day in June. Our close friend Elizabeth Alexander, the poet who'd written a poem for Barack's first inauguration, spoke to the class, which meant that Barack and I got to sit back and just feel. I was proud of Malia, who was soon to head off to Europe to travel for a few weeks with friends. After taking a gap year, she'd enroll at Harvard. I was proud of Sasha, who turned fifteen that same day and was counting down the hours to the Beyoncé concert she was going to instead of having a birthday party. She would go on to spend much of the summer on Martha's Vineyard, living with family friends until Barack and I arrived for vacation. She'd make new friends and land her first job, working at a snack bar. I was proud, too, of my mom, who sat nearby in the sunshine, having managed to live in the White House and travel the world with us while staying utterly and completely herself.

I was proud of all of us, for almost being done.

Barack sat next to me in a folding chair. I could see the tears brimming behind his sunglasses as he watched Malia cross the stage to pick up her diploma. He was tired, I knew. Three days earlier, he'd attended a funeral and paid tribute to a friend from law school who'd worked for him in the White House. Two days later, an extremist would open fire inside a gay nightclub in Orlando, Florida, killing forty-nine people and wounding fifty-three more. The gravity of his job never let up.

He was a good dad, dialed in and consistent in ways his own dad had never been. But there were also things he'd sacrificed along the way. He'd entered into parenthood as a politician. His constituents and their needs had been with us all along.

It had to hurt a little bit, realizing he was so close to having more freedom and more time, just as our daughters were beginning to step away.

But we had to let them go. The future was theirs, just as it should be.

IN LATE JULY, I flew through a violent thunderstorm, the plane dipping and diving on its approach to Philadelphia, where I was going to speak for the last time at a Democratic convention to support Hillary Clinton. It was perhaps the worst turbulence I'd ever experienced, and while Caroline Adler Morales, my very pregnant communications director, worried that the stress of it would put her into labor and Melissa—a skittish flier under normal circumstances—sat shrieking in her seat, all I could think was *Just get me down in time to practice my speech*. Though I'd long grown comfortable on the biggest stages, I still found huge comfort in preparation.

Back in 2008, during Barack's first run for president, I'd rehearsed and re-rehearsed my convention speech. I'd never given a speech on live television like that, and the stakes felt so high. I was stepping onto the stage after having been criticized for being an angry Black woman who didn't love her country. My speech that night gave me a chance to explain who I was in my own voice, slaying the distorted images and stereotypes with my own words. Four years later, at the convention in Charlotte, North Carolina, I'd spoken earnestly about what I'd seen in Barack during his first term—how he was still the same principled man I'd married, how I'd realized that "being president doesn't change who you are; it reveals who you are."

Hillary Clinton, Barack's opponent in the brutal 2008 primary, had gone on to become his loyal and effective secretary of state. I'd never feel as passionately about another candidate as I did about my own husband, but when it came to speaking publicly about anything or anyone in the political sphere, I maintained a code for myself: I said only what I absolutely believed and what I absolutely felt.

Once we arrived at the convention center, I stepped out and spoke my truth. I talked about the fears I'd had early on about raising our daughters in the White House and how proud I was of the intelligent young women they'd become. I said that I trusted Hillary because she understood the demands of the presidency and had the character to lead, because she was as qualified as any nominee in history.

Since childhood, I'd believed it was important to speak out against bullies while also not stooping to their level. We were now up against a bully. Donald Trump was a man who demeaned minorities, women, and prisoners of war, and challenged the dignity of our country with his every word. I wanted Americans to understand that words matter—that the hateful language they heard coming from their TVs did not reflect the true spirit of our country and that we could vote against it. It was dignity I wanted to make an appeal for—the idea that as a nation we might hold on to the core thing that had sustained my family, going back generations. Dignity had always gotten us through. It was a choice, and not always the easy one, but the people I respected most in life made it again and again, every single day. There was a motto Barack and I tried to live by, and I offered it that night from the stage: *When they go low, we go high.*

Two months later, just weeks before the election, a tape would surface of Donald Trump bragging to a TV host in 2005 about sexually assaulting women. The language used was so crass and vulgar that it violated the decency standards that media have to follow. In the end, those standards of decency were simply lowered in order to make room for his voice.

When I heard it, I could hardly believe it. And then again, there was something painfully familiar in the menace and boys' club aggression of that tape. *I can hurt you and get away with it.* It was an expression of hatred that had generally been kept out of polite company, but it still lived deep down in our supposedly open-minded society. Every woman I know recognized it. Every person who's ever been made to feel "other" recognized it. It was precisely what so many of us hoped our own children would never need to experience, and yet probably would. That kind of dominating power, even the threat of it, is dehumanizing. It's the ugliest kind of power.

My body buzzed with fury after hearing that tape. At a campaign rally for Hillary the following week, I felt compelled to try to address Trump's words directly—to counter his voice with my own.

I worked on my remarks while sitting in a hospital room at Walter Reed, where my mom was having back surgery. I'd been mocked and threatened many times, cut down for being Black, female, and vocal. I'd felt ridicule directed at my body, the literal space I occupied in the world. I'd watched Donald Trump stalk Hillary Clinton during a debate, following her around as she spoke, standing too close, trying to diminish her presence with his. *I can hurt you and get away with it.* Women regularly suffer these indignities—in the form of catcalls, groping, assault, oppression. These things injure us. They leave scars, some huge, some barely visible, that we carry everywhere—to and from school and work, at home with our families, at our places of worship, anytime we try to move forward.

For me, Trump's comments were another blow. I couldn't let his message stand. Working with Sarah Hurwitz, my brilliant speechwriter, I channeled my fury into words. After my mom had recovered from surgery, I delivered them one October day in New Hampshire. Speaking to a high-energy crowd, I made my feelings clear. "This is not normal," I said. "This is not politics as usual. This is disgraceful. It is intolerable." I expressed my rage and my fear, along with my faith that Americans understood the true nature of what they were choosing between in this election. I put my whole heart into giving that speech.

I then flew back to Washington, praying I'd been heard.

AS FALL CONTINUED, Barack and I began making plans for our move to a new house in January, having decided to stay in Washington so that Sasha could finish high school. Malia, meanwhile, was in South America on a gap-year adventure, feeling the freedom of being as far away from politics as she could. I urged my staff in the East Wing to finish strong, even as the battle between Hillary Clinton and Donald Trump grew more intense and distracting by the day.

On November 7, 2016, the evening before the election, Barack and I traveled to Philadelphia to join Hillary and her family at a final rally before an enormous crowd on Independence Mall. The mood was positive, expectant. I took heart in the optimism Hillary represented that night, and in the many polls that showed her with a comfortable lead. I presumed nothing, but I felt good about the odds. For the first time in many years, Barack and I had no role to play on election night. There was no hair, makeup, or wardrobe to be tended to, no late-night speech being prepped for delivery. We had nothing to do, and it thrilled us. This was the beginning of our stepping back, a first taste of what the future might be like. We cared, of course, but the moment ahead wasn't ours. It was merely ours to witness. Knowing it would be a while before results came in, we invited Valerie Jarrett over to watch a movie in the White House theater.

I can't remember a thing about the film that night. We were just passing time in the dark. My mind kept turning over the reality that Barack's term as president was almost finished. What lay ahead most immediately were good-byes—dozens and dozens of them, all emotional, as the staff we loved and appreciated so much would begin to rotate out of the White House. Our goal was to do what George and

Laura Bush had done for us, making the transition of power as smooth and friendly as possible. Already, our teams were beginning to prepare briefing books and contact lists for their successors. Before they left, many East Wing staffers would leave handwritten notes on their desks, giving a friendly welcome and a standing offer of help to the next person coming along.

We were still deeply involved in our work, but we'd also started to plan for what lay ahead. Barack and I were excited to stay in Washington but would stay connected to the South Side of Chicago, which would become home to the Obama Presidential Center. We planned to launch a foundation as well whose mission would be to encourage and embolden a new generation of leaders. The two of us had many goals for the future, but the biggest involved creating more space and support for young people and their ideas. I also knew that we needed a break: I'd started scouting for a private place where we could go to relax for a few days in January, immediately after the new president got sworn in.

We just needed the new president.

As the movie wrapped up and the lights came on, Barack's cell phone buzzed. I saw him glance at it and then look again, his brow furrowing just slightly.

"Huh," he said. "Results in Florida are looking kind of strange."

There was no alarm in his voice, just a tiny seed of awareness. The phone buzzed again. My heart started to tick faster.

I watched my husband's face closely, not sure I was ready to hear what he was going to say. Whatever it was, it didn't look good. I felt something heavy take hold in my stomach, my anxiety hardening into dread. As Barack and Valerie started to discuss the early results, I announced that I was going upstairs. I walked to the elevator, hoping to do only one thing, which was to block it all out and go to sleep. I understood what was probably happening, but I wasn't ready to face it.

As I slept, the news was confirmed: American voters had elected

Donald Trump to succeed Barack as the next president of the United States.

The next day, I woke to a wet and dreary morning. A gray sky hung over Washington. I couldn't help but interpret it as funereal. Time seemed to crawl. Sasha went off to school, quietly processing her shock. Malia called from Bolivia, sounding deeply rattled. I told both our girls that I loved them and that things would be okay. I kept trying to tell myself the same thing.

In the end, Hillary Clinton won nearly three million more votes than her opponent, but Trump had captured the Electoral College. I am not a political person, so I'm not going to attempt to offer an analysis of the results. I won't try to speculate about who was responsible or what was unfair. I just wish more people had turned out to vote. And I will always wonder about what led so many women, in particular, to reject an exceptionally qualified female candidate and instead choose a man who spoke of and treated women so badly as their president. But the result was now ours to live with.

As had happened so many times before, Barack was called upon to step forward as a symbol of steadiness to help the nation process its shock. Around noon, he delivered a serious but reassuring speech to the nation from the Rose Garden, calling—as he always did—for unity and dignity. He asked Americans to respect one another as well as the institutions built by our democracy.

That afternoon, I sat in my East Wing office with my staff, all of us crammed into the room. My team was made up largely of women and minorities, including several who came from immigrant families. Many were in tears. They believed thoroughly in the causes they worked on. I tried to tell them that they should be proud of who they are, that their work mattered, and that one election couldn't wipe away eight years of change.

Everything was not lost. This was the message we needed to carry forward. It's what I truly believed. It wasn't ideal, but it was our reality—the world as it is. We needed to keep our feet pointed in the direction of progress.

WE WERE AT the end now, truly. I found myself caught between looking back and looking forward, mulling over one question in particular: What lasts?

We were the forty-fourth First Family and only the eleventh family to spend two full terms in the White House. We were, and would always be, the first Black one. I hoped that when future parents brought their children to visit, the way I'd brought Malia and Sasha, they'd be able to point out some reminder of our family's time here, like the stunning yellow, red, and blue abstract painting by Alma Thomas—*Resurrection*—which became the first work of art by a Black woman to be added to the White House's permanent collection. I thought it was important to register our presence within the larger history of the place.

Our most lasting mark lay outside the walls. The garden had persisted through seven and a half years now, producing roughly two thousand pounds of food annually. It had survived heavy snows, sheets of rain, and hail. When winds had toppled the forty-two-foot-high National Christmas Tree a few years earlier, the garden had survived intact. Before I left the White House, I wanted to give it even more permanence. We expanded it to more than double its original size. We added stone pathways and wooden benches, plus a welcoming arbor made of wood sourced from the estates of Presidents Jefferson, Madison, and Monroe and the childhood home of Dr. Martin Luther King Jr. And then, one fall afternoon, I set out across the South Lawn to officially dedicate the garden for the future.

Joining me that day were supporters and people who'd helped with our nutrition and childhood health efforts over the years, as well as a pair of students from the original class of fifth graders at Bancroft Elementary School, who were now practically adults. Most of my staff was there, including Sam Kass, who'd returned for the occasion.

Looking out at the crowd in the garden, I was emotional. I felt grateful to all the people on my team who'd given everything to our work. I'd seen many of them take on more responsibility and blossom both professionally and personally, even under the glare of the harshest lights. The burdens of being "the first" didn't fall only on our family's shoulders. For eight years, these optimistic young people—and a few seasoned professionals—had had our backs. Melissa, who had been my very first campaign hire nearly a decade ago and someone I will count on as a close friend for life, remained with me through the end of the term, as did Tina, my remarkable chief of staff. Kristen Jarvis had been replaced by Chynna Clayton, a hardworking young woman who quickly became another big sister to our girls and was central to keeping my life running smoothly. I considered all of them, current and former staff, to be family. And I was so proud of what we'd done.

For every video that went viral—I'd mom-danced with Jimmy Fallon, Nerf-dunked on LeBron James, and college-rapped with Jay Pharoah—we'd focused ourselves on doing more than trending for a few hours on Twitter. And we had results. Forty-five million kids were eating healthier breakfasts and lunches; eleven million students were getting sixty minutes of physical activity every day through our Let's Move! Active Schools program. Children overall were eating more whole grains and produce.

Through my work with Jill Biden on Joining Forces, we'd helped persuade businesses to hire or train more than 1.5 million veterans and military spouses. Following through on one of the very first concerns I'd heard on the campaign trail, we'd gotten all fifty states to collaborate on keeping military spouses' careers from stalling every time they moved.

When it came to education, Barack and I had directed billions of dollars to help girls around the world get the schooling they deserve. In the United States, my team and I had helped more young people sign up for student aid, supported school counselors, and raised College Signing Day to a national level.

Barack, meanwhile, had managed to turn around the worst economic crisis since the Great Depression. He'd helped to negotiate the Paris Agreement on climate change, brought tens of thousands of troops home from Iraq and Afghanistan, and effectively shut down Iran's nuclear program. Twenty million more people had health insurance. We'd managed two terms in office without a major scandal. We had held ourselves and the people who worked with us to the highest standards of ethics and decency, and we'd made it all the way through.

For us, some changes were harder to measure but felt just as important. Six months before the garden dedication, Lin-Manuel Miranda, the young composer I'd met at one of our first arts events, returned to the White House. His hip-hop riff on Alexander Hamilton had exploded into a hit musical, and with it he'd become a global superstar. *Hamilton* was a musical celebration of America's history and diversity, changing our understanding of the roles minorities play in our national story, highlighting the importance of women who'd long been overshadowed by powerful men.

Lin-Manuel brought most of his cast along with him to Washington, a talented multiracial ensemble. The performers spent their afternoon with young people who'd come from local high schools— budding playwrights, dancers, and rappers kicking around the White House, writing lyrics and dropping beats with their heroes. In the late afternoon, we all came together for a performance in the East Room. Barack and I sat in the front row, surrounded by young people of all different races and backgrounds, the two of us overwhelmed by emotion as Christopher Jackson and Lin-Manuel sang the ballad "One Last Time" as their final number. Here were two artists, one Black and one Puerto Rican, standing beneath a 115-year-old chandelier, bracketed by towering antique portraits of George and Martha Washington, singing about feeling "at home in this nation we've made." The power and truth of that moment stays with me to this day.

Hamilton touched me because it reflected the kind of history I'd lived myself. It told a story about America that allowed the diversity in. I thought about this afterward: So many of us go through life with our stories hidden, feeling ashamed or afraid when our whole truth doesn't live up to some established ideal. We grow up with messages that tell us that there's only one way to be American. If our skin is dark or our hips are wide, if we don't experience love in a particular way, if we speak another language or come from another country, then we don't belong. That is, until someone dares to start telling that story differently.

I grew up with a disabled dad in a too-small house with not much money in a starting-to-fail neighborhood, and I also grew up surrounded by love and music in a diverse city in a country where an education can take you far. I had nothing or I had everything. It depends on which way you want to tell it.

As we moved toward the end of Barack's presidency, I thought about America this same way. I loved my country for all the ways its story could be told. For almost a decade, I'd been privileged to move through it, experiencing its bracing contradictions and bitter conflicts, its pain and persistent idealism, and above all else its resilience. My view was unusual, perhaps, but I think what I experienced during those years is what many did—a sense of progress, the comfort of compassion, the joy of watching the unsung and invisible find some light. A glimmer of the world as it could be. This was our bid for permanence: a rising generation that understood what was possible—and that even more was possible for them. Whatever was coming next, this was a story we could own.

EPILOGUE

BARACK AND I WALKED OUT OF THE WHITE HOUSE FOR the last time on January 20, 2017, accompanying Donald and Melania Trump to the inauguration ceremony. That day, I was feeling everything all at once—tired, proud, upset, eager. Mostly, though, I was trying just to hold myself together, knowing we had television cameras following our every move. Barack and I were determined to make the transition with grace and dignity, to finish our eight years with both our ideals and our poise intact. We were down to the final hour.

That morning, Barack had made a last visit to the Oval Office, leaving a handwritten note for the next president. We'd also gathered on the State Floor to say good-bye to the White House's permanent staff—the butlers, ushers, chefs, housekeepers, florists, and others who'd looked after us with friendship and professionalism and would now extend those same courtesies to the family due to move in later that day. These farewells were particularly rough for Sasha and Malia. They'd seen many of these people nearly every day for half their lives. I'd hugged everyone and tried not to cry when they presented us with a parting gift of two United States flags—the one that had flown on the first day of

Barack's presidency and the one that had flown on his last day in office, symbolic bookends to our family's experience.

Sitting on the inaugural stage in front of the U.S. Capitol for the third time, I worked to hold in my emotions. The vibrant diversity of the last two inaugurations was gone. In their place was the kind of overwhelmingly white and male crowd I'd encountered so many times in my life—especially in the more privileged spaces I'd found my way into since leaving my childhood home. What I knew from working in these professional environments—from recruiting new lawyers at my old law firm to hiring staff at the White House—is that sameness leads to more sameness, until you make a thoughtful effort to counteract it.

Looking around at the three hundred or so people sitting on the stage that morning, the guests of the incoming president, it felt clear to me that in the new White House, this effort wasn't likely to be made. Someone from Barack's administration might have said that the optics there were bad—that what the public saw didn't reflect the president's reality or ideals. But in this case, maybe it did. Realizing it, I made my own optic adjustment: I stopped even trying to smile.

A TRANSITION IS exactly that—a passage to something new. A hand goes on a Bible; an oath gets repeated. One president's furniture gets carried out while another's comes in. Closets are emptied and re-filled. Just like that, there are new heads on new pillows—new temperaments, new dreams. And when your term is up, when you leave the White House on that very last day, you're left in many ways to find yourself all over again.

I am now at a new beginning, in a new phase of life. For the first time in many years, I'm free from political obligations and other people's expectations. I have two nearly grown daughters who need me less than they once did. I have a husband who no longer carries the weight of the nation on his shoulders. The responsibilities I've felt—to Sasha and Malia, to Barack, to my career and my country—have shifted in ways that allow me to think differently about what comes next. I've had more time to reflect, to simply be myself. I am still in progress, and I hope that I always will be.

For me, becoming isn't about arriving somewhere or achieving a certain aim. I see it as forward motion, a means of evolving, a way to reach continuously toward a better self. The journey doesn't end. I became a mom, but I still have a lot to learn from and give to my children. I became a wife, but I continue to adapt to and be humbled by what it means to truly love and make a life with another person. I have become, by certain measures, a person of power, and yet there are moments still when I feel insecure or unheard.

It's all a process, steps along a path. Becoming requires equal parts patience and rigor. Becoming is never giving up on the idea that there's more growing to be done.

Because people often ask, I'll say it here directly: I have no intention of running for office, ever. I've never been a fan of politics, and my experience over the last ten years has done little to change that. I continue to be put off by the nastiness—the tribal segregation of red and blue, this idea that we're supposed to choose one side and stick to it, unable to listen and compromise, or sometimes even to be civil. I do believe that at its best, politics can be a means for positive change, but it is just not for me.

That isn't to say I don't care deeply about the future of our country. Since Barack left office, I've read news stories that turn my stomach. I've lain awake at night, fuming over what's come to pass. It's been distressing to see how the behavior and the political agenda of the current president have caused many Americans to doubt themselves and to doubt and fear one another. It's been hard to watch as carefully built, compassionate policies have been rolled back, as we've alienated some of our closest allies and left vulnerable members of our society exposed and dehumanized. I sometimes wonder where the bottom might be.

What I won't allow myself to do, though, is to become cynical. In my most worried moments, I take a breath and remind myself of the dignity and decency I've seen in people throughout my life, the many obstacles that have already been overcome. I hope others will do the same. We all play a role in this democracy. We need to remember the power of every vote. I continue, too, to keep myself connected to a force that's larger and more potent than any one election, or leader, or news story—and that's optimism. For me, this is a form of faith, an answer to fear. Optimism thrived in my family's little apartment on Euclid Avenue. I saw it in my dad, in the way he moved around as if nothing were wrong with his body, as if the disease that would some-day take his life just didn't exist. I saw it in my mom's stubborn belief in our neighborhood, her decision to stay rooted even as fear led many of her neighbors to pack up and move. It's the thing that first drew me to Barack when he turned up in my law office, wearing a hopeful grin. It helped me overcome my doubts and vulnerabilities enough to trust that my family would stay safe and happy even while living in the public eye.

And it helps me now. As First Lady, I saw optimism in surprising places. It was in the wounded warrior at Walter Reed who pushed back against pity, reminding everyone that he was both tough and hope-ful. It lived in Cleopatra Cowley-Pendleton, who directed some part of her grief over losing her daughter into fighting for better gun laws. It was there in the social worker at Harper High School who made a point of shouting out her love and appreciation for students each time she passed them in the hall. And it's there in the hearts of young people who wake up each day believing in the goodness of things, in the magic of what might be. Together, we will stay strong and keep working to create a more fair and humane world. We need to remain both tough and hopeful, to acknowledge that there's more growing to be done.

There are portraits of me and Barack now hanging in the National Portrait Gallery in Washington. This fact humbles us both. I doubt that anyone looking at our two childhoods would ever have guessed we'd land in an art museum. The paintings are lovely, but what matters most is that they're there for young people to see—that our faces help change the idea that in order to be an important part of history, you have to look a certain way. If we belong, then so can many others.

I'm an ordinary person who found herself on an extraordinary journey. In sharing my story, I hope to help create space for other stories and other voices, to widen the pathway for who belongs and why. I've been lucky enough to get to walk into stone castles, urban classrooms, and Iowa kitchens, just trying to be myself, just trying to connect. For every door that's been opened to me, I've tried to open my door to others. And here is what I have to say, finally: Let's invite one another in. Maybe then we can begin to fear less, to make fewer wrong assumptions, to let go of the biases and stereotypes that unnecessarily divide us. Maybe we can better embrace the ways we are the same. It's not about being perfect. It's not about where you get yourself in the end. There's power in allowing yourself to be known and heard, in owning your unique story, in using your authentic voice. And there's grace in being willing to know and hear others. This, for me, is how we become.

ACKNOWLEDGMENTS

As with everything I've done in my life, this memoir would not have been possible without the love and support of many people.

I would not be who I am today without the steady hand and un-conditional love of my mom, Marian Shields Robinson. She has always been my rock, allowing me the freedom to be who I am, while never allowing my feet to get too far off the ground. Her boundless love for my girls, and her willingness to put our needs before her own, gave me the comfort and confidence to venture out into the world knowing they were safe and cherished at home.

My husband, Barack, my love, my partner of twenty-five years and the most lovingly committed dad to our daughters, has been a life partner I could only have imagined. Our story is still unfolding, and I eagerly await the many adventures left to come. Thank you for your help and guidance with this book . . . for reading chapters carefully and patiently, and for knowing exactly when to give a gentle steer.

And to my big brother, Craig. Where do I begin? You have been my protector since the day I was born. You have made me laugh more than any other person on this earth. You are the best brother a sister could ask for, a loving and caring son, husband, and dad. Thank you for all the hours you spent with my team peeling back the layers of our childhood. Some of my best memories of writing this book will be our time together, with Mom, sitting in the kitchen reliving so many old stories.

There is absolutely no way that I could have completed this book in my lifetime without an incredibly gifted team of collaborators whom I simply adore. When I first met Sara Corbett a little over a year ago, all I knew about her was that she was highly respected by my editor and knew very little about politics. Today I would trust her with my life not just because she has an amazing and curious mind but because she is a fundamentally kind and generous human being. I hope that this is just the beginning of a lasting friendship.

Tyler Lechtenberg has been a valuable member of the Obama world for more than a decade. He came into our lives as one of the hundreds of hopeful young Iowa field organizers and has been with us as a trusted adviser ever since. I have watched him grow into a powerful writer with an incredibly bright future.

Then there is my editor, Molly Stern, whose enthusiasm, energy, and passion instantly drew me to her. Molly kept me buoyed by her unwavering faith in my vision for this book. I am forever grateful to her and the entire Crown team, including Maya Mavjee, Tina Constable, David Drake, Emma Berry, and Chris Brand, who supported this effort from the beginning. Amanda D'Acierno, Lance Fitzgerald, Sally Franklin, Carisa Hays, Linnea Knollmueller, Matthew Martin, Donna Passannante, Elizabeth Rendfleisch, Anke Steinecke, Christine Tanigawa, and Dan Zitt all helped make *Becoming* possible.

For this young readers' edition, I'd like to additionally thank the team at Delacorte Press/Random House Children's Books, which includes Beverly Horowitz, Rebecca Gudelis, Jake Eldred, Alison Kolani, Andrea Lau, April Ward, Denise DeGennaro, Tim Terhune, Linda Palladino, Judith Haut, Barbara Marcus, and Felicia Frazier, as well as the Marketing, Publicity, Sales, and foreign and subsidiary rights groups, and David Drake, Emma Berry, Chris Brand, and Madison Jacobs at Crown for their ongoing contributions.

I also want to thank Markus Dohle for putting all the resources of Penguin Random House behind this labor of love.

I would not be able to function successfully in this world as a mom, wife, friend, and professional without my team. Anyone who knows me well knows that Melissa Winter is the other half of my brain. Mel, thank you for being by my side through every step of this process. More importantly, thank you for loving me and my girls so fiercely. There is no me without you.

Melissa is the chief of staff of my personal team. This small but mighty group of smart, hardworking women are the folks who make sure I'm always on point: Caroline Adler Morales, Chynna Clayton, MacKenzie Smith, Samantha Tubman, and Alex May Sealey.

Bob Barnett and Deneen Howell of Williams and Connolly were invaluable guides to the publishing process, and I am grateful for their advice and support.

A special thanks to all those who helped bring this book to life in so many other ways: Pete Souza, Chuck Kennedy, Lawrence Jackson, Amanda Lucidon, Samantha Appleton, Kristin Jones, Chris Haugh, Arielle Vavasseur, Michele Norris, and Elizabeth Alexander.

In addition, I want to thank the incredibly resourceful Ashley Woolheater for her thorough research and Gillian Brassil for her meticulous fact-checking. Many of my former staff also helped confirm critical details and time lines throughout this process—there are too many to name, but I am grateful to each of them.

Thank you to all the amazing women in my life who have kept me lifted up. You all know who you are and what you mean to me—my girlfriends, my mentors, my "other daughters"—and a very special thanks to Mama Kaye. All of you have supported me during this writing process and have helped me become a better woman.

The hectic pace of my life as First Lady left little time for traditional journaling. That is why I am so grateful to my dear friend Verna Williams, who is currently serving as the interim dean and Nippert Professor of Law at the University of Cincinnati College of Law. I relied heavily on the roughly 1,100 pages of transcripts resulting from our biannual recorded conversations during our White House years.

I am so proud of all that we accomplished in the East Wing. I want to thank the many men and women who dedicated their lives to help our nation, the members of the Office of the First Lady—policy, scheduling, administration, communications, speechwriters, social office, correspondence. Thank you to the staffs, White House Fellows, and agency detailees who were responsible for building each of my initiatives—Let's Move!, Reach Higher, Let Girls Learn, and, of course, Joining Forces.

Joining Forces will always hold a special place in my heart because it gave me rare exposure to the strength and resilience of our outstanding military community. To all of the service members, veterans, and military families, thank you for your service and sacrifice on behalf of the country we all love. To Dr. Jill Biden and her entire team— it was truly a blessing and a joy to work side by side with you all on this very important initiative.

To all of the nutrition and education leaders and advocates, thank you for doing the thankless, everyday hard work of making sure all our children have the love, support, and resources they need to achieve their dreams.

Thank you to all of the members of the United States Secret Service, as well as their families, whose daily sacrifice allows them to do their jobs so well. Particularly to those who have and continue to serve my family, I will be forever grateful for their dedication and professionalism.

Thank you to the hundreds of men and women who work hard each day to make the White House a home for the families who have the privilege of inhabiting one of our most treasured monuments—the ushers, chefs, butlers, florists, grounds crew, housekeeping, and engineering staffs. They will always be an important part of our family.

Finally, I want to thank every young person I ever encountered during my time as First Lady. To all the promising young souls that touched my heart over those years—to those who helped my garden grow; to those who danced, sang, cooked, and broke bread with me; to those who remained open to the love and guidance I had to give; to those who gave me thousands of warm, delicious hugs, hugs that lifted me up and kept me going even during my most difficult moments. Thank you for always giving me a reason to be hopeful.

PHOTOGRAPH CREDITS

FRONT ENDPAPER: All photographs courtesy of the Obama-Robinson Family Archive

BACK ENDPAPER: (*from left*) Courtesy of the Obama-Robinson Family Archive (three images); © Callie Shell/Aurora Photos; © Susan Watts/New York Daily News/Getty Images; © Brooks Kraft LLC/ Corbis/Getty Images; Photo by Ida Mae Astute © ABC/Getty Images

INSERT 1

PAGES 1 TO 3: All photographs courtesy of the Obama-Robinson Family Archive

PAGE 4: (*top and bottom left*) Courtesy of the Obama-Robinson Family Archive; (*bottom right*) Photo by Kat Peeler

PAGES 5 TO 8: All photographs courtesy of the Obama-Robinson Family Archive

INSERT 2

PAGE 1: (*top*) Courtesy of the University of Chicago School of Medicine; (*bottom*) Courtesy of the Obama-Robinson Family Archive

PAGE 2: (*top*) © David Katz 2004; (*middle*) © Anne Ryan 2007; (*bottom*) © Callie Shell/Aurora Photos

PAGE 3: (*top*) Courtesy of the Obama-Robinson Family Archive; (*middle*) © Spencer Platt/Getty Images; (*bottom*) © David Katz 2008

PAGE 4: Photo by Chuck Kennedy, McClatchy/Tribune

PAGE 5: © Mark Wilson/Getty Images

PAGE 6: (*top*) Official White House Photo by Joyce N. Boghosian; (*middle*) Official White House Photo by Pete Souza; (*bottom*) © Karen Bleier/AFP/Getty Images

PAGE 7: (*top and bottom*) Official White House Photo by Chuck Kennedy

PAGE 8: (*top and middle*) Official White House Photo by Pete Souza; (*bottom*) Official White House Photo by Samantha Appleton

INSERT 3

PAGE 1: (*top*) Official White House Photo by Sonya Hebert; (*middle*) Official White House Photo by Lawrence Jackson; (*bottom*) Official White House Photo by Amanda Lucidon

PAGE 2: Official White House Photo by Samantha Appleton

PAGE 3: (*top*) Official White House Photo by Chuck Kennedy; (*middle and bottom*) Official White House Photo by Pete Souza

PAGE 4: (*top*) Official White House Photo by Chuck Kennedy; (*middle and bottom*) Official White House Photo by Pete Souza

PAGE 5: (*top*) Official White House Photo by Samantha Appleton; (*bottom*) Official White House Photo by Pete Souza

PAGE 6: Courtesy of the Obama-Robinson Family Archive

PAGE 7: Official White House Photo by Lawrence Jackson

PAGE 8: Official White House Photo by Pete Souza

ABOUT THE AUTHOR

Michelle Robinson Obama served as First Lady of the United States from 2009 to 2017. A graduate of Princeton University and Harvard Law School, Mrs. Obama started her career as an attorney at the Chicago law firm Sidley & Austin, where she met her future husband, Barack Obama. She later worked in the Chicago mayor's office, at the University of Chicago, and at the University of Chicago Medical Center. Mrs. Obama also founded the Chicago chapter of Public Allies, an organization that prepares young people for careers in public service.

The Obamas currently live in Washington, D.C., and have two daughters, Malia and Sasha.

becomingmichelleobama.com